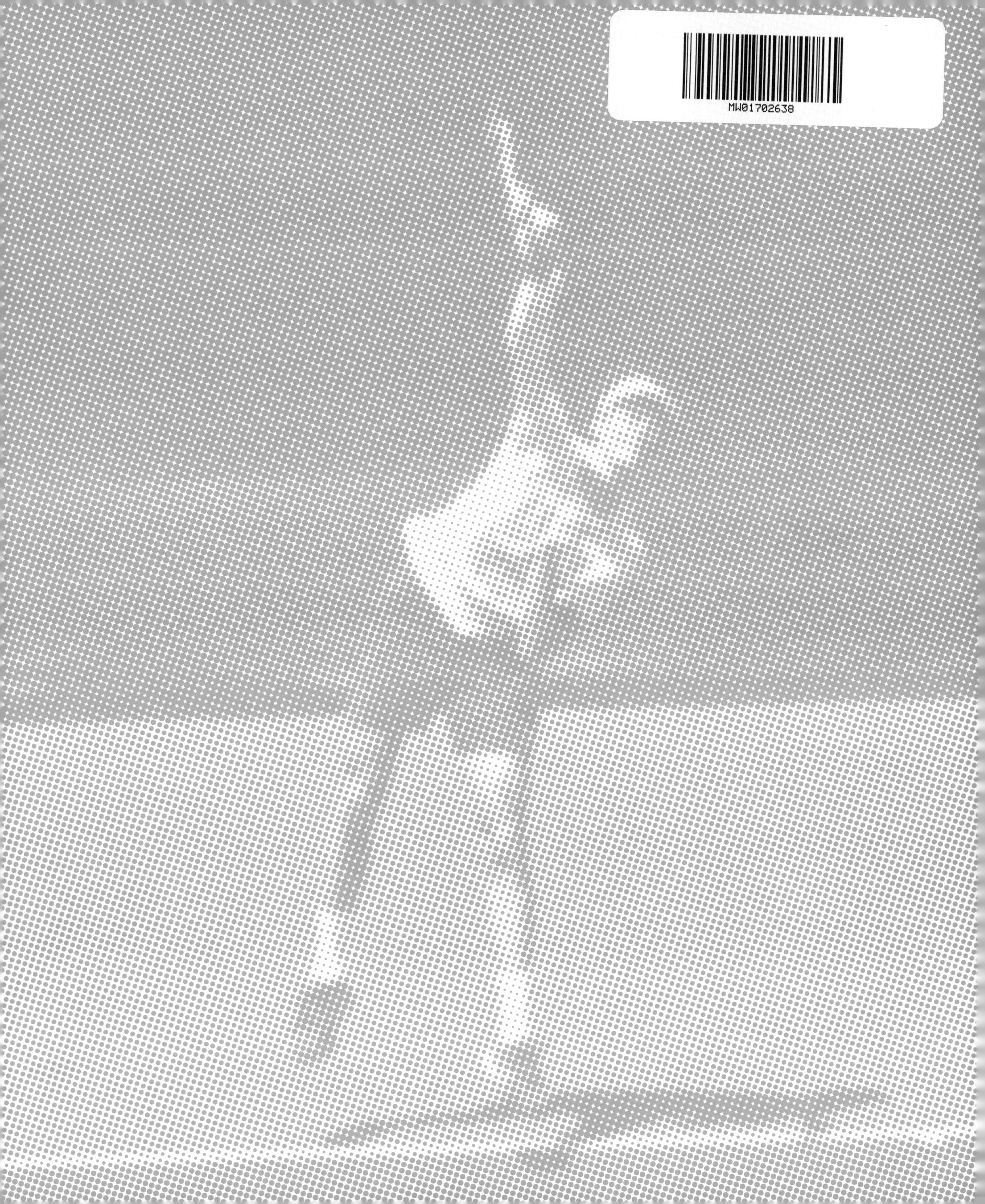

ACE

ACE

THE TIMES & STYLE OF TENNIS

SUNITA KUMAR NAIR

ABRAMS, NEW YORK

CONTENTS

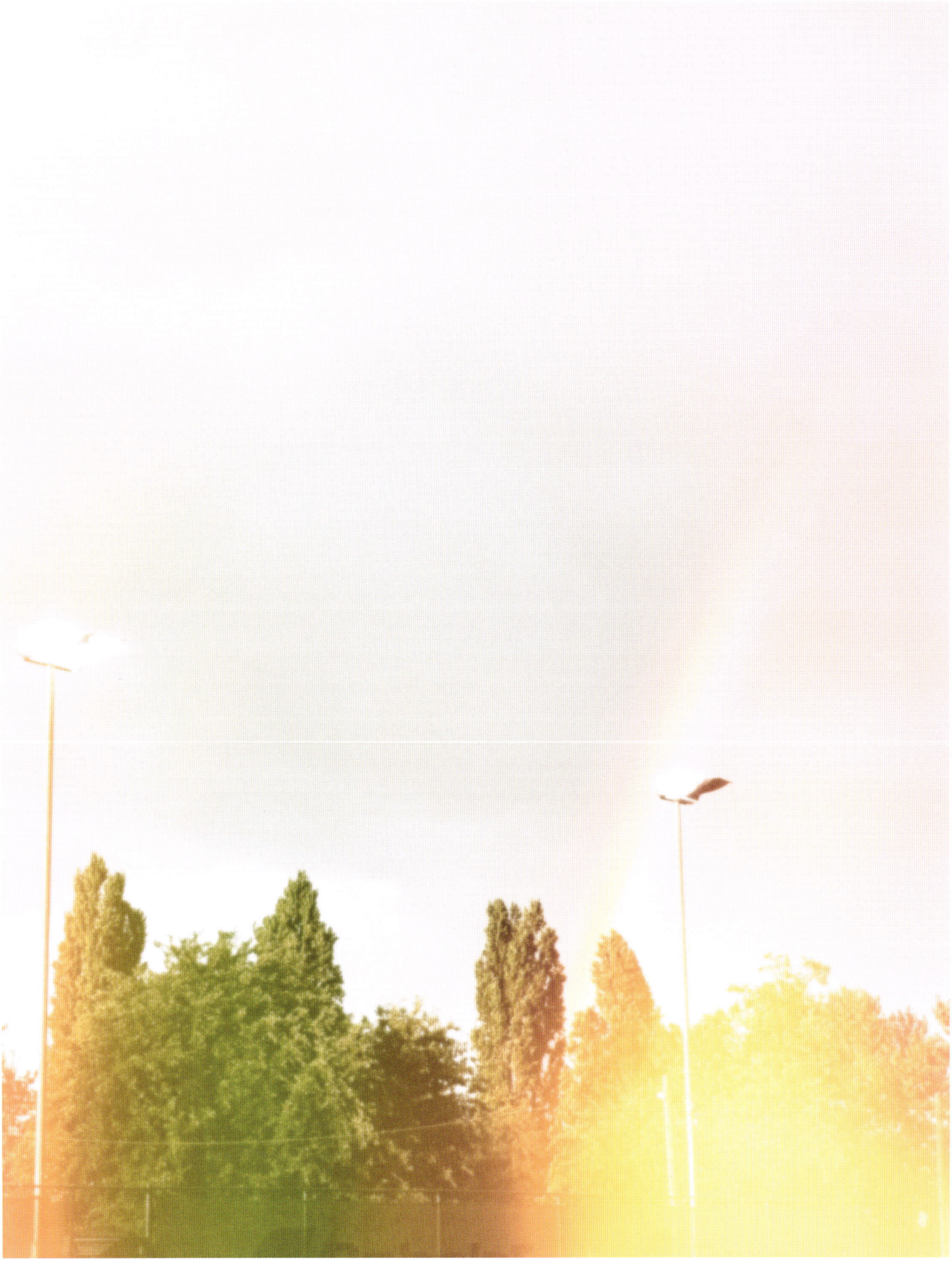

BEFORE ANY GAMES BEGIN,

something happens in the players' tunnel. It's a telling few minutes; the televised camera always takes us, the spectator, there. Zooming in on the athlete, it is here that an inner transformation, from human into some physical paranormal state, occurs: eyes fixed, mind engaged, a limbering of limbs, the muscle memory called to action, the trained target now chalked up in real time. As we witness this catalytic conversion between the athletic mind and body, it feels primeval and relatable, because we can all connect to it in some basic, intrinsic way—this is *Homo sapiens*, preparing to take flight or fight. To me, this is where the match has already unfolded, the score decided, the trophy doled out. It is only the fates who can intervene by twisting and turning any presumed outcome into the unthinkable.

While researching *ACE*, I had the chance to walk through a football tunnel at the adidas HQ in Herzogenaurach, Germany—a phantom energy of past players ran beside me. I felt the same as a classics student walking through the Roman Colosseum: *Greatness* has happened here. Literature has told it, but the third eye feels it: an epitaph to humankind's ability to transcend any physical limit through the rigors and excellence of sport.

There is another phase to this metamorphosis, and that is the "walk-on" moment. Here, the athlete strides into their arena, the stage where the games will play out and the victor will be declared. The tunnel walk connects the body and mind to action, but it is the court's runway that calls the athlete's persona to action. What the athlete wears enables this superego conversion. The sports gear is called *performance* for this very reason. Together, the tunnel and walk-on moments summon the alchemy of physique and might.

A runway show of the athlete's prowess as they walk on, their attire becomes a brief window into their inner psyche and that of the brands who sponsor them. This union of brand and athlete is part parade, part functional, a peacocking to the predator on the other side. The one with the best dress will surely succeed. Why? Because if you look and feel good, you will play well. Every single sports brand that I visited uttered similar mantras.

The performance aspect of a design is always a challenging one—comparable to the work of couture ateliers. Every detail is painstakingly addressed: neckline, armholes, length, seams, sleeves. The holy grail is next-to-skin sensation: the ultimate design endpoint, and often the difference between winning and losing. Integrating fashion into performance design introduces a layered complexity—one that often necessitates the direct involvement of fashion designers themselves. Sport and fashion are distinct disciplines; merging them into a single garment demands an unspoken cooperation. It's not called a collaboration for nothing.

And the sport that began this affair with fashion first? Tennis. Players began to understand that aligning with fashion designers (in the 1920s to 1960s), and later with sports brands (from the 1960s onward), would elevate their social status and, crucially, enhance their game on court. This cultural relevance off-court is a sequel of the pro and their celebrity; it serves as a style mnemonic to the crowd, which we can later buy—a brief portal into their heroic magic for us to play out in our daily lives. Together, these components form the operating system that powers *ACE*.

Casting the style categories for the athletes—the Classics, the Mavericks, and the Cool—proved easy for me. Their on-court fashions were a reflection of their time, their personalities, or both.

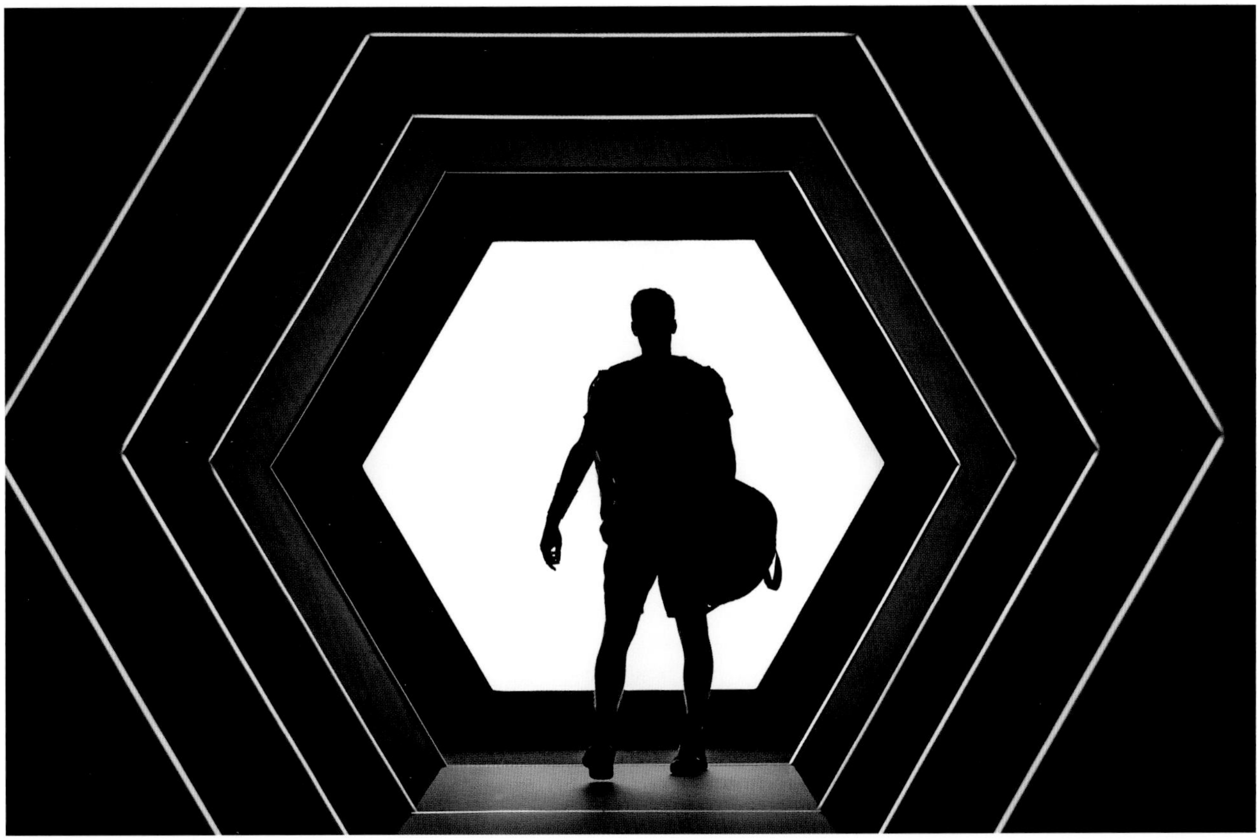

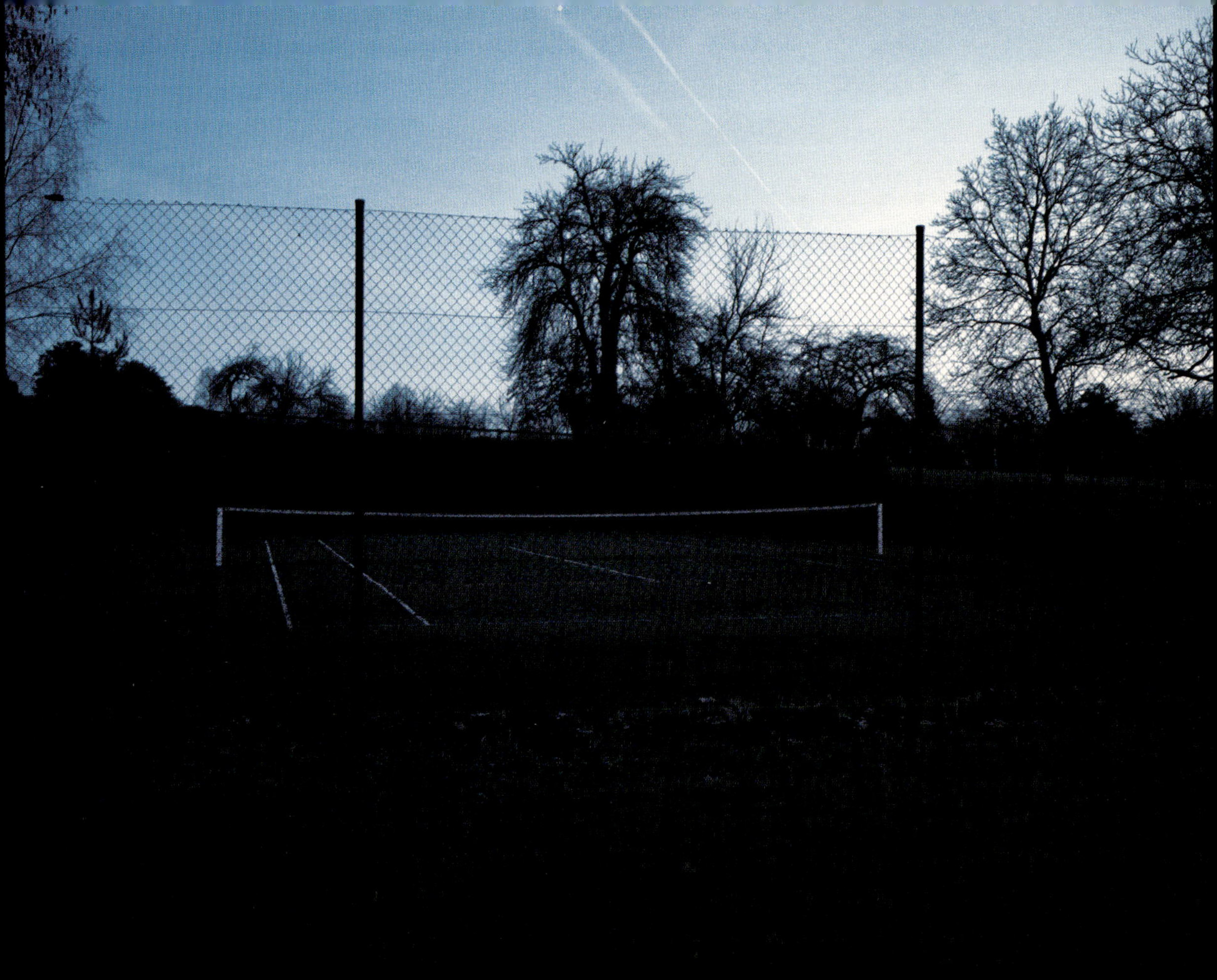

GREATNESS HAS HAPPENED HERE

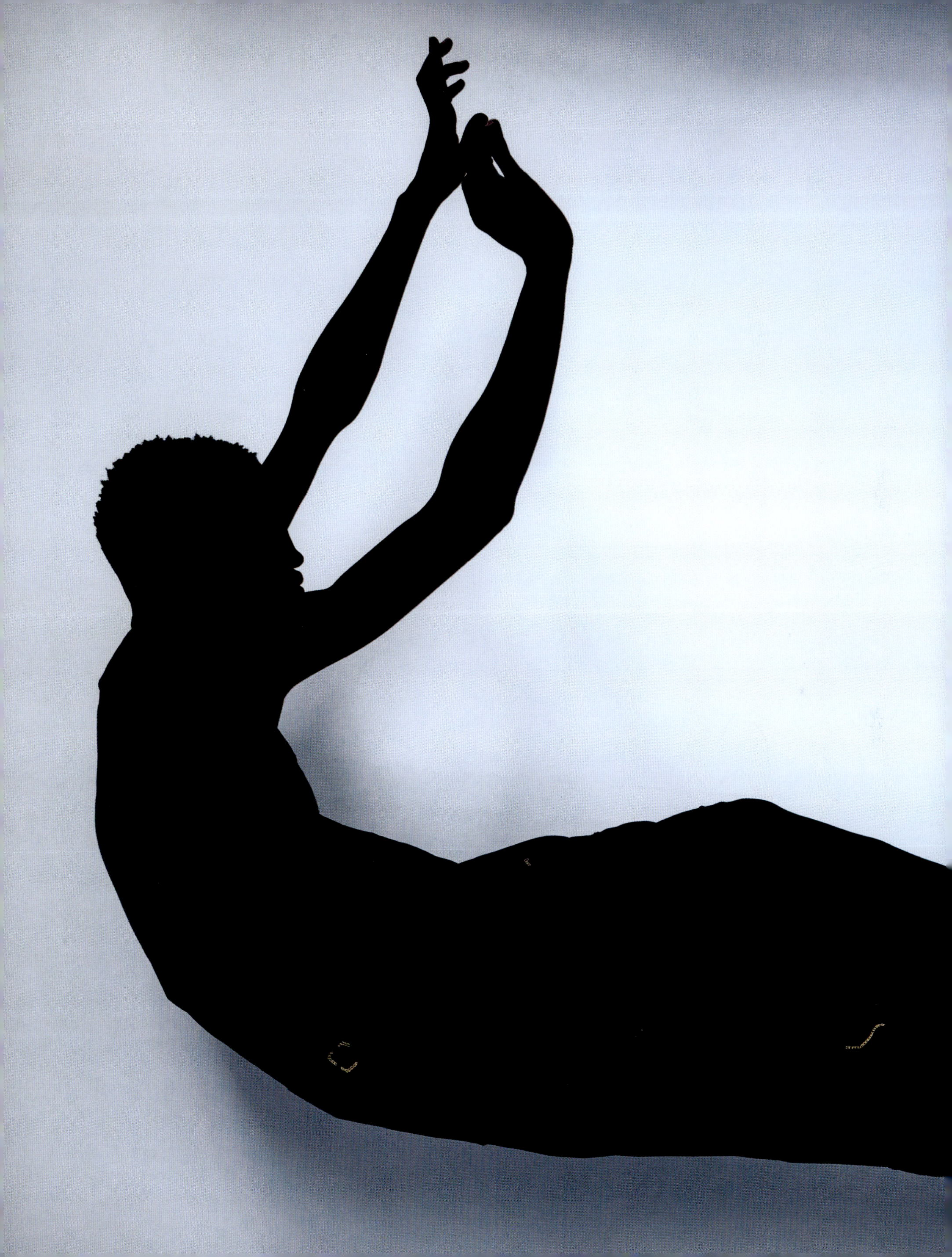

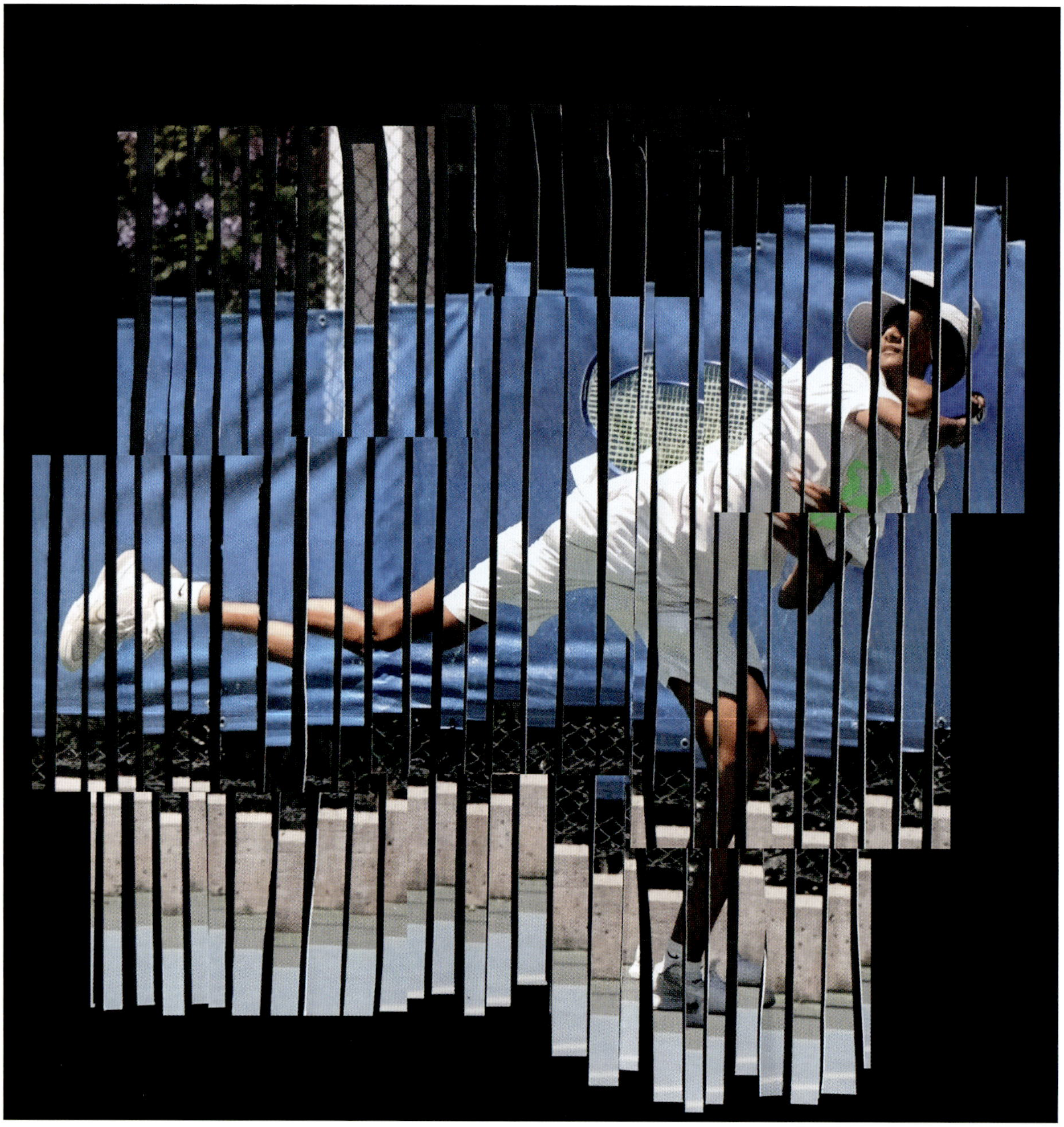

Tennis began and endures with the Classics. Like the silent majesty of an elder oak tree, tennis sowed its seeds in privileged soil. The societal dress codes nearly stunted its growth, but the players' will to win ultimately prevailed. Today, we still hark back to this world of the English aristocrat, the American WASP, the Hollywood glitterati, and the European jet-set with retro varsity wear.

The Mavericks broke free from the Classics. Players were no longer fenced in by the four walls of the country club; their design language spoke with every strain of their own identities and philosophies. It was a new breath in tennis style.

And those who needed neither of the above? The Cool. They quietly impress via their play, beliefs, or brand, and their design codes can be found in every stratum of our world today, whether it's fashion, film, music, art, or the hype world. It's the unwritten playbook on the story of fashion and sport.

ACE, the word, came to me first, before I actualized the players and their respective kingdoms. I watched my young son one day unfailingly practice his serve—nowhere near making an ace, yet the set motions were becoming ingrained in his brain. Muscles, the body's own database, will eventually synchronize these steps into a single impactful movement. One misstep, however, and it all falls apart.

I realized that the control, skill, and accuracy of this stroke captured the very essence of the sport—a perfect fusion of physical mastery and mental tenacity. Making an ace is peak performance. I wondered as I was writing *ACE* what the word would mean to pro players. Each one, of course, had their own unique response. As for me? I play but not well, as my son often reminds me, but visually, when I see a pro executing an ace, it's invariably made at the eleventh hour—a crucial point when the die is not quite cast on whether they will win or lose. For when you choose to serve an ace, you are ultimately betting on your best self, the part that will win without any doubt. Because if you don't take that mental gamble on yourself, what else is there?

SKN

SUNITA KUMAR NAIR

I.

THE CLASSICS

Classics is where the story emerged: with the upper echelons of society, namely in England and America, in the latter part of the 1800s. Old-money gentry had access to play; the apparel rules enforced this class system, with both men and women tied into restrictive formalwear—until the athleticism part required them to push past these codes. It's the very definition of power dressing for sports. This genre today harks back to that elite, sophisticated, moneyed world now known as *retro*. Royalty and Hollywood alike, from Princess Diana to Grace Kelly, played out this quiet luxe with quintessential grace.

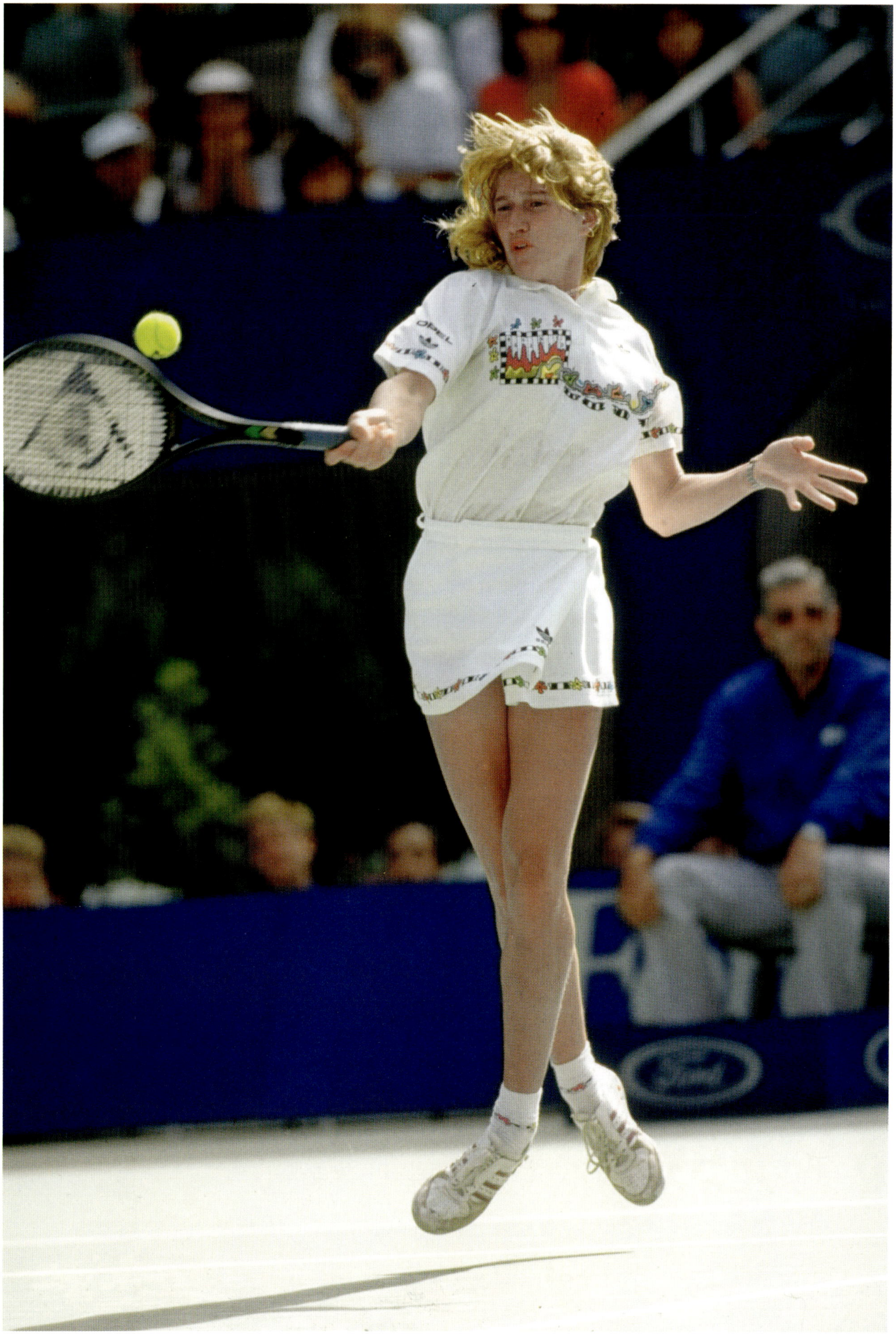

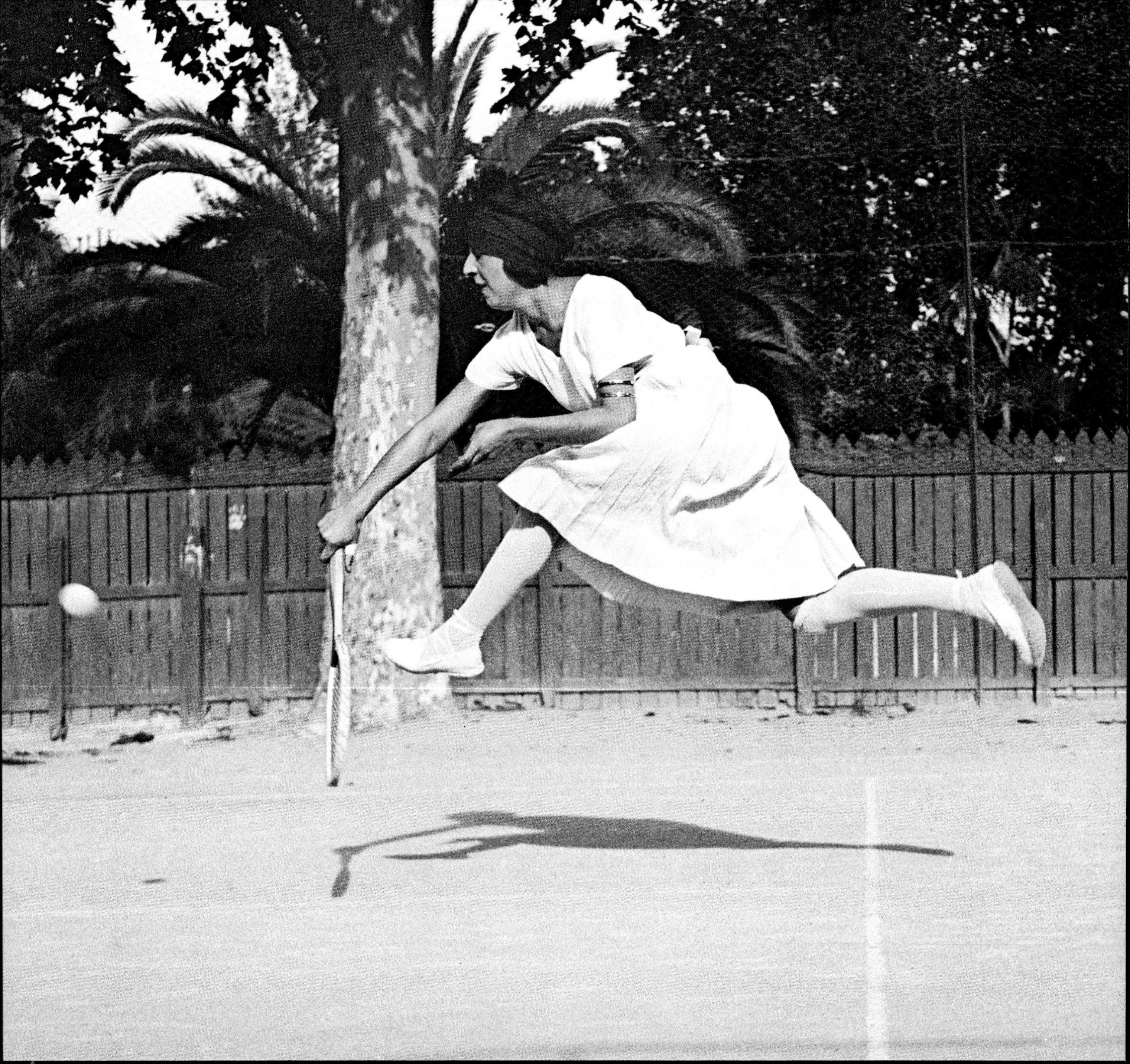

SUZANNE LENGLEN (1899—1938) WAS AN EIGHT-TIME GRAND SLAM WINNER, OLYMPIC GOLD MEDALIST, AND AUDACIOUS ALL-ROUND HARD-BALL HITTER. JEAN PATOU (1887—1936) WAS A VISIONARY FRENCH COUTURIER AND FASHION INNOVATOR.

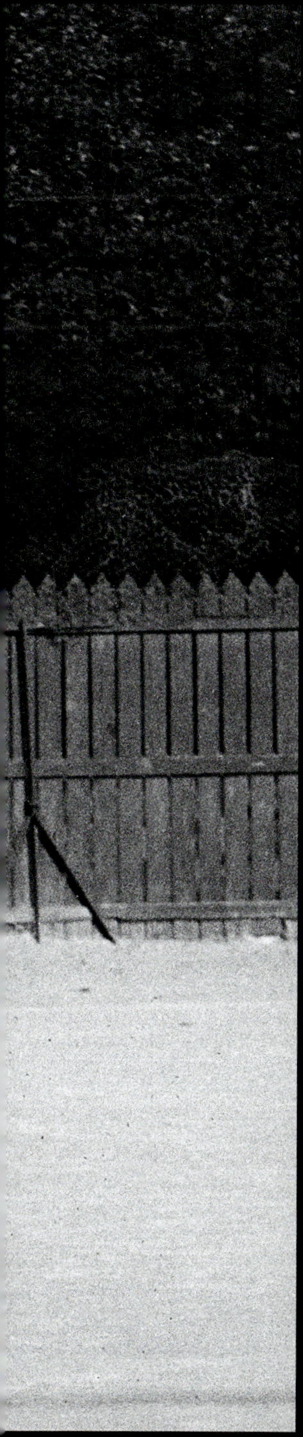

MISS SUZANNE LENGLEN & JEAN PATOU

Her name sounded like her game: *Lenglen*, a long lengthening of limbs. Unorthodoxly, she trained predominantly with men—King Gustav V of Sweden and navigator Alain Gerbault, no less. Suzanne Lenglen mastered precise, hard-ball play along with her acrobatic skills. Her impressive stats reflected her relentless chase for the ball: 250 championships, 83 singles, 74 doubles, and 93 mixed doubles, one with René Lacoste. In short, from 1919 to 1926, she lost just one match. The *International Herald Tribune* petitioned that "it had earned her the right to be ranked alongside top male players in history."

Compared to a brilliant meteor by fashion designer and friend Ted Tinling, Lenglen blinded those in her shadow with her courtside antics—swigging flasks of brandy in between points to calm her nerves, berating opponents and umpires, reapplying her siren-red lipstick, and routinely arriving on court clad in fur. The godmother of tennis, crowned "La Divine" by all, she set the mold: a child prodigy of an ambitious tennis parent, a consecutive Grand Slam winner, a fashion brand ambassador, a sports celebrity, an influencer, and a women's advocate. Her limbs unfurled into every domain now claimed by modern athletes.

I begin as Lenglen would have wanted: with her tennis. But it was her downright love of the sport—and more so of winning—that incited her fashion intelligence in play. Insisting that clothes must "free the body," she did exactly that, arriving to her first 1919 international match at Wimbledon in a Jean Patou dress. Up until that point, women were obliged to play in garden party attire: full-length skirt, blouson-sleeved shirt, corset, and broad hat. Lenglen shed them all for tennis.

Patou, the revolutionary French couturier, modified his design specs specifically for a tennis player. Lenglen blithely walked on the grass in a cap-sleeved dress—arm free for serves, a scoop-neck bodice—that revealed her sun-kissed skin. The straight-lined, dropped-waist silhouette enabled her hips a wider rotation range as she played. The midcalf hemline gave her further agility: the accordion-pleated skirt increased the scope of mobility and retained her genteel modesty. The fine white silk jersey fabric provided aeration and breathability. Her return to Wimbledon in 1920 was equally brazen, the dress shorter, sleeveless, and made of a translucent silk, which she accessorized with a crêpe georgette silk turban. Worn in a panoply of colors, it became signature Lenglen.

Patou experienced an extraordinary spike in sales while dressing Lenglen. American *Vogue* reviewed "the freedom, appropriateness, and excellence of its [the dress] simple lines" and included patterns of her dress for women to sew themselves. Lenglen's on-court look partly inspired the off-court "La Garçonne" aesthetic, consisting of boyish haircuts and hips disguised within dropped-waist dresses that fell a little over the knee. Driven by sales, Patou finessed this fledging luxury performance sportswear market—whch Gabrielle "Coco" Chanel had begun with her Deauville boutique—and opened Le Coin des Sports, a corner dedicated to all modes of sportswear (golf, skiing, swimming, and tennis) at his salon. Lenglen's endorsement of Patou continued off court; she adored fashion, once absentmindedly replying, "You should see this black-and-white evening dress—it's a masterpiece," when asked about her tennis form by a reporter. Royalty, Hollywood, and creatives entertained Lenglen—the famed photographer Jacques-Henri Lartigue even captured her magic moves—and yet the media always rallied back to the same shot:

"WHAT HAS NOT BEEN SAID ABOUT MY CHIC? I PROBABLY GET MORE COMPLIMENTS FOR MY ATTIRE THAN MY PLAYING. IT'S ALMOST IRRITATING. I DO BELIEVE THAT PATOU'S SUCCESS IS NO LESS THAN MY OWN."

—SUZANNE LENGLEN, 1926

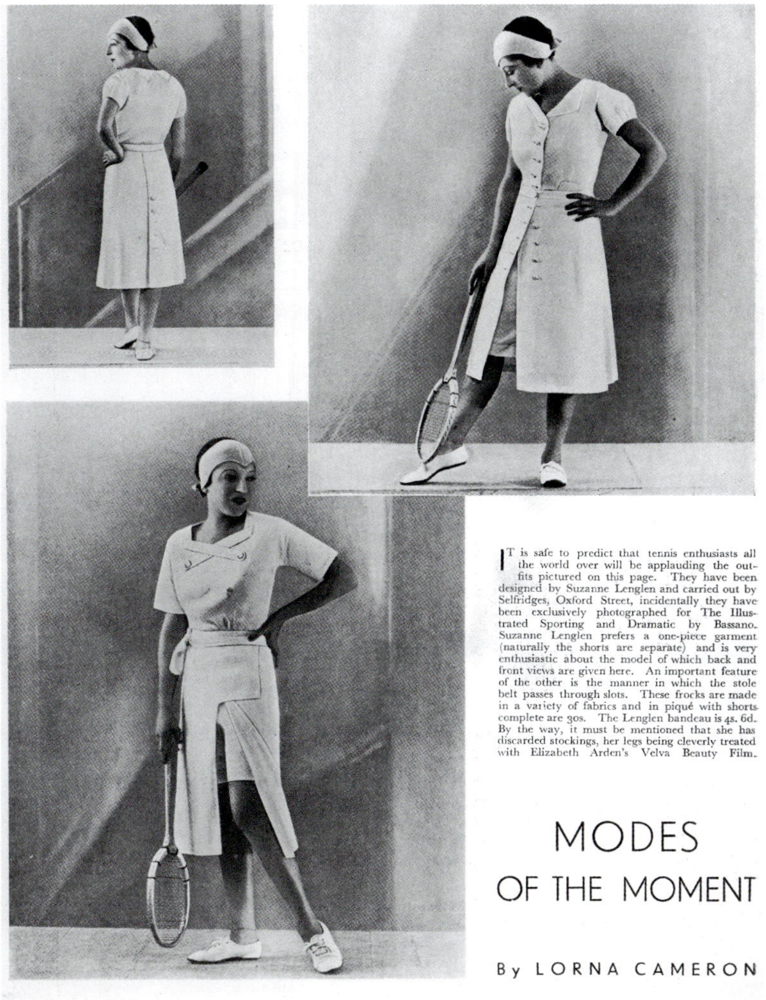

IT is safe to predict that tennis enthusiasts all the world over will be applauding the outfits pictured on this page. They have been designed by Suzanne Lenglen and carried out by Selfridges, Oxford Street, incidentally they have been exclusively photographed for The Illustrated Sporting and Dramatic by Bassano. Suzanne Lenglen prefers a one-piece garment (naturally the shorts are separate) and is very enthusiastic about the model of which back and front views are given here. An important feature of the other is the manner in which the stole belt passes through slots. These frocks are made in a variety of fabrics and in piqué with shorts complete are 30s. The Lenglen bandeau is 4s. 6d. By the way, it must be mentioned that she has discarded stockings, her legs being cleverly treated with Elizabeth Arden's Velva Beauty Film.

MODES

OF THE MOMENT

By LORNA CAMERON

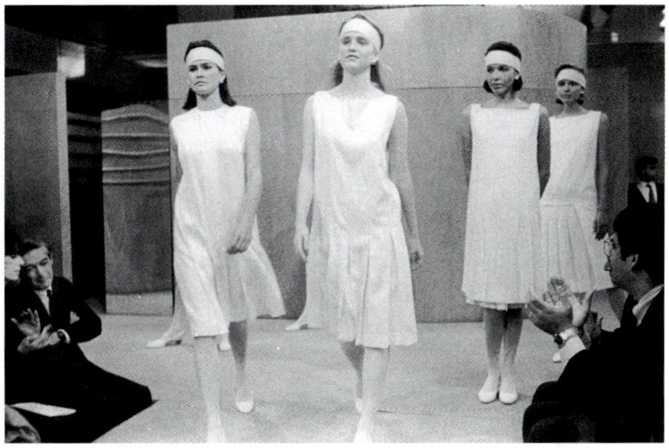

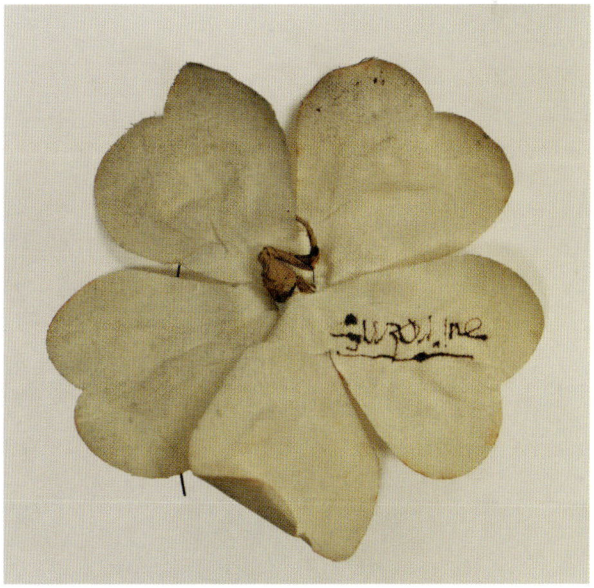

LEFT

SUZANNE LENGLEN MODELING HER OWN DESIGN FOR SELFRIDGES & CO.,SHOWN EXCLUSIVELY IN ILLUSTRATED SPORTING AND DRAMATIC NEWS, 1993

TOP RIGHT

PERRY ELLIS' TENNIS BRIDESMAIDS, INSPIRED BY LENGLEN'S LOOK, 1984

BOTTOM RIGHT

LENGLEN'S BROOCH, DATE UNKNOWN

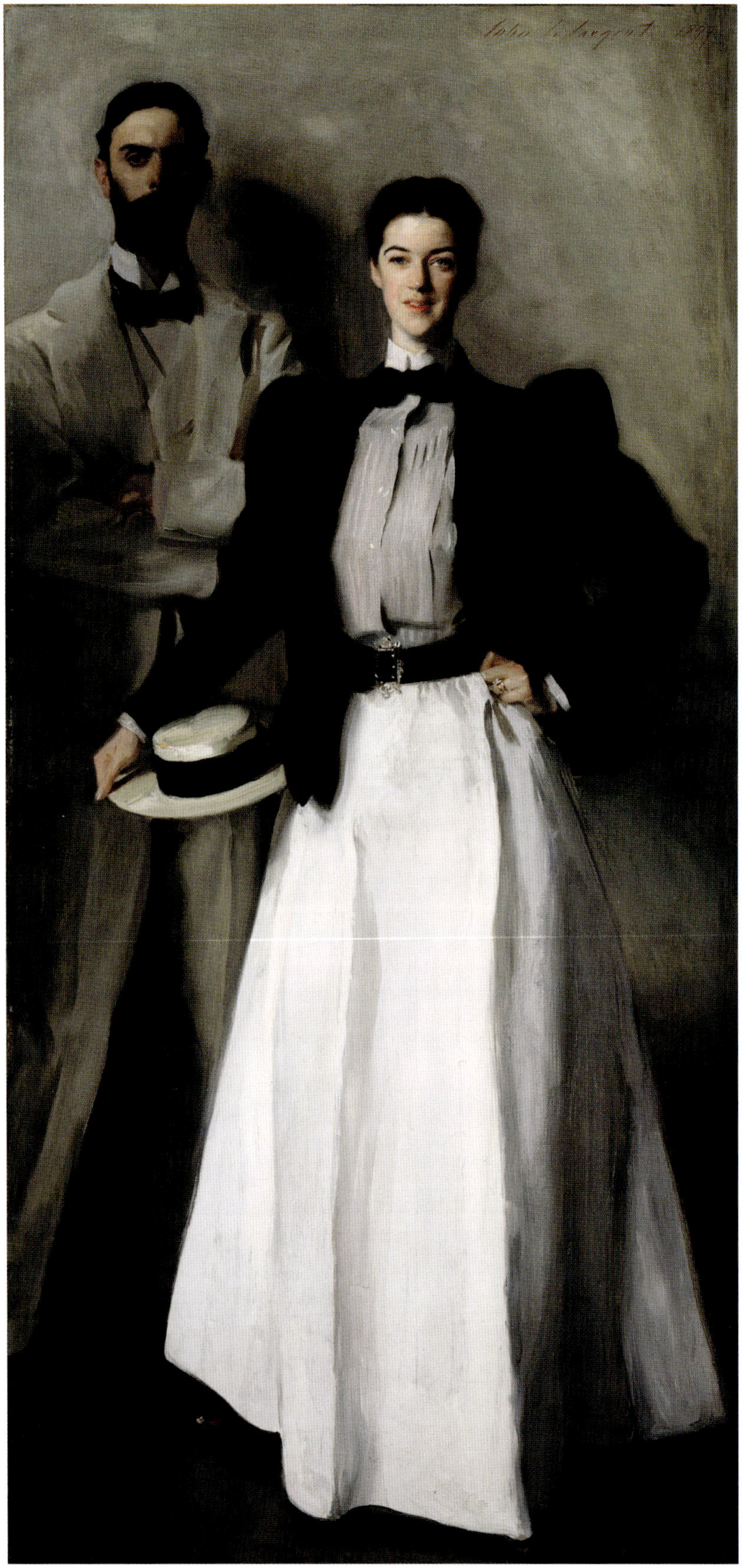

THE SKIRT

It's a basic instinct: to move to catch a ball when it's thrown to you. The physics of any sport is the body in motion, and the fashion of sport should enhance that movement. Not so for tennis. Born from high society's manicured grounds, there was a gamut of respectable clothing requirements that oppressed female players and their bodies. Their desire to move, however, without restraint, eventually reigned supreme. A quiet revolution was at play, for every inch that the tennis skirt hemline rose, it marked a step up in women's social standing. What could be more compelling in fashion and sports history than to witness this cultural influence?

TIME

The sportswomen spoke out as early as 1887. Lottie Dod, five-time Wimbledon champion, asked, "How would one ever hope to play a sound game when their dresses impeded the free movement of every limb?" She and others before her were decked out in full skirts, petticoats, bustles, long-sleeved blousons—and corsets. The corset's purpose was to cater to the male gaze—cinching in the waist, amplifying the bosom—but to play tennis in it seemed unfathomable. But play they did. Perhaps the tennis word *changeover* arose from these women physically changing out of their bloodied corsets into fresh ones? The game was slow-paced, with ball speeds clocking no more than 40 mph. Maybe women didn't need to run? With both torso and limbs securely contained by a corset and long skirt, there was no chance.

MR& MRS PHELPS STOKES BY JOHN SINGER SARGENT, 1897

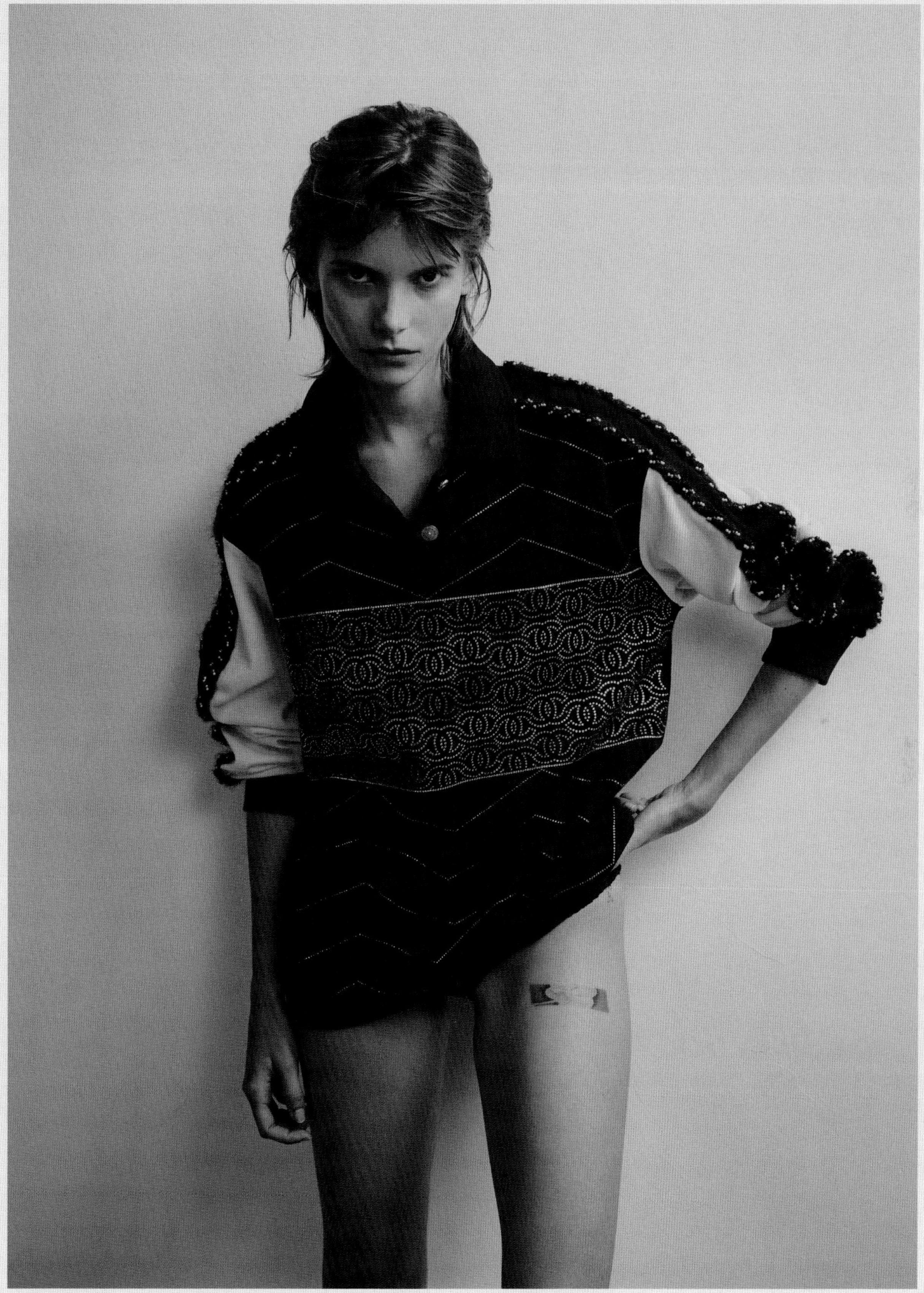

LOVE–15

A painting in 1897 signaled a small shift in women's social standing. Those who sat for John Singer Sargent, the famed American portraitist to the gentry, usually dressed their best: in evening attire. Mrs. Phelps Stokes, however, was rendered in her street or sportswear—how rad. The mismatched cloth outfit and its color were clues that she had just returned from playing a sport (most likely tennis): a long white cotton broadcloth maxi skirt; a short black wool Eton jacket and pleated light-gray cotton wing-collar shirt; a short necktie; and a straw boater. Her stance is strong, cheeks and nose clearly flushed—is she perspiring? Her husband disappears behind her, shadowlike, his clothing a mimicry of hers. This woman is standing as an equal to her counterpart, and she too can play sport just like him.

15–ALL

The skirt hem finally got the cut, thanks to the fashion teamwork between European designers and players. Suzanne Lenglen and couturier Jean Patou were the first perfect doubles pairing in 1919. Specifically with performance play in mind, he raised the hem, dropped the waist, and created a tennis dress. Helen Wills favored Patou too. Rhapsodizing on the pleating technique—a firm design feature for tenniswear—she said, "It has a classic simplicity, and in action is most comfortable and pleasing to the onlooker." Patou deftly demonstrated that couture form could seamlessly follow function.

Gabrielle "Coco" Chanel, an accomplished sportswoman herself, also made her own tennis rendition. She even detailed the ideal specs: "Dress should be adapted to the freedom of movement which the game demands, and 'l'élégance' consists much more in the harmony of proportions and lines than in any detail of decoration." Tennis was now in vogue, literally and culturally. Chanel often designed for the Ballets Russes; one particular production, *Le Train Bleu*, centered around the sporting life and featured a Lenglen-inspired character. This on-court silhouette organically spun off-court and contributed to the 1920s flapper fashion trend. By 1924, women were partaking in the Olympics, and even Jeanne Lanvin—renowned for her "robe de style" dresses with voluminous skirts and fitted bodices—couldn't resist this new liberated line; she designed the "Championnat" dress to celebrate. Thanks to this silhouette, shapely limbs were on show everywhere, and a sporting consciousness became widespread. All this exercise also unfortunately resulted in sweating, and so the respective ateliers created their own eau de parfums. Traveling to far-flung locations to swim, play tennis, or golf was de rigueur and a new market developed, courtesy of another fashion creative, Lucien Lelong. His focus: leisurewear.

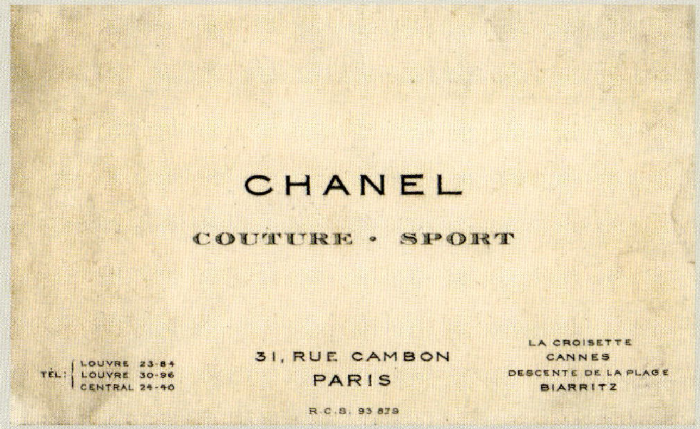

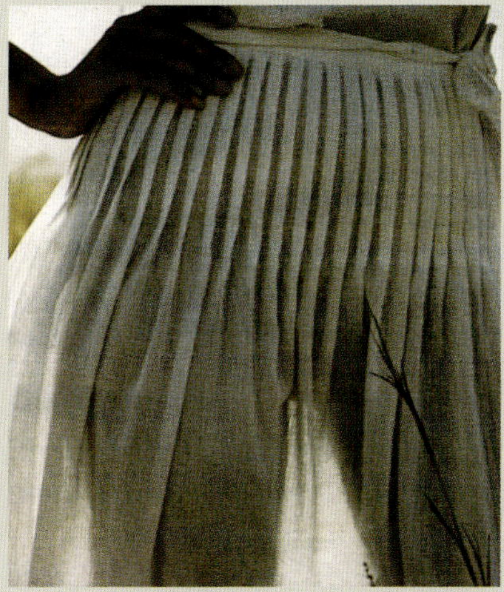

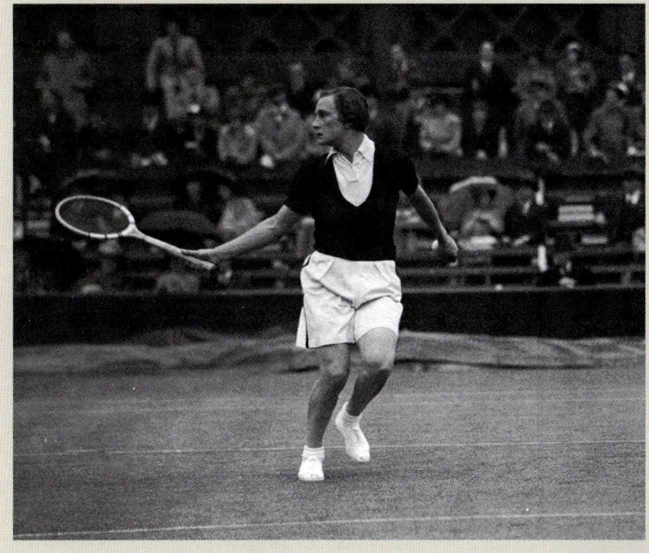

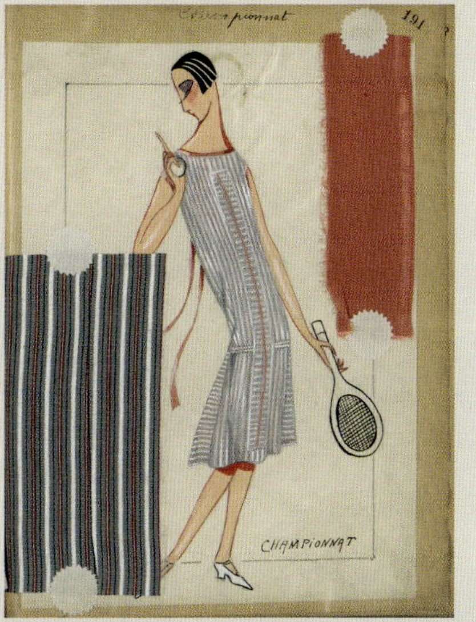

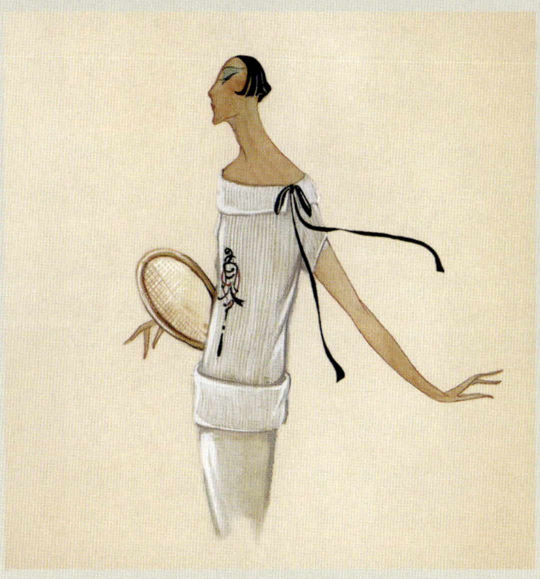

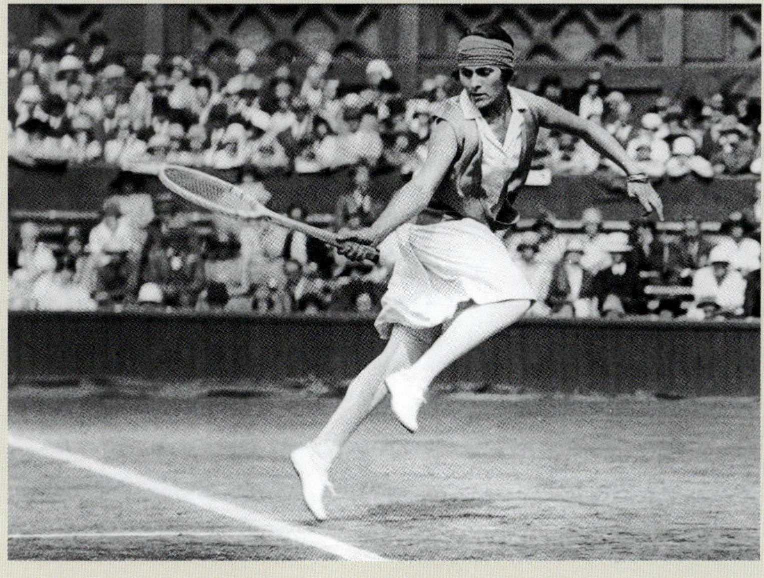

CLOCKWISE, FROM TOP LEFT

CHANEL COUTURE SPORTS CARD, 1920S, PATRIMOINE DE CHANEL, PARIS © CHANEL

HARRI PECCINOTTI

CHAMPIONNAT DRESS, 1924
© LANVIN HERITAGE

LILÍ ÁLVAREZ AT WIMBLEDON WEARING SCHIAPARELLI, 1926

LANGRUNE DRESS, 1923-24
© LANVIN HERITAGE

HELEN JACOBS AT WIMBLEDON WEARING SHORTS, 1936

15–30

Improved racket design by 1937 led to faster ball speeds and some topspin on groundstrokes. Elsa Schiaparelli had already cemented her reputation as an avant-garde designer; when she dabbled in sportswear, she inadvertently pushed the game further afield. The parameters of dressing remained firmly within the confines of the female wardrobe until Lilí Álvarez, winner of the French Open, was diplomatically described as wearing "a divided skirt." Schiaparelli bluntly corrected it to a "trouser skirt." The reactions were close to violent—the *Daily Express* in London declared, "If any woman comes to Wimbledon in that divided skirt, they should be soundly beaten." What the hell were women doing wearing men's clothing? What would be next? If women were chasing balls instead of babies—a crime Lenglen had already committed—what would be the future of mankind? All these players were photographed like sporty theatrical ingenues—limbs midflight, their dresses flowing in fluidity, their newfound freedom, tangible.

15–40

It was only a matter of time for shorts to take their turn. The varsity sports uniform of a polo shirt with shorts was the preference of American players like Alice Marble and Helen Hull Jacobs. Jacobs felt she had to validate this risqué choice, citing it as "a tremendous advantage." Practically, it helped her to be "cooler" and "faster." She was pictured on the front cover of *Time* magazine in September 1936—a global seal of approval.

MATCH POINT

This kinetic impact between sport, fashion, and the fabric of society was a breakthrough for female tennis pros. After all, in the words of Chanel: "Fashion does not exist only in dresses; fashion is in the air, it is borne on the wind, you can sense it, you can breathe it, it's in the sky and on the highway, it's everywhere, it has to do with ideas, with social mores, with events." It was a masterful collaboration of performance playwear and Parisian fashion design. Only Pierre Balmain failed to adapt his designs to suit his player's body; excessive pleating and reams of heavy fabric hindered Gussie Moran's mobility.

In 1947, however, came a new Paris fashion horizon: Christian Dior's cinched waists and voluminous skirts, marketed as the "New Look"; here, ladylike aesthetics prevailed over comfort. There was no conceivable manner in which this trend could support the sportswoman's apparel path. When one hem falls, another will rise—isn't that how the saying goes? Over to Ted Tinling, who would make and take the cut further.

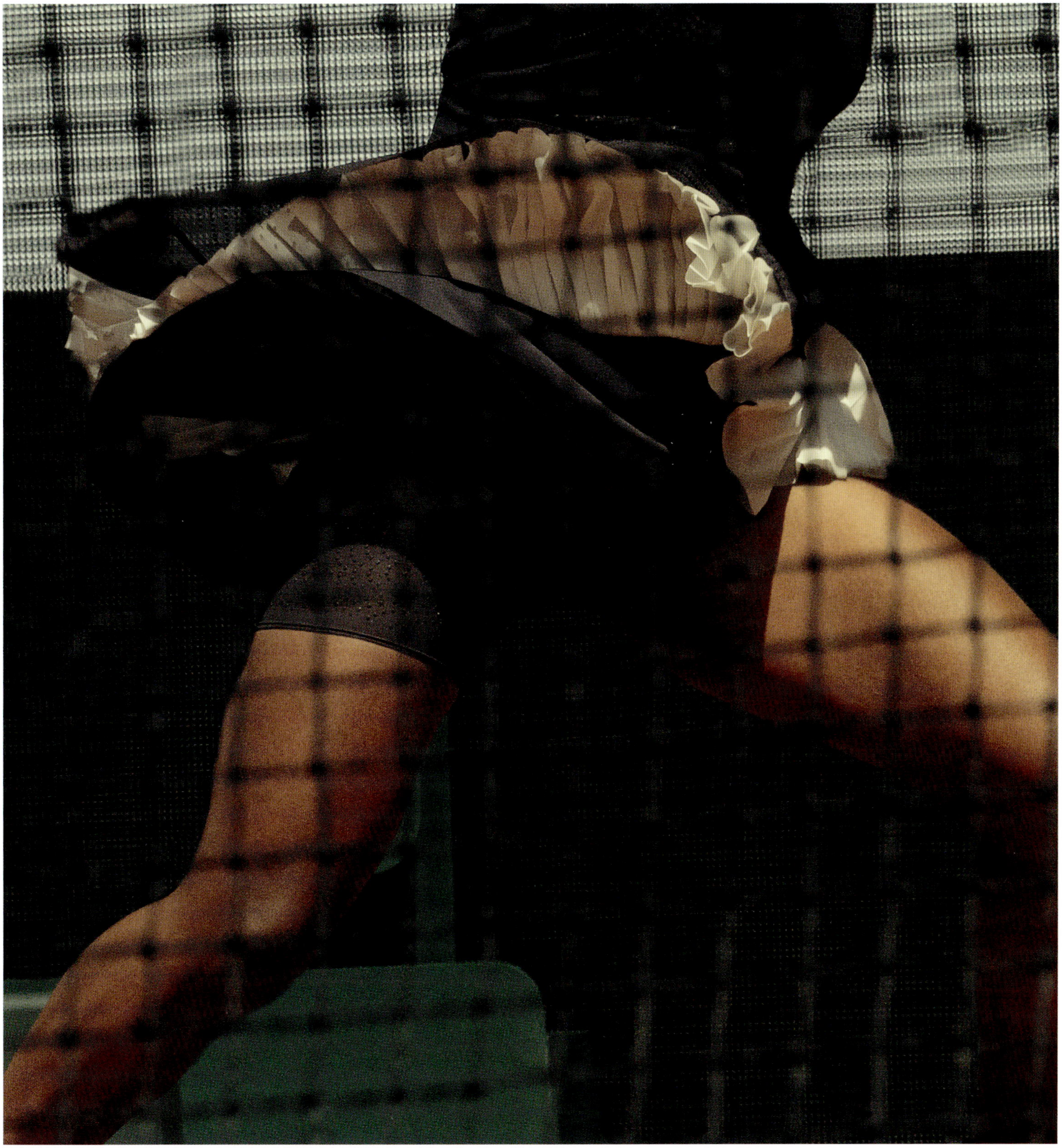

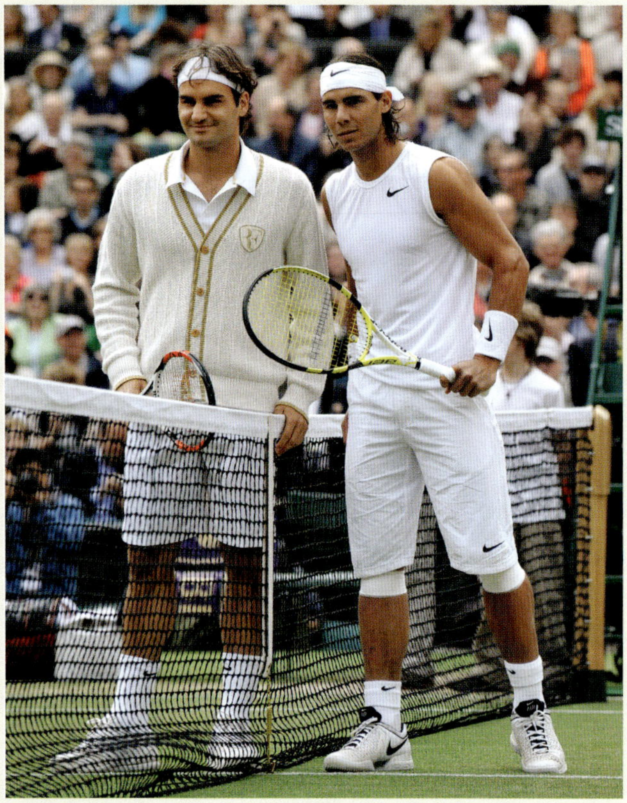

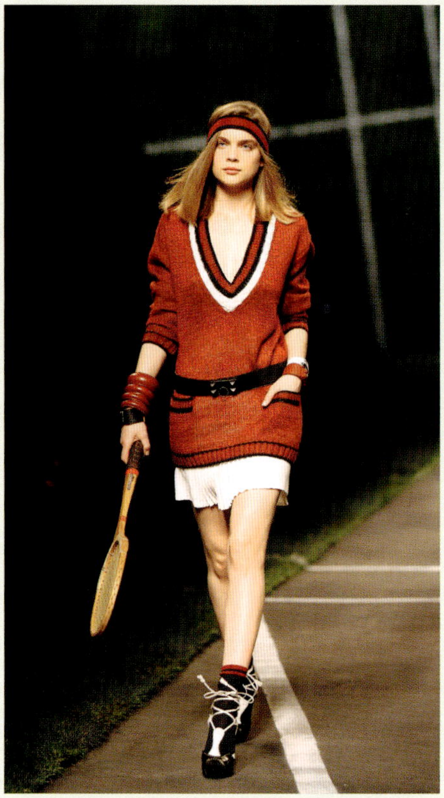

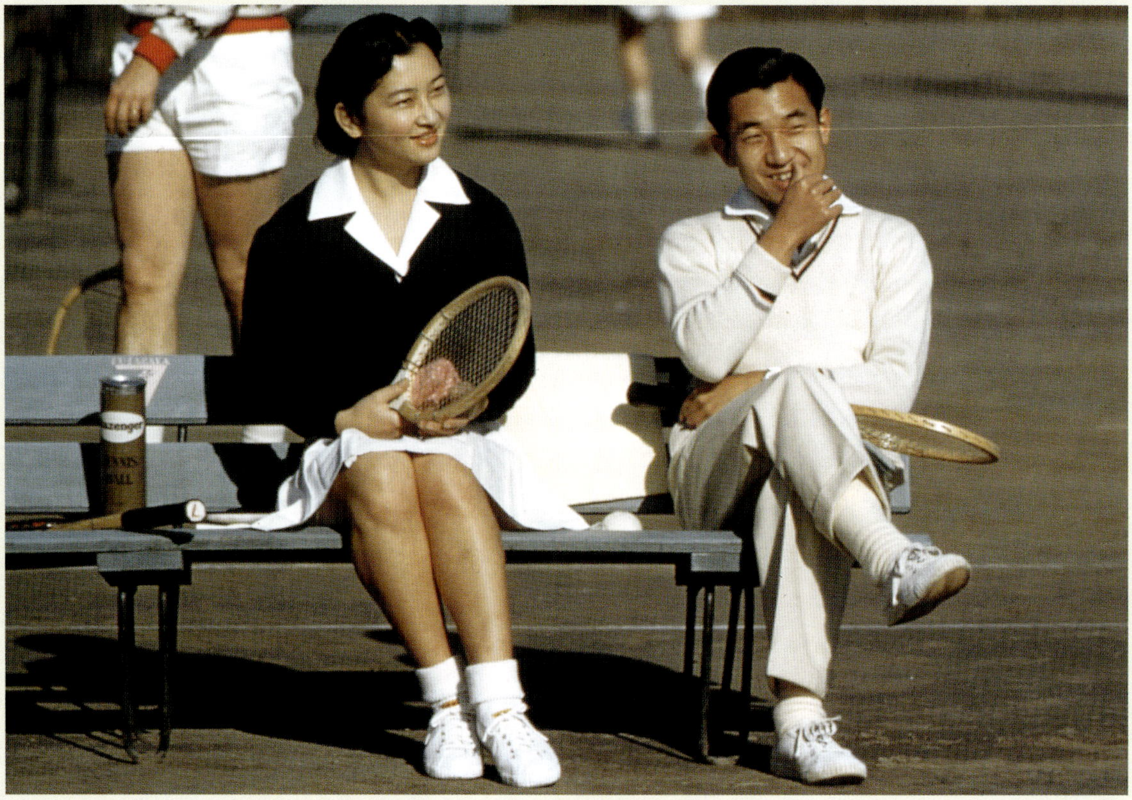

THE SWEATER

A fashion fable tends to begin with humble, deviant, disenchanted beginnings. It's the spine on which most fashion stories are made—the mundane is divined into the extraordinary, magically cast with a new thread of luxury by the fashion designer. And so 'twas the begotten beginnings of the tennis sweater not from court, but from sea, off the rugged shores of the British Isles, where the wives of fisherfolk did knit Aran sweaters, each tight stitch a shield against the raging seas, each pattern a tale of kin and coast. Somewhere along this fashion timeline, an infiltration occurred. The fisherman's cabled covering most likely leapt from the seas to the shore—onto a cricket field, to be exact, where the aristocracy learned the sport from their laborers; it then later moved on to a tennis court. A versatile piece made with a lighter knit to enhance fluidity and beat the unruly British climes.

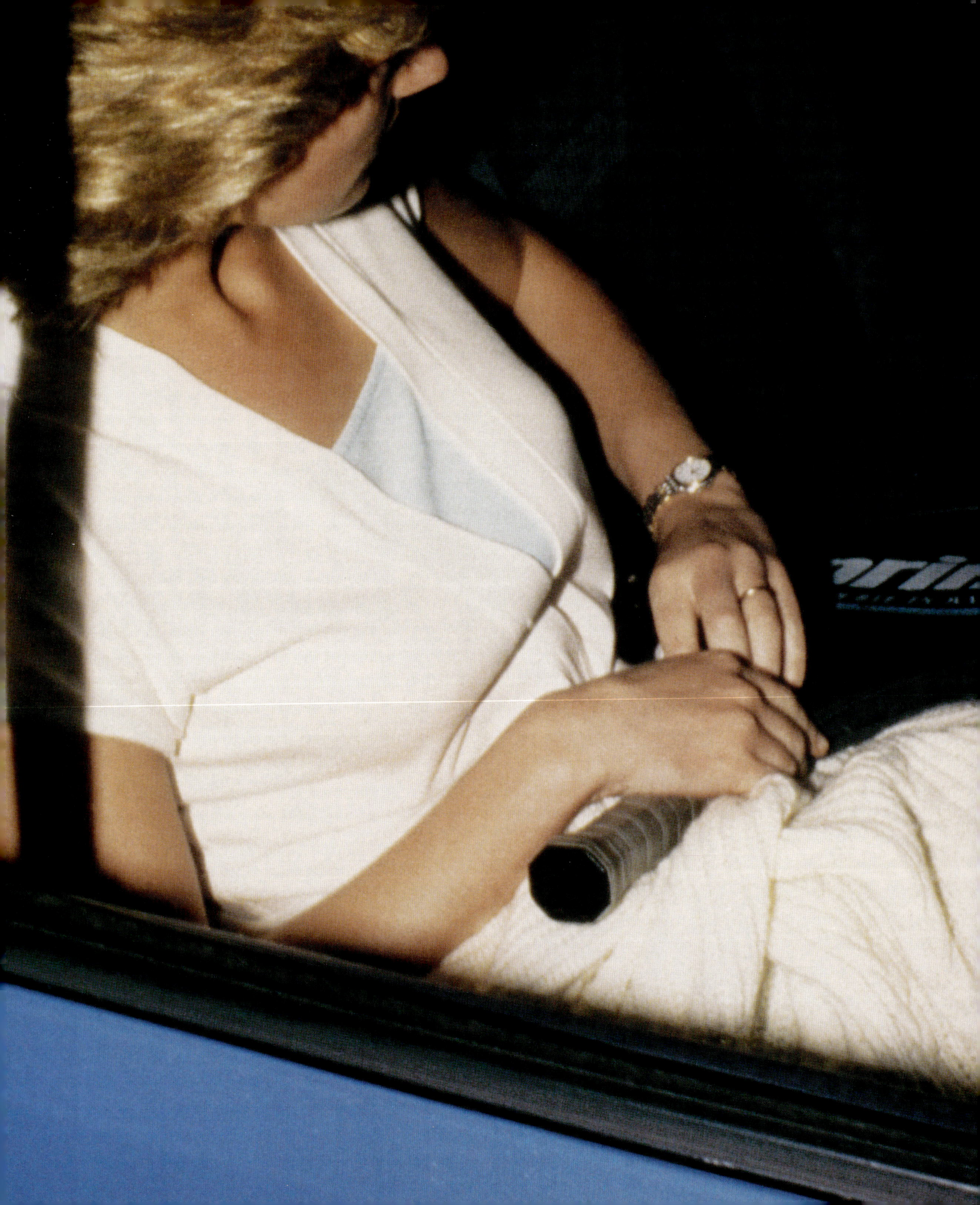

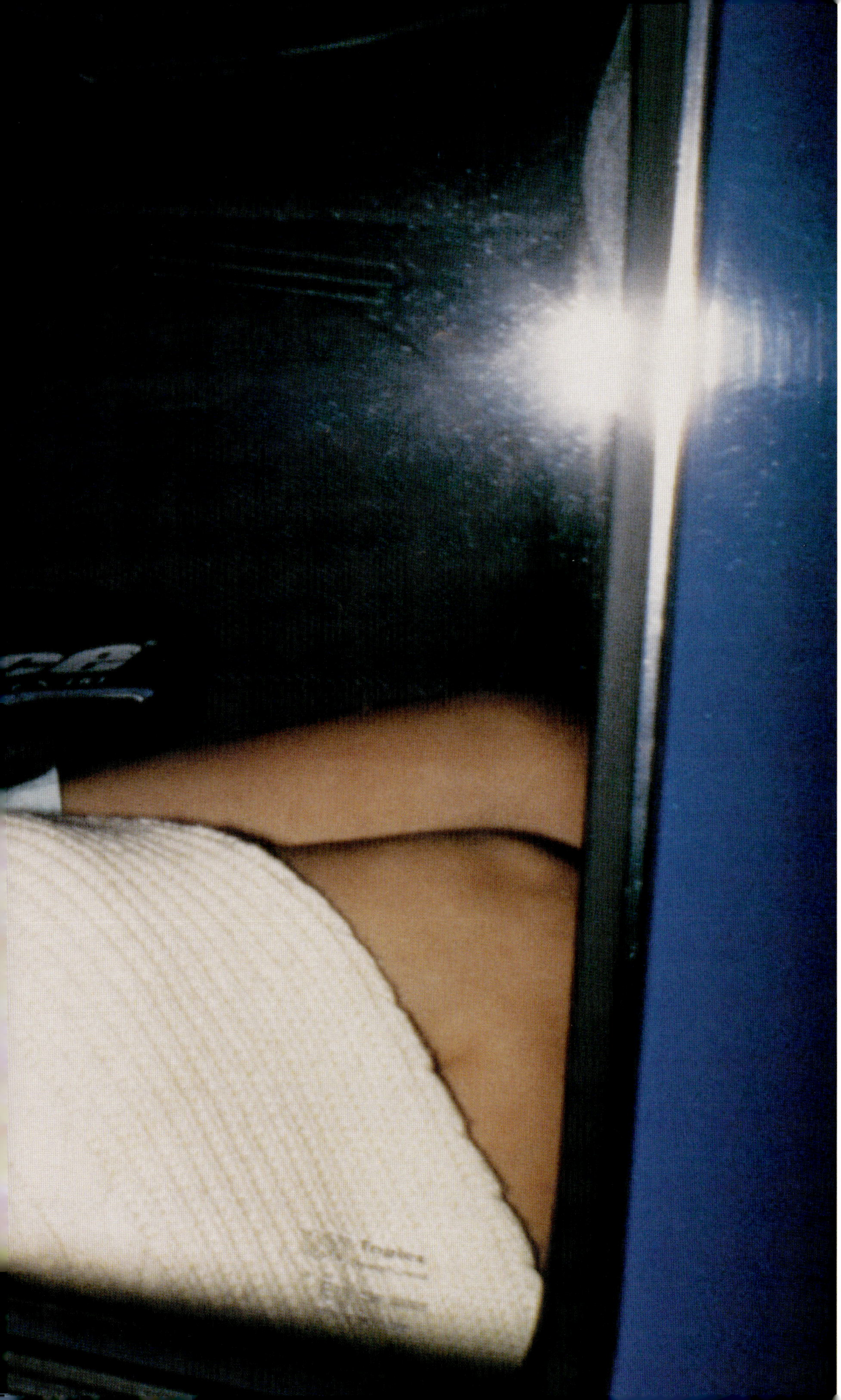

THE STRIPES

Stripes were often knitted along the V-neck of the sweater (the *V* shape gave better scope to the arms), a style flag that marked a school, university, or club affiliation. Blazers and caps with wider stripes were already part of the academia sporting uniform in the early 1900s, a chic badge of elite belonging and honor.

If men could play sport, so could women; what better symbol of modernity could there be? So if she had to loot from her brother's, father's, husband's, or lover's wardrobe, she did. Chanel first borrowed from her lover, Boy Capel—she made his clothing hers, reconfigured the masculine lines and later sold them for women. Sweaters and cardigans served utilitarian purposes, but in Chanel's and Patou's hands, their status became luxury. Remodeled in fine wool or silk jersey, with sophisticated logos subtly combined, it instantly elevated the knitwear genre: a happily-ever-after fashion fairy tale, if ever there was, with the tennis sweater still holding fort on and off the court.

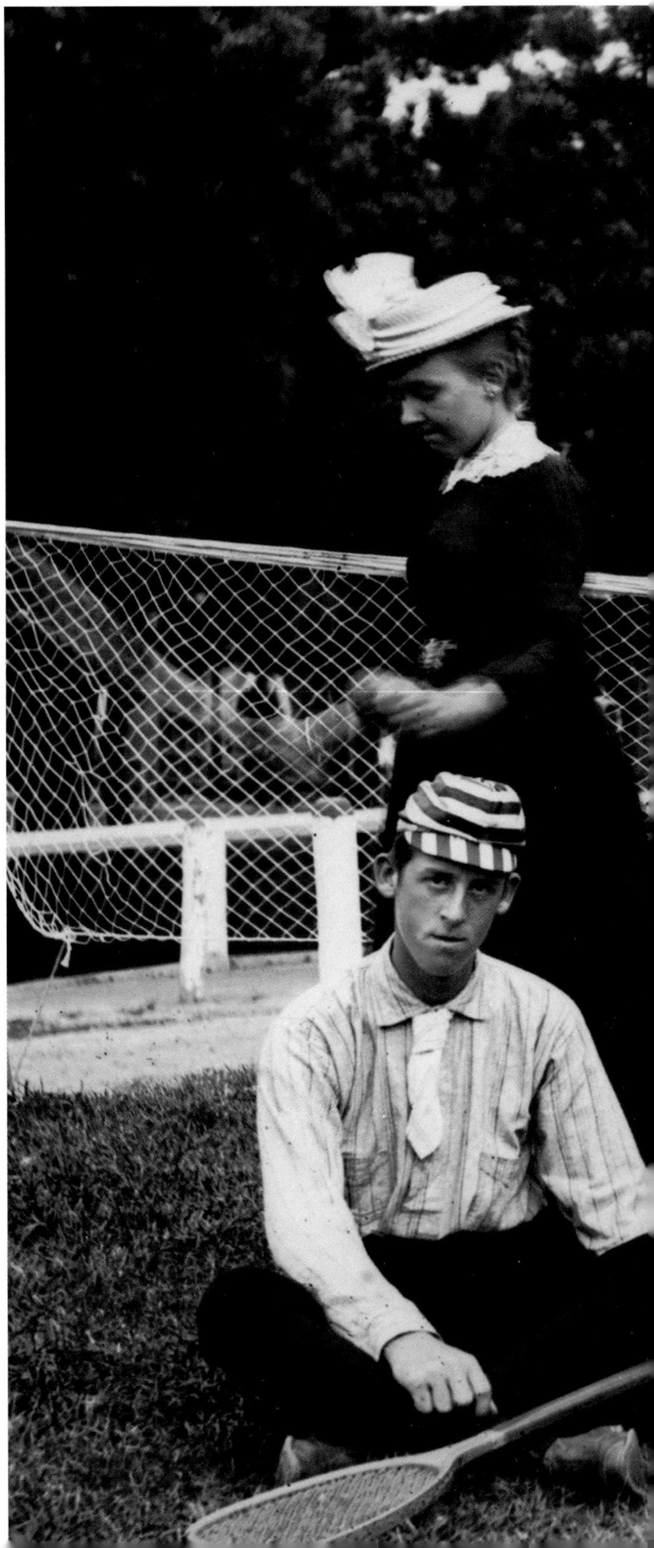

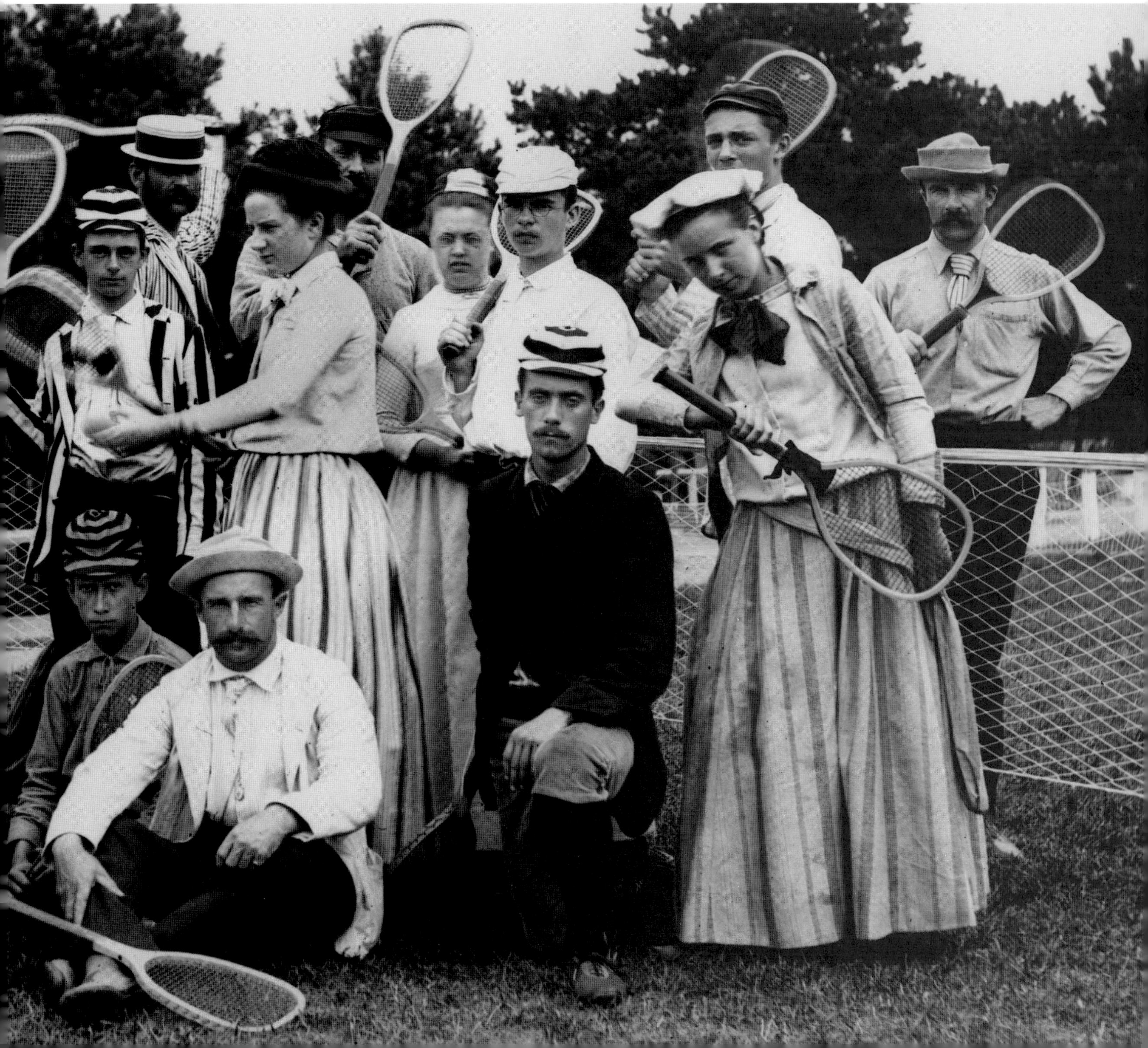

MR. BUNNY AUSTIN & THE CALL FOR SHORTS

BUNNY AUSTIN WAS A QUICK, ATHLETIC ALL-ROUNDER AND BOTH A WIMBLEDON AND US OPEN FINALIST (1906–2000).

Where you could play a sport determined *if* you could play it, especially in the 1910s. Tennis, golf, and swimming required specific venues that were afforded only by the affluent. Club uniforms symbolically served as visual reinforcements to this social order: Compulsory men's sports gear included long-sleeved flannel shirts, pleated trousers, knitted vests, cricket jumpers on court, and for post-play, wool or cotton blazers.

Football, on the other hand, could be played anywhere. Yes, it began on the gilded grounds of elite British schools like Harrow and Eton, but because you can literally kick a ball anywhere, the game quickly spread across all demographics. Football kits consisted of jerseys, knickerbockers (short pants), and matching long socks. The jerseys were embroidered with crests placed on the left side of the chest panel—the rough locale of the human heart and easy eye-level visibility—an open declaration of allegiance to a club or school. The knickerbockers were made of wool, which retained moisture and heat but would also shrink—and so the evolution of shorts could have been attributed to a happy laundry error. The Football Association was established in 1863, but by 1904 shorts were formalized as part of the football kit for both genders.

Male tennis pros had to sit on a sartorial knife edge before they got to wear shorts. An unknown, Brame Hillyard, bravely walked onto Court 10 at the All England Lawn Tennis and Croquet Club (Wimbledon) in 1930 while wearing a pair; the year before, the Men's Dress Reform Party had determined that heavy-duty fabrics were tight, unventilated, and virtually unwashable, making them unhygienic and impractical for sport. Pro player Bunny Austin also supported this progressive thinking, but it took him a good two years after Hillyard to summon up the courage to wear shorts publicly. Austin recounts the Shakespearean torment he went through as he was about to leave his hotel room for his professional match in Forest Hills, New York, in 1932: "I hovered in my bedroom . . . putting them on, taking them off, putting them on again, wrestling with the problem of *Hamlet*: *To be or not to be*." Finally, he left his room, wearing an overcoat to hide his legs. A nearby porter apparently rushed to his aid and said, "Excuse me, sir, but I think you have forgotten your trousers."

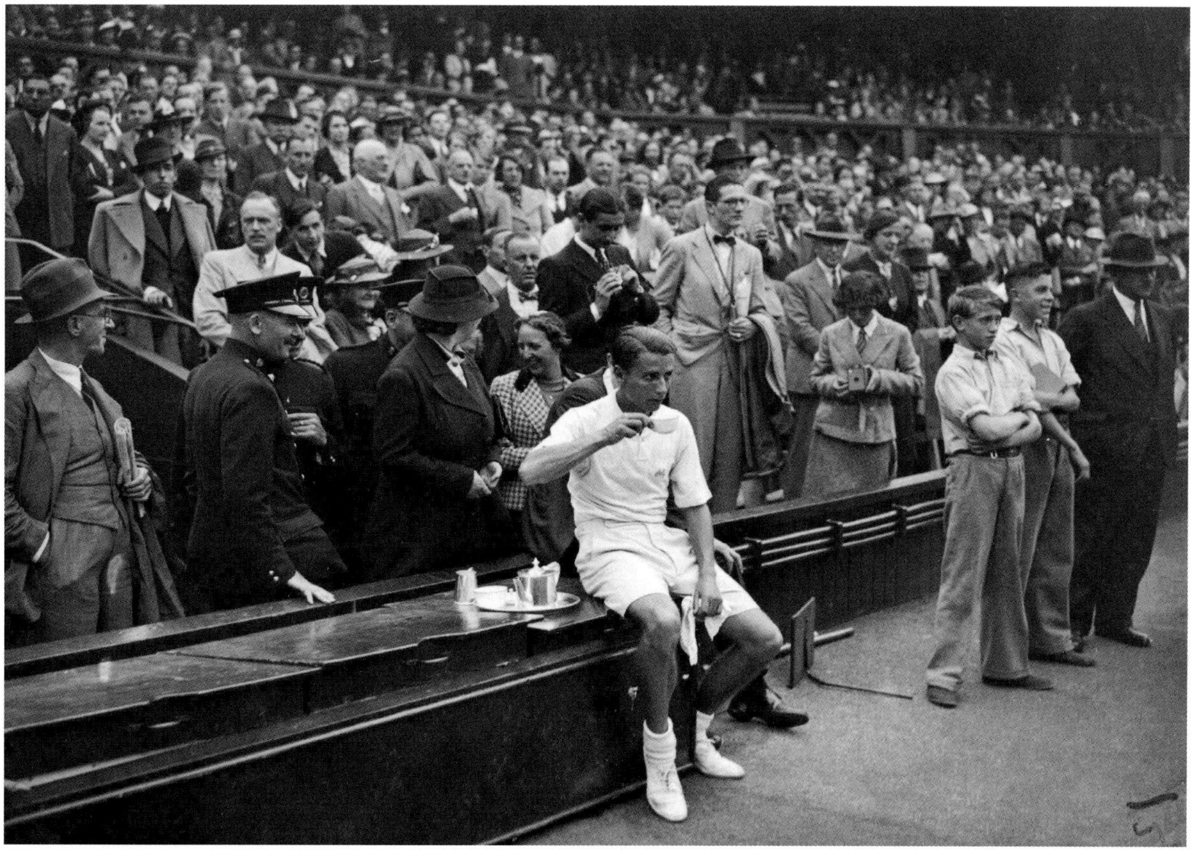

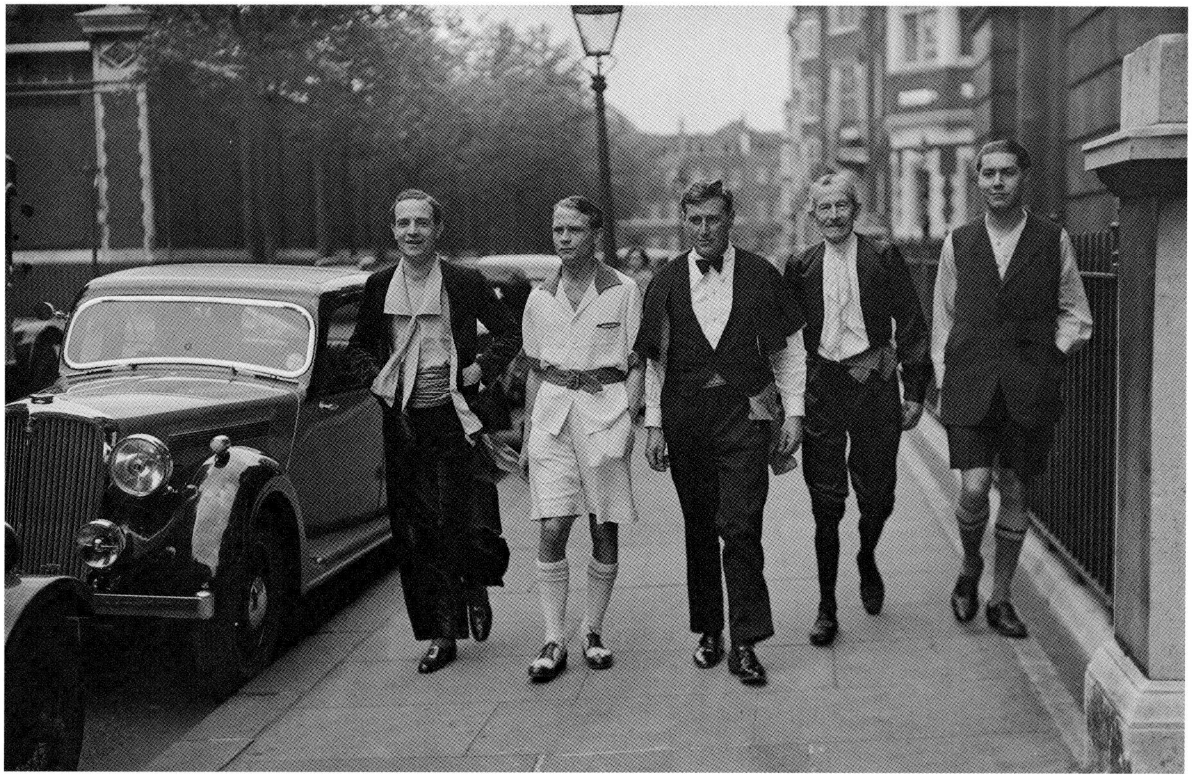

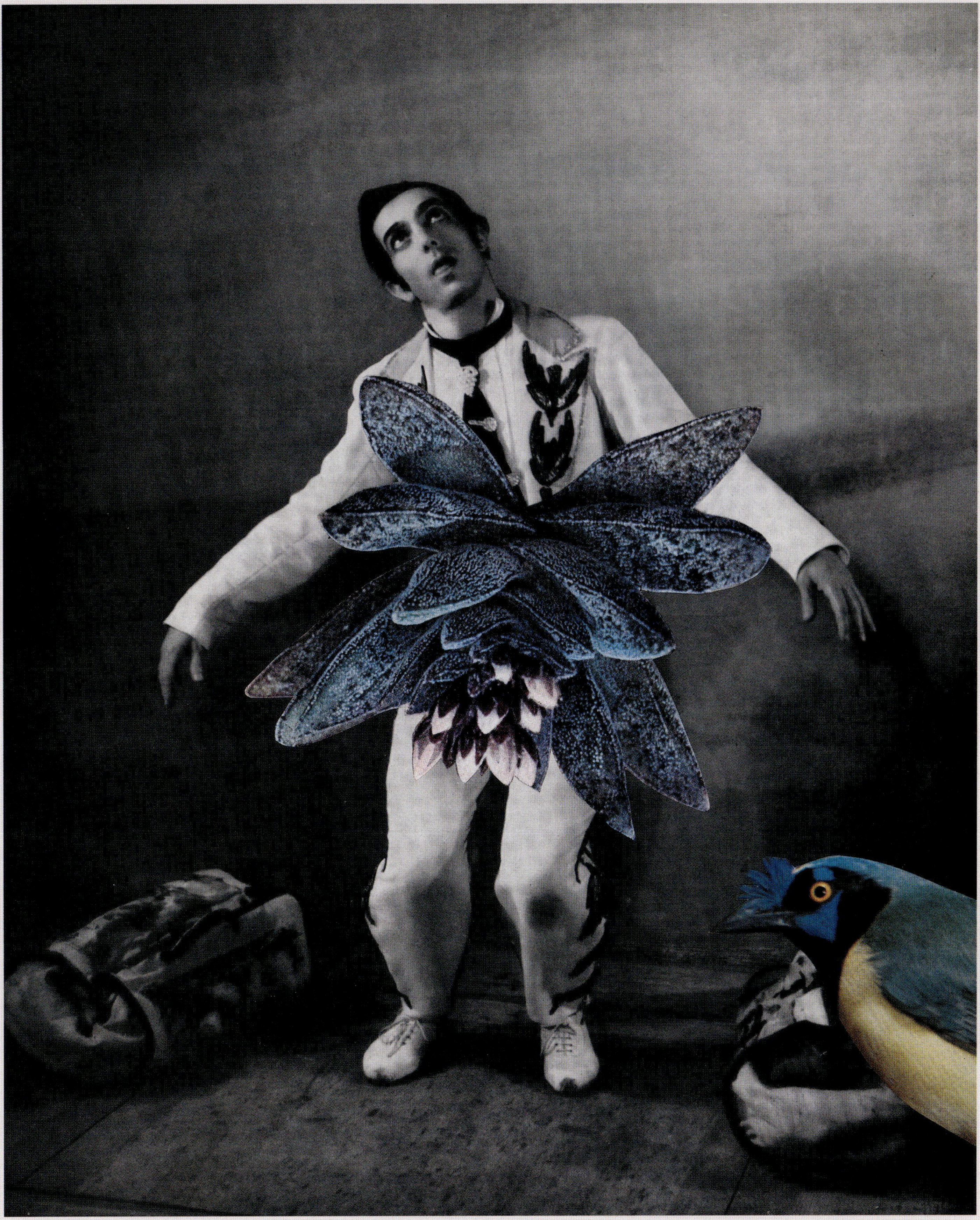

MISS HELEN WILLS & THE MUSE IN MOTION

HELEN WILLS (1905–1998) WAS A NINETEEN-TIME GRAND SLAM WINNER, OLYMPIC GOLD MEDALIST, AND A CONTROLLED, AGILE, AND BALANCED MOVER ON COURT.

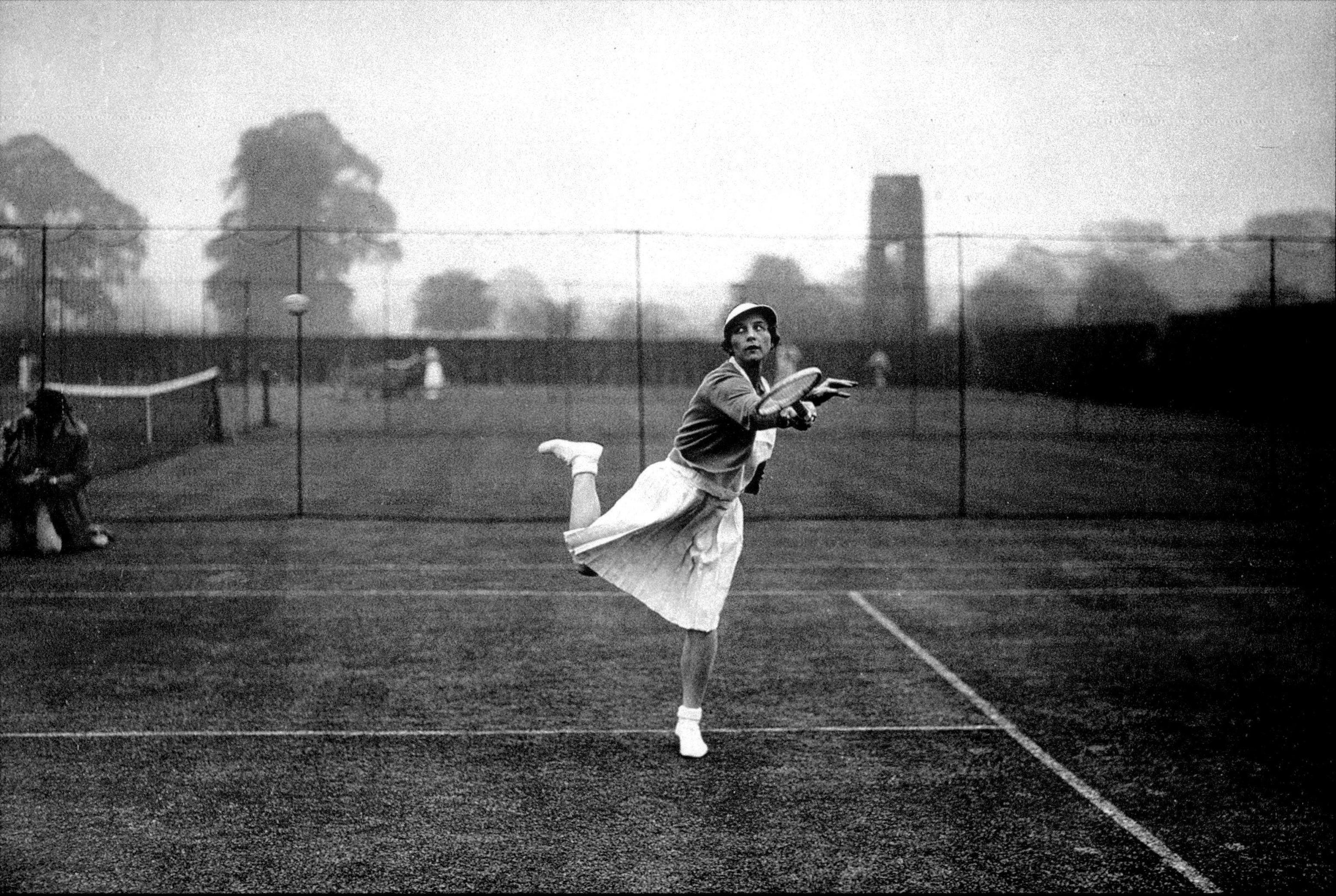

It could have been a match made in rivalry heaven—if Suzanne Lenglen hadn't been at the end of her career and American Helen Wills at the beginning of hers, when the two historically played against each other in 1926. It was billed as a clash of nations (Europe and America), style (both wore Patou), and eras (one a seasoned champion—the other, a rising star). At the Carlton Club in Cannes, the grounds were packed with spectators and press—some even climbing trees. Lenglen ultimately won, 6-3, 8-6, yet Wills was distinguished for her poise and play. Her style reflected her game: clinical and minimal, with functionality reining over frivolity. She represented modern athleticism as the unflappable American, captivating her audiences and gaining worldwide fame. Her play later inspired creatives like renowned sculptor Alexander Calder, who created two wire sculptures (*Helen Wills 1* and *Helen Wills II*) capturing her movement, literary writers from Ernest Hemmingway to F. Scott Fitzgerald, who pondered her play, and even actor and director Charlie Chaplin, the master of the silent movies, who remarked when asked about the most beautiful sight he had ever seen: "The movement of Helen Wills playing tennis."

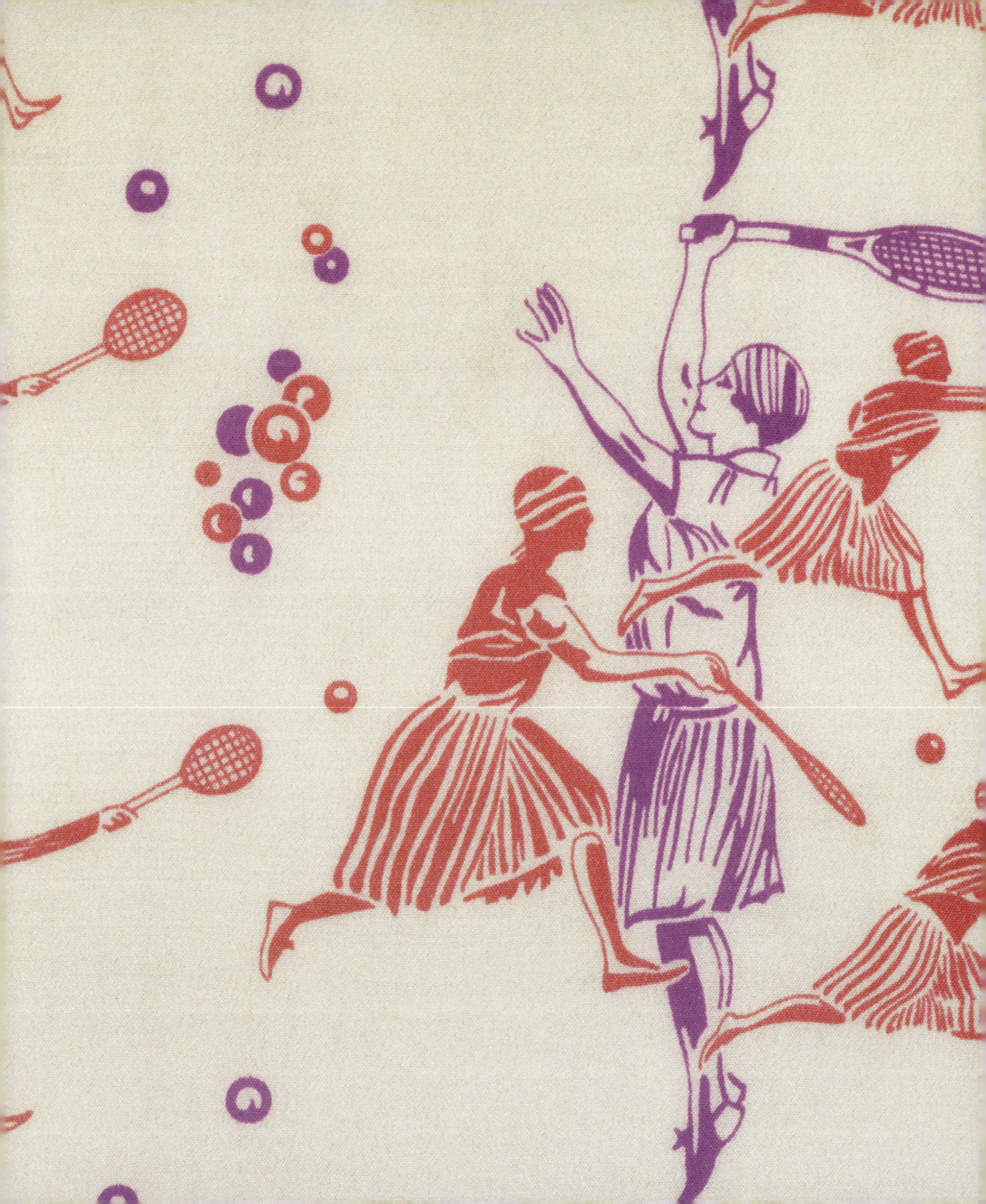

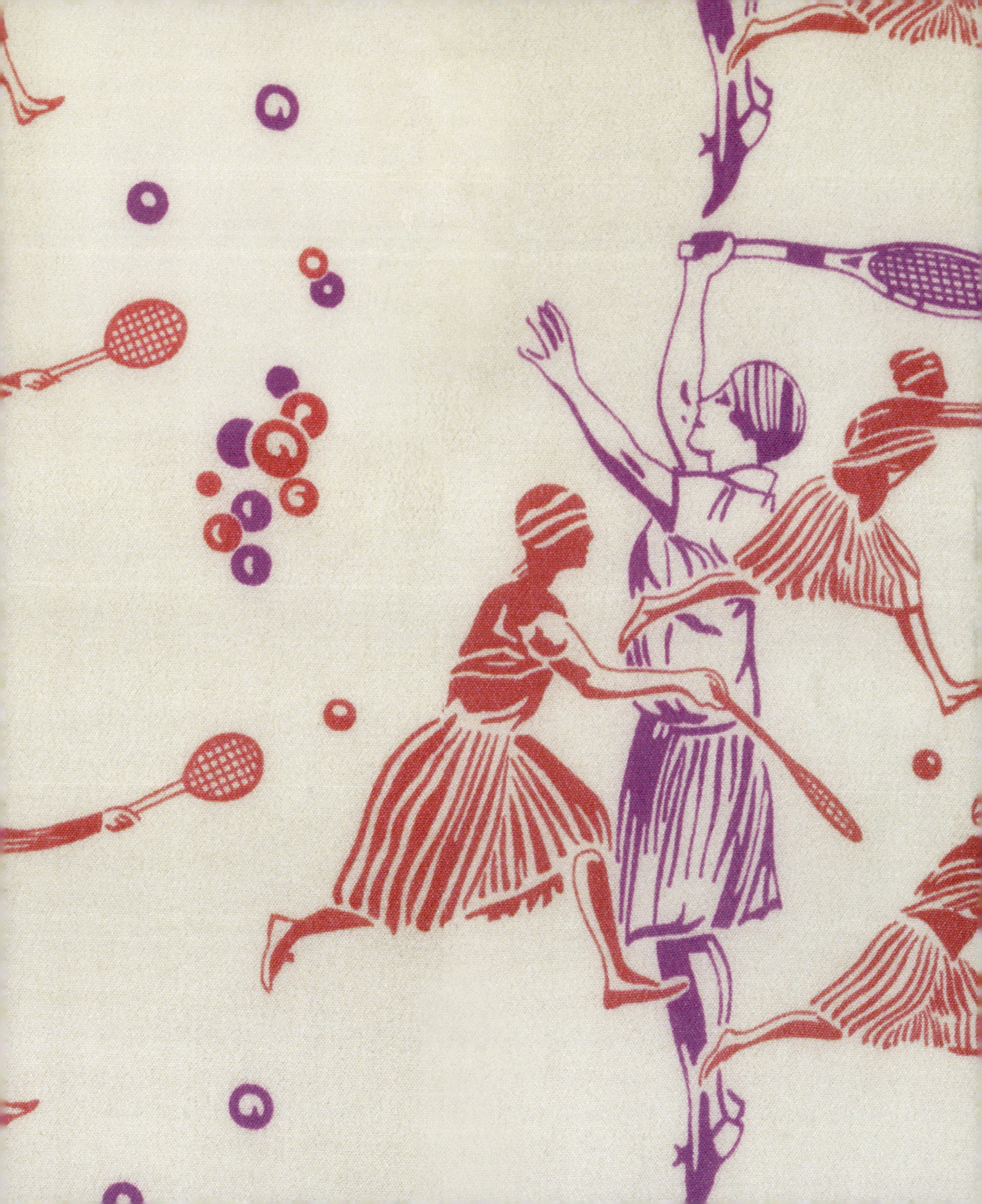

HRH THE DUKE OF KENT

PRESIDENT OF THE ALL ENGLAND LAWN TENNIS AND CROQUET CLUB FROM 1969 TO 2021.

Wimbledon has been part of the Kent family since my father, the Duke of Kent, began as its president in 1929, following the Prince of Wales. I took over as president after my mother, Princess Marina of Greece and Denmark, died in 1962, for fifty years. My wife, Katharine, accompanied me for most of it. As the president of the Football Association for twenty-five years as well, I have always thought that sports is a great unifier of people.

At Wimbledon, I was fairly indifferent as to who would win, but you couldn't help rooting for the fighter. The [Rafael] Nadal versus [Roger] Federer match in 2007 was a fantastic example of that. I have always had enormous admiration for the stamina of the players. I will always hold Wimbledon dear to my heart.

LADY HELEN TAYLOR

DAUGHTER OF THEIR ROYAL HIGHNESSES THE DUKE & DUCHESS OF KENT.

I made my first visit to Wimbledon at age eight in 1972; Stan Smith was in the final. It was very exciting as a child to watch him play and to meet him afterward. He had such star quality. I was lucky enough to watch many of the finals from 1972 to 1982, with tennis greats like Jimmy Connors, Ilie Nastase, John McEnroe, Björn Borg. Evonne Goolagong was memorable not only for her play but famous for her frilly Ted Tinling knickers. Martina Navratilova, Chrissie Evert . . . My other childhood memory from the Royal Box is of these wastepaper baskets brimming with sweets, which would be passed along below eyeline. We had to unpeel the wrapper when there was clapping and then bend down and pop it into our mouths without anyone seeing—it was a bit of a game. Of course, I remember the fantastic teas, which are memorable to this day too—no one misses tea.

Wimbledon Centre Court has such a rarefied atmosphere—you feel it when you sit there. You just feel it.

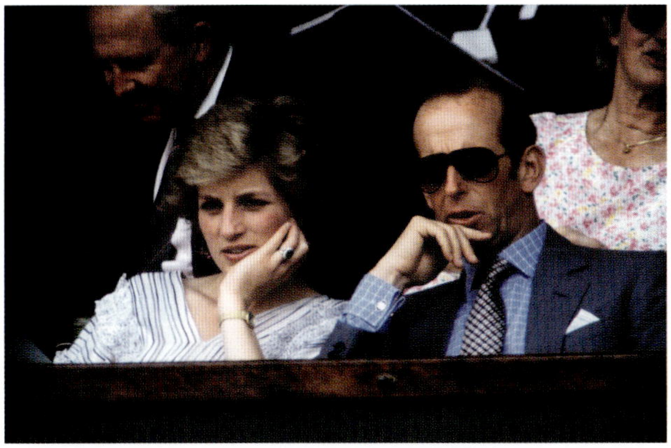

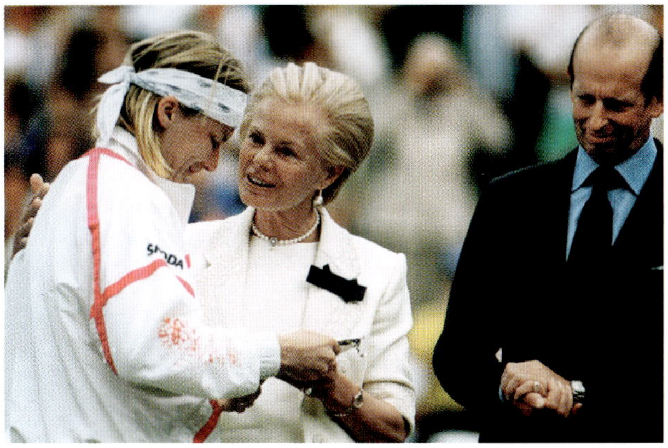

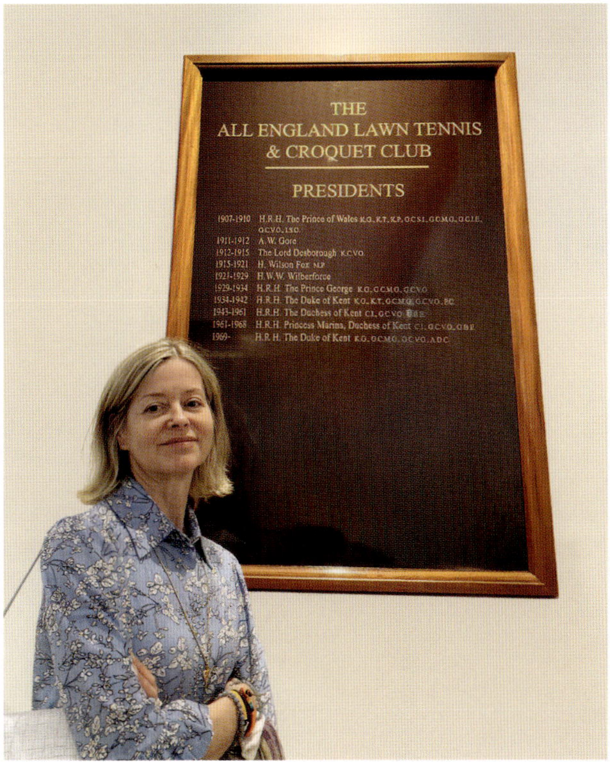

ON HER PARENTS

My parents would meet the players when they were at the peak of their emotions after the finals and would hand out the trophies. My mother would always connect with the runner-up—she was compassionate that way. There was that famous moment with Jana Novotná when Novotná cried on my mother's shoulder; she was delighted when Novotná won a few years later. My parents took their roles seriously, because they were representing the Queen. It's that little fairy dust of royalty that makes Wimbledon unique. My father was keen to invite the Queen so that she could support British players playing on Centre Court; when she came, it put another layer of magic to Wimbledon. He did away with the curtseying and bowing at the Royal Box. It didn't feel right anymore, and most of the players were international anyway. My mother always made sure she planned her outfits in advance; she had to think of the English summer, which could be very hot or wet, and with no roof at the time, you never knew how the weather would be. She would think about the practicalities—for example, making sure that the fabric wouldn't crease when sitting for a long time. She would sell the previous year's looks to finance the next; it was a very efficient process. She had some stunning pieces from Catherine Walker, Bellville Sassoon, and even a Courrèges dress!

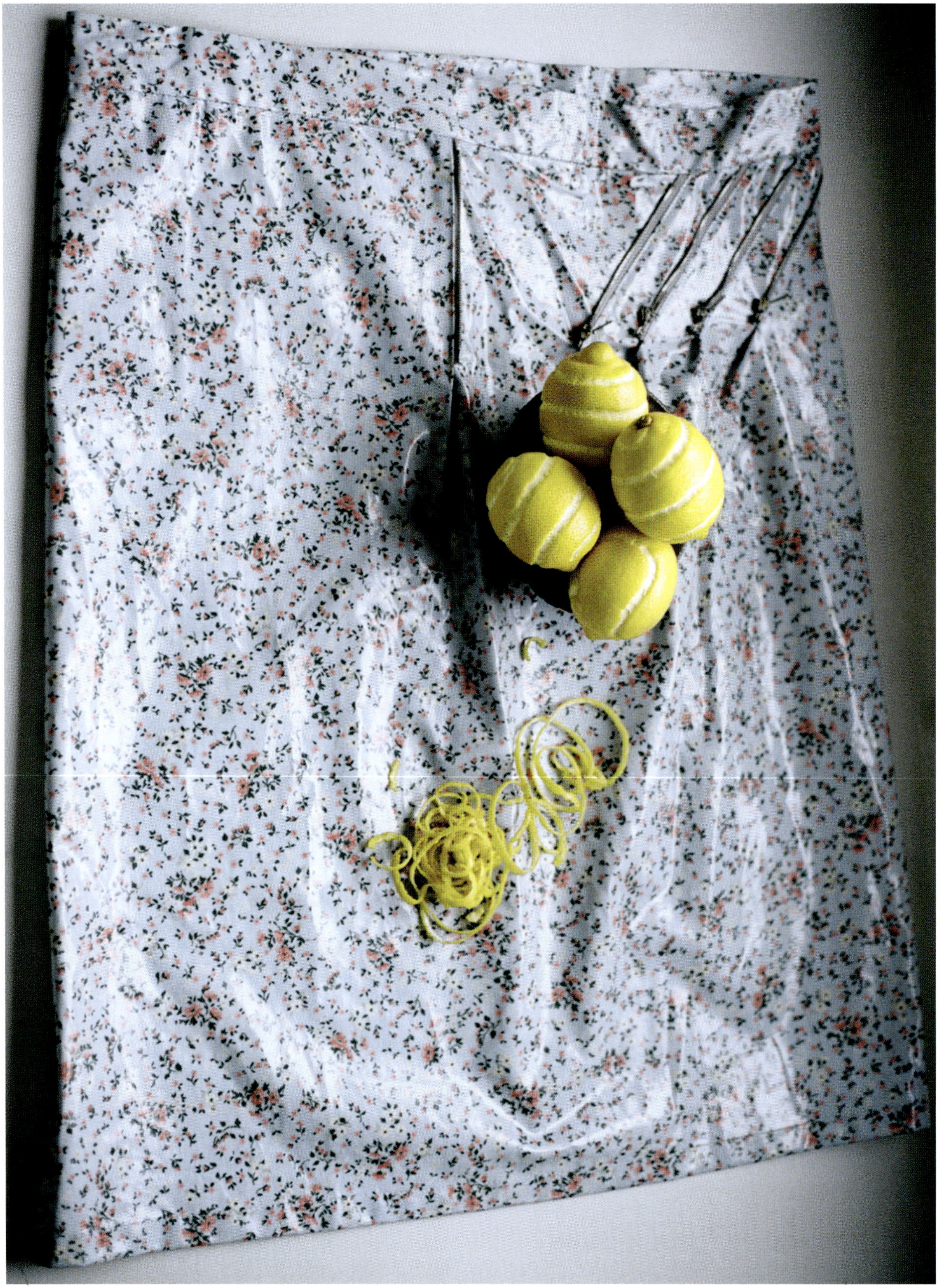

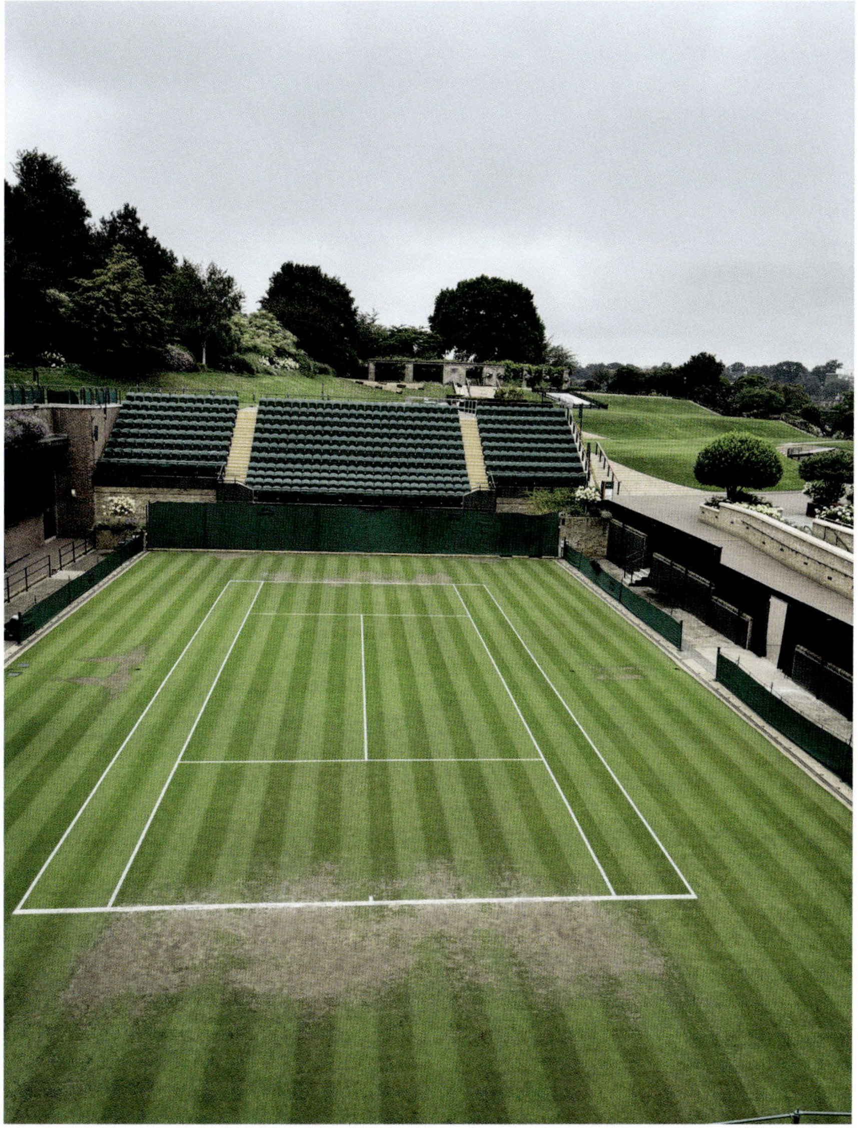

MISS ALTHEA GIBSON & THE REST OF THE WORLD

ALTHEA GIBSON (1927—2003) WAS AN ELEVEN-TIME GRAND SLAM WINNER, KNOWN FOR HER EXPLOSIVE ATHLETICISM AND FLAT GROUND SHOTS.

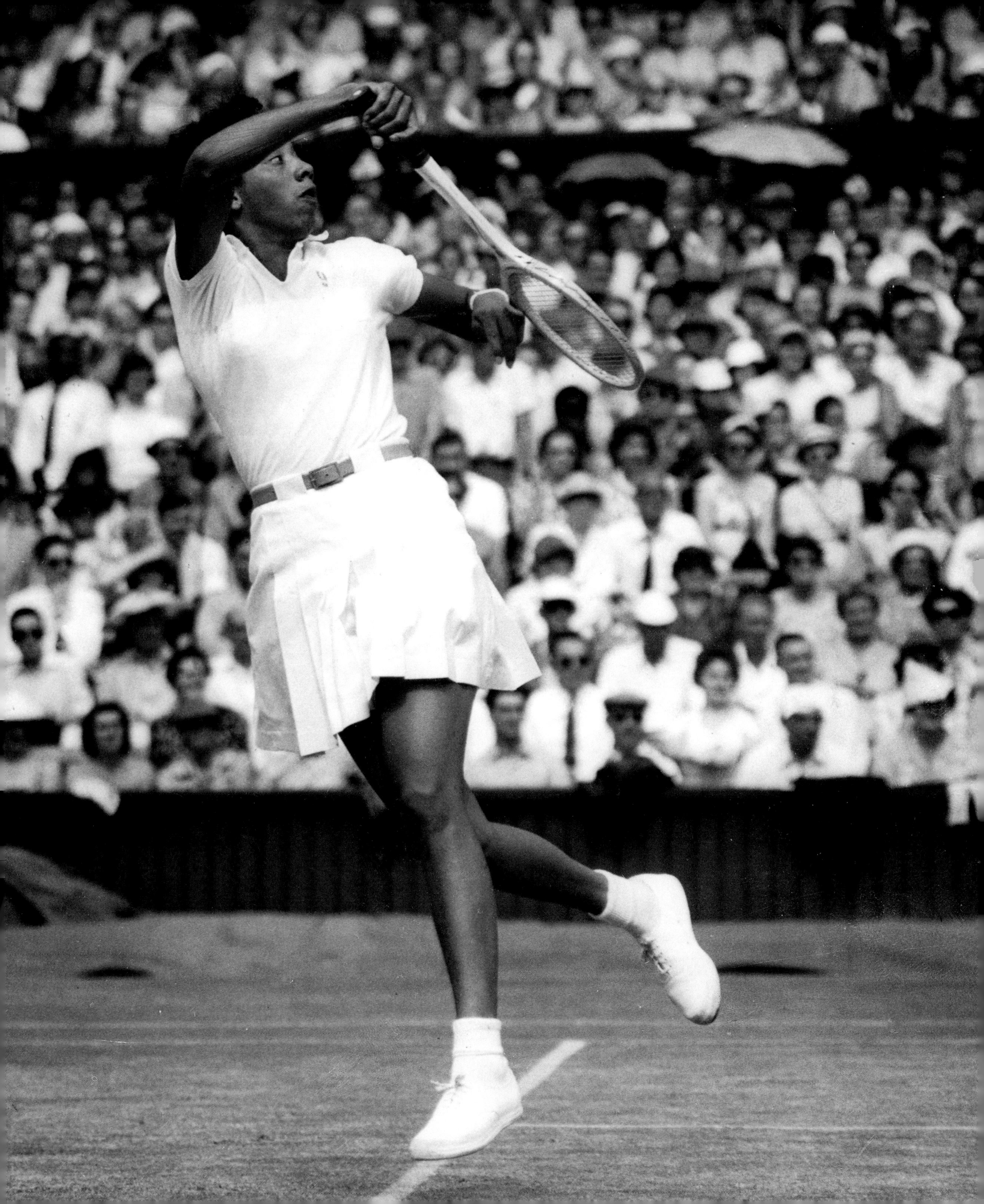

Shaking hands with the Queen of England, waving to bystanders during a ticker-tape celebration parade in her honor on Broadway in New York City, and appearing on the front covers of *Sports Illustrated* and *Time*—these were all firsts for the first African American woman to win Wimbledon in 1957. She jubilantly declared to awaiting press, "I have got what I have wanted, to have an identity. I'm Althea Gibson, the tennis champion. I hope it makes me happy."

HAPPY HOPES

Gibson was described as "a pioneer in every sense, [with an] unprecedented difficulty to overcome. She needed extraordinary determination and resilience to combat the discrimination which placed her in virtual isolation." Prior to her Wimbledon win, she was barred from using the changing rooms at the all-white tennis clubs; instead, she changed in her car. When she endured endless heckles and hisses from spectators as she walked on court, she feigned courage. Openly ostracized by her fellow sportsmen if she approached them, she instead found an equally skilled doubles partner in Angela Buxton—a Jewish player, also treated as an outlier—with whom she won two doubles Grand Slams. Both counterbalanced open prejudice from spectators and chose instead the soothsaying attire of varsity cardigans, polo shirts, and preppy pleated skirts. Gibson's tailored elegance and streamlined silhouette accentuated her statuesque, athletic build. What better way to coerce the collective than with bourgeois regalia?

Despite winning eleven Grand Slam titles, she bitterly observed, "Being the queen of tennis was all well and good, but you can't eat a crown." Amateur tennis rarely provided prize money, and with no lifeline of family income, her dream to live "a normal life" appeared to slip away from her tenuous grip; she died in 2003 in virtual poverty. The fates of tennis mythology decreed that Gibson was the one, but the spoils of money and happiness were not allotted for her. She was ordained to be the first, so that many like her could follow.

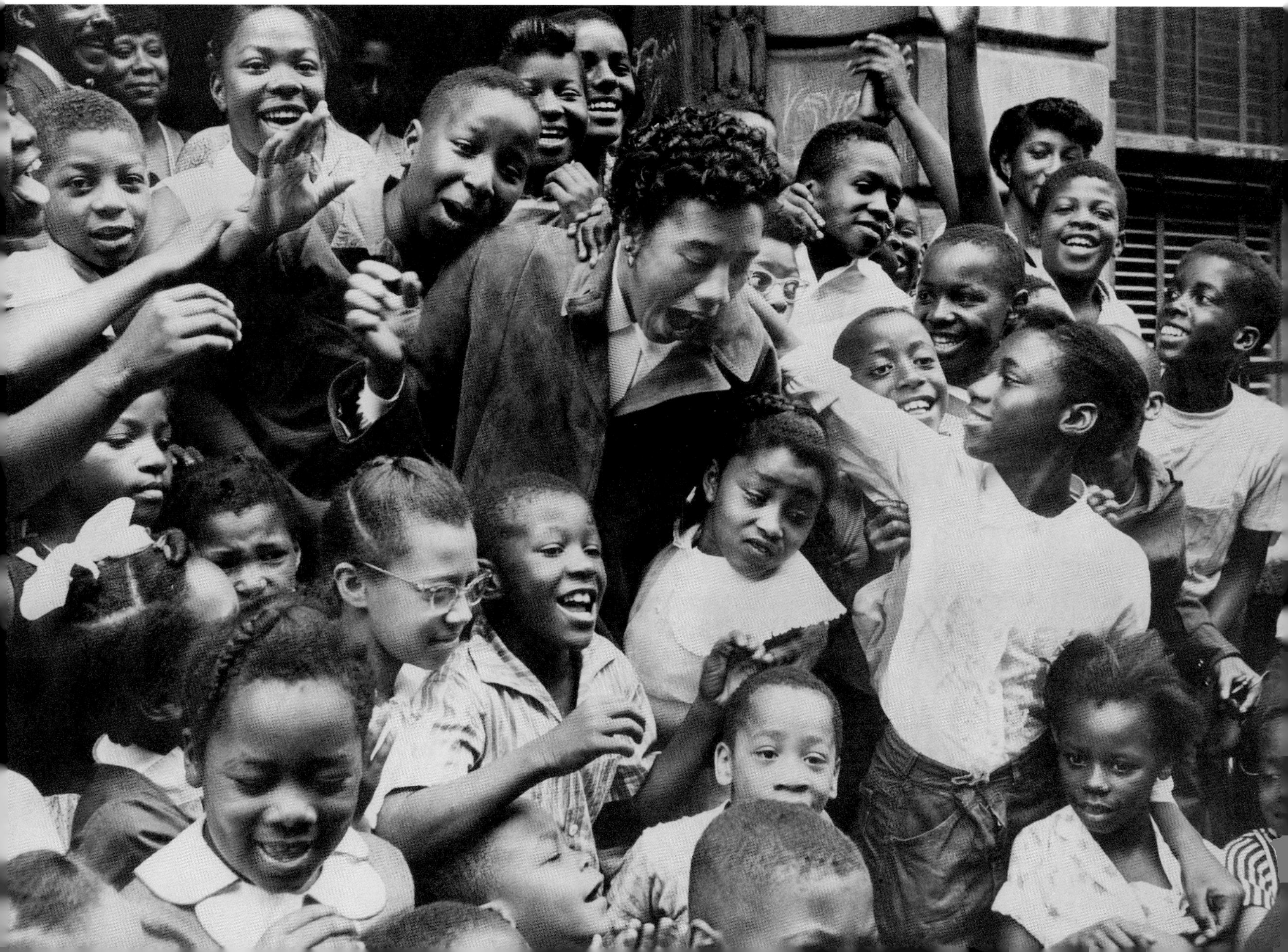

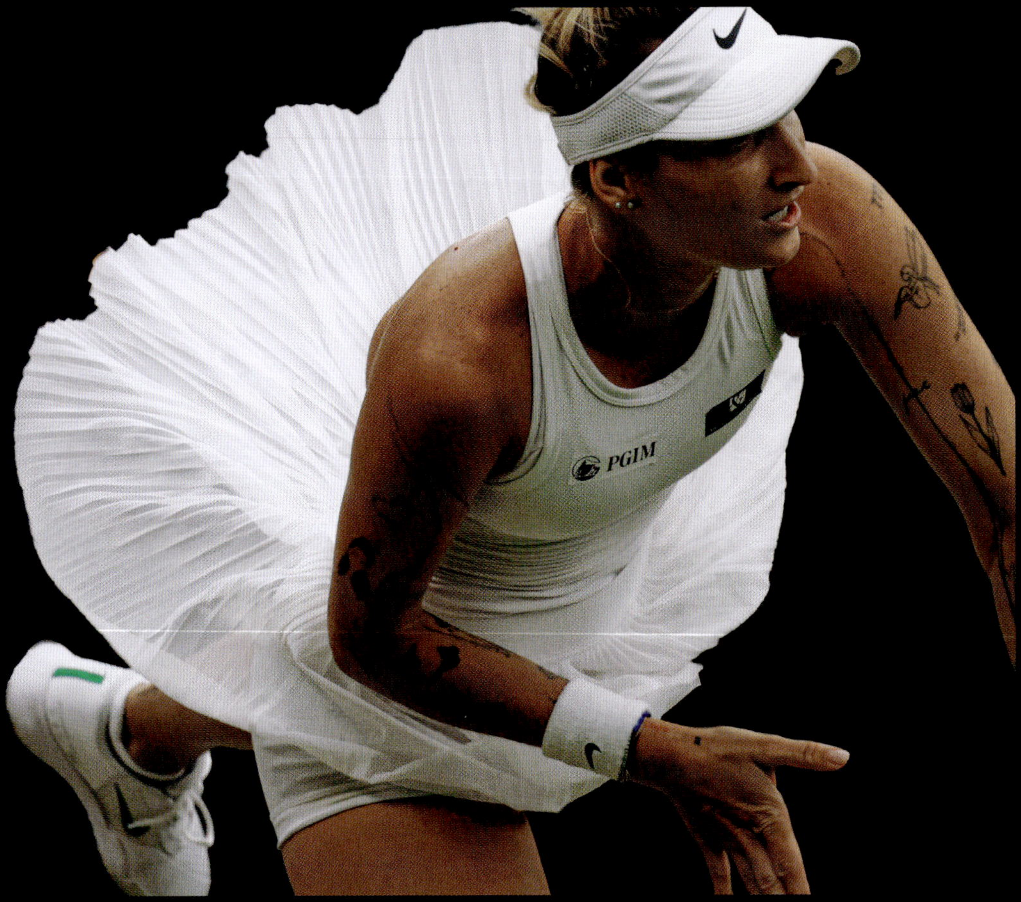
PGIM

THE WHITES

"The actor on Broadway, the singer at La Scala, and the dancer at the Bolshoi Theatre will understand what the tennis player at Wimbledon feels." Wimbledon is the tournament every player wants to win first—this is the homeland of tennis, where sportsmen become legends, hallowed grounds tell a thousand stories, and countless tests must be passed. And the most notorious of all?

THE STRICT RULE OF WEARING WHITE

1877, the year the All England Lawn Tennis and Croquet Club was established—and with it, the requirement that members dress in white. Then, the color carried countless social connotations: Only the wealthy could afford to wear, own, and maintain it. The rest had neither the means nor the staff to have and keep separate athletic attire. This was upheld until 1962, when designer Ted Tinling—ironically an ex-member of the club—dared to introduce color. Maria Bueno came on court in a white Tinling dress, but its lining and undershorts were not the same—they were pink. Wimbledon retaliated with its "predominantly white" rule in 1962, which meant all competitors had to wear almost white.

There have been acts in flagrante of this rule since: Pat Cash famously won Wimbledon wearing a black-and-white checkered headband in 1987, and Anne White wore a white Lycra unitard designed by Ted Tinling the same year. Andre Agassi defiantly boycotted the championships altogether from 1988 to 1990. "I resent rules, especially arbitrary rules. Why should I wear white? What should it matter what I wear?" Agassi said. (He did, however, manage to find and wear an all-white outfit in 1991 and win in 1992.)

Two indelible stains came to mark Wimbledon history in 2012 and 2013, when a stricter mandate of an "almost entirely white rule" was enforced on undergarments, bras, knickers, straps, lace, soles, other accessories, including a 1-cm colored trim around the neckline, cuffs, outside seam of shorts, tracksuit bottoms and skirts. The first violation occurred when Serena Williams appeared (and won) in a white dress, but wore bright purple-and-pink patterned undershorts *and* matching sweatbands. The second occurred with Roger Federer's footwear; his white Nike V8 shoes revealed a shocking orange sole—he was asked to change out of them.

The ban on colored undershorts was particularly dated. Billie Jean King, ever the advocate for women, told CNN, "When we have a menstrual period . . . we are always checking whether we are showing." Menstruation is female biology, a fact, and it's not progress to introduce colored shorts; it's a basic dignity. Joanne Simons, professional manager of the AELTC, explained, "We received feedback that this was a source of anxiety for female players. We listened, reviewed, and made the necessary rule change to help alleviate those concerns. The topic was also gaining wider attention across other sports. For example, in the lead-up to the Women's World Cup, players in football were speaking out about similar issues, leading to positive change across all sports." Simons works closely with the brands and designers to help them with their designs the year before Wimbledon.

Surely the all-white rule hinders creativity? To scale uncharted designs and concepts, there must be complete creative freedom? Ben Herath, vice president of design for adidas, relishes the exercise, and explains that all doors need not be open to innovate: "When you remove something or you limit something like color, it pushes you to explore texture. When you turn something off, it helps to turn other things up. And so making white look distinctive is always a challenge."

Call it what you will—when one walks into the Club, one knows. There is a tinge of a librarian hush in the air, the muffled pop of picnic champagnes uncorked across the courts, the clean scent of the cut pastoral green lawns, and the pictorial gleam of competitors wearing crisp white—this is the All England Lawn Tennis and Croquet Club, ladies and gentlemen, as it was, is, and ever shall be.

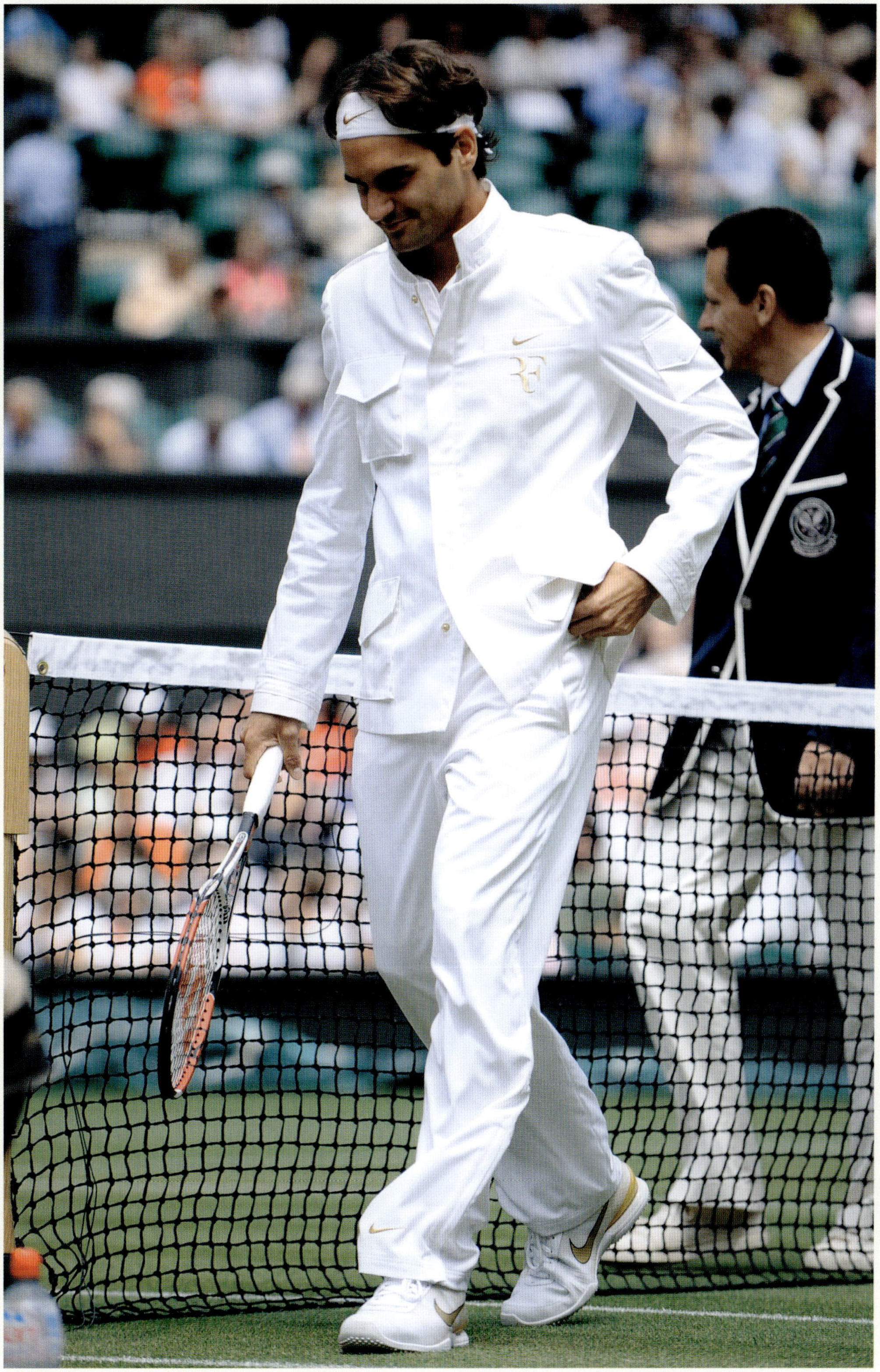

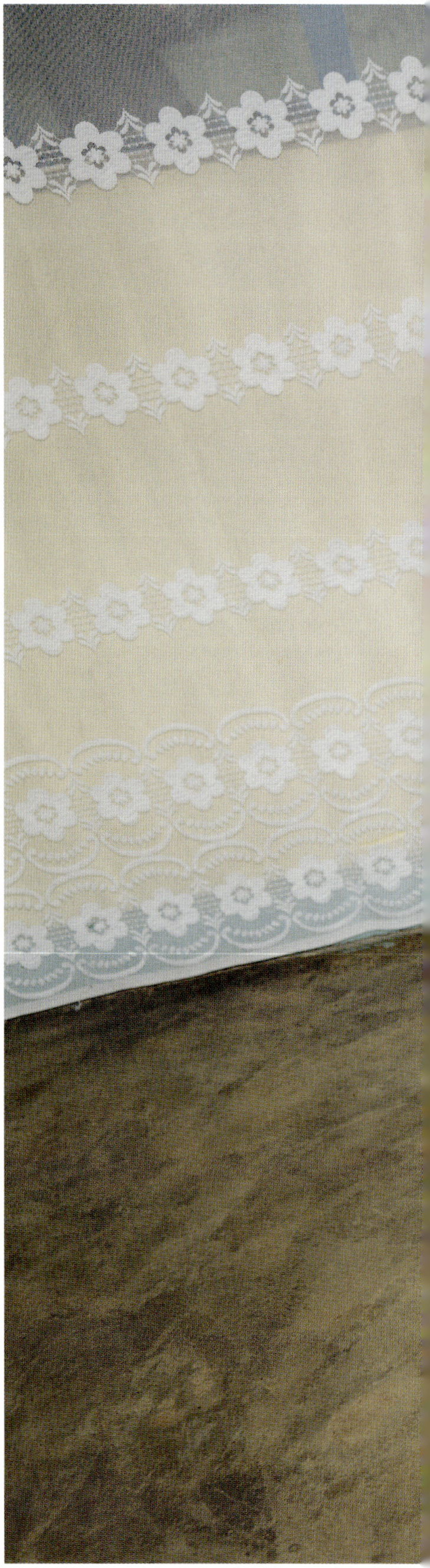

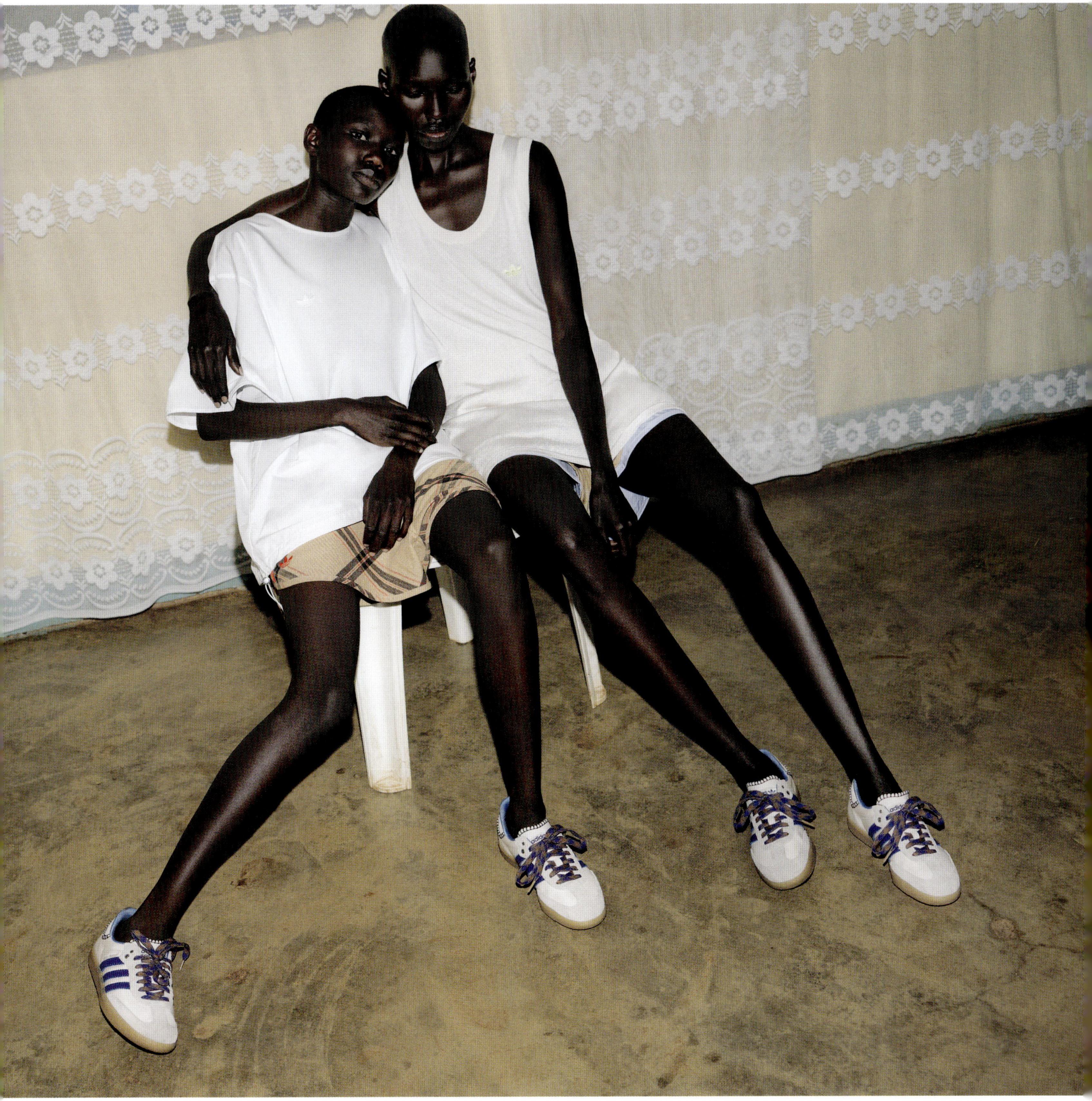

DAME ANNA WINTOUR, DBE

ANNA WINTOUR IS GLOBAL EDITORIAL DIRECTOR OF *AMERICAN VOGUE* AND CHIEF CONTENT OFFICER FOR CONDÉ NAST.

SKN: You've helped to position tennis players alongside the likes of Hollywood actors and rock stars, in terms of visibility and cultural status. What inspired that focus, and how do you see fashion continuing to influence how athletes are perceived globally?

AW: I've simply been a huge fan of tennis for my entire life, and I've been so lucky to have the privilege to meet all these amazing athletes. In my world, tennis players *are* rock stars, and fashion and sports—all sports, really—are inspired by each other. Fashion has been influenced by sport and movement more than ever, and sports and athletes are looking to fashion to help them express themselves. It's been an amazing development to witness.

SKN: Sport is about freedom of movement, yet for so long women had to fight—sometimes literally—for the right to move freely on the court. What's your perspective on how far we've come, and how fashion has either helped or hindered that journey?

AW: Fashion, of course, is a reflection of its time and ethos, and thankfully we're long removed from those days at the dawn of the twentieth century when women still wore corsets at Wimbledon. Almost without exception, the evolution of what women have worn on the court since has been a straight progression toward freedom, toward self-expression, and toward fun. One can argue in favor of this dress or against that color story—or one could choose to wear something extremely boring and not be part of this conversation at all—but I think there's no question that fashion has helped players express themselves, define themselves, and occasionally simply draw attention to themselves. And I think that's a wonderful thing.

SKN: The French couturiers Jean Patou, Gabrielle "Coco" Chanel, Jeanne Lanvin, and Lucien Lelong were innovators in performance wear and leisurewear for tennis, and now designers are collaborating with players again—it feels like a golden age. How do you see this shaping the future of both tennis and fashion?

AW: There have been so many small revolutions—in fit, in fabrics and the technology used to make those fabrics, in style and cut. I also think we're finally beyond any stigma that may have existed within the world of professional sports about fashion being frivolous or somehow a distraction, and the best players aren't simply billboards for brands—they work closely with those brands to make clothes that work the way they want them to work and look the way they want them to look. It's part of a lineage that goes back to the designers you mention and extends forward to stylish players from René Lacoste and Andre Agassi to Roger Federer, Jannik Sinner, Coco Gauff, and Carlos Alcaraz, to name just a few.

SKN: Finally, what are your best tennis memories—your most memorable match, played or watched, and on-court outfit?

AW: My favorite match would have to be Roger Federer's win over Andy Roddick in the Wimbledon final in 2009—16–14 in the fifth set—to win his fifteenth Major and break Pete Sampras's record. It's the only match in Grand Slam history where someone (in this case, Andy) lost a match despite having their serve broken only once—in the final game of the match.

As far as on-court outfit: I'll take Serena's style, always.

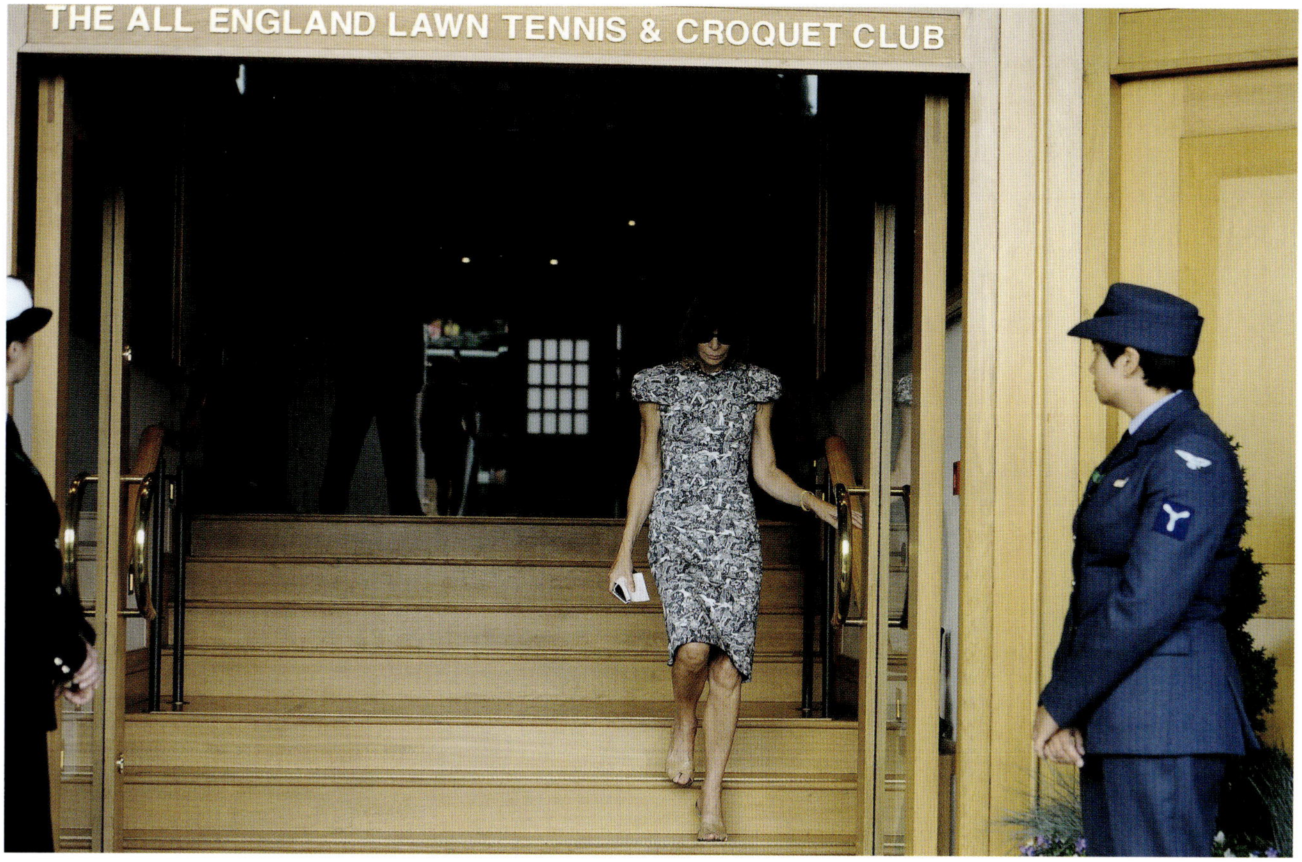
THE ALL ENGLAND LAWN TENNIS & CROQUET CLUB

RALPH LAUREN

Visualize this: a man on horseback at a gallop, a mallet raised in his left hand while he grips the reins with his right. Scale it down, place it on a shirt, and this is Polo—or Ralph Lauren, the brand—which began in 1967. What does this symbol mean to you? Where does it take you? Most sports logos carry a myriad of messages, and it's generally up to us to pick the ones that define who and what we are. The Polo insignia, however, doesn't necessarily reference a person, but a lifestyle. Ralph Lauren is very good at taking you somewhere else, somewhere you would rather be. As Lauren said, "Think about the people who play polo: wealthy, cosmopolitan, chic. I wanted to create a concept for the name"—which he did in 1968. Drawing from the formal attire of 1900s aristocratic England—preppy blazers, pinstripe shirts, cable-knit sweaters—and the Old Hollywood glamour of chinos and double-breasted suits made in luxurious yarns, Lauren did it the American way: casual. This school of thought was cemented previously in the 1940s by the American designer Claire McCardell, with her classical sportswear separates for women.

Middle-class America was all-in for Lauren. And while most had likely never been on a polo field (or even had any inclination to be on one), it promised a certain kind of life. Perhaps it was Lauren's: He was perpetually sun-kissed, with silken silver hair. He had a ranch here, a Hamptons home there, a ski chalet somewhere. It wasn't just his stores in which you could visit Lauren's world; you could experience it at the movies too. In *Annie Hall* (1977), a Woody Allen love story with the dapper Diane Keaton playing the lead, the actor wore Ralph Lauren menswear-inspired clothing throughout. Oversize jackets, tailored waistcoats teamed with neckties, and double-pleated pants were just too cool. This cohesive look rippled through the tennis court scene: A perfectly loose fitted shirt—tucked in, the collar up, half sleeves exactly half folded—is chicly unbuttoned to reveal a peek of a white vest with a center bow, teamed with high-waisted white paper-bag shorts. It was the epitome of dandy femme chic. Allen, who played the hapless love interest, wore stiff white tennis attire with mid white socks to match, oblivious to her coquettish tennis play and outfit. Annie Hall was Ralph Lauren—or perhaps his tomboy sister.

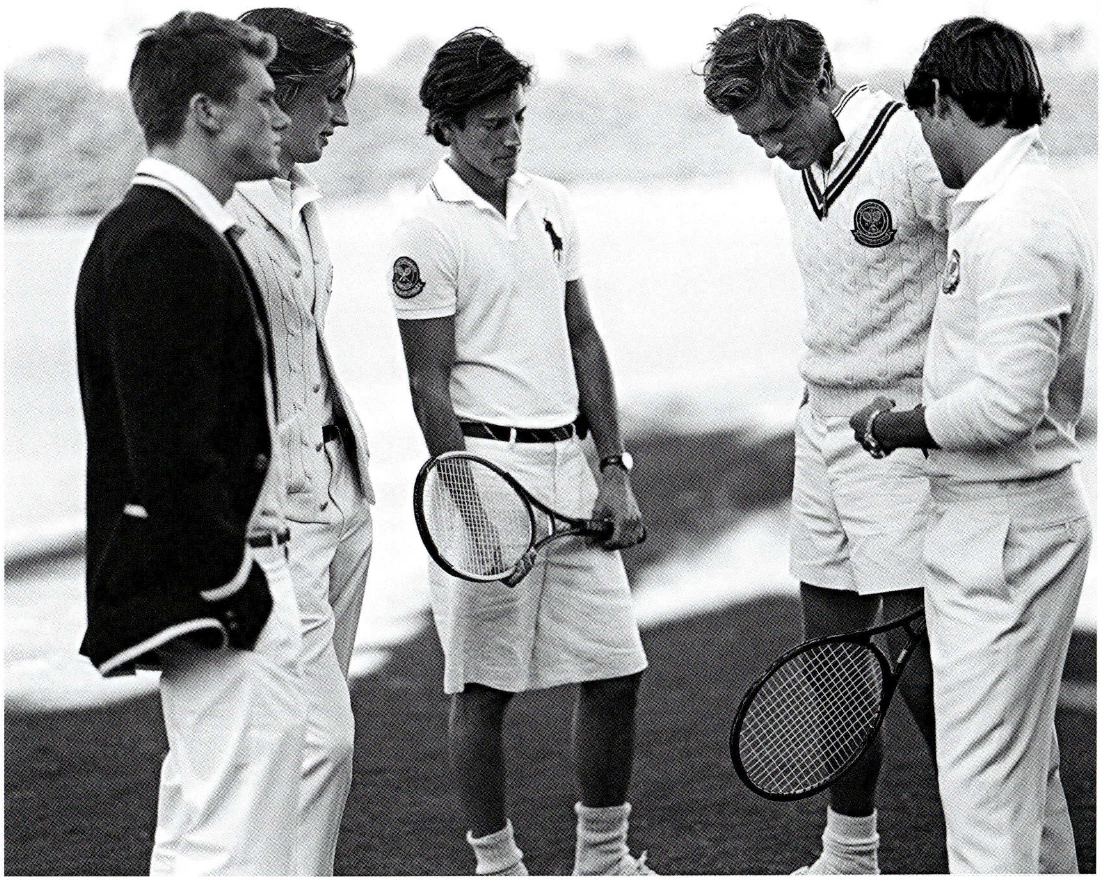

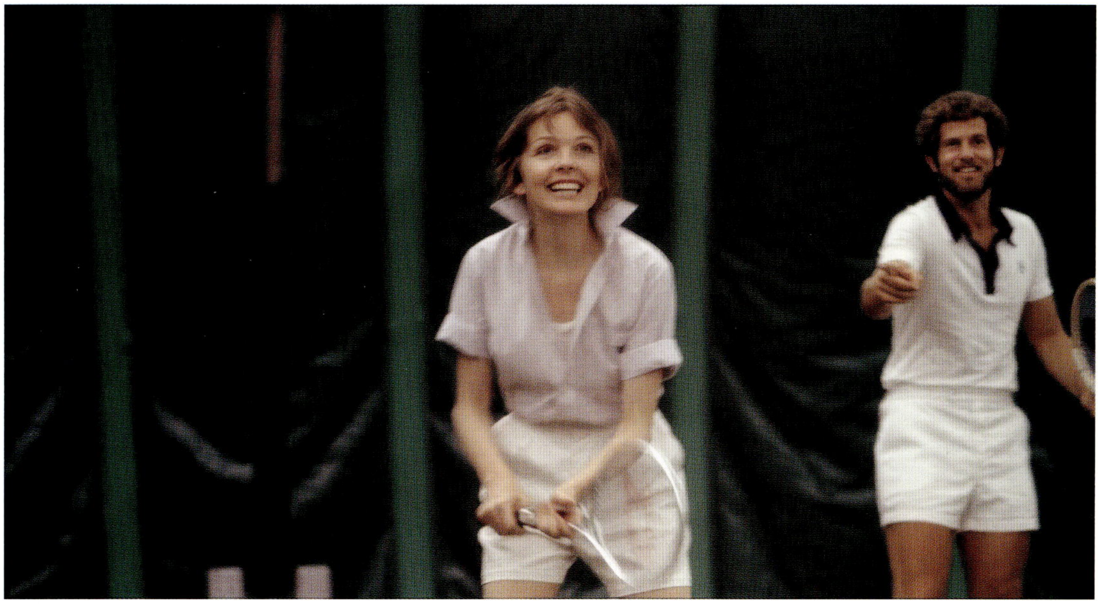

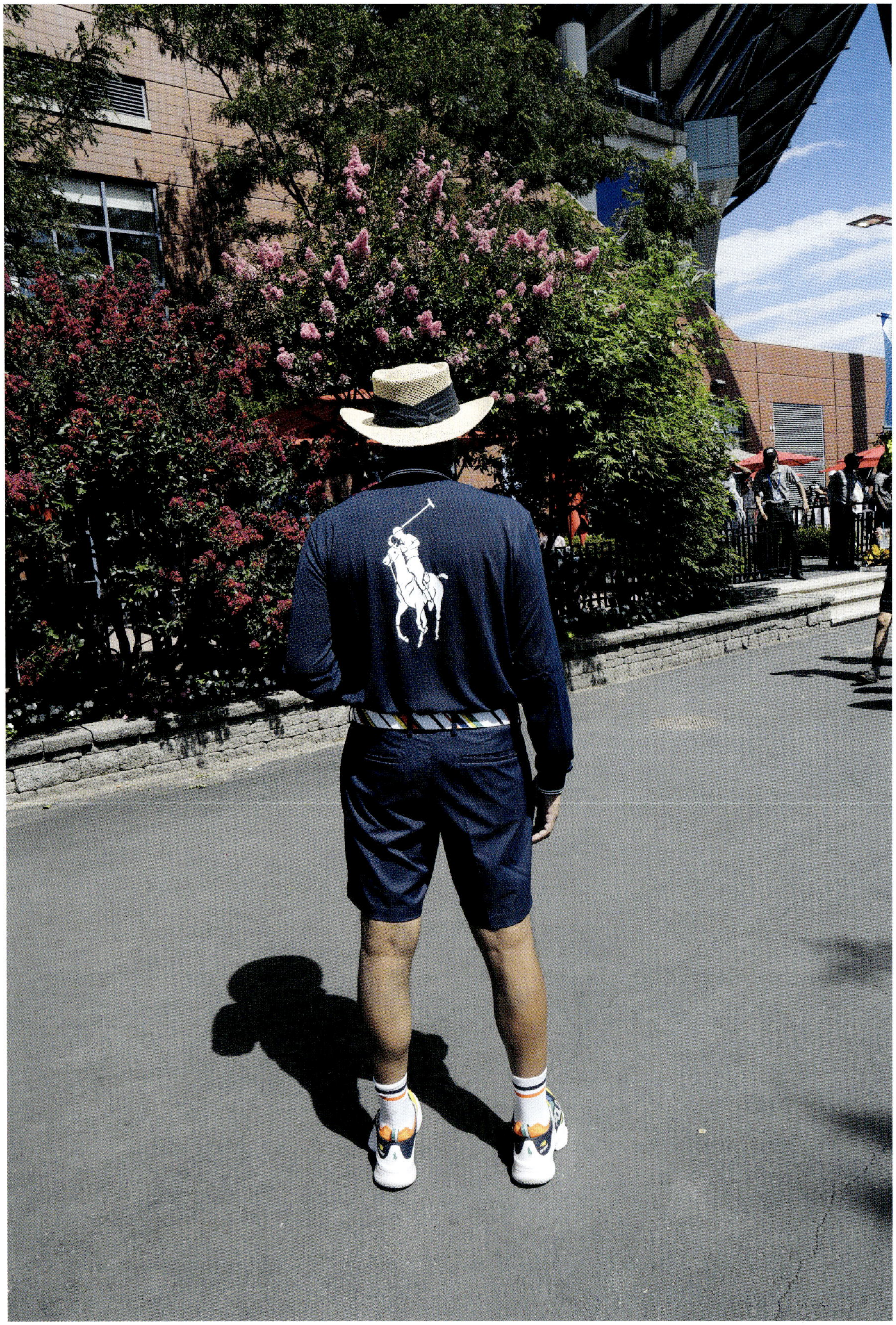

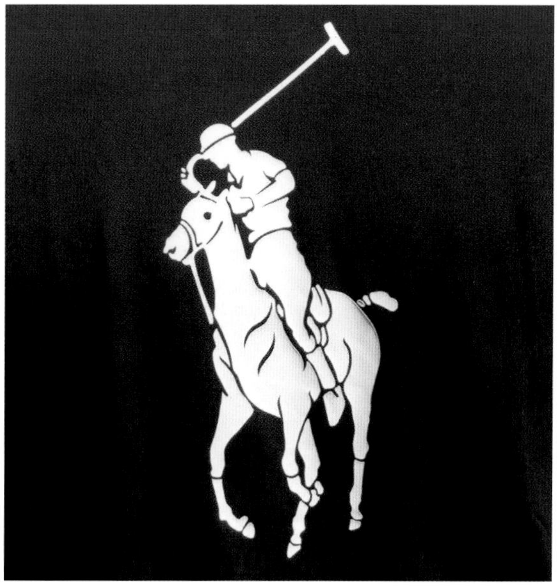

It was the polo shirt introduced in 1971 that made the brand. Lauren deftly circled back to where the story began—on the polo fields of India. The Indian ruling class was rich enough to rear exquisite polo horses and had equal chutzpah to finance the sport. When British colonial rule took over in 1858, it wasn't just Indian realms and estates that came under their control; the British poached the raj's sport too. Sportsmen would button down their shirt collars (or invert them) so that they wouldn't flap about while playing, and at some point, long sleeves were functionally cut short. It wasn't until the 1920s, when Lacoste spotted an aristocrat wearing his polo shirt to play tennis in, that Lacoste cleverly recast the garment for tenniswear. Lauren, some forty years later, did what all American designers are intrinsically good at (aside from being astutely creative): marketing. First, he created the Polo motif and used it in his womenswear. Then he applied it to his Polo shirt, which used a softer cotton-mesh fabric and employed a tennis-tail silhouette (where the back panel is longer than the front). Finally, he rebranded the shirt in an array of bold colors. It was an invitation for the rich, or those who aspired to be, to come play—on a boat, on a tennis court, on horseback, or on a golf course.

Lauren's fantasia didn't stop there—it couldn't. Why? Simply because any good lifestyle concept will have the ability to seep into every corner of our existence. Lauren outfitted the grounds staff at the US Open in 2005, but it was his entrée into Wimbledon 2006 that felt pivotal. The All England Lawn Tennis & Croquet Club had staunchly refused explicit advertising since its inception in 1868, but Lauren would prove that his brand's presence at Wimbledon "embodied elegance and classicism" and was a natural reflection of the club. Much like the cast of a movie, there appeared a sea of ball boys in preppy navy polo shirts and legions of groundsmen sporting white-and-blue pinstripe shirts and navy blazers topped with brass buttons. The double-cream color sightings of chinos and flat caps made one think: Did we time travel back to Edwardian Wimbledon? Not quite. Yes, they were all dressed in Ralph Lauren, but this was the All England Lawn Tennis & Croquet Club reimagined, this time through the refined eyes of an American designer and his sensibility.

With the American and British Grand Slams under his flat cap, Lauren took on the Australian Open too. The US Olympic team followed in 2008—Lauren's sporty, sophisticated paintbrush was prolific. Pinstripes and tweed suits with neckties were spotted even in the Royal Box in 2024: actors perched on the highest spectator branch, their patterned markings telltale signifiers of the brand. It was picture-perfect. Even today, we are subtly reminded of the Ralph Lauren manifesto nearly everywhere. It is, after all, a lifestyle brand, not a sporting one, that has successfully managed to cross-pollinate its vision into global sporting events—as well as our homes and personal wardrobes. Leaving us to wonder: Where next for the man astride his horse, playing polo?

"OUR DEEP CONNECTION TO TENNIS IS REFLECTED IN OUR ENDURING PARTNERSHIPS WITH THE WORLD'S MOST PRESTIGIOUS TOURNAMENTS: WIMBLEDON, THE US OPEN, AND THE AUSTRALIAN OPEN.

EACH TOURNAMENT CARRIES ITS OWN RICH HISTORY AND TRADITIONS, REFLECTING THE GLOBAL INFLUENCE OF THE GAME AND SERVING AS THE FOUNDATION FOR OUR COLLECTIONS EACH YEAR. FROM THE PRISTINE GRASS COURTS OF THE ALL ENGLAND CLUB TO THE ELECTRIC ENERGY OF NEW YORK CITY TO THE VIBRANT SPIRIT OF MELBOURNE, WE HONOR THESE DISTINCT LEGACIES WHILE BRINGING OUR OWN TRADITION OF TIMELESS STYLE AND CRAFTSMANSHIP TO THE WORLD OF TENNIS.

WHEN DESIGNING FOR WIMBLEDON, FOR EXAMPLE, WE HAVE ALWAYS BEEN INSPIRED BY ITS SPIRIT OF OLD-WORLD SOPHISTICATION AND SPORTY ELEGANCE. BREATHING NEW LIFE INTO THE ROMANCE AND NOSTALGIA OF A BYGONE ERA, RALPH LAUREN HAS REDEFINED THE TOURNAMENT'S IDENTITY OF STYLE—CRISP WHITE POLOS, STRUCTURED JACKETS, AND TAILORED TROUSERS—HONORING ITS STORIED PAST WHILE INSPIRING FUTURE GENERATIONS."

—DAVID LAUREN,
CHIEF BRANDING AND INNOVATION OFFICER, RALPH LAUREN

MISS MARIA SHARAPOVA X NIKE

MARIA SHARAPOVA IS AN AGGRESSIVE AND INTENSE BASELINE PLAYER, FIVE-TIME GRAND SLAM WINNER, OLYMPIC SILVER MEDALIST, AND AN ELITE ATHLETE SPONSORED BY NIKE.

MS: I've worked with Nike since I was twelve years old. They didn't have a kids' line back then, so my mom had to roll up the skirts or cut the length or sew a few pieces together to make it fit. As I gained success, I realized that it wasn't just about playing tennis—it was about these brand partnerships. I sat in on these meetings because I really thought about the people around me, including my brand partners. How were they helping me shape my story? Do they even know what their end is? So many brands want that immediate instant gratification, a return on their investment, and in sports it just takes patience.

When I used to do interviews in different parts of the world—for example, in Asia or Europe—they'd ask, why do you think tennis isn't developed? I would reply that it takes years to develop generational talent. You have to train for over ten years on [say] Court 32 just to have a chance to step on Centre Court. The brands have to be prepared for that.

SKN: How has growing up with a brand reshaped the experience of young female athletes on the circuit?

MS: I played with the Women's Tennis Association for many years, and they have a health department. As a young girl, you have a team to whom you can ask questions without feeling like you weren't smart or good enough, whether it's about subjects like fertility or real-life questions. If there are leagues and organizations that can provide pockets of support, that adds so much value to a player's health, their outlook, and their careers in life. Women—and in particular, female athletes—now have the resources and tools to guide them and help them make thoughtful decisions about how they want to lead and prolong their careers.

I've never had the mentality that I'm going to change the way I feel, or that I'm going to work differently, because of inequality elsewhere, or because I'm paid less. I just put my head down and work hard and try to be the best in my field, and whether on that day you make a dollar less or five hundred dollars less, if you gave everything you have and you are fulfilled by your efforts and input—that gives me joy. I did everything I could as an individual in my craft, in my career, and I knew that one day I'd be rewarded for it, and I didn't think of my reward compared to others, whether they were female or male.

SKN: Do you think that women in tennis, whether they are the player, coach, or tennis parent, are often portrayed negatively for showing traditional male traits of grit or aggression?

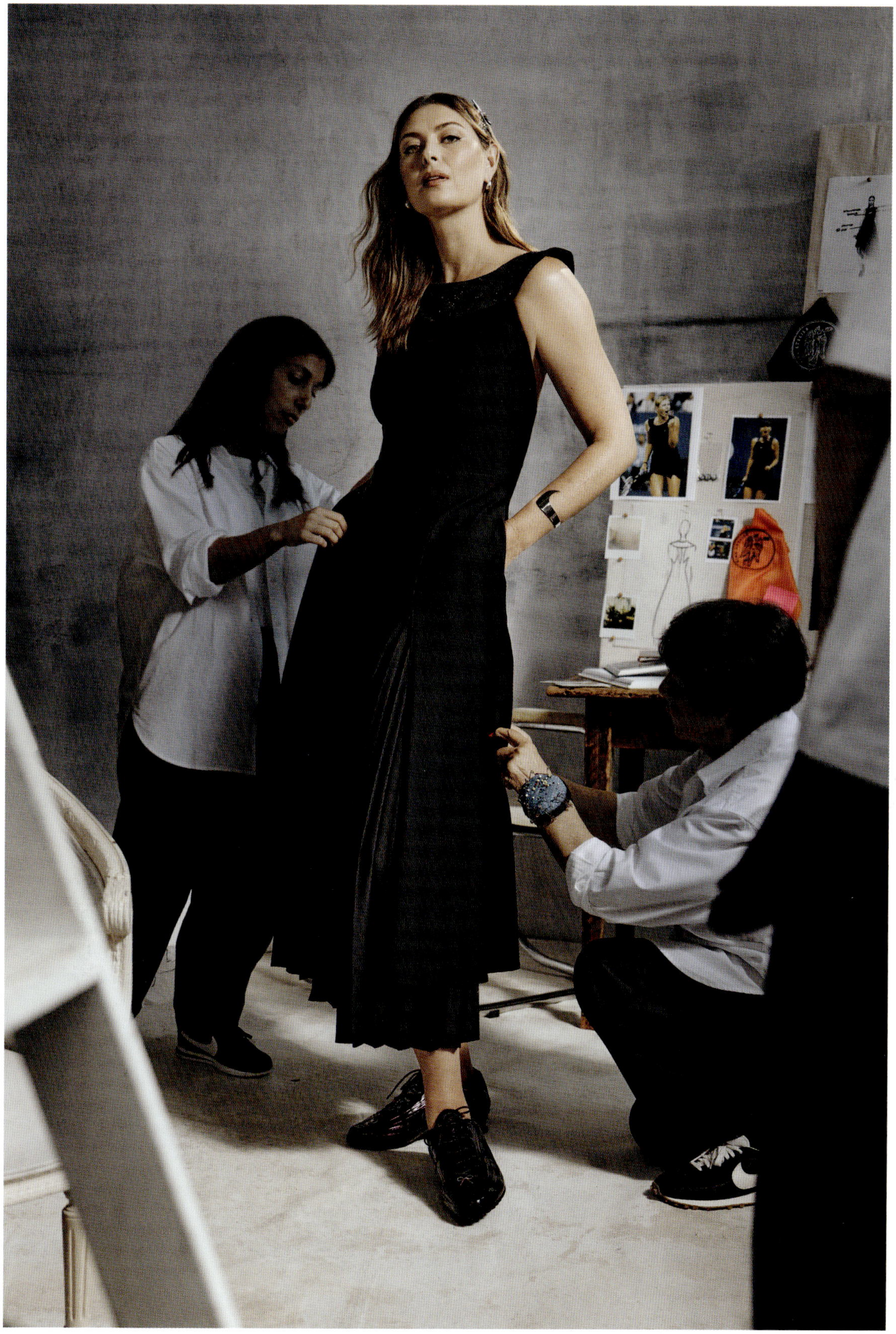

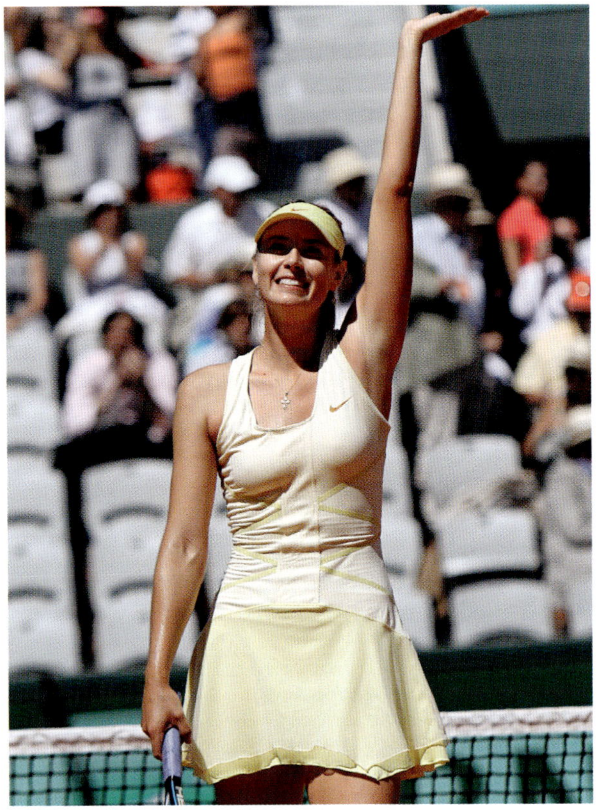

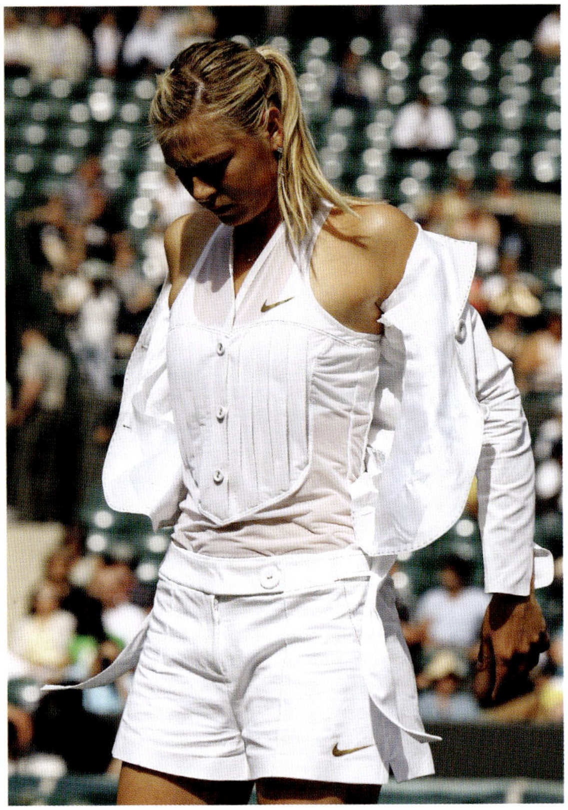

MS: I can definitely relate to showcasing passion with a strong fist-pump and a loud grunt. I wanted to stand out. I wanted to be different. If everyone was wearing black, I wanted to wear red; if everyone was working on something in the gym one way, I wanted to do it differently. I wanted to push the boundaries, and I didn't feel I had to apologize for wanting to do it my way. If someone sees a woman in a situation and she is fighting hard because she's putting in so much work, and it's an important match in her career and in that minute, she's showing that kind of emotion, that is beautiful to me. And if anyone has something to say, then that's their opinion. As athletes, you work so much away from the spotlight. When you are on the battlefield, that's your moment, and if you're showing your true character, isn't that pretty damn cool? I led my career with authority and by taking ownership of my wins and losses and being gritty about it, and if that meant that the world was to see it that way, then that's the way it was. I apply that now to everything I do.

SKN: You had a stellar relationship with Nike throughout your career, together you were positioned as a serious force at the intersection of fashion and sport—would you agree?

MS: Tennis hasn't evolved in many ways, but fashion is part of an athlete's storytelling, and it gives athletes permission to be more than just an athlete—it gives them character, playfulness, a point of view with the fans and the outside world. It's huge and important. I got a firsthand view of understanding that a brand is about the athlete, and it was very reciprocal. When I was in the locker room, I wanted to feel like I was not worried about my outfit. I was not thinking about it, because everything was perfect: It was engineered and designed months before, so that when I get to that moment in the locker room before a very big match, I feel like it's my second skin, like it's part of my body.

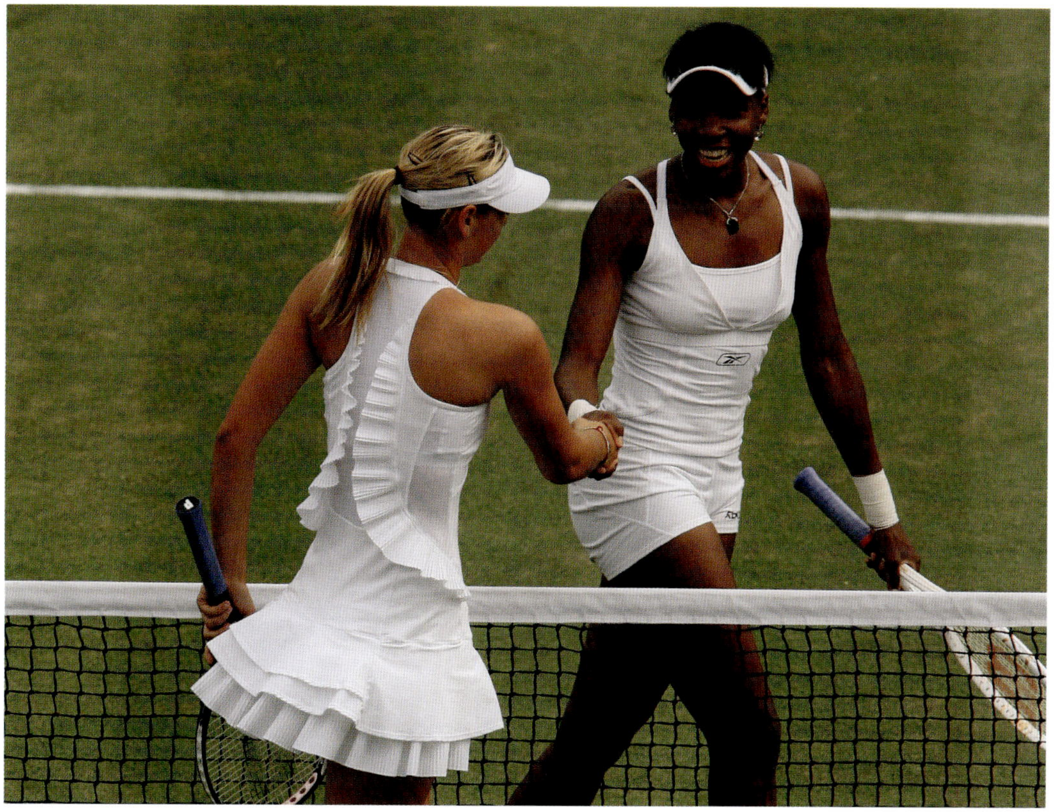

I guess we can go back to my first understanding of taste and fashion, which was all based on my mom and grandmothers. I didn't have siblings, so they were my style inspirations. My mom was very elegant, simple in a way—we didn't come from a lot of money, no wealth of jewels, diamonds, or gold. But she bought pieces that she lived with for a very long time, and I have that same aesthetic in tennis in some ways. I think every meeting I had with Nike [for designing my commercial pieces], they related to me being at center court of the US Open. The fans want to be part of that moment, and I also wanted to apply this to their lives and create pieces that would complement them, whether they were playing in a doubles league or in a junior tournament. But it's hard to design for everyone including yourself.

We took some chances; comfort was not something that I took chances on, so we focused on details. When Wimbledon came around, we would discuss what the unique elements were that we could use given the certain restrictions to play, and then we would look at textures and materials. This was fifteen, twenty years ago, and innovation has changed so much—all we had was Dri-FIT!

SKN: And a bit of Lycra if you were lucky, right?

MS: Exactly! A big part of designing was the R&D [research and development] on materials, because I was really pushing to make sure the meshes were breathable—because you would think that they are naturally breathable, right? But actually, when you try to pull it, it doesn't pull—it's as tight as a drum. So before we even looked at a shape or a silhouette, we made sure that certain materials went through wear and tear.

SKN: When I assessed your tennis looks, some seem to carry this pre-Raphaelite painting quality—the diaphanous detailing or the lace overlay. How would you describe your own style?

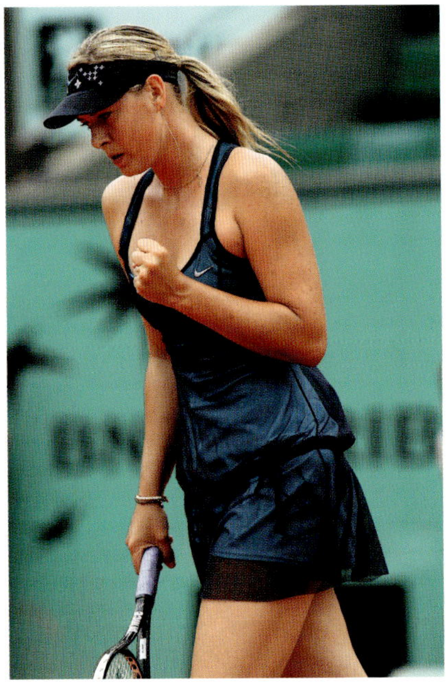

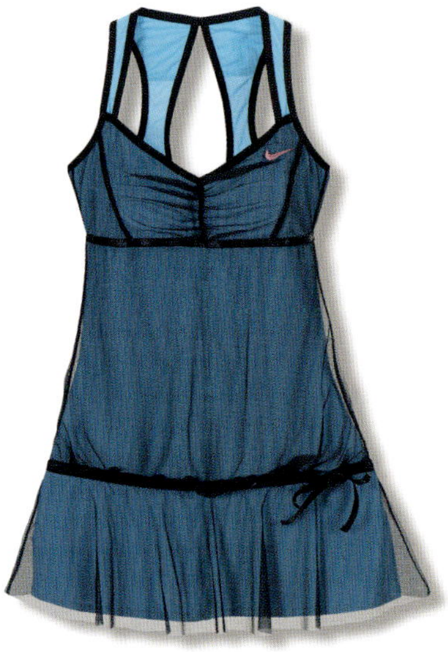

PREVIOUS PAGE:

MARIA SHARAPOVA X NIKE ATELIER 25

LEFT (LEFT TO RIGHT):

2007 FRENCH OPEN

FLAT OF SEA BLUE OVERLAY DROP-WAISTED DRESS IN MESH TRICOT

MS: I would say *classic*. I grew up watching and admiring rhythmic gymnastics, and at the end of their performance, where they would blow kisses to the crowd—standing kind of statuesque, with their backs bent backward—it was such an elegant form, and I always thought of that moment. As I won more matches, I started feeling that I was like them, and you appreciate the crowd, and you thank them for the support. So that was my moment of going back and saying, *These athletes were so beautiful at the end of their performance*. And that's how I felt about my clothes. I want these textures and materials to feel like they were part of my body. Perhaps it goes back to gymnastics suits, right? That it's just like a suit, an envelope around your body, and it's part of your skin.

SKN: Ah, yes—I can see you with the wave! Did you ever feel like some of the revealing outfits put you at risk of being disempowered with a beauty-first narrative?

MS: I was comfortable with it. When you are competing and you are running side to side and you're sweating, you're already vulnerable. So I'm not gonna worry about if my shorts are too short or is the V-neck too low—I never really sweated that. And yeah, a big part of being a female athlete is vulnerability and showcasing a female body, which is beautiful at any level and at any stage of life and not because of how you're showing it, but because of how you've worked for it and what you did to get there.

SKN: I noticed that there were repeat looks which worked well for you. A certain silhouette but rotated in different color ways?

MS: Yes, there were definitely shapes like a small waist, and I wanted a skirt that didn't have too much volume because I didn't like things flying and moving around too much. So the silhouette was quite skinny.

LEFT AND BELOW:

WRAP-OVER TOP FOR TIERED DRESS FROM THE 2007 FRENCH OPEN

SKETCH OF LAYERED, TIERED DRESS BY NIKE DESIGNER NATALIE CANDRIAN

FLAT OF THE TIERED 2007 FRENCH OPEN DRESS

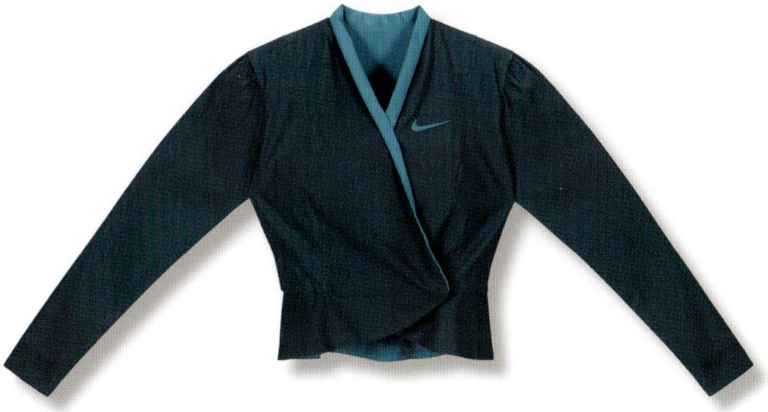

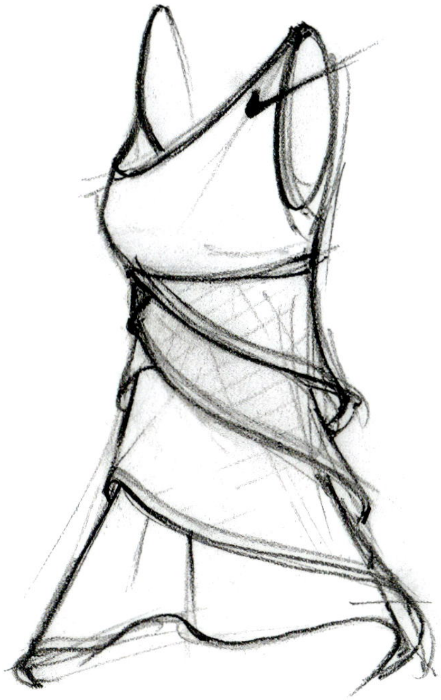

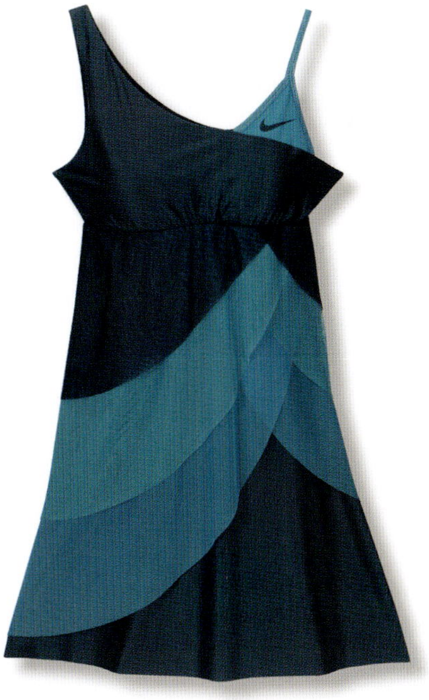

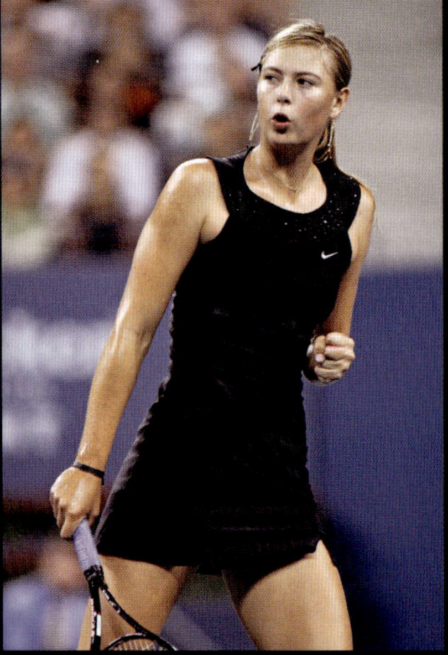

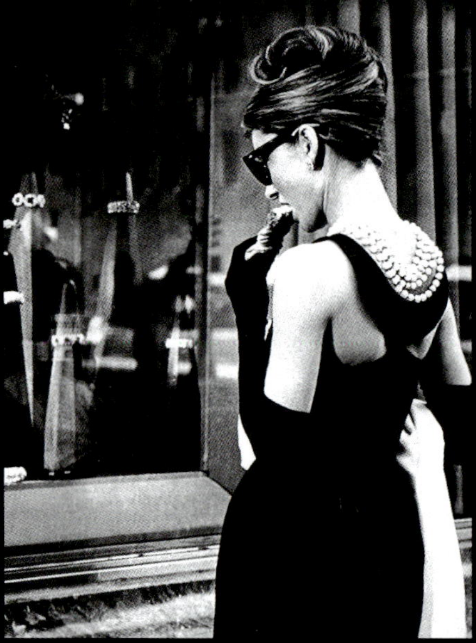

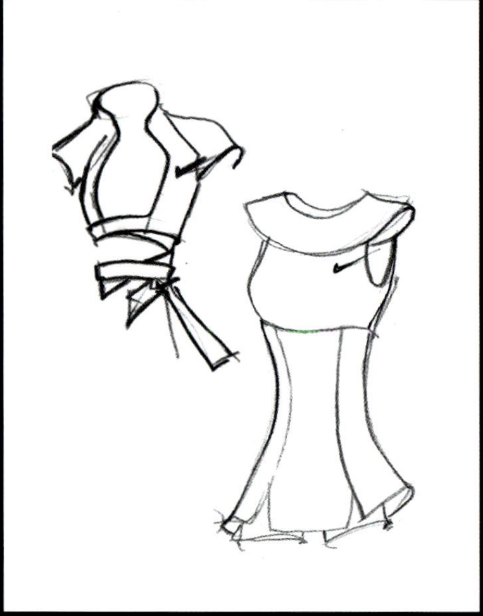

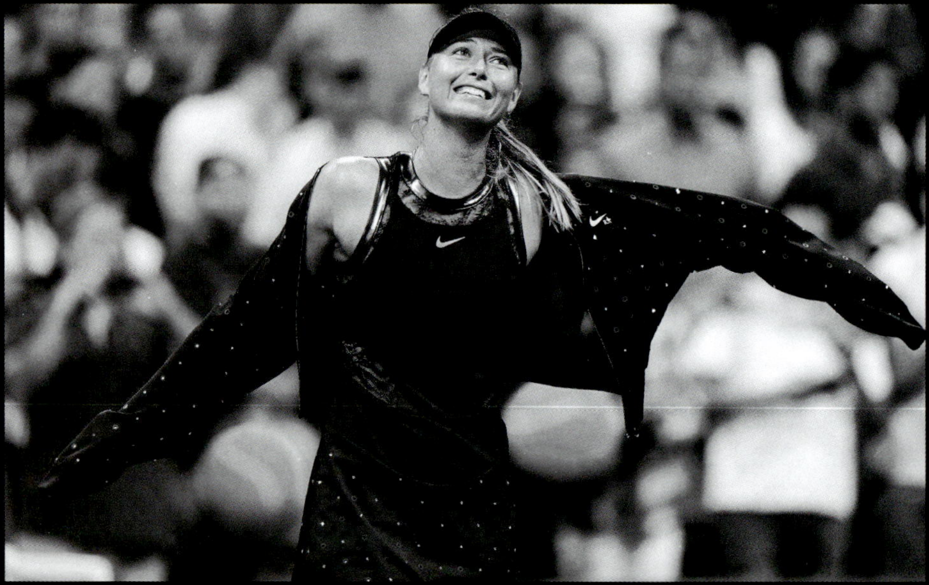

CLOCKWISE FROM LEFT:

2006 US OPEN

AUDREY HEPBURN IN BREAKFAST AT TIFFANY'S, WEARING HUBERT DE GIVENCHY, 1961

SKETCH OF THE 2006 US OPEN DRESS, NATALIE CANDRIAN

2017 US OPEN NIKE X RICCARDO TISCI STADIUM DRESS

SKN: What were your favorites?

MS: I have to go back to the meeting with Riccardo Tisci. Having him sit in my living room and talk about my designs was pretty mind-blowing. It was a night match at the US Open, so there's a significance to that, but I was the first athlete who wore a nighttime outfit for the US Open. There were crystals on the dress, and it was definitely more of a moment as you're walking down the tunnel and you feel it, you feel the excitement around—like, **What is she gonna wear?**

SKN: Maria, this book is called *ACE*: what does it mean to you?

MS: When I think of an ace, I think of someone really going for it. You don't hit an ace unless you have a purpose or a mission or a goal of giving it everything you have, whether that's power, precision, placement, and it seems like it's a combination of all those things. It's also synergy, but it's like the perfect shot: There is a lot that goes into it and a lot of guts as well.

THE LBD IN TENNIS

When a dress works, it works: silently, deftly, and precisely. If it embodies a distinct design DNA that can be recrafted and reinterpreted across eras, it earns its place as a timeless fashion classic—like the little black dress.

Couturier and fashion designer Hubert de Givenchy's 1961 floor-length black satin sheath dress with a fitted bodice and distinctive neckline was not quite "little," but it was a definitive black dress moment. Its atypical boatneck curved into a V, revealing the upper- and mid-back with sleek daring. At dawn on New York City's Fifth Ave, actress Audrey Hepburn ate her *Breakfast at Tiffany's* in this full black tie. This was her walk of glory, not shame. The scene, the dress, the film—made cult status. Apt, perhaps, that Sharapova drew on this iconic clip for her dress in the 2006 US Open final, working with Nike performance designer, Martin Lotti. This was her nighttime party after all, and she was going to wear an LBD for it. The dress was short and tailored to the body. The Givenchy collar was reinterpreted with crystal studs while the back of the dress had a subtle surprise aperture trimmed with a satin bow. Former Givenchy creative director, Riccardo Tisci, created the next iteration in 2017. Renowned for his love of gothic romance, he included eyelet perforations, laser-cut lace panels trimmed with soft leather, and delicate Swarovski crystals, which shimmered across her match ensemble. He later reflected that the design was "elegant, minimal, but strong." Lotti returned to work on Sharapova's final tennis fashion reprisal for her induction into the International Hall of Fame in 2025. This bespoke piece fused timeless performance with modern luxury. The dress's buttons were crafted using advanced algorithmic design features while Nike's signature "tech fleece" was chosen for the jacket. This cross-pollination of sport and fashion resulted in a modern reinterpretation of the little black dress, an effortless blend of house DNA and innovation.

MR. RENÉ LACOSTE & LACOSTE

RENÉ LACOSTE (1904–1996) WAS A STRATEGIC, METHODICAL BASELINE PLAYER WHO WON SEVEN GRAND SLAM TITLES.

Point by point, the tennis player plots—games, sets, and the match is eventually won. A solitary sport, the win is all on you. Excelling physically is a given, but it's the mind that truly holds court and dictates that final result. René Lacoste won seven Grand Slam titles from 1925 to 1929, but he succeeded primarily because he was a brilliant note taker, strategizing after each win and loss. Acknowledging his lackluster physicality, he said, "I was not incredibly talented or robust, but I was an inventor and could invent shots that bothered my opponents." He wore his opponent down—like a crocodile grasping its prey by its jaws and crushing it. Lacoste appreciated the comparison so much that he had an embroiderer sew a motif of the reptile on his cream wool blazer pocket—who knew?

Lacoste's tennis career was short; a respiratory illness cut him off from a pro career. His next innovation would be off court sometime in the 1920s. He recounts, "One day I noticed my friend the Marquess of Cholmondeley wearing his polo shirt on the court . . . a practical idea, I thought to myself. It was so practical, in fact, that I commissioned an English tailor to whip up a few shirts in both cotton and wool. Soon everyone was wearing them."

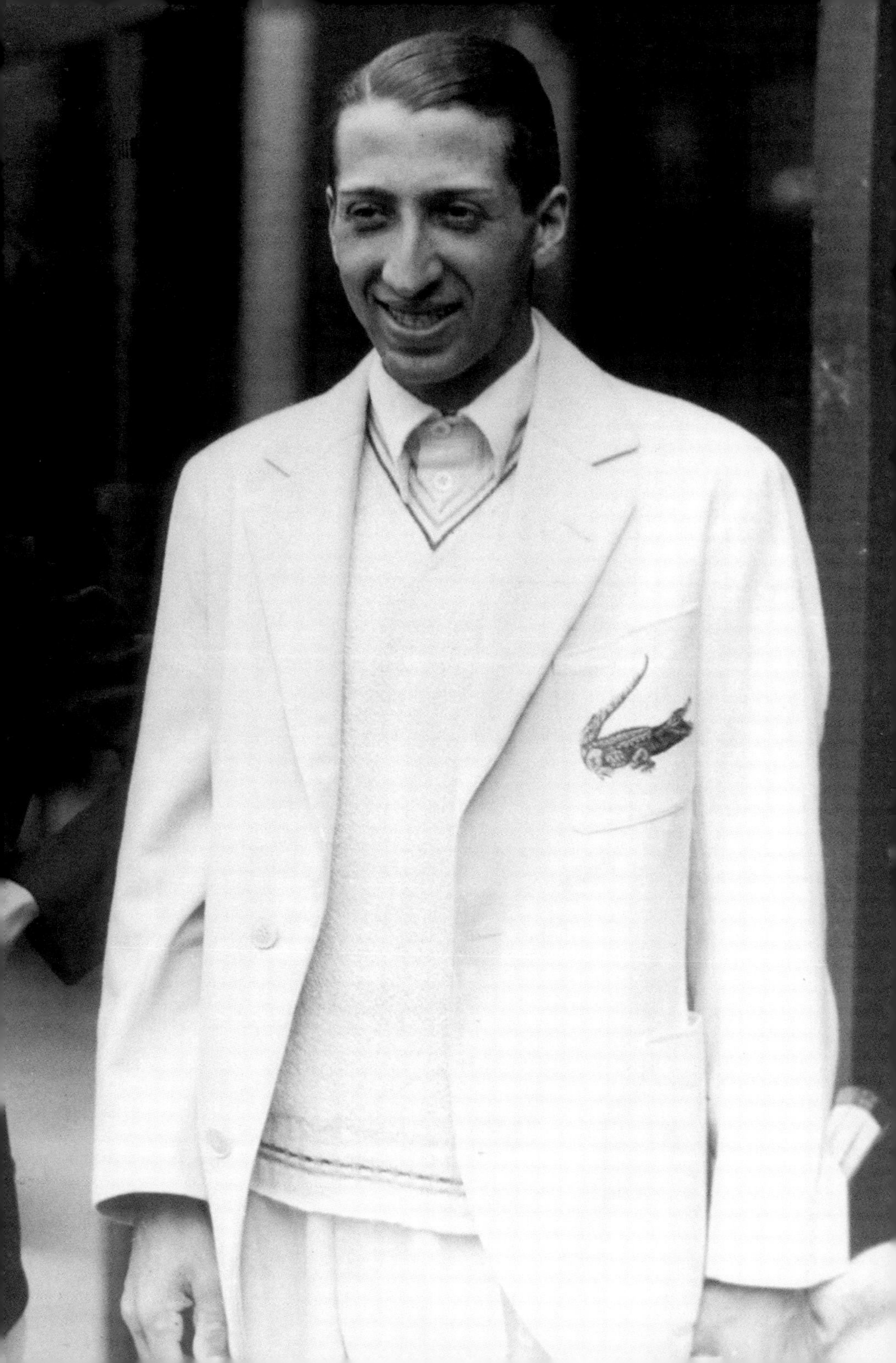

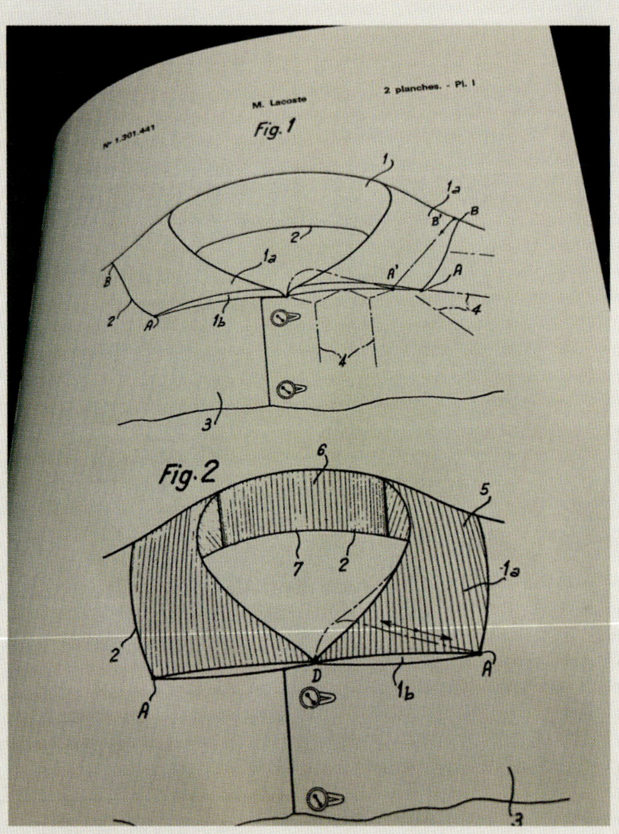
N° 1.301.441
M. Lacoste
2 planches. - Pl. I
Fig. 1
Fig. 2

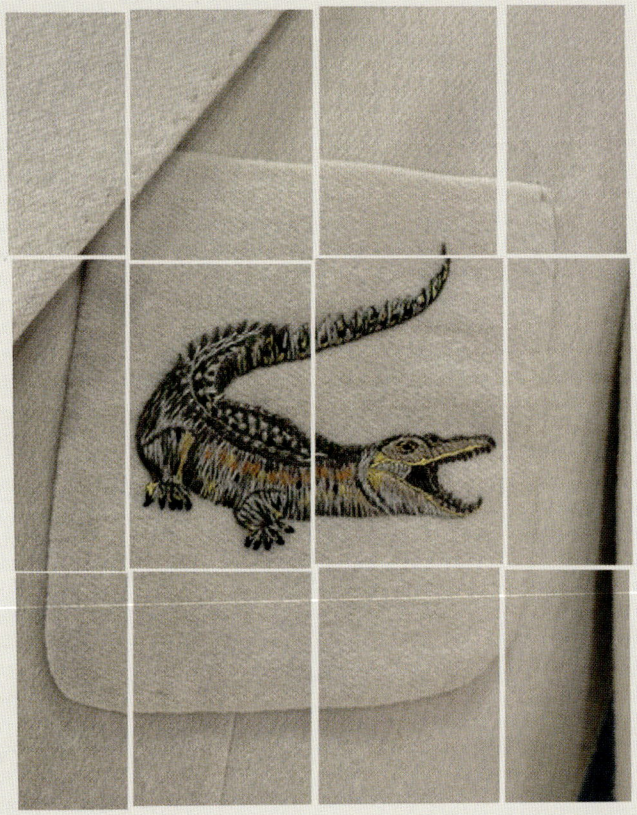

Lacoste's new short-sleeved shirt debuted at the US Open in 1926: practical, essential, and imperative to better performance, a final good riddance to the long-sleeved flannel shirts previously worn by men. He had discovered a loose cotton knit known as piqué that would stretch and allow for breathability and took facets from a regular button-down shirt by adding a double-knit collar and a front placket with buttons. The polo tails were made slightly longer in the back than the front so that it could be tucked in neatly into the trousers. The final result was the L.12.12: *L* for Lacoste, 1 for the knit, 2 for the shirt's sleeve design, and 12 for the number of prototypes that were made. The fashion topper? The crocodile icon, of course, an identifiable moniker of his label, a frontrunner statement in a newly defined sports market. Was this our first whiff of sport and style making the sweet scent of a new concept? The symbol was a subtle key to an exclusive sophisticated world where only the moneyed had access.

The style language of the polo shirt meant one could wear it to play tennis on court in the morning, sit in a café at lunch, and then sail off on a yacht in the evening. It was a sartorial scene-stealer that paved the way for a new, sportier life. Lacoste didn't stop with just the polo shirt: He devised the all-important grip for a tennis racket; he invented the ball machine; and significantly, he (with Wilson) developed the tubular steel prototype racket frame that would change the pace and style of the game forever. René Lacoste died in 1996.

By the 2000s, Lacoste the brand had lost its bite. Spread too thinly over too many product ideas, its teeth needed sharpening—urgently. When brands lose their way, a time-out is crucial to regroup back to its core aesthetic and re-strategize. The decade redefined sportswear with the designer collaboration concept. Puma started it first—not for tennis, but with the King soccer shoe under the minimalist and cerebral designer Jil Sander. And second entered Christophe Lemaire who led Lacoste into a fashion-forward paradigm. His work revitalized the brand into conceptualizing fashion but with a sports directive. A refined functionalist, he reimagined the polo in unexpected colorways and with quiet detailing. The label became part of the fashion runway calendar and so the collections expanded to outerwear, suiting, and knitwear. Lacoste was moving toward a new milieu: repositioned as a fashion brand, but always with the sport of tennis at the back of its mind (and jaws).

"PSYCHOLOGICALLY, THE COLOR OF WHAT I WEAR IS VERY IMPORTANT . . . I LIKE THE IDEA OF CAMOUFLAGE AND ALWAYS TRY AND PICK THE COLOR THAT IS CLOSEST TO THE SHADE OF THE COURT."

— NOVAK DJOKOVIC

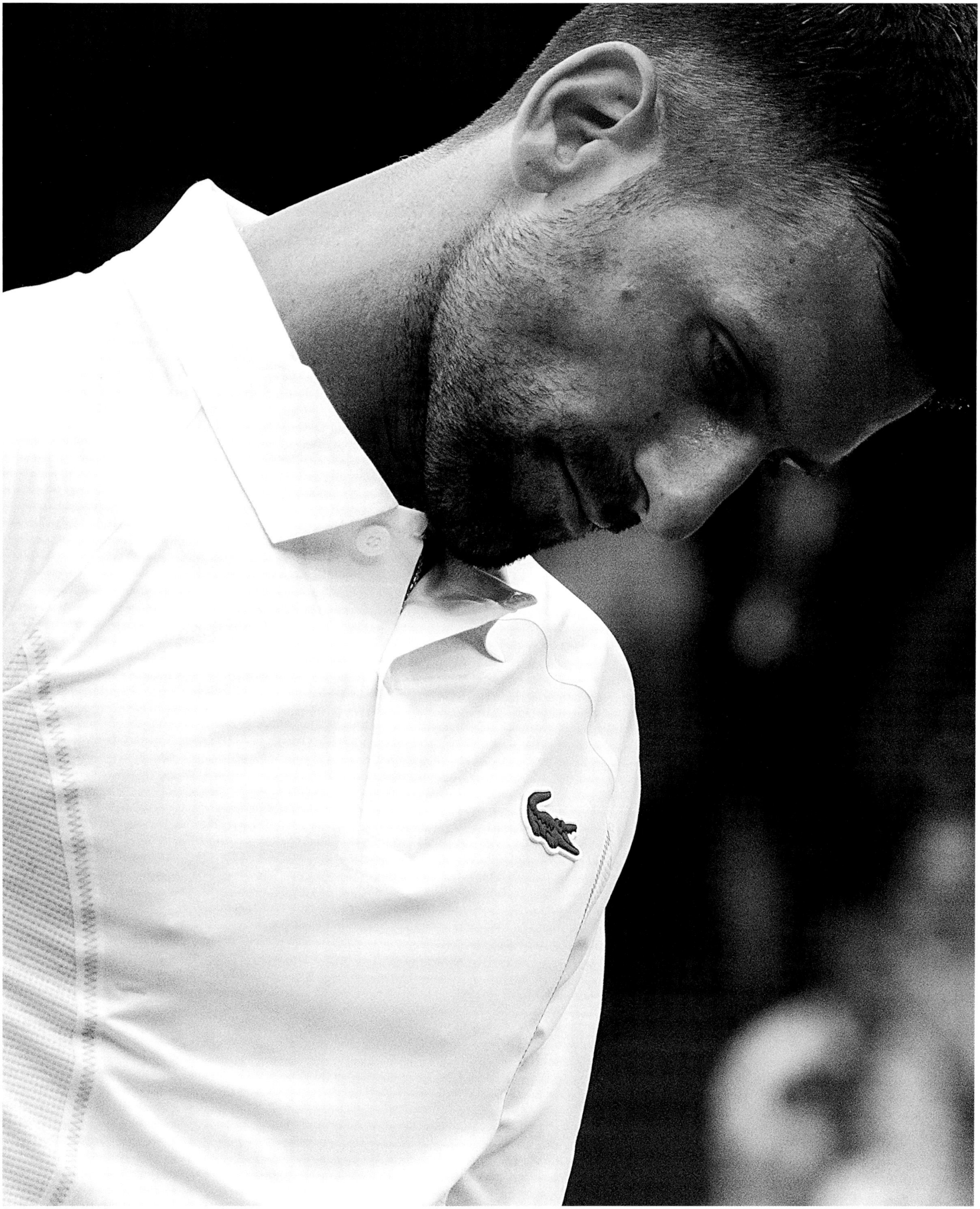

PELAGIA KOLOTOUROS

PELAGIA KOLOTOUROS IS THE CREATIVE DIRECTOR AT LACOSTE.

I would describe my design thinking as storytelling—I fall in love with either an image from Lacoste's extensive archive or an attitude and build around that. I think in chapters or film sequences, and I first start with visualizing the landscape or the characters around it. Lacoste's life's work and the game of tennis inspire me to keep delving deep into the mindset of innovation, effortless elegance, and technical apparel blended with heritage [tech heritage]. I love how fashion reflects culture: We are shifting our mindsets, wanting to live longer and healthier. Playing sports helps, and layering in fashion elements creates a new rising desire. It is this intersection of fashion and sport that is inherently Lacoste's DNA, and I'm cultivating it by respecting and disrupting the codes as Lacoste did with the polo shirt or steel racket, which he invented. I like to imagine my collections for Lacoste as akin to aces. René was an ace in my book, and expanding the brand's expertise to craft silhouettes that are tech-heritage and authentic while embodying simplicity.

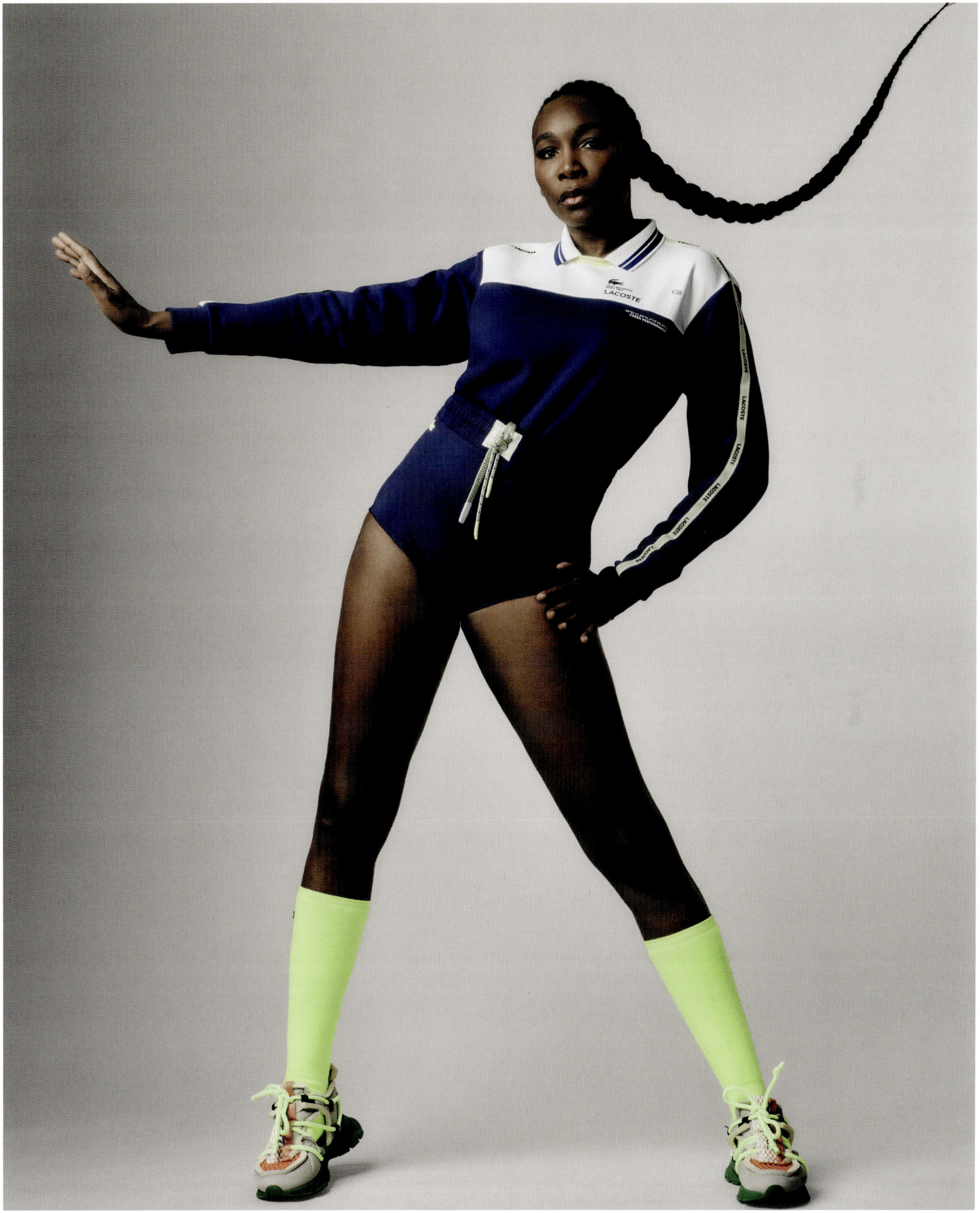
LACOSTE

MISS CHRIS EVERT & THE TENNIS BRACELET

CHRIS EVERT IS THE WINNER OF EIGHTEEN GRAND SLAM TITLES AND A BONA FIDE REVELER IN FEMININE FINERY WHO WORE DIAMONDS ON COURT AND BEGAN THE TENNIS BRACELET PHENOMENON.

Men run, fight, and partake in games to display their valor, strength, and virility—and the reward? Why, the hand of a fair maiden or a laurel wreath. The very premise of the Olympic Games in ancient literature was the ritual and celebration of male heroic feats, their physical prowess a measure of their masculinity and worth. Nothing wrong with that, but what if a woman felt inclined to do the same? Would that rob her of her beauty? Would she no longer be the fair maiden? Simone de Beauvoir, feminist extraordinaire, observed: "Man is defined as a human being and a woman as a female; whenever she behaves as a human being, she is said to imitate the male."

Social stereotyping has always been central to the narrative of tennis, particularly in the early twentieth century. Both sexes began playing around the same time, yet there was so much court for the woman to cover—metaphorically and physically. Viewed through the male lens as fragile childbearers, their physical ability was often reduced to grace over grit. The 1960s and 1970s were a time when women realized they could do both—play fiercely and look feminine. Jewelry became a firm fixture for all athletes from the 1950s onwards, with necklaces and bracelets becoming visual signifiers of personal superstition or spirituality. Donning diamonds on court, however, wasn't just a decoration, but a declaration of women's social positioning at the time.

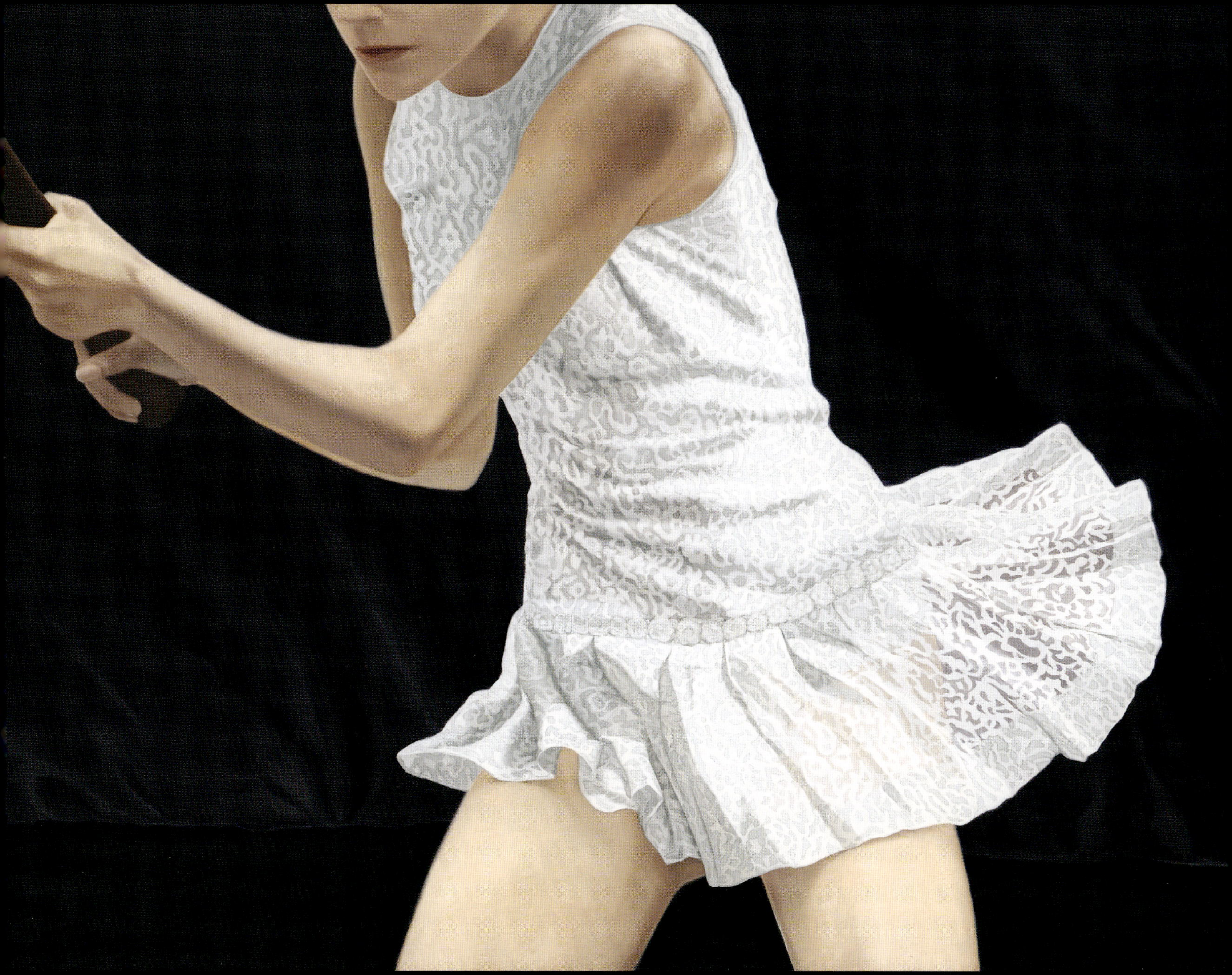

SKN: During the years you played, female athletes often seemed to face this intense pressure to over-emphasize their beauty and appearance—as if their athleticism alone needed softening.

CE: You have to understand that women in sports were a totally new concept in the 1970s. Tennis was the first women's professional sport. I remember my mother always dressed me in the prettiest tennis clothes, lace, ruffles—you name it. I had these socks with little pom-poms on them, and I wore my hair in a ponytail with a ribbon. It was important for me, because I was going out there and doing some pretty athletic moves. Nobody had muscles back then, but we would go to the gym to get stronger and we were sweating profusely, because we were running around like maniacs, falling down in front of a lot of people. I was a teenager when I first played, and I wanted boys to like me, so yeah, it was important for me to be feminine, to wear nail polish and jewelry. I didn't go so far as wearing makeup, because that's a bit gross—it would come off the towel with the sweat—but I made an effort.

SKN: Chrissie, the 1970s marked the normalization of diamonds for daywear, but did it feel decadent to take them on court at this point?

CE: I wasn't the only one—the top players were all wearing some kind of jewelry, like Billie Jean [King], Rosie Casals. But I can say that I bought my diamond bracelet for myself.

SKN: Which was probably rare at the time—for you to be able to afford that yourself—since it was heavily advertised then that he bought jewelry and she would wear it.

Can we talk about the design specifically? Pictures in 1977 show that you are wearing what appears to be a hexagonal cuff with a line of diamonds on the top—you wore the very same one for your US Open win in 1978. It's not technically a bracelet?

CE: I don't think that's the one—the one is what Monica and I have now designed.

SKN: Can you tell us the legendary story?

CE: It was for the US Open. I believe I was playing Pam Shriver, and I was wearing my diamond-and-gold bracelet. I remember the green tennis court with the white lines—it was at Forest Hills—and I was sweating profusely! I lost the bracelet at midpoint, and the game was stopped so I could find it.

SKN: Afterward, a reporter asked you why the match was stopped, and your offhand reply was, "Oh, that was my tennis bracelet!" History was made right then in jewelry terms—forget about all your incredible Grand Slam wins!

CE: Exactly!

SKN: And so you designed this line with Monica Rich Kosann. You also wore a BABE necklace for that match—were those diamonds as well?

CE: No, that was from Burt Reynolds.

SKN: The term *tennis bracelet* came about because of what happened to Chris, but there are women who don't even play tennis who wear one. What's the draw, Monica?

MRK: The appeal of a tennis bracelet is its timelessness. They are very delicate-looking, and yet they are so strong and powerful. The way the diamonds are made and set on the wrist makes it technically strong. There's something very classic and elegant about it.

SKN: The great Helen Wills had a charm bracelet with a Cartier tennis racket charm; the tennis ball charm is another popular motif, both have obvious connotations to tennis, whether you like tennis or not. There are many nuances in these tokens that also connect emotionally to an elite, rich world—would you agree?

CE: Maybe. Those kinds of charms have been around forever—I remember even as a teenager that I won a tournament, and I got a trophy and a little gold tennis racket charm with a diamond on the strings; it could go on a bracelet or a necklace.

SKN: What about women pros on court now? What's your take on the bling factor? There is some heavy artillery out there.

CE: I've seen Sloane Stephens wearing a diamond necklace. Donna [Vekić] too. It's becoming very common now. I think it's great if it doesn't bother them, especially with the sexy attire, the hair and nails all done up.

SKN: Yes, everyone is a winner—they can wear what they want, right?

CE: Yes, fitness and exercise is also inspiring not just what they wear, but women flaunt their muscles, and they flaunt their femininity at the same time. You can do both. Look at ice skating: The outfits are so revealing, such great athletic bodies wearing rhinestones and diamonds. I feel that's the direction tennis is moving toward.

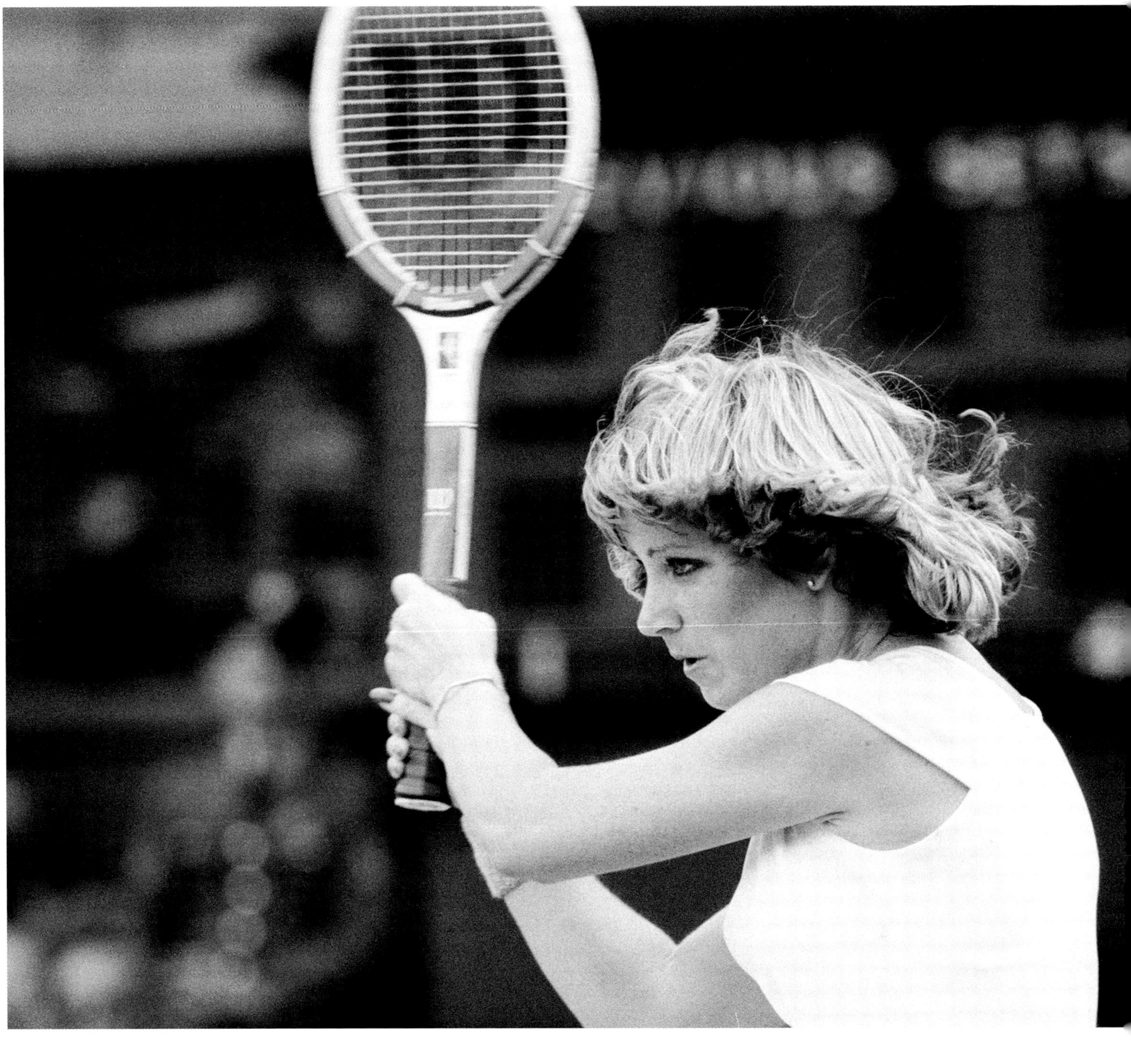

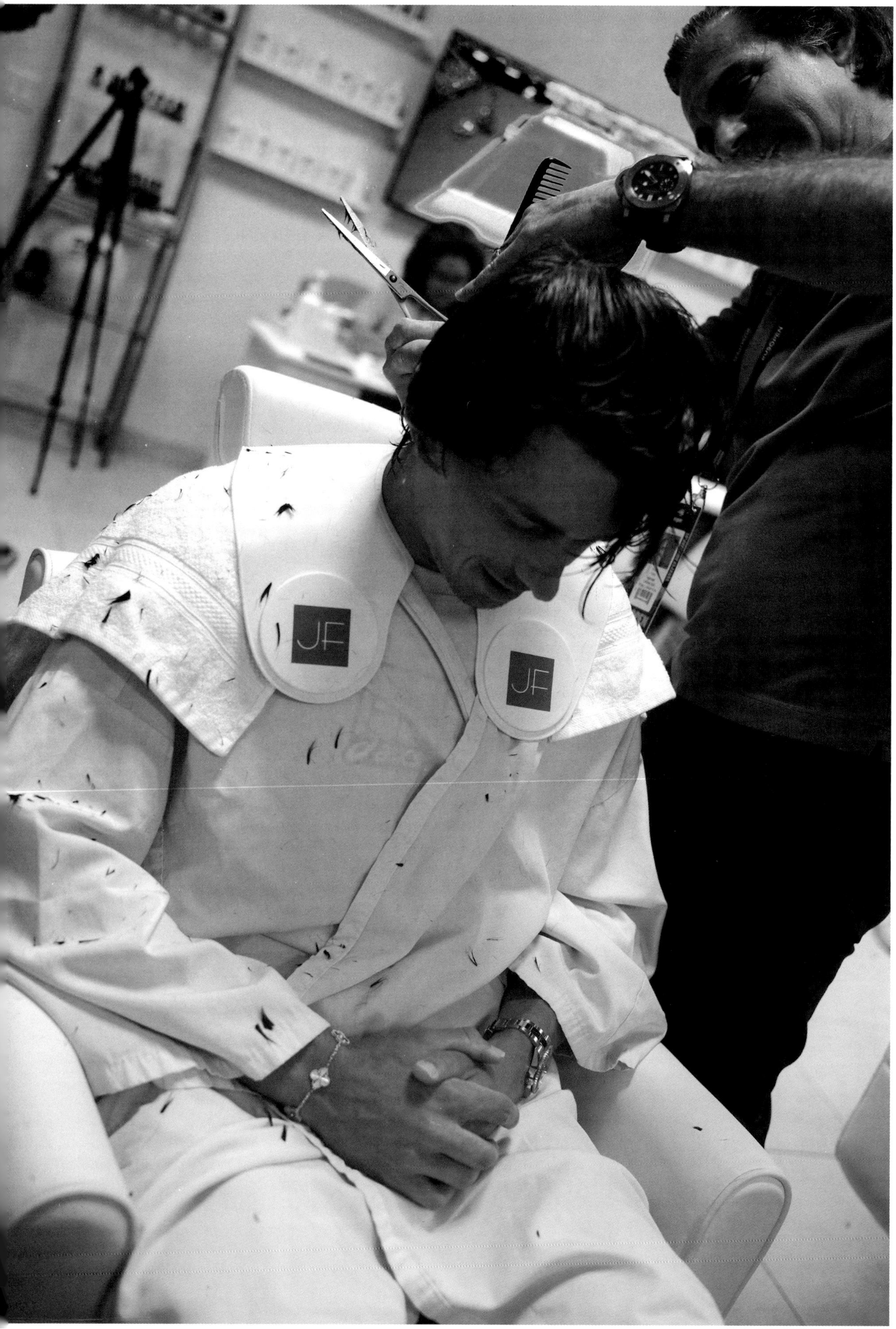

"PRIMING THE BODY FOR MATCH PLAY IS NOT JUST THE PHYSICAL TRAINING—IT CAN BE GETTING A HAIRCUT OR WEARING SOMETHING LUCKY TO FEEL CONFIDENT. IT IS ALL PART AND PARCEL OF THE GAME."

—JULIEN FAREL,
HAIRSTYLIST FOR US OPEN PLAYERS SINCE 2007

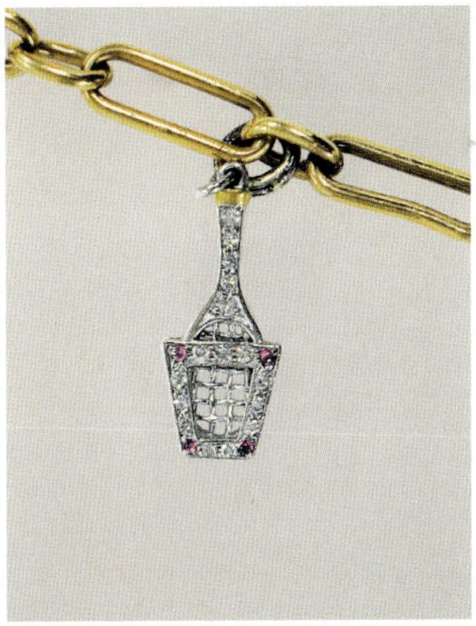
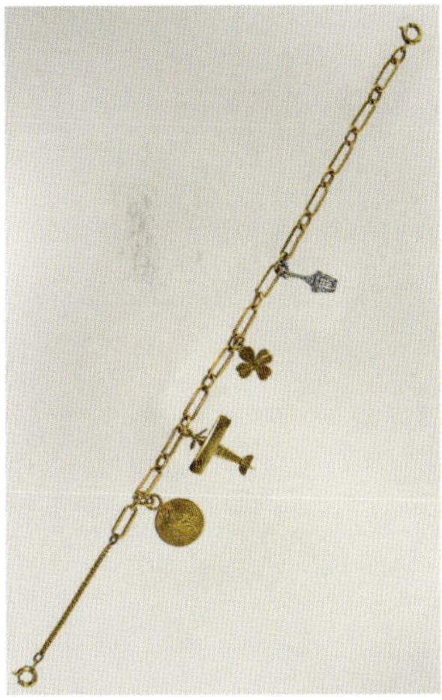
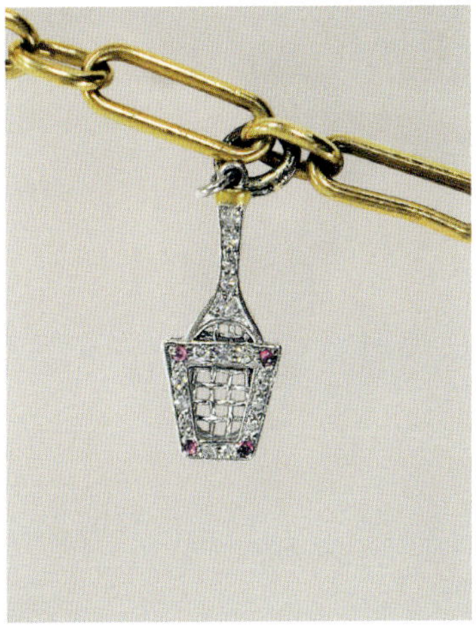
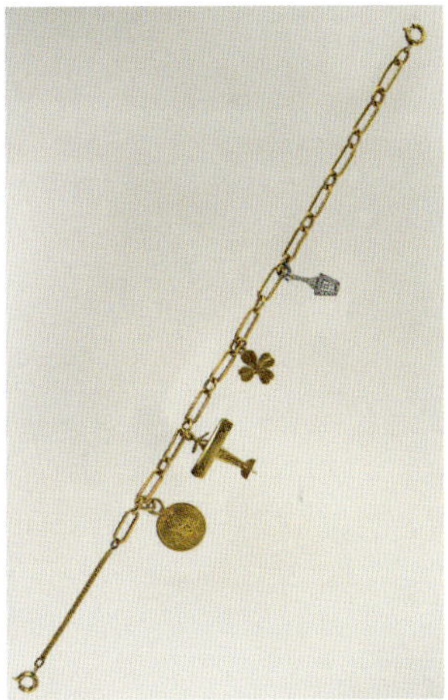

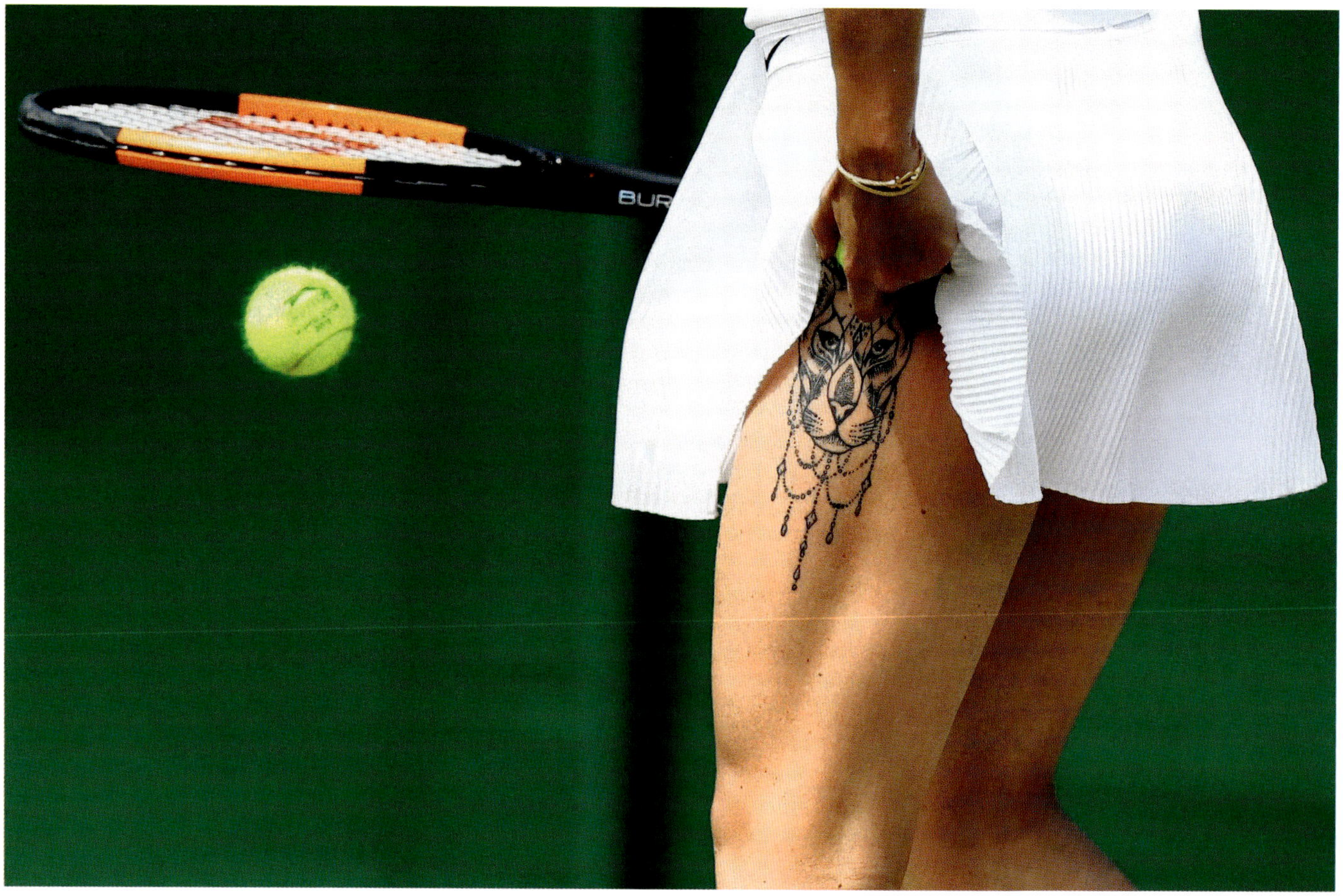

THE TATTOO CULT

Fashion history is littered with shards of sartorial satire—the tattoo cult on court is no different. Once worn by the lower ranks of society—prisoners, soldiers, and sailors from the 1800s—tennis players today are choosing to adorn their bodies with the same, a marker that the game once steeped in privilege is now inclusive to all classes. In the 1990s, footballers like David Beckham and Neymar Júnior famously extended their personal identities with tattooed tributes to their families and inspirational mottos and images. Tennis athletes soon followed in the 2000s: Kim Clijsters has her husband's initials inked on her wedding ring finger, Nick Kyrgios has tattoos running the lengths of both arms like sleeves, and Elina Svitolina and Aryna Sabalenka each sport tattooed tigers—each inking personal in its own right. Their athletic body, a temple; their performance, a meditation between mind and muscle; their tattoos, morphing into a second sheath of skin inscribed by their own mortal hand.

THE WATCH

VICTORIA GOMELSKY IS THE EDITOR IN CHIEF OF *JCK MAGAZINE*.

Rolex has always associated itself with winners—when people think of achievements and big milestones in their lives, they think of Rolex. The brand has cleverly aligned itself with high-end luxury sports like golf, motor racing, yachting, equestrianism, and of course tennis, and here's the thing: With the exception of yachting, they're never team sports. They're always the sports focused on individual excellence. That connection goes back to 1927, when Rolex's cofounder Hans Wilsdorf arranged for the swimmer Mercedes Gleitze to cross the English Channel wearing the brand's newest watch—called the Oyster, because it shut like a clam—pioneering and proving its water-resistance. Rolex is not just a branding powerhouse, however. It is the maker of arguably the finest Swiss watches in the world, and as a result Rolex utterly dominates the Swiss watch industry.

Today, most leading pro players are sponsored by watch brands. Most wear the watch after a Major match; Rafael Nadal wore his Richard Mille watch while playing, an excellent example of high-performance watchmaking. The RM 27-01 Tourbillon Rafael Nadal was designed for the tennis champ. The piece weighs just 18.83 grams, and even though the tourbillon is a delicate complication, Rafa has proved that the watch can hold up to whatever he is doing with his playing hand.

We've been living through a mechanical watchmaking renaissance since the 1990s—a high-end luxury watch is a status symbol, a totem of personal achievement, a stylish fashion accessory, and often all of the above. It's no surprise that the greatest tennis players in the world want to show off what's on their wrists!

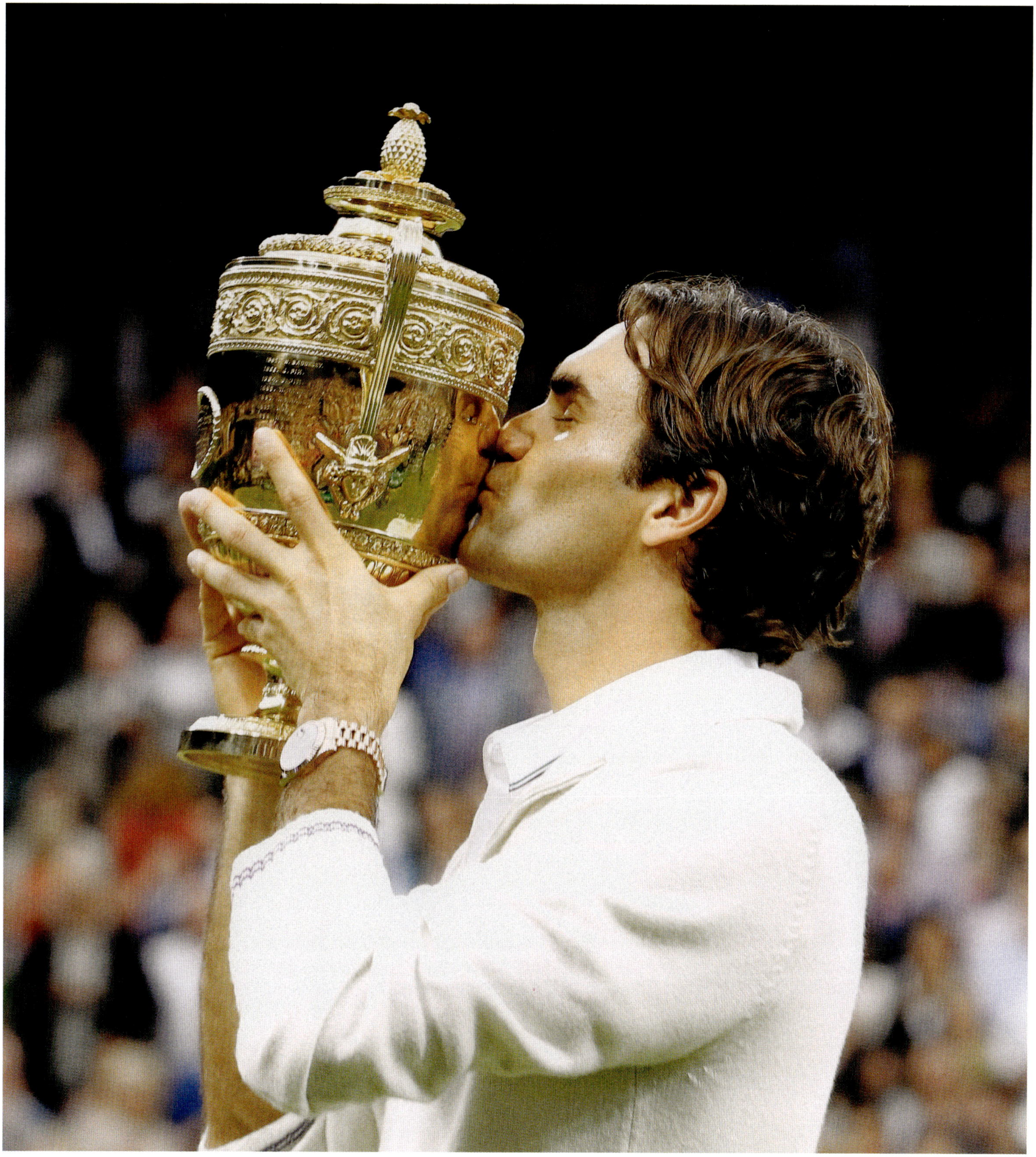

MISS MARTA KOSTYUK

&

WILSON

MARTA KOSTYUK IS AN AGGRESSIVE ALL-COURT PLAYER WITH ONE WOMEN'S TENNIS ASSOCIATION TITLE.

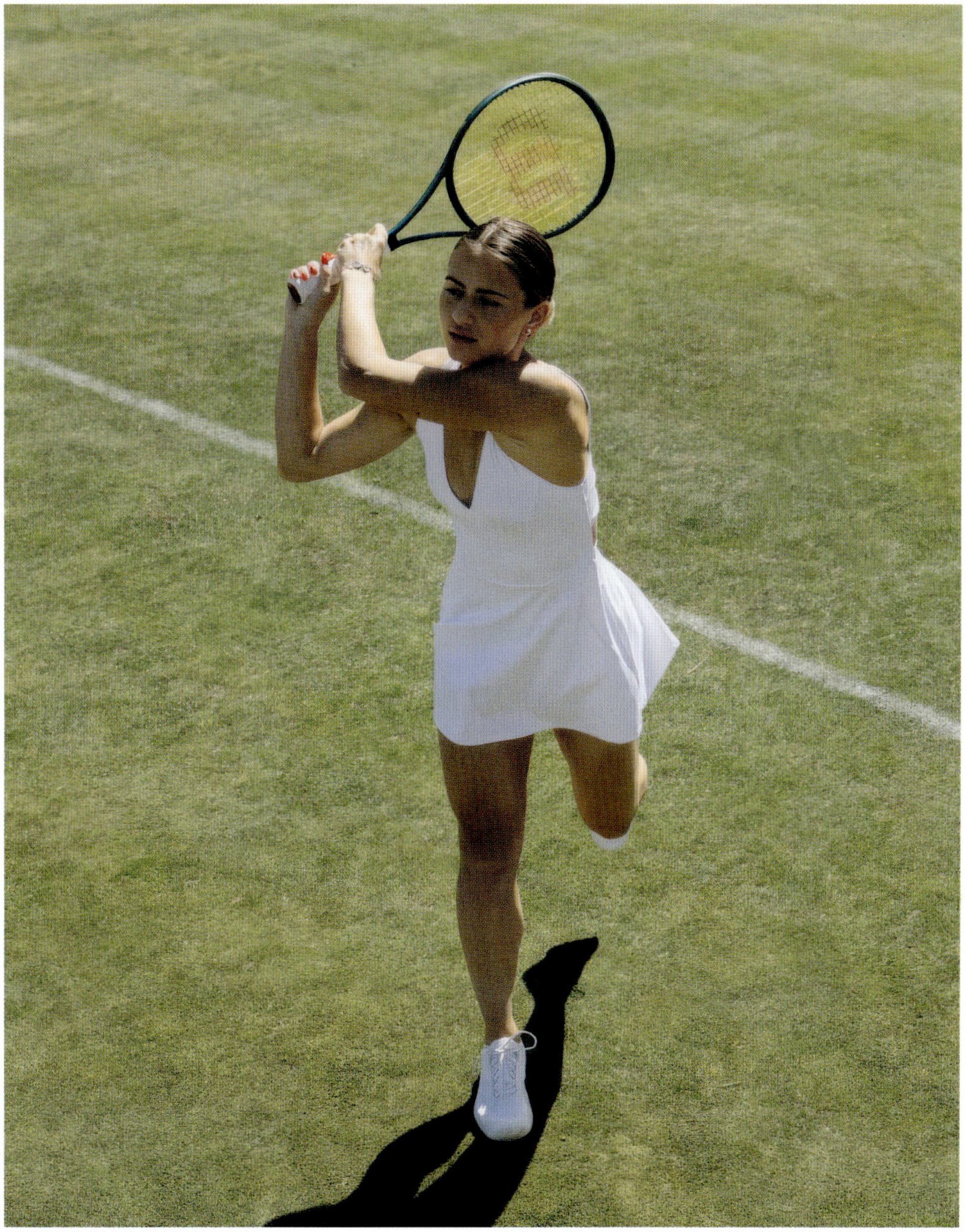

“THE MOST ICONIC PART OF THIS PROJECT FOR ME WAS THAT, AT FIRST, TURNING A TENNIS DRESS INTO A WEDDING DRESS WAS NOT ON THE TABLE AT ALL. IT WAS A VERY NATURAL TRANSITION FROM MY “JOB” ON-COURT TO THE MOST IMPORTANT DAY OF MY LIFE. THESE TYPES OF STORIES ARE VERY SPECIAL BECAUSE YOU DON’T PLAN FOR IT—IT FALLS INTO PLACE NATURALLY. WE WERE ABLE TO CREATE A BEAUTIFUL STORY FOR THE SPORT OF TENNIS AND FOR FASHION IN GENERAL. I AM VERY INTO FASHION MYSELF. MY STYLE HAS EVOLVED OVER THE YEARS, BOTH ON AND OFF THE COURT. I HAVE FULL TRUST IN JOELLE AND THE WILSON TEAM WHEN THEY BUILD MY KITS; IT’S A GREAT POSITION TO BE IN!”

—MARTA KOSTYUK

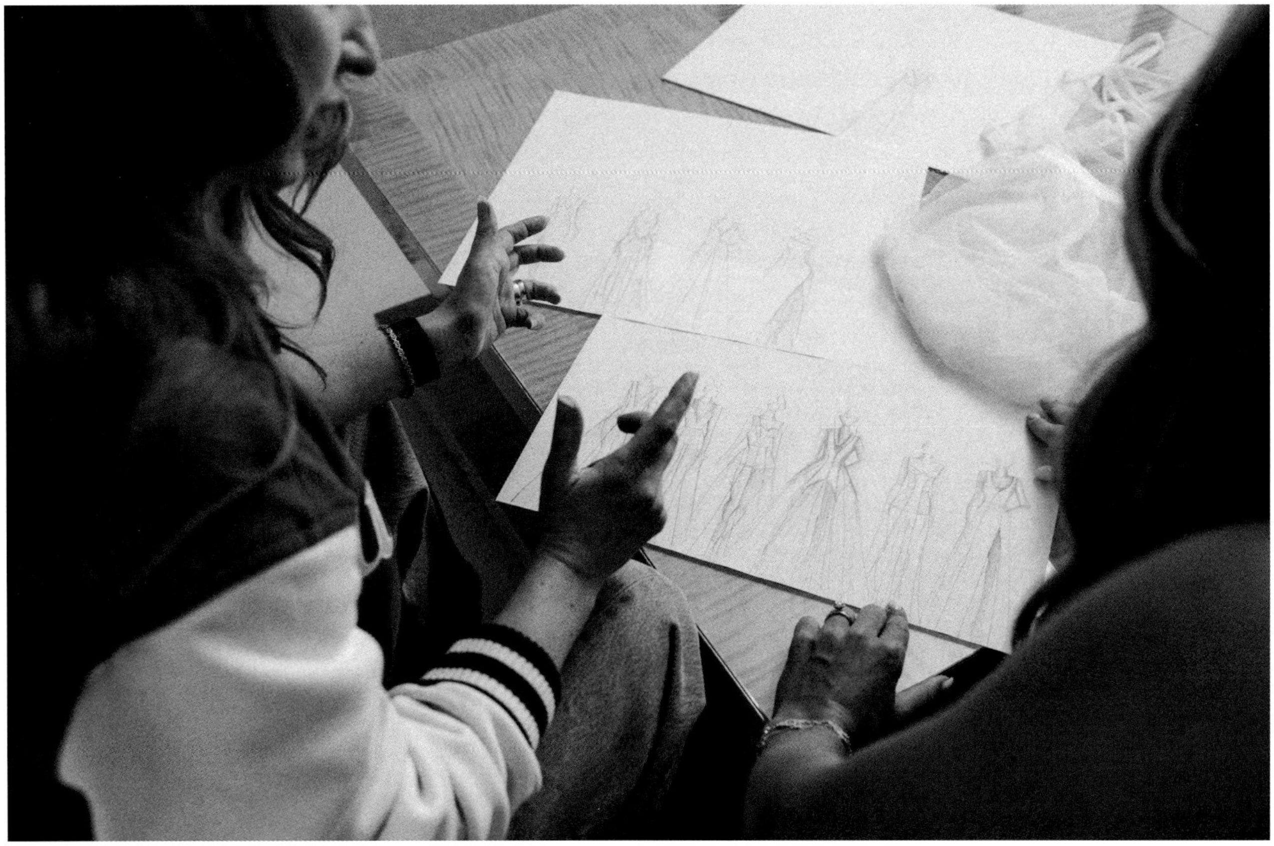

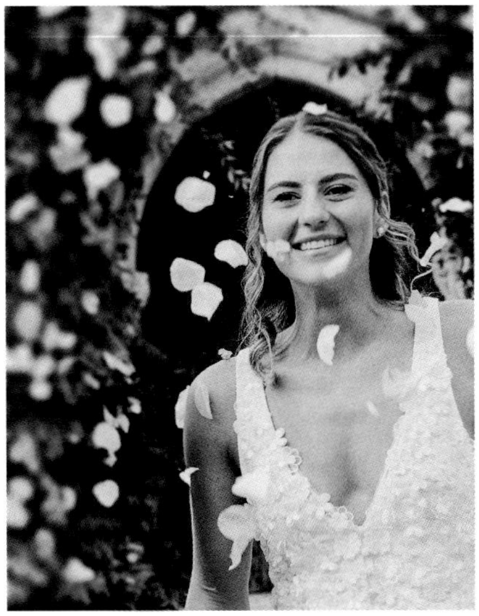

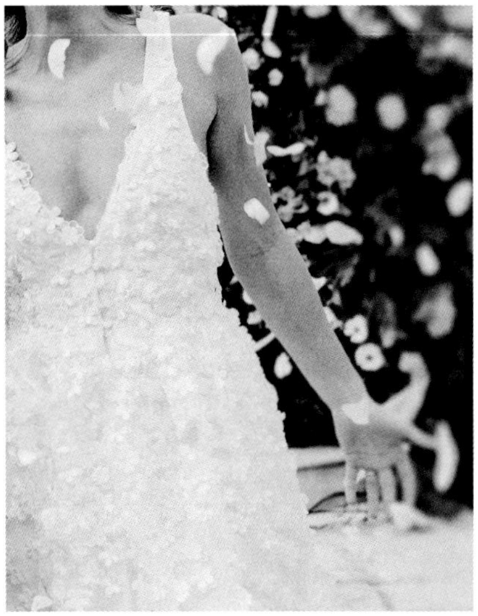

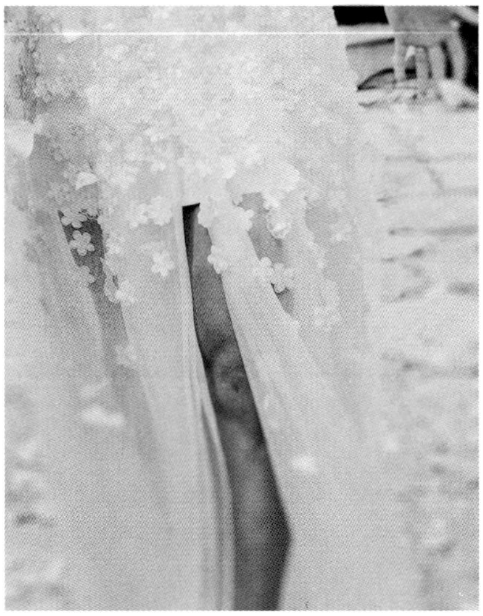

"MARTA AND I HAD ALREADY ESTABLISHED A CLOSE WORKING RELATIONSHIP BEFORE WE COLLABORATED ON HER WEDDING DRESS. THE BASE WAS ROOTED IN TENNIS DESIGN—FUNCTIONAL, LIGHTWEIGHT, AND MOVEMENT-FRIENDLY. WE USED TECHNICAL MATERIALS TO ENSURE COMFORT, BREATHABILITY, AND EASE OF MOVEMENT, SHE DIDN'T WANT A SUPER HEAVY WEDDING DRESS. THE SILK ORGANZA OVERLAY, WHICH COULD BE REMOVED LIKE A JACKET, WAS DESIGNED WITH VERSATILITY IN MIND. THE UNDER DRESS WAS MADE OF AN ITALIAN PERFORMANCE FABRIC. THE OUTER WAS MADE OF A SILK ORGANZA THAT WAS HAND EMBELLISHED WITH CASCADING FLOWERS. THE ACTUAL DRESS SHE WORE AT WIMBLEDON WAS A VERSION OF THE SHORTER DRESS BUT WITH A BUILT-IN LINER AND LIGHTER WEIGHT FABRIC FOR HIGH SWEAT AND SUPPORT."

—JOELLE MICHAELOFF,
VICE PRESIDENT OF DESIGN AT WILSON SPORTSWEAR

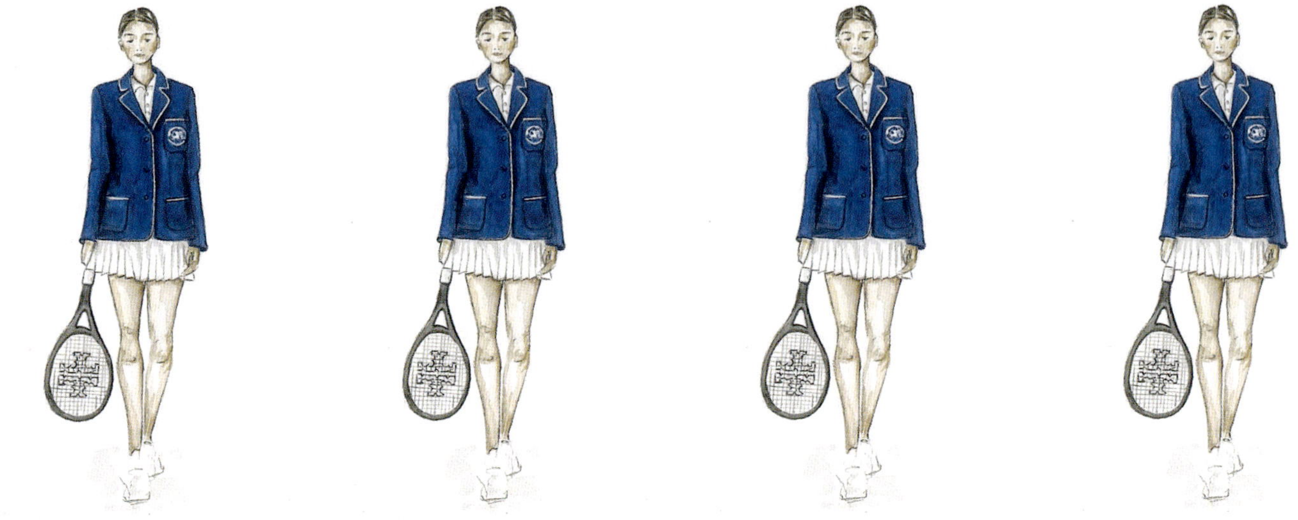

TORY BURCH

TORY BURCH IS THE EXECUTIVE CHAIRMAN AND CHIEF CREATIVE OFFICER OF TORY BURCH AND THE FOUNDER OF THE TORY BURCH FOUNDATION, WHICH PROVIDES WOMEN ENTREPRENEURS IN THE UNITED STATES WITH CAPITAL, EDUCATION, AND COMMUNITY. A LIFELONG TENNIS PLAYER, SHE LAUNCHED TORY SPORT IN 2015 WITH A COLLECTION OF TENNIS, GOLF, AND ACTIVEWEAR.

I grew up on a farm in Pennsylvania with my brothers, and we had a red clay tennis court. I started playing when I was four years old. I was pretty competitive in high school, captain of the tennis team. It taught me about teamwork, leadership, tenacity, grit, and focus—it gave me a lot of character. I remember the camaraderie, team playing, and rooting for others.

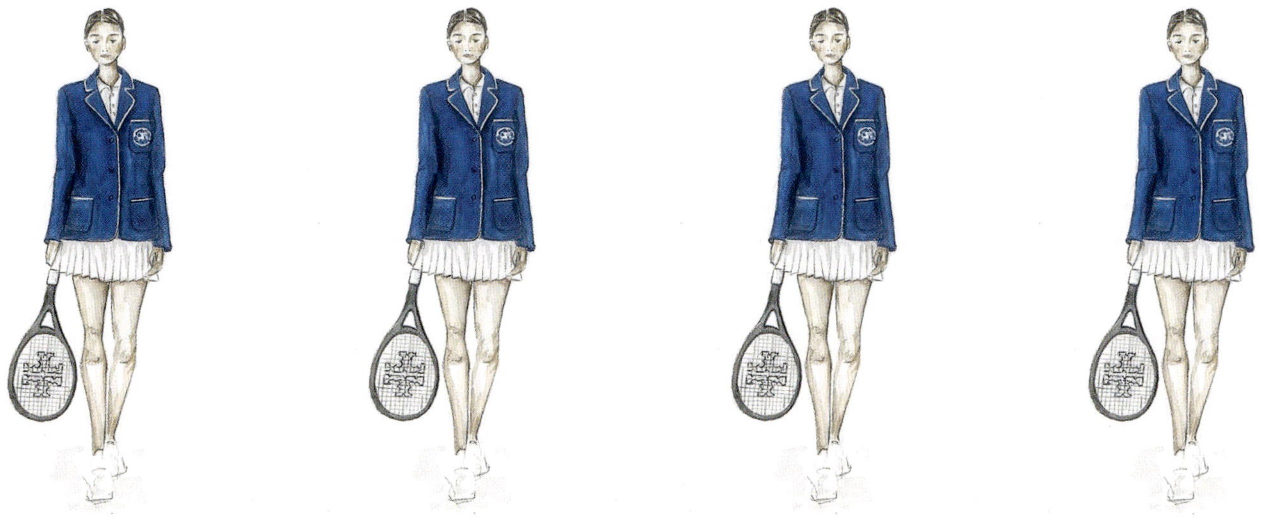

SPORTSWEAR

It's about confidence. When a woman feels beautiful and confident, that's everything to me. I have always been inspired by Claire McCardell's ingenuity and entrepreneurial spirit. She invented American sportswear in the 1940s and forever changed the way we dress. While other designers looked to Paris couture for inspiration, McCardell elevated the practical needs of American women: She gave them fabrics that were soft and durable, sleeves that could be rolled up, and silhouettes that moved with the body, not against it. Everything was intentional, nothing was frivolous, and comfort was as vital as glamour.

TORY SPORT LINE

I have always been passionate about sports. I love athletes, and I like thinking about the different fabrics and silhouettes and reimagining classical shapes with modern technology. Our Tory Sport line launched in 2015. I knew I wanted to focus more on creativity and the creative process. I grew up admiring Billie Jean King, and I'm still in awe of her, so our partnership was very exciting. She is a champion of equality, and what she's done with Title IX has changed women's lives. Our partnership started in 2022; we were the official outfitter of the Billie Jean King Cup and worked on a winner's jacket in "Billie Blue." We were inspired by the classic green Masters jacket, and the blue came from Billie's sneakers at the Battle of the Sexes match in 1973. I don't think there should be a pay disparity between men and women in sports. The fact that we are still talking about women's equality means we certainly haven't come far enough.

NEW BALANCE

SPEAKERS

CD: CHRIS DAVIS,
Brand President and Chief Marketing Officer

BL: BRIAN LYNN,
global vice president of lifestyle

EZ: EVAN ZEDER,
director of global sports marketing for tennis and baseball

JW: JOSH WILDER,
senior product manager for tennis

TS: TEDDY SANTIS,
founder, Aimé Leon Dore

CD: We want to be the brand that is the most inspiring and fun. We are striving to be the most premium athletic brand in the world. We have a strong entrepreneurial spirit and great long-term collaborations; we want partnerships, not sponsorships. We identify these artists, curators, visionaries—they represent the fun we're striving to evoke, and we elevate them to a global scale, demonstrating that we have our finger on the pulse of culture.

We've never tried to be the biggest; we've always tried to be the best. It's like casting a movie, a way to show the values and emotions that we're trying and striving to attain every day. So we've got two prominent luxury Italian brands: Miu Miu and Loro Piana. Miu Miu exemplified our desire to innovate through trend creation, and Loro Piana exemplified our innovation in premium materials and craftsmanship through trend validation. But they're both saying something that we stand for.

SKN: You had over fifty collaborations last year, though. Is it too many? Does the core message get diluted with consumers?

CD: If you have to ask why a collaboration exists, then it shouldn't exist. All of our collabs sell out immediately—we sold 5,000 units of [the] $1,500 [Loro Piana] shoe, and now it's on Stock X for $10,000. This is happening because the values we are communicating are honest, and the consumer sees that.

SKN: *ACE* is about the intersection of sports and fashion, something that New Balance does very well.

CD: I think we can all agree the worlds of sport, streetwear, and luxury have never been more intertwined. You can probably attribute that to the NBA walking-out moments or to footballers carrying Goyard purses or wearing Hermès scarves, and to the globalization of sport and fashion through social media and athletes becoming more than just athletes. How does New Balance do this? It goes back to our values. It's really easy to make connective tissues when every component works. There's nothing better than getting a retro tennis silhouette like the T500, which was codesigned by Aimé Leon Dore, a streetwear brand that is beloved in New York City fashion, and launching it at the US Open with Coco Gauff. We took a global sports moment, a global athlete at her pinnacle, and a loved streetwear brand, and that marriage was all authentic. If one of those things was not right, it wouldn't have worked.

SKN: The new T500 hits that intersection of performance and lifestyle. Why did you feel New Balance needed a lifestyle tennis shoe?

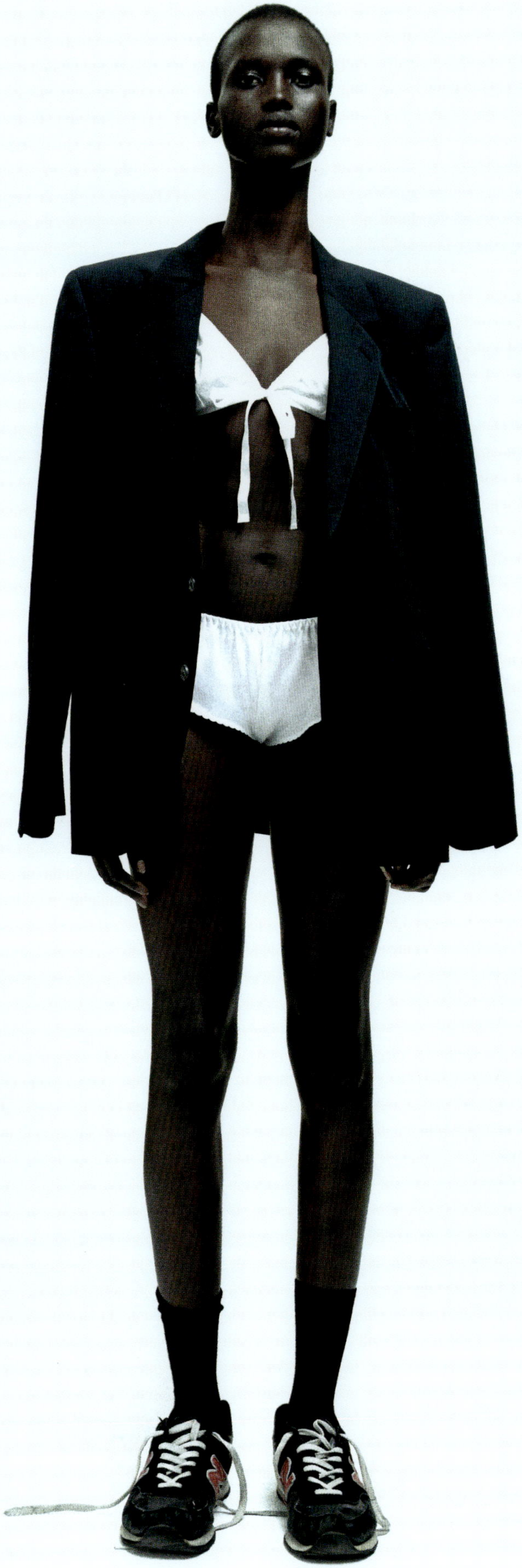

BL: Most of our lifestyle shoes have been running-inspired. The T500 had that classic tennis look, but the old T500 was incredibly uncomfortable. I think a few players wore it back in the 1980s, like Virginia Wade and Roy Emerson. The on-court tennis is mirroring the off-court retro style, the old money trend, away from the bling. We get back to timeless outfits and style, which is where the T500 fits in.

TS: The T500 has a simple silhouette and a uniform appeal; this brings a versatility in styling it. It's a timeless court aesthetic that balances heritage and innovation and makes it classic and relevant today. When we were working on the shape, it was about minimizing the toe spring, a sport-performance feature that we made into a lifestyle element. We matched the slightly square, top-down toe shape one-to-one with the original. With this, we were preserving an important archival design detail—and it was also one of the shoe's most recognizable visual characteristics. Our brand, Aimé Leon Dore, has built a reputation of being part of reviving New Balance heritage silhouettes through a fresh lifestyle lens.

ON COCO GAUFF AND TENNIS PERFORMANCE

SKN: You signed Coco Gauff when she was fourteen and have been with her since. How did you make this decision? Did you think she would get to the point she is at right now?

[Chris Davis shows SKN a thank-you card that Gauff wrote after her first visit to the New Balance factory.]

CD: [reading] "Dear Mr. Chris, I just wanted to say thank you for the visit to the factory headquarters, it was very insightful. Love, Coco Gauff."

I sent a picture of this to her when she won the US Open. A lot of the time athletes don't realize it [their potential], but this note says everything you need to know. Today, whether she is number 2 or number 40 in the world, it was unequivocally the right decision to partner with her, because of who she was as a person. I will say it again: Our partners are a reflection of our values. If we look at the individual first and foremost, we make the best decision, because the partnership is intrinsic to our mutual values, respect, and vision. The only thing we can control is the character of the individuals who come into the brand. I can't win the US Open for Coco, but I can say that we have been able to see her grow into a young lady who has shown nothing but dignity and respect with the whole world watching her, and we are incredibly proud of her.

SKN: How do you nurture a young junior tennis player to a pro? The family-like culture at New Balance certainly helps.

EZ: It takes time to foster relationships, not just with the player but also with the parents. We are always aware of not putting too much pressure on the child. Tennis has to be fun, always. When you play professionally, it still has to be fun. It's a very lonely sport—we at New Balance want to be the fun part. I know it myself from growing up and playing it. When you open a sneaker box, you are that kid all over again, and that's what it should be about: going back to that moment of happiness. It's building a trusting relationship early on and encouraging [the athletes] to give us negative feedback. We want to make a product better and know that we're doing everything in our power to make sure that they're performing at their best. I look at footwear as equipment, just like a tennis racket, so you have to perform your best with these, and I think apparel is an incredible modem for storytelling in the fashion element.

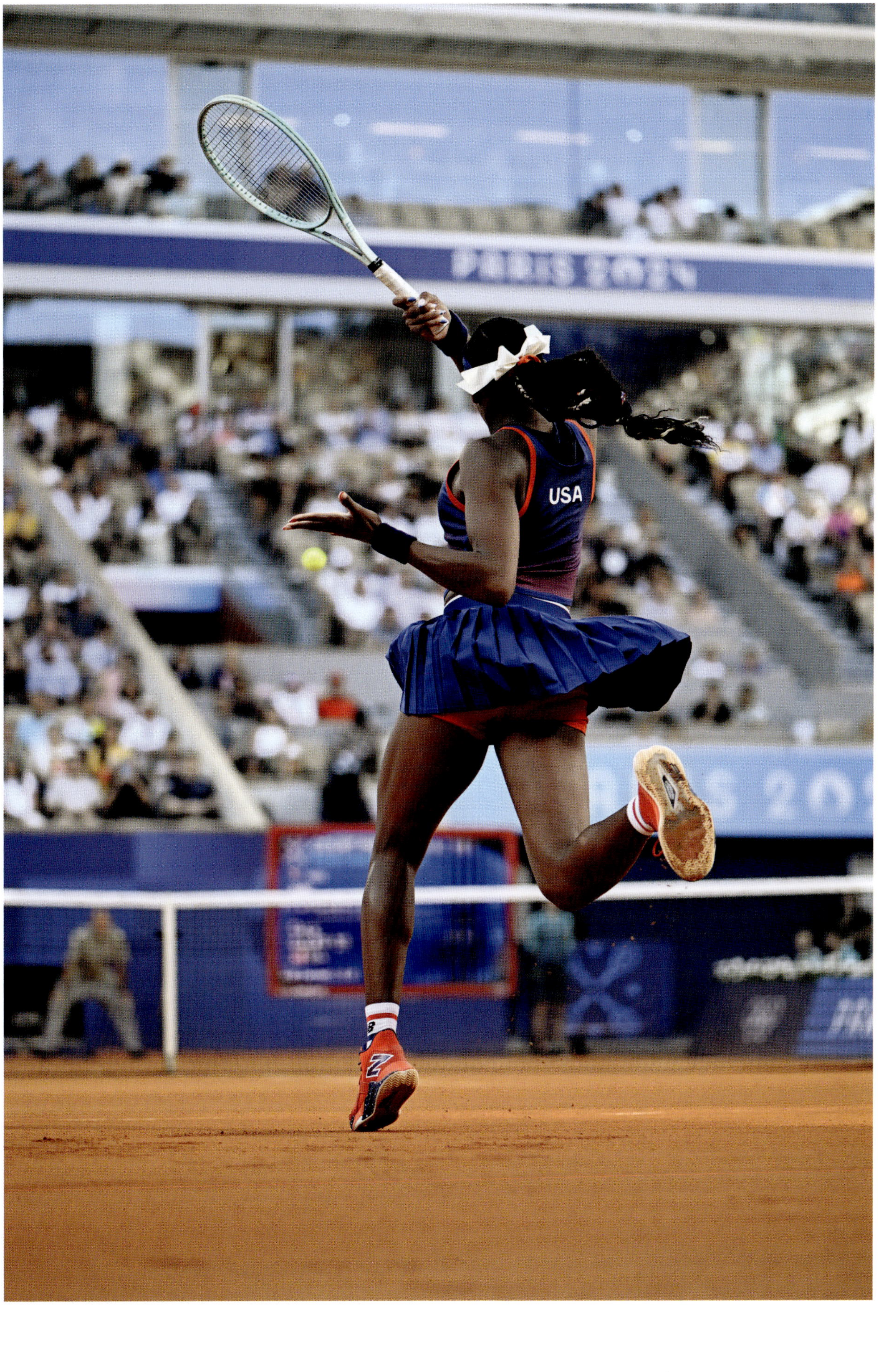
PARIS 2024
USA

ON FEMALE ATHLETES

SKN: Can we discuss the disparity in pay between male and female tennis players? What do you believe can be changed to address that?

CD: We're changing it through our actions. Coco's the highest paid female athlete in the world, and who's our primary partner in New Balance? It's Coco. We activate her in global and lifestyle-specific campaigns and collaborations for the brand, and it's all over Fashion Week and all across the board. Same with Gabby Thomas, Cameron Brink. New Balance views women's sports as sports. Women have an equal voice to men at New Balance.

SKN: But how can it change across the board?

CD: It's like a rising tide that lifts all ships: Activation is critical to demonstrate how marketable they are, and networks and the media need to do a better job of providing visibility, particularly in prime-time moments. But I also feel like it's the responsibility of the brands and those participating in the space of sport to provide equitable opportunities from an investment standpoint: sponsorship, marketing, and so forth. Coco is the only female on tour right now with a signature shoe. If you look at our top-ten highest paid New Balance athletes, a lot of them are women.

NEW BALANCE AND PERFORMANCE DESIGN

EZ: Because Coco is so involved in the design phase, she knows immediately how to speak eloquently and confidently about it. You are rooting for a person in tennis, and that's super special; we are invested in Coco the person, not in a team. It's a commitment and an investment—you need the right athlete to do it with.

ON THE PERFORMANCE SHOE

JW: To design a signature shoe for her, which takes two years out to plan and make, she had to have some credibility first, so it was either a top-ten ranking or win an Open.

COCO CG1

JW: She was really into the 1990s basketball silhouette, which we were on the fence about, because it was different from anything you've seen before in tennis shoe design; it's mid-cut versus low-cut. The Coco hand signature was important to her, because so many players sign with just a squiggle. We made this graphic graffiti print with fades and gradients. There was a lot of color in her first vision meeting; it ranged from neons to metallics to graffiti. Easter egg details feature in the design: the track logo, because her mother was a pentathlete, and a basketball logo at the bottom of the shoe for her dad, who played for Georgia State. Her brothers' names are at the ends of her laces. On the front of the shoe, there is the geographical location of her home court in Miami. In terms of technology, we combined all these elements of carbon fiber technology in the Energy Arc, which is used in all our running and basketball models, but this time it was specifically tailored. The Arc provides better energy return and torsional stability because of the load-and-explode factor and the way Coco slides. CG1 was a unisex shoe.

COCO CG 2

JW: Coco went from wild to mild in style. She wanted the shoe to be wearable on court and off court as well as high-performance. CG2 was a nice blend of all the things CG1 was.

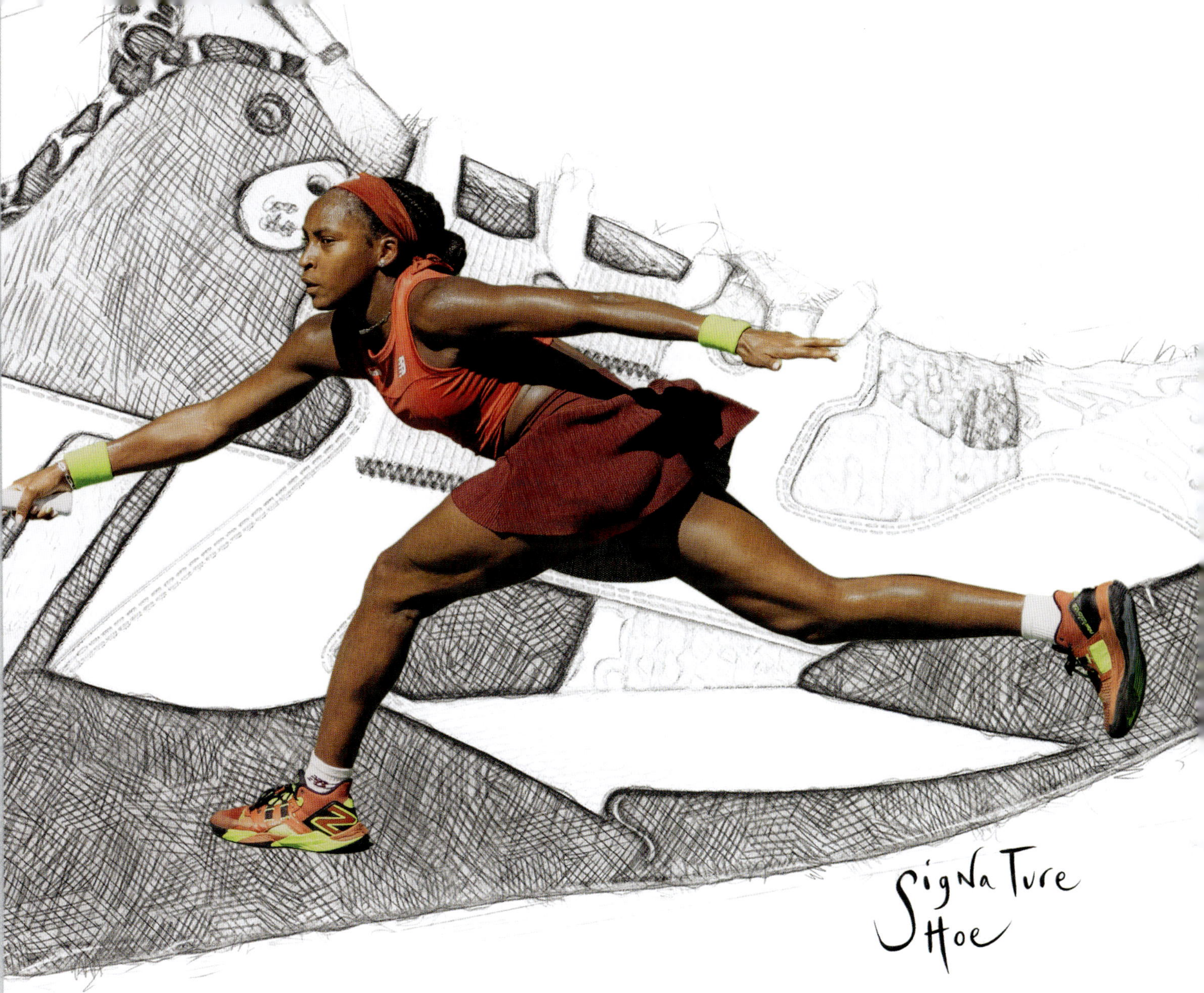

Signature Shoe

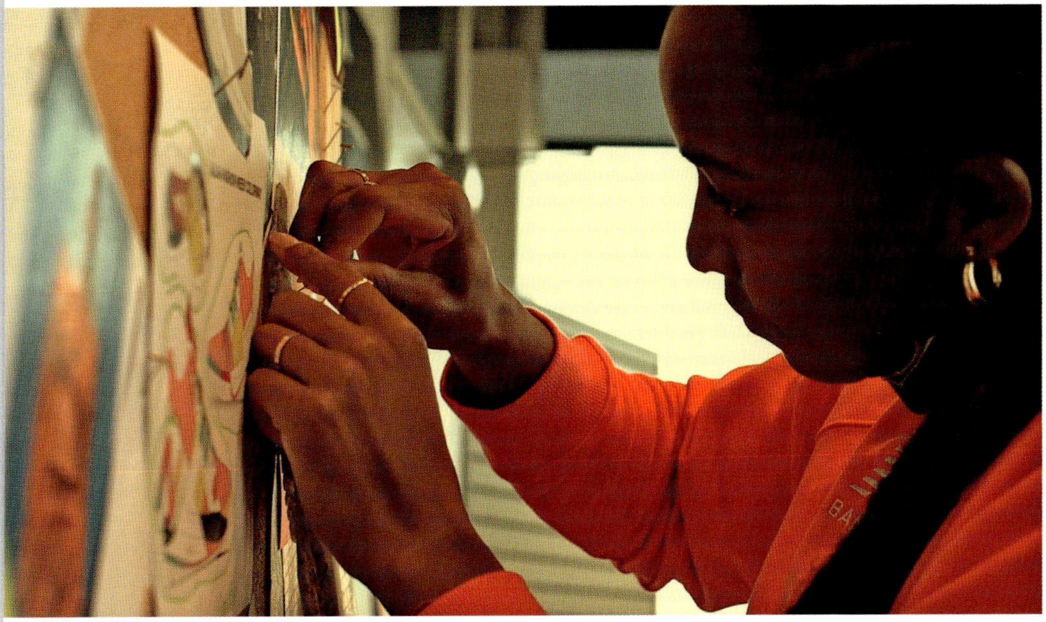

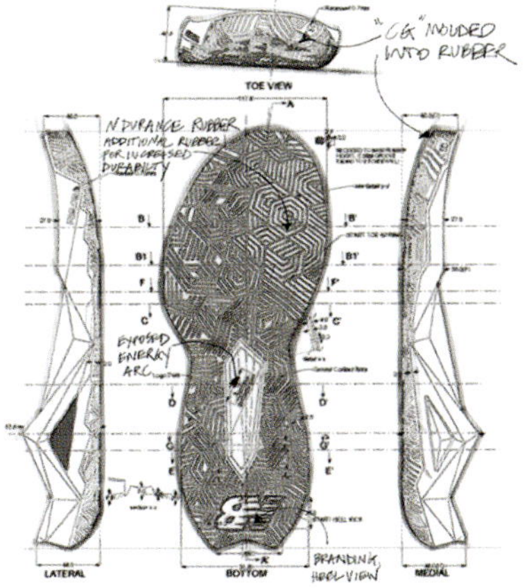

midsole → pentathlete - mother
motifs ↘ Basketball - father
Family | eastereggs

NEW BALANCE APPAREL

THE APPAREL TEAM WORKS IN TANDEM WITH THE PERFORMANCE SHOE DESIGNERS, ALIGNING FABRIC SWATCHES WITH SHOE EXTERIORS TO ENSURE VISUAL AND FUNCTIONAL COHESION. DESIGN CRITERIA ARE CATEGORIZED INTO EASE, FIT, COVERAGE, AND COMFORT. GAUFF FAVORS SPECIFIC SILHOUETTES—BODICES THAT ARE OFTEN STRUCTURED, LIKE A BUILT-IN CORSET, OR FORM-FITTING, LIKE A BODYSUIT. THESE MOLD TO HER FRAME WHILE LEAVING HER ARMS FREE FOR A FULL RANGE OF CIRCUMFERENTIAL MOTION. HER TWO-HANDED BACKHAND IS WORLD-CLASS: COMPACT, COMMANDING, AND CLEAN. SKIRTS ARE FREQUENTLY CONSTRUCTED FROM MESH MICRO PLEATING, OFFERING BREATHABILITY AND FLUIDITY DURING HIGH-INTENSITY PLAY. THIS MODULAR BESPOKE SYSTEM, WHERE SIX TO EIGHT PIECES CAN BE BUILT INTO VERSATILE OUTFITS AND CREATE UP TO TWENTY-FOUR DIFFERENT LOOK OPTIONS, GIVING COCO EXTRA CHOICES ON THE DAY OF THE GAME.

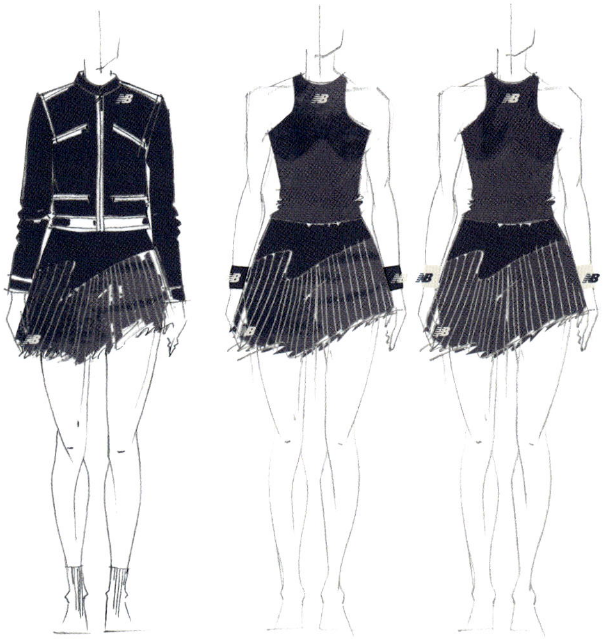

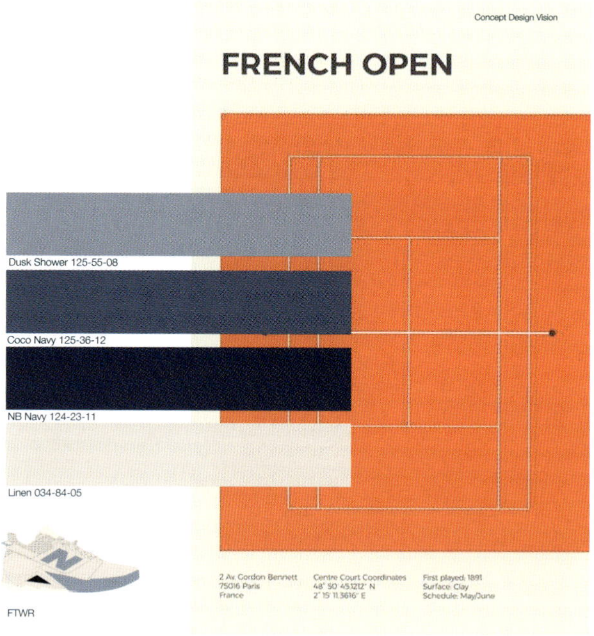

THE 2025 FRENCH OPEN

BLEU DE FRANCE, THE FLEUR-DE-LIS FLOWER, AND FRENCH EXPRESSIONIST HENRI MATISSE'S CUT-OUT IMAGERY WERE SOME OF THE SOURCES OF INSPIRATION FOR COCO'S OUTFIT AT THE 2025 FRENCH OPEN. THE FITTED BODICE SHAPE HAS REMAINED CONSISTENT THROUGH MOST OF COCO'S CAREER SO FAR—BECAUSE WHEN IT WORKS, WHY CHANGE IT?

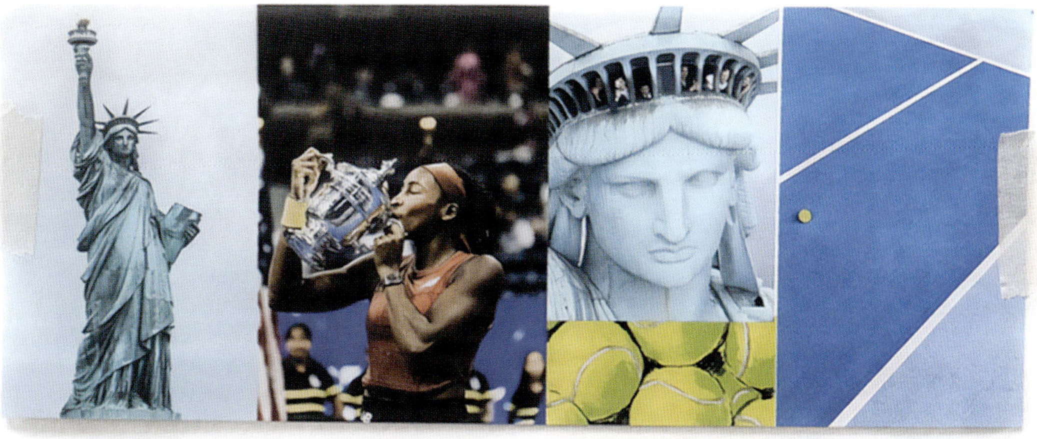

aRm Freee

cRoss Strappings

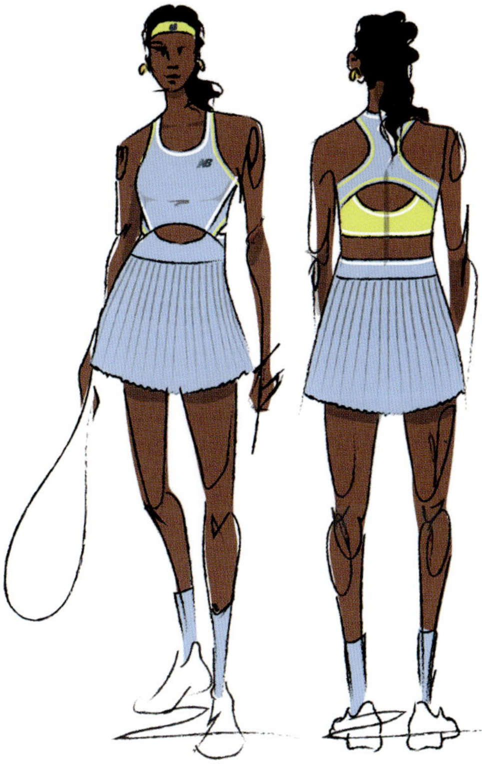

side seam →
armhole front →
underarm sleeve seam →
NO STITCH

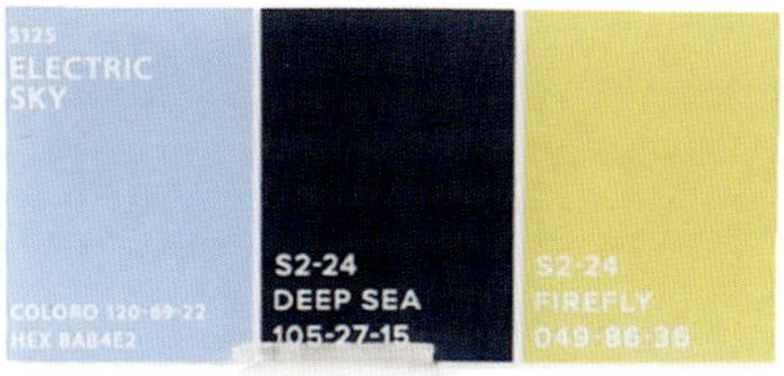

US OPEN

Fitted BodiCE

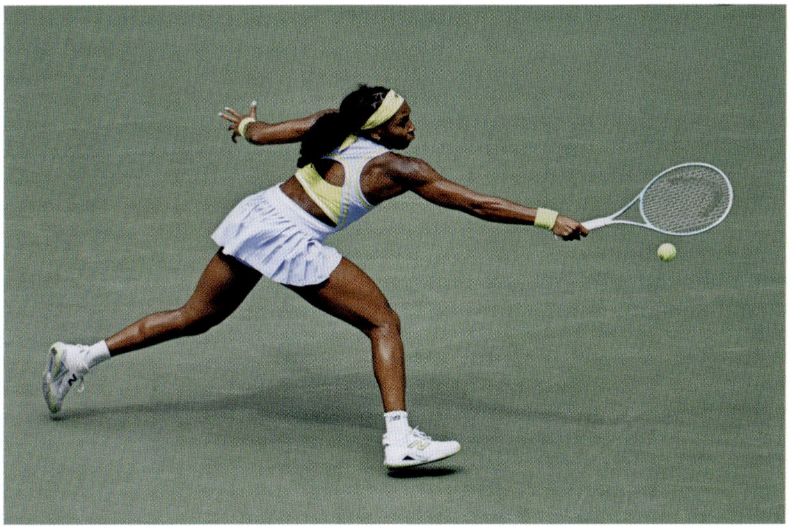

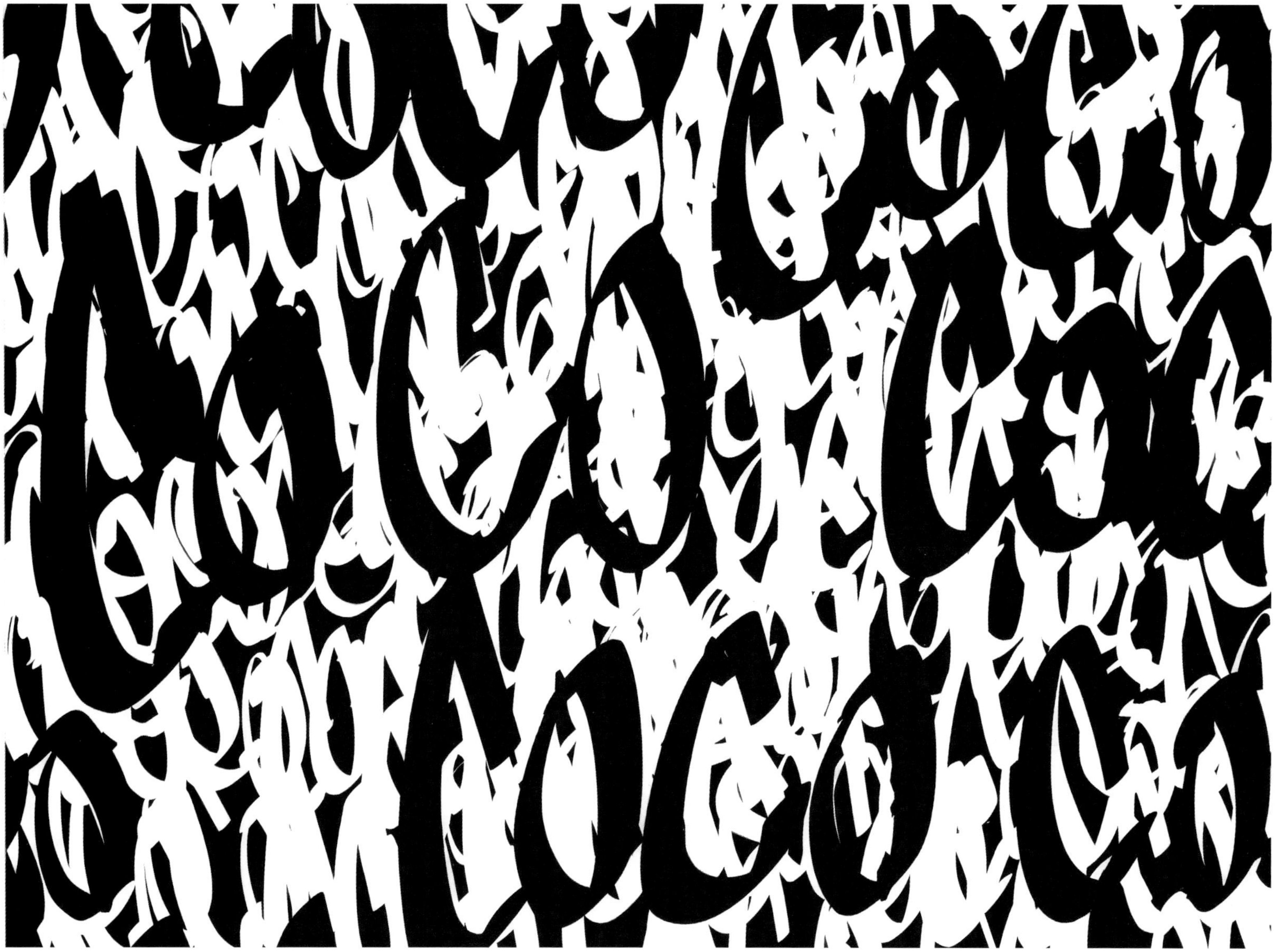

"'YOU CAN CHANGE THE WORLD WITH YOUR RACKET,'" WAS SOMETHING HER FATHER SAID TO HER, AND WE'VE USED THIS QUOTE A FEW TIMES ON THE OUTSOLES OF HER SHOES."

—JOSH WILDER,
SENIOR PRODUCT MANAGER FOR TENNIS, NEW BALANCE

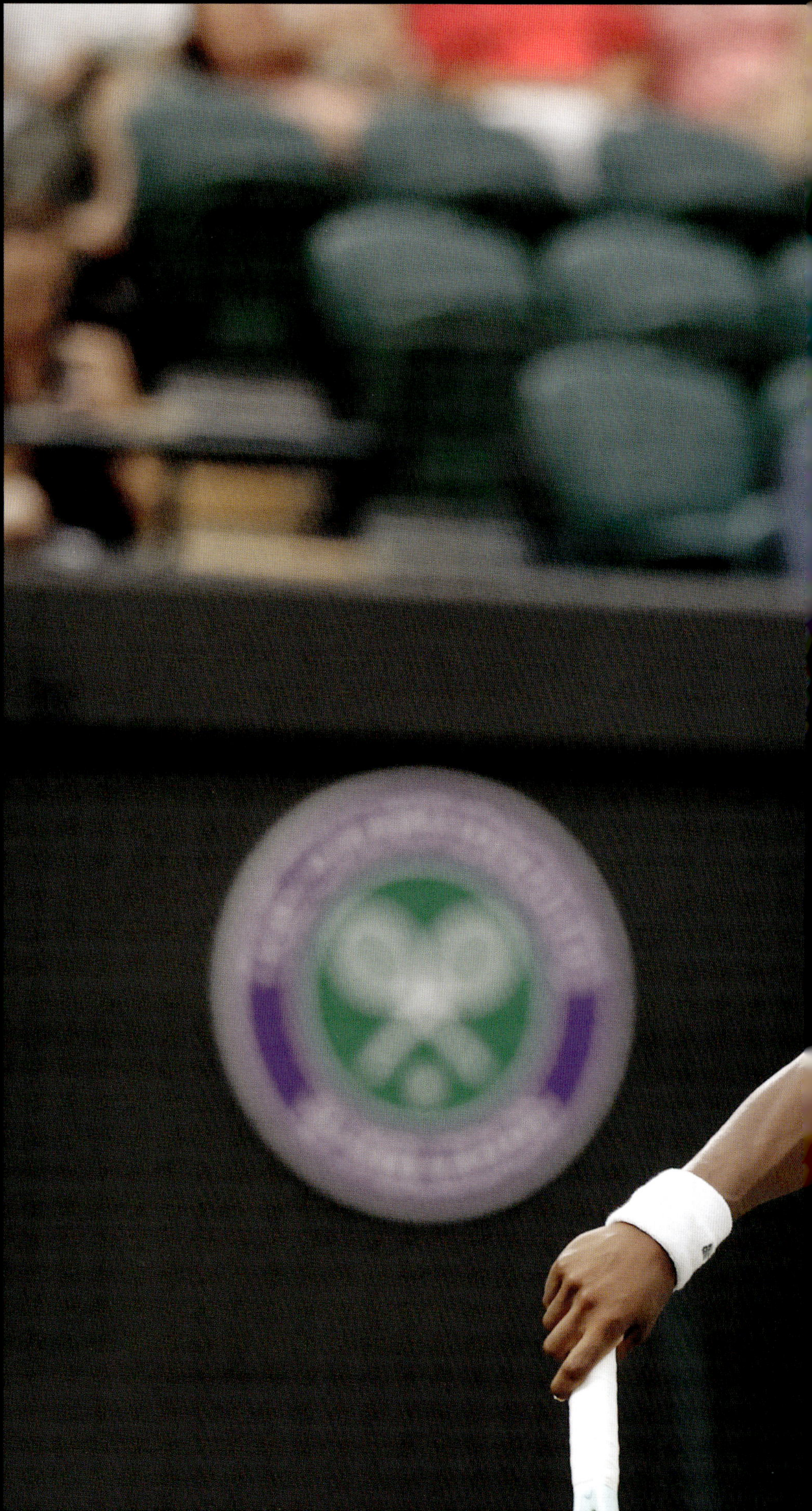

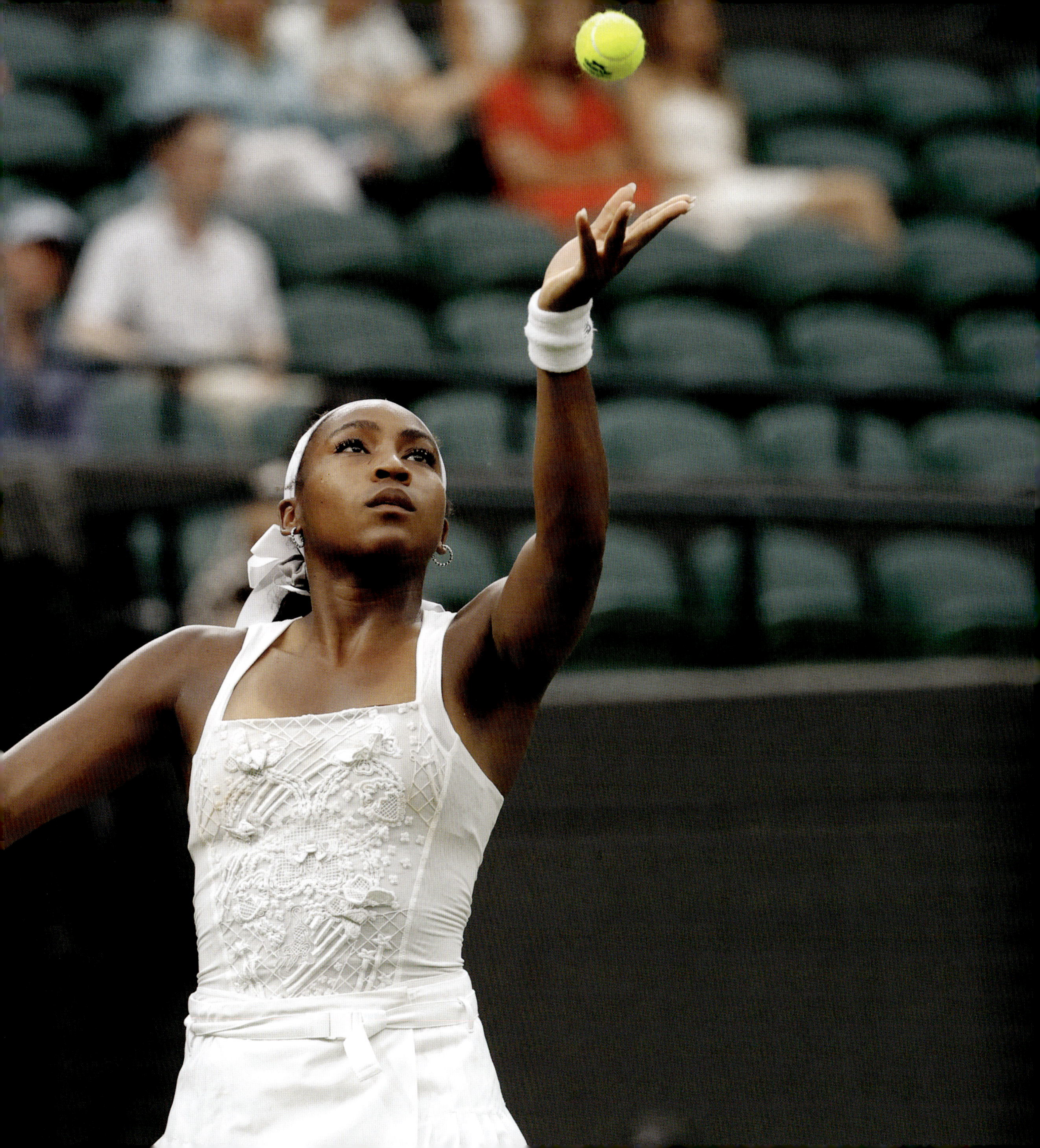

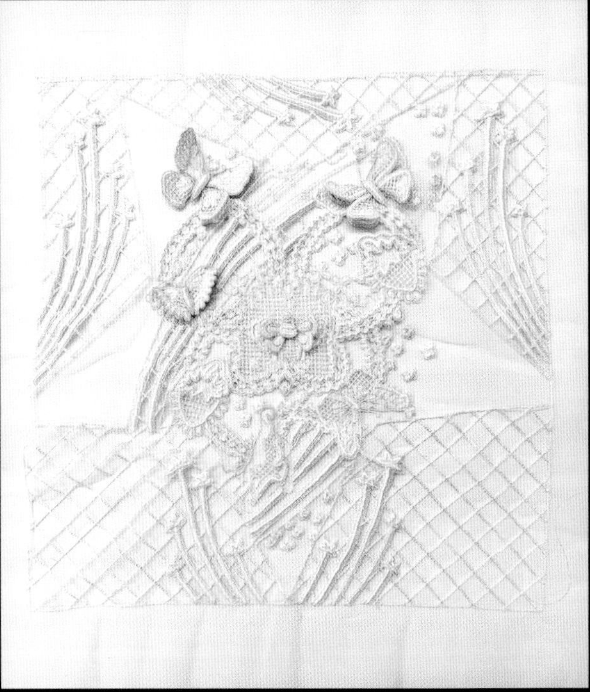

THE WEIGHT OF WIMBLEDON HISTORY OFTEN WEAVES SEAMLESSLY INTO THE DESIGN FOUNDATION OF ANY GRAND SLAM APPAREL. NEVERTHELESS, IT IS THE INTERTWINING OF CONTEMPORARY REFERENCES AND INSPIRATIONS THAT BECOMES THE VITAL THREAD TO MODERN DESIGN. THE NEW BALANCE TEAM DID EXACTLY THIS FOR THEIR 2025 COLLECTION FOR GAUFF. THEY CALLED IN THE SPIRITS OF BRITISH PUNK, VIVIENNE WESTWOOD, ROCK AND ROLL, AND THE RUGGED ROMANCE OF THE SCOTTISH HIGHLANDS FOR GAUFF'S WIMBLEDON WARDROBE. IT'S ALL THERE WITH A CUSTOM LACE EMBROIDERY PIECE INTERLACED WITH WIMBLEDON STRAWBERRIES, BEES, THE STARS AND STRIPES, AND FAVORITE GAUFF MEMORABILIA SUCH AS MARVEL MOTIFS. IT LINES A CORSET-SHAPED PERFORMANCE TOP, MELDING ATHLETIC FUNCTION WITH COUTURE ARTISANSHIP. AN EXPOSED BACK IS A CLASSIC GAUFF DETAIL. THE FINE-WOOL SKIRT IS PERMANENTLY PLEATED TO CREATE THIS DYNAMIC FAN EFFECT, BUT IT'S THE CLASSIC KILT SILHOUETTE THAT IS THE PERFECT HARMONY OF HERITAGE AND MODERNITY.

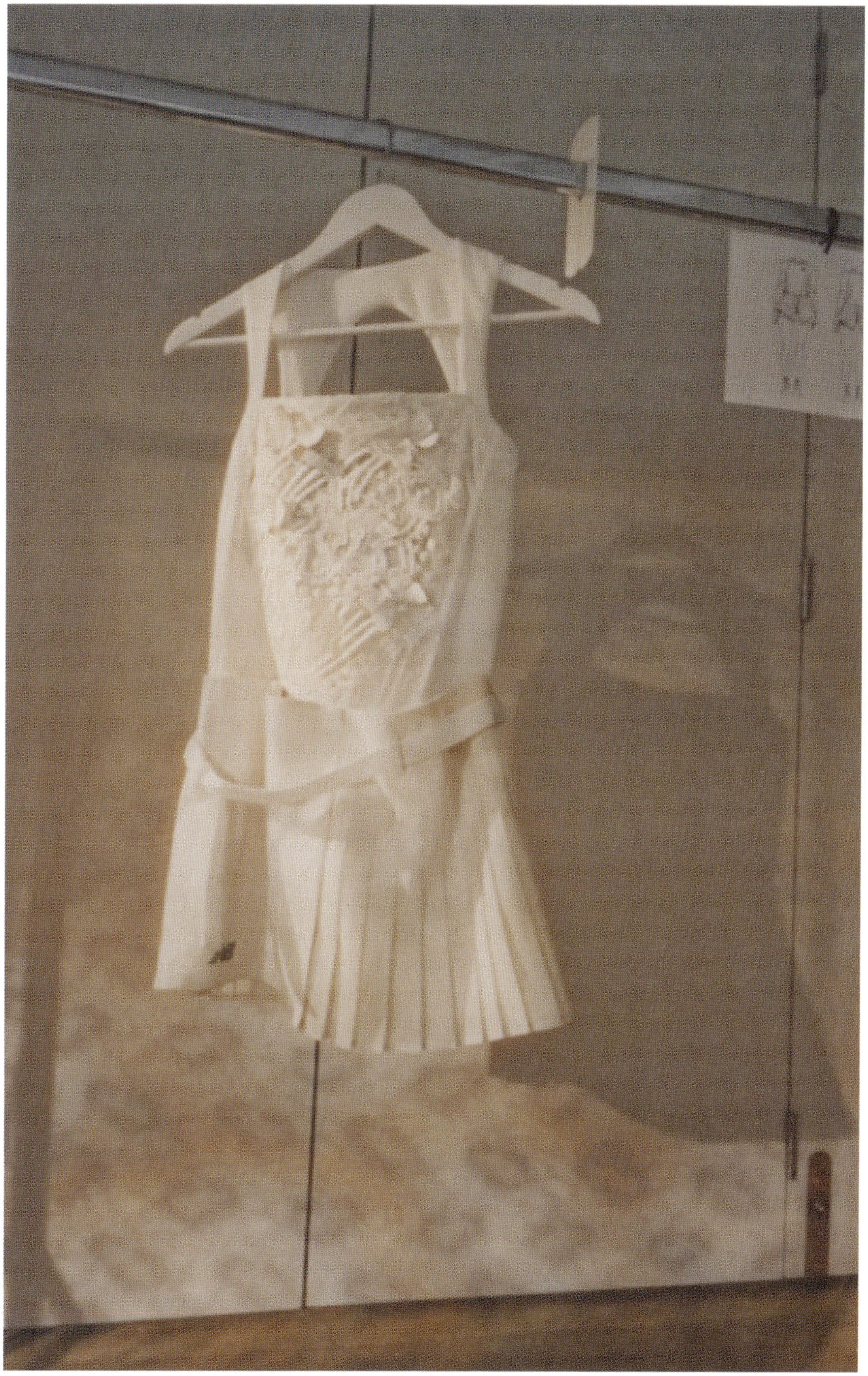

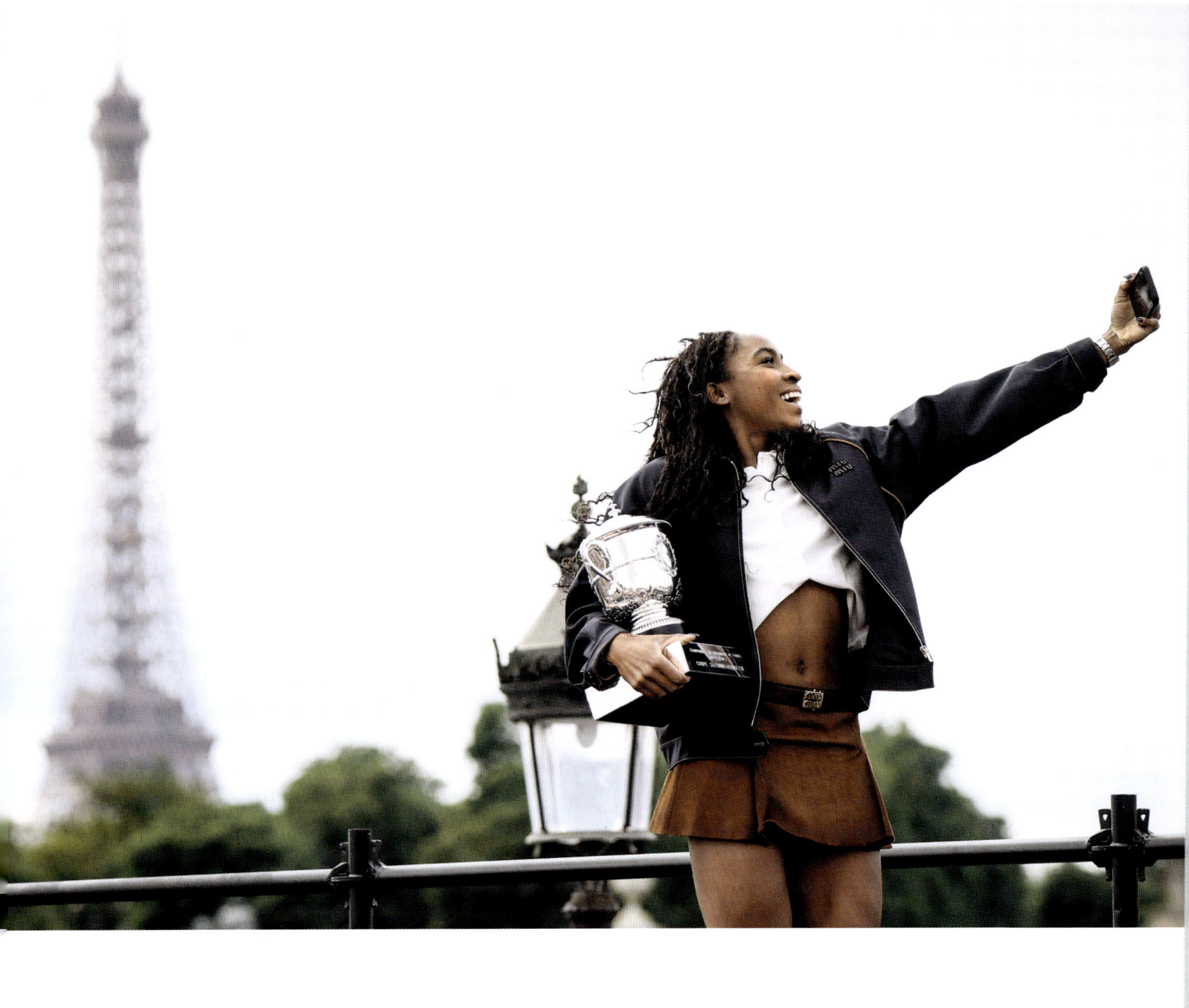

THE COCO GAUFF X MIU MIU ON-COURT COLLAB COULD BE THE MATCH MADE IN FASHION HEAVEN. THEIR RECENT DESIGNER SHOE DROPS WITH NEW BALANCE SENT SNEAKERHEADS AND FASHIONISTAS INTO A EUPHORIC TAILSPIN. MRS. PRADA EXPLAINED THAT THE COLLABORATION WAS "EMPHASIZING CONSTRUCTION THROUGH DECONSTRUCTION." GAUFF IS THE BRIGHT YOUNG THING WHO STREAKS LIGHT-YEARS AHEAD OF US AND NOW WITH MIU MIU AS HER DESIGN COPILOT IT WILL ONLY PROPEL HER FURTHER. WHEN A LUXURY POWERHOUSE ALIGNS ITS VISION WITH AN ATHLETE'S CREATIVE VOICE, IT TRANSCENDS COLLABORATION AND BECOMES SELF-AUTHORED STYLE, LEGACY DRESSING IN THE SPIRIT OF LENGLEN AND PATOU. THE COLLECTION LEANS INTO THE '80S DANCEWEAR AESTHETIC WITH PUNCHY PRIMARY COLORS; THE SHELL FABRIC TEXTURES CHOSEN FOR THE WARMUP OUTFITS GAVE IT THE VITAL STREET CRED THAT GAUFF HAS PERSONALLY FAVORED. HER FIRST *VANITY FAIR* PARTY DRESS FOR THE OSCARS SHARED A SIMILAR STYLE VOCABULARY TO HER ON-COURT LOOKS: A LIME-GREEN BEJEWELED SHEATH DRESS IN A PLUSH SILK SATIN. BUT IT WAS THE SPAGHETTI STRAPS, SCULPTED BODICE, AND THE CUT-OUT DETAILED BACK THAT WAS PURE COCO GAUFF. THE WOMAN. THE PLAYER. A BRAND UNTO HERSELF.

Mrs Prada –"emphasising construction through deconstruction"

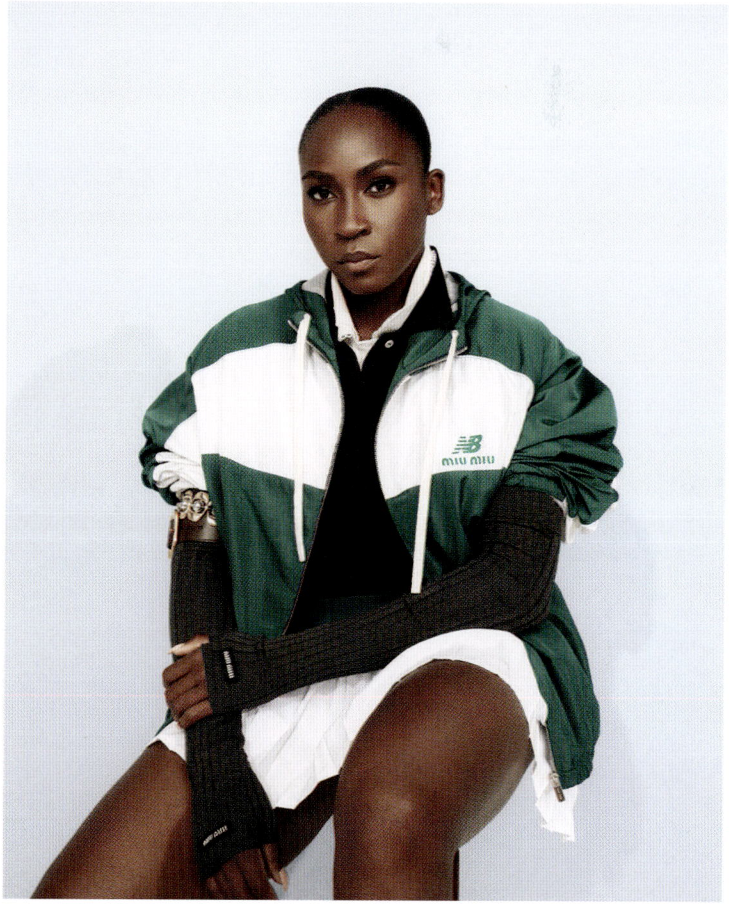

MISS COCO GAUFF

COCO GAUFF IS AN EXPLOSIVE, DYNAMIC ALL-ROUNDER AND TWO-TIME GRAND SLAM WINNER.

SKN: You started with New Balance when you were fourteen; you have grown with them, and they have grown with you. How has this relationship formed you personally and professionally?

CG: Yeah, I started with them when I was fourteen years old. Now I'm twenty-one, so it feels like it's gone fast. Serena was my idol; she still is. She was very much into designing her kits, and she always had nice outfits, so I always knew I wanted to be like that. And as I've gotten older, New Balance has let me be a part of the creative process every step of the way, which I feel is rare for a brand, because sometimes they just say, This is what you're wearing. And that's it. I got my first custom kit with NB when I was fifteen, and it's been [a collaboration] ever since. So I'm very grateful to them for trusting my vision, and also for trusting a teenage girl with the representation of their brand. And obviously, it's grown into something great.

SKN: What outfits have empowered your play and fed your fashion eye?

CG: There was one from the Australian Open, a bodysuit with an orange skirt. I had lost first round, and I was so upset, because I really liked it. In another Australian Open, I had an orange dress that faded into blue, and I lost the fourth round. But yeah, the Australian Open has good looks.

SKN: Is there a connection to how you play and what you wear? Does it fuel you in some way?

CG: One hundred percent. Sometimes I feel more pressure when I have a good outfit, to even perform better.

SKN: I love that you chose your grandmother to feature in your New Balance Delray commercial. You're clearly close to your mom too. What have you learned from them, personally and stylistically?

CG: My grandmother is still very youthful. She likes to stay up with the trends. Actually, in that commercial, it's her own dress that she's wearing. Apparently they brought outfit choices for her, and she didn't like any of them, because she doesn't fit into the grandma stereotype. And my mom, she's very chic, with a feminine, classic type of style, which is kind of the opposite of what I am—more street, and younger. When I get older, I'll be like [my mom]. I like her style; I steal her clothes a lot. She's who I aspire to be like.

SKN: Who else informs your style? Are there any people who you look up to that are your age—musicians, artists, fashion people?

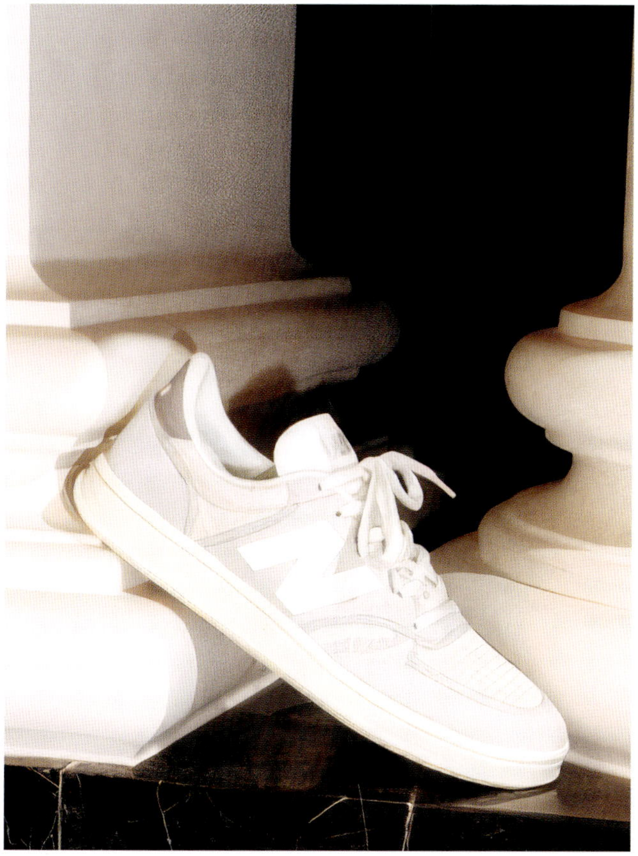

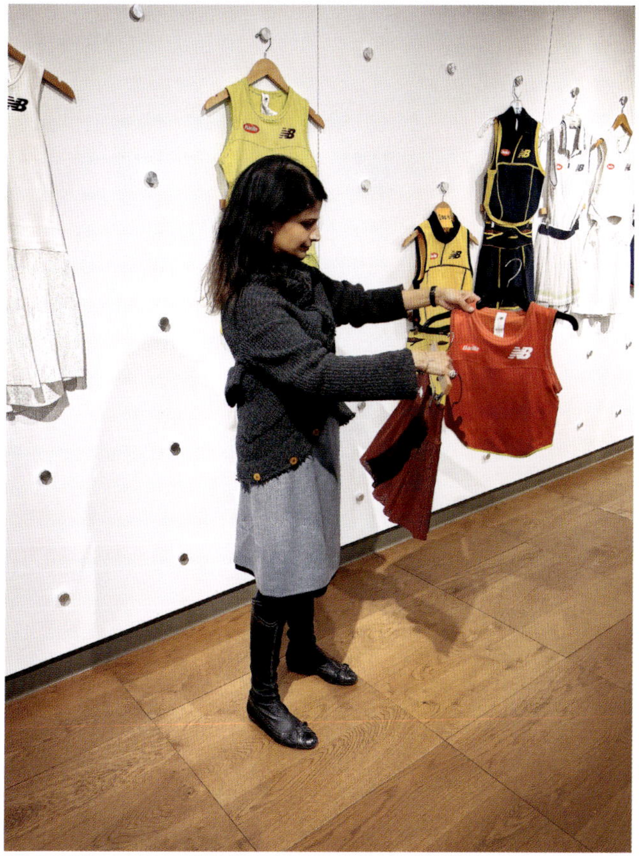

CG: In fashion, I really like Zendaya and Rihanna. I like Tyler, the Creator—his style choices are cool, and I like his brand a lot. I usually lean toward more streetwear vibes. But I'm going to Europe—actually, tomorrow. So when I go there, I feel like I have to be more chic and classy. You know the vibe in Paris—they're wearing trench coats and things like that, which I actually do enjoy. But for some reason, when I'm home in the US, I'm just like, **I can't, I don't want to do it**. But when I go there, I feel like I want to be a part of that world.

SKN: Oh, that's interesting! So you're a bit of a chameleon—you change with your environment.

CG: Yes, and I go through different phases during the year where sometimes I'll be more feminine, and other times I'll be more masculine.

SKN: That's cool and pretty true to yourself, fashion-wise. So you just go with how you are feeling, your moods? That must make you feel really confident—changing your style as you feel, rather than sticking to one aesthetic, regardless.

CG: I always say to people, one day in an outfit I feel great, and the next day, if I'm just not in the mood, then I feel awful. I probably look the same in it, but it just **feels** different.

SKN: It's the only way, but maybe not for your stylist! You once said to give yourself grace, which I loved—you have such a major following with young kids, especially children of color. How did you give yourself grace as you grew up? What's your message to them?

CG: Sometimes I'm a little bit hard on myself, and I'm a bit of a perfectionist. So as I've gotten older, I've learned that I actually do better when I give myself grace and allow myself to make mistakes. Because if you make mistakes, that means you're still learning, and you don't want to get to a point in life where you stop learning. Rejection is just redirection, and a mistake just means you're still learning. I saw a quote that said "Every great scientist has a failed experi-

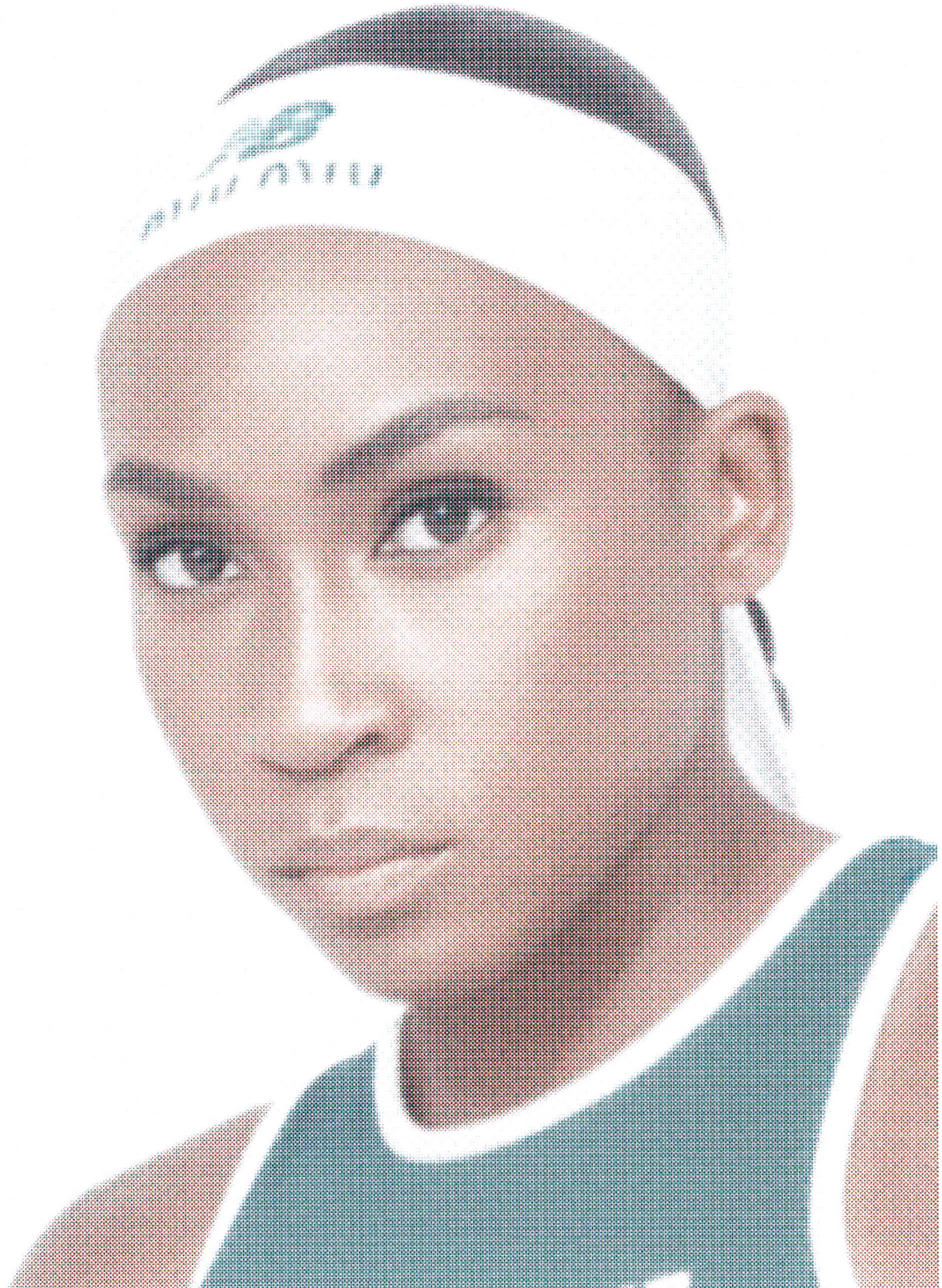
miu miu

ment." So I try to think of life like that. And every champion, no matter how great they are, has lost at some point in their life.

SKN: You've spoken about making children's tennis more accessible and diverse. What's your hope in pushing this ideal further forward? There is so much to do, it's so apparent.

CG: Yeah, it is. As many public tennis courts that are in the US, especially in Florida, it's still a very expensive sport, with the equipment and things like that. For me, it starts first with representation, and just having me and other POC pros continuing to be that representation, but also providing that kind of direction by diving into their communities. I'm a big believer in starting in your own community and expanding elsewhere. I always feel such a strong connection with my community; I feel like I am involved with them. I'm continuing to rehabilitate public tennis courts. It's important—a lot of times they do exist, but they're not great. So one of the things we did with the [United States Tennis Association] was help refurbish those courts, and I did a park in Atlanta. I want to continue to do that and help people become involved in the sport.

SKN: Now with your move to William Morris Endeavor agency, there seems to be a new energy with this chapter. Are there any creative ambitions that you have or are dreaming up, fashion wise? Because you're so vocal about your love for fashion.

CG: I've always been a fan of Miu Miu and wanted to collaborate with a big fashion brand on my kit. Luckily, I get to do that with them. Our first kit will be in Rome. I'm super excited for that. I think only Serena has done something like that before, so I'm very excited for that. And so that's one of my big fashion dreams. And then the *Vogue* cover was one of my dreams too, and I got to do that. So I'm very blessed.

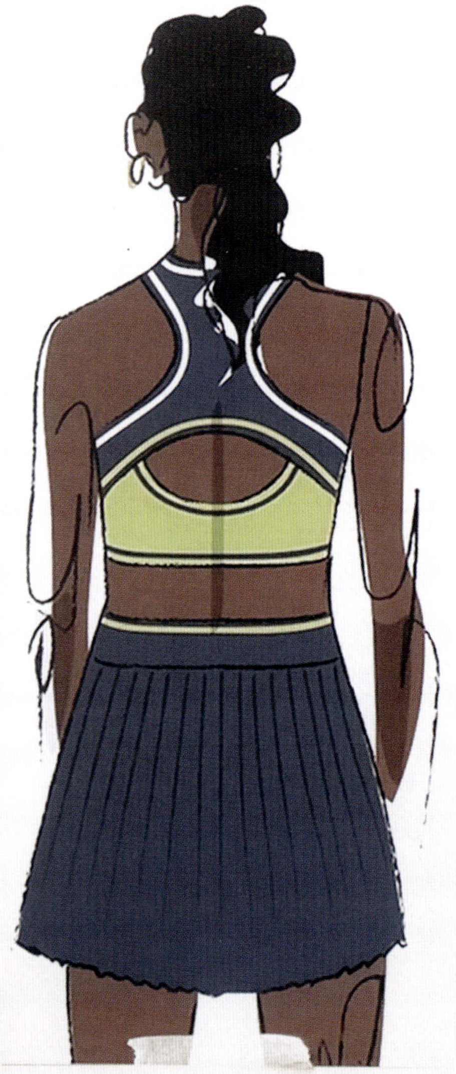

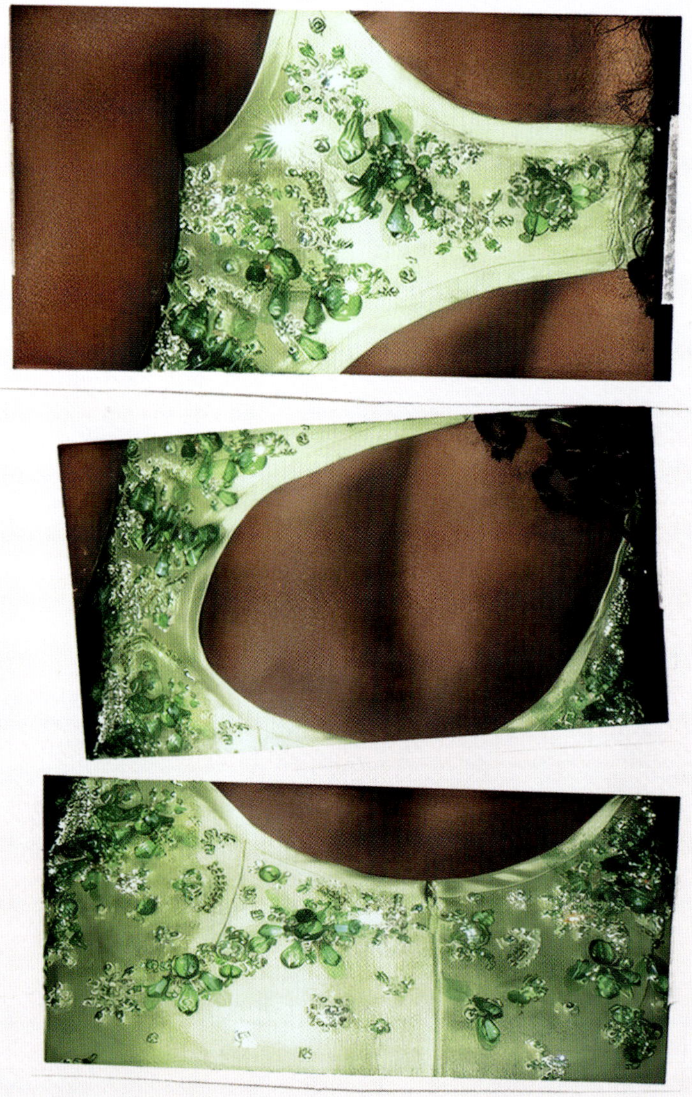

miu miu oscars dress 25

SKN: Annie [Leibovitz] captured your essence so well. Did you feel like yourself? Is it the same feeling—walking on court and being on a photo shoot?

CG: Annie gave me a lot of confidence, because she was a very nice person. I obviously knew who she was and her work. But I never know how these big people in fashion are gonna be, and I'm not Gigi Hadid or Anok [Yai], like a great model. She gave me a lot of direction, and ever since then, I've been using that in my other shoots.

SKN: That's awesome. Yes, it can be quite nerve-racking on set, when I am styling certain celebs or models; if they are not comfortable, it will always translate photographically and stylistically. I noticed that your Oscars dress mirrored some tennis dress features: the spaghetti strap, the open tie cross detail at the back. I can identify your tennis design preferences having seen all the looks at NB. Do you intentionally channel your on-court aesthetic off court?

CG: On court, I like things to be fitted to the skin, and I like cutouts. I like to show skin on court, and then off court, I do like that too, but I like to mix it up more—if it's tighter at the top, I like it to be looser at the bottom, so things like that. But the Oscars look, the V cutout of the neck was inspired by what I wear on court. I feel like that's such a classic type of silhouette, the V-neck dress. And then obviously we had to Oscar-fy it. It was very fun. Green has been one of my favorite colors lately, so though I had the choice of doing different colors, I chose that one, and I was happy.

SKN: It was very you, Coco; it was perfect.

So this book is called *ACE*. What does the word mean to you?

CG: For me, it's just exceeding at the highest level. I'm someone who liked school, so I liked to get A's and stuff. And obviously in the literal sense, in tennis, it's the most satisfying way to win a point, hitting an ace. It's just exceeding at the highest level in whatever you do.

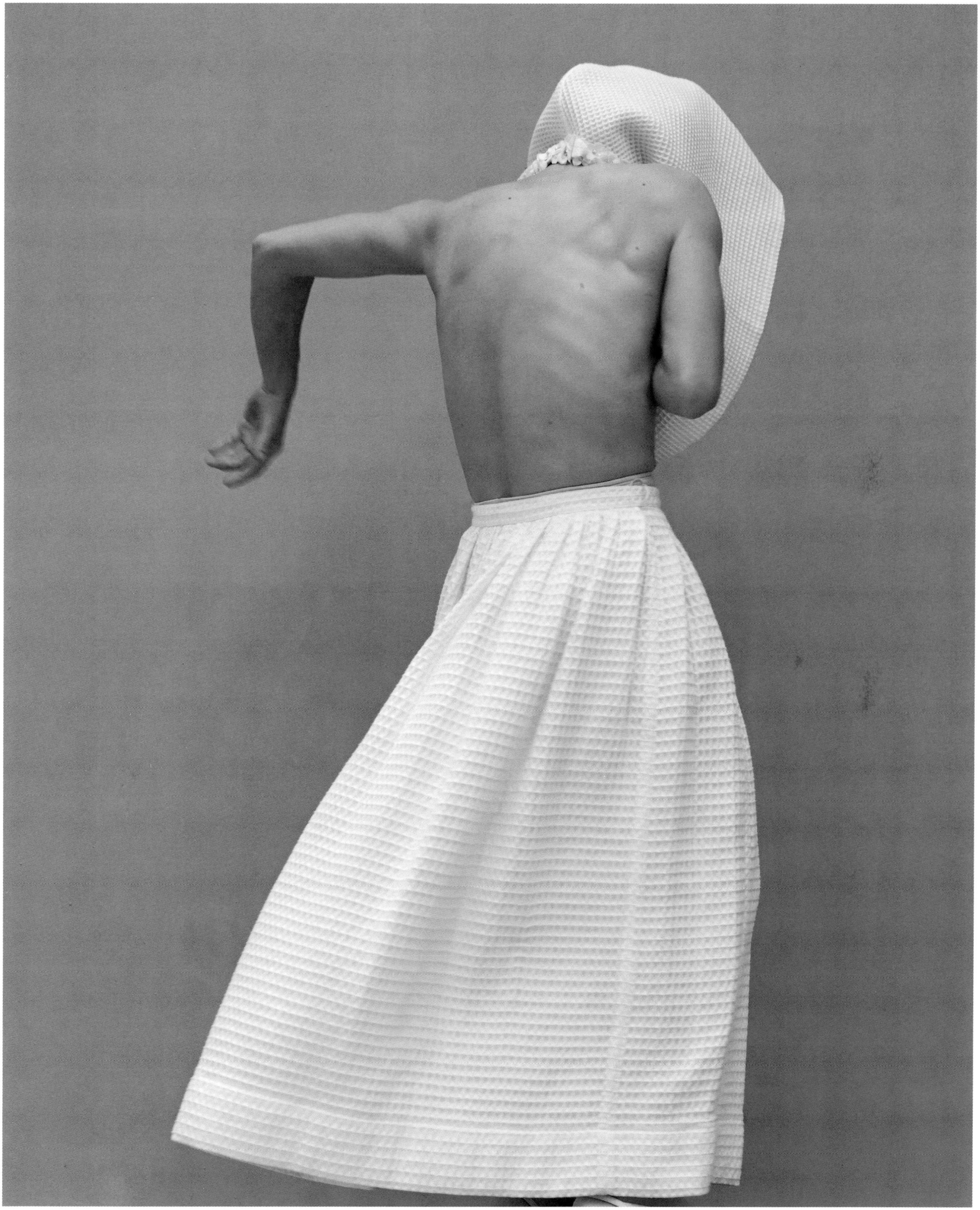

II.

THE MAVERICKS

Mavericks lead us from the grass to the global and public tennis courts. They repositioned the sport into the four corners of the world. The players who fall into this category allowed their subliminal selves to dictate their play and style. There is no order to this world. The playbook of style is tried and tested. The game's institutional custodians, shaken from their quiet complacency, would try to crush this spirit with periodic bans or public condemnations. It is here where players become design muses, and they find their respective interpreters—fashion designers—with their own swagger and style.

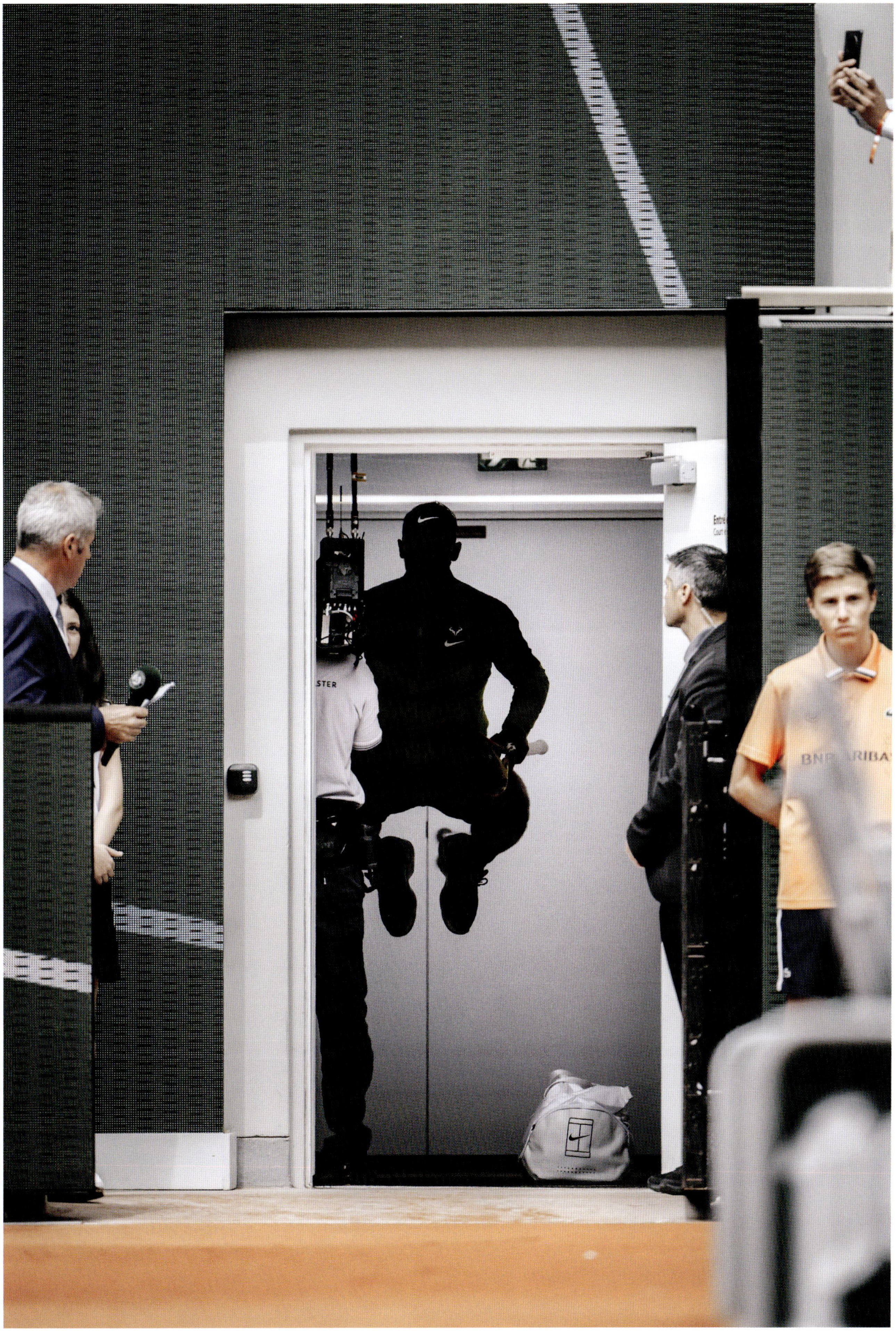

TED TINLING

A disco ball of a diamond stamped to his left ear, his six-foot-seven towering frame decked out in one of his prized razor-sharp suits, a constellation of color and print. His silken bald head mirroring Magritte-like clouds above him. This is Ted Tinling stepping onto center court as the first dedicated sport couturier.

British-born Tinling's tennis story started in 1924, when, at thirteen, he was appointed as the exclusive umpire to the inimitable and undefeatable tennis champion Suzanne Lenglen. In his own words: "There is always one lad in every stable who, by some unaccountable bond of telepathic sympathy, can hold the bridle of the star runner in peace and calm."

Tinling noted that aside from Lenglen's extraordinary athleticism, "She taught me that tennis was showbiz, and clothes had to be dramatic too." The Wimbledon administration named him player's liaison, a role he held from 1927 until 1949, when he was fired for a dress that went too far. He apparently emerged from World War II as a spy, only to redirect his bridal-dress design pathway to sportswear that was part practical (because fabric rationing was still in effect) and part dire necessity. Sportswomen were languishing in sterile masculine separates post-war until Tinling.

His natural design predisposition was always as a couturier. He redefined technical textiles through endless experimentation with what his player would feel comfortable playing in—lamé, leather, lace, vinyl, polyester, taffeta—and added meticulous embellishments such as rhinestones and personalized embroidery, motifs that became essential components to his design's oeuvre. Each piece was unabashedly feminine and unique; the meticulous fit sessions rivaled that of an atelier seamstress. And yet the women could play in the clothes, citing comfort and versatility in Tinling's choice of fabrics, which could be washed, crease-free and ready for the next game day. A successful player himself—he was in the Wimbledon doubles finals four times—Tinling reasoned that "when you dress a player, you must take into account both her personality and the way she hits a ball. I would never dress a player without seeing her play, and sometimes the person and player can be quite contradictory."

Flamboyance was signature to his design; it also reflected his sexual orientation, which he neither disguised nor publicly discussed. In his quest for the best designs, he flexed every romantic muscle he had. Nothing stood in his way, not even the strict dress rules of Wimbledon. Despite being a member of that very establishment, he did what he could to defy it and play his own game.

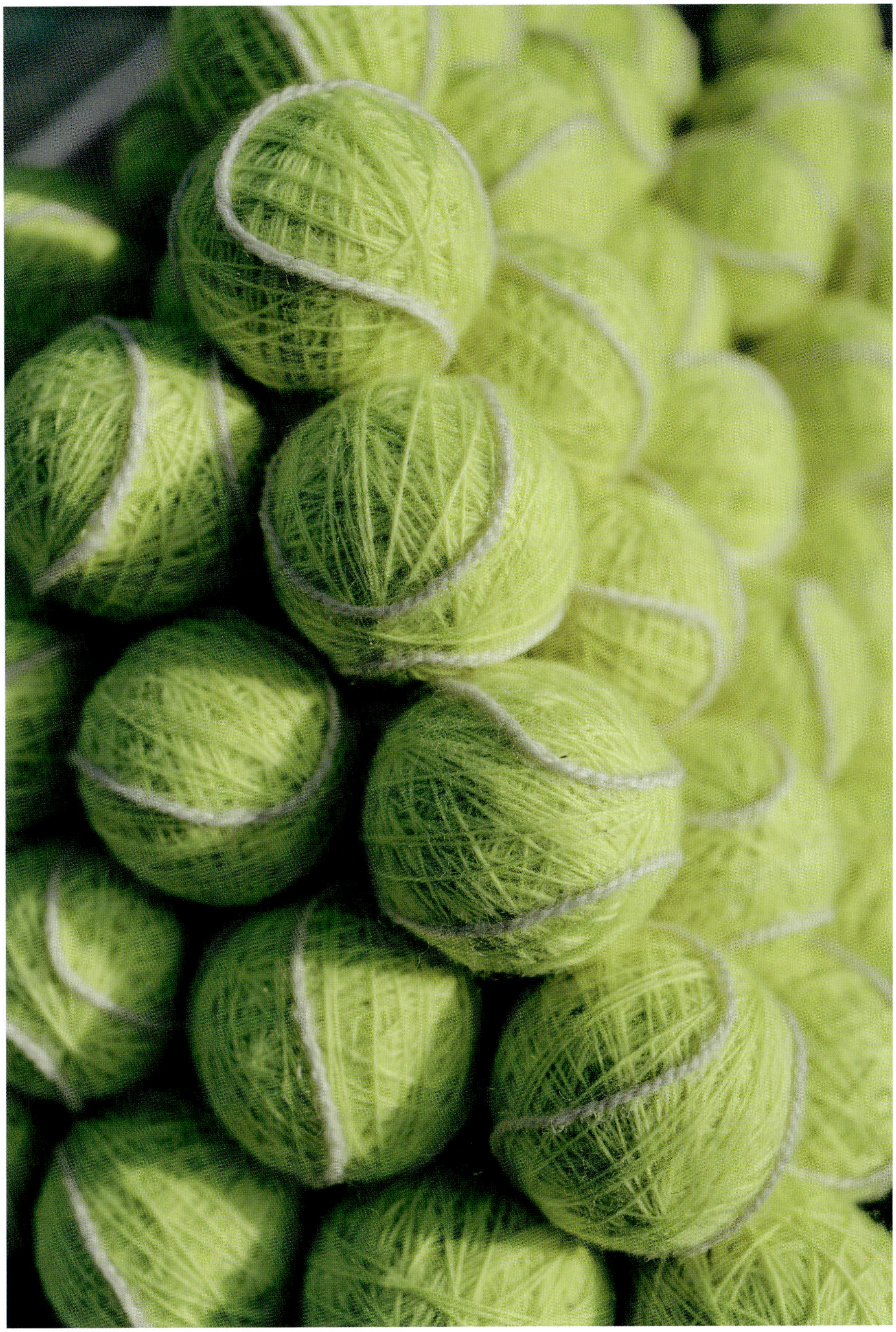

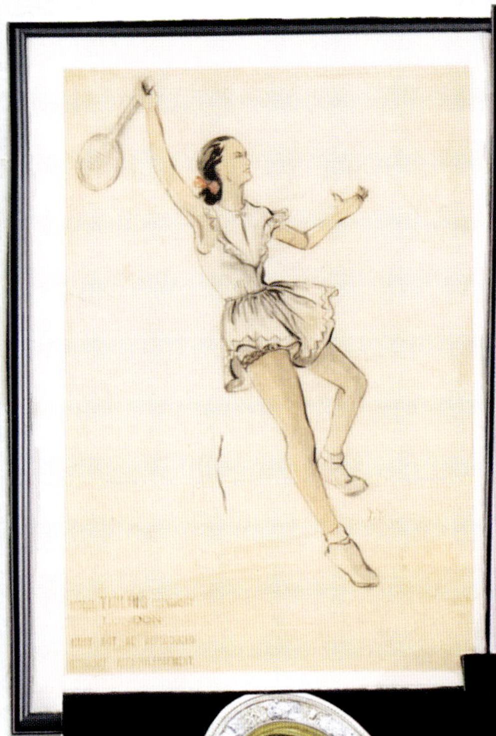
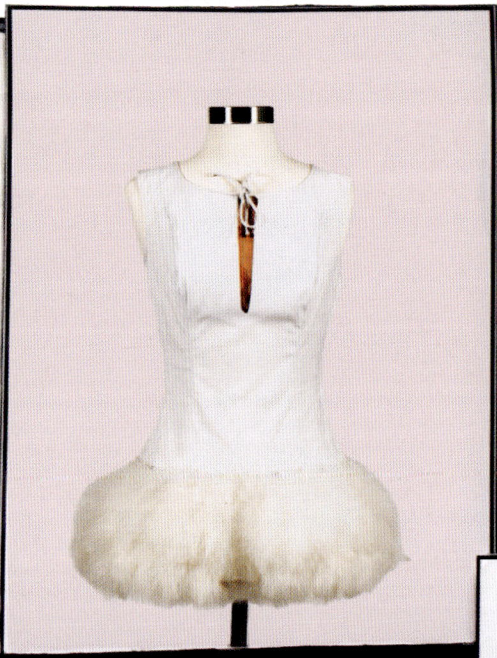
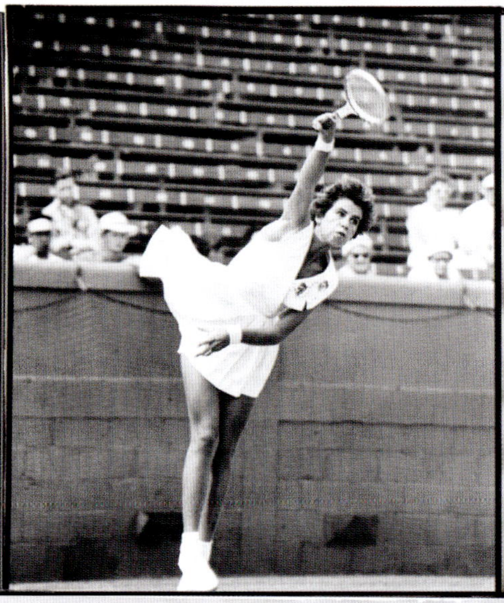
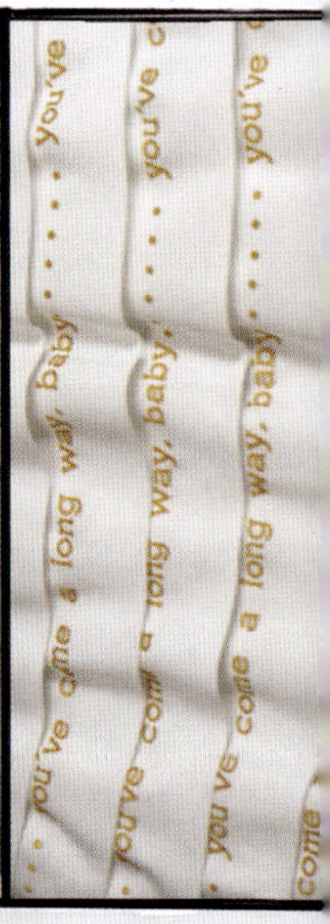

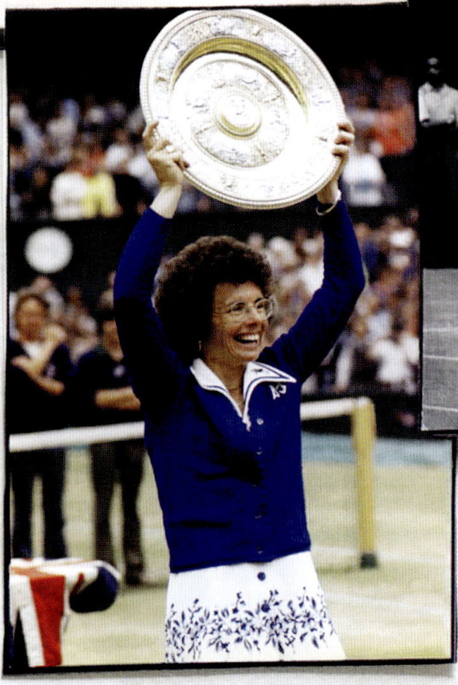
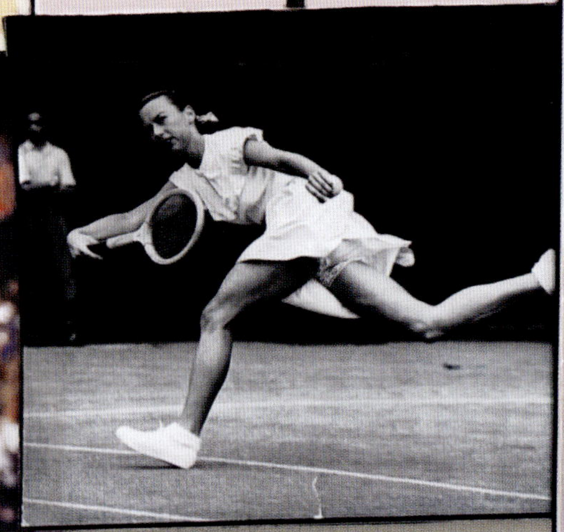
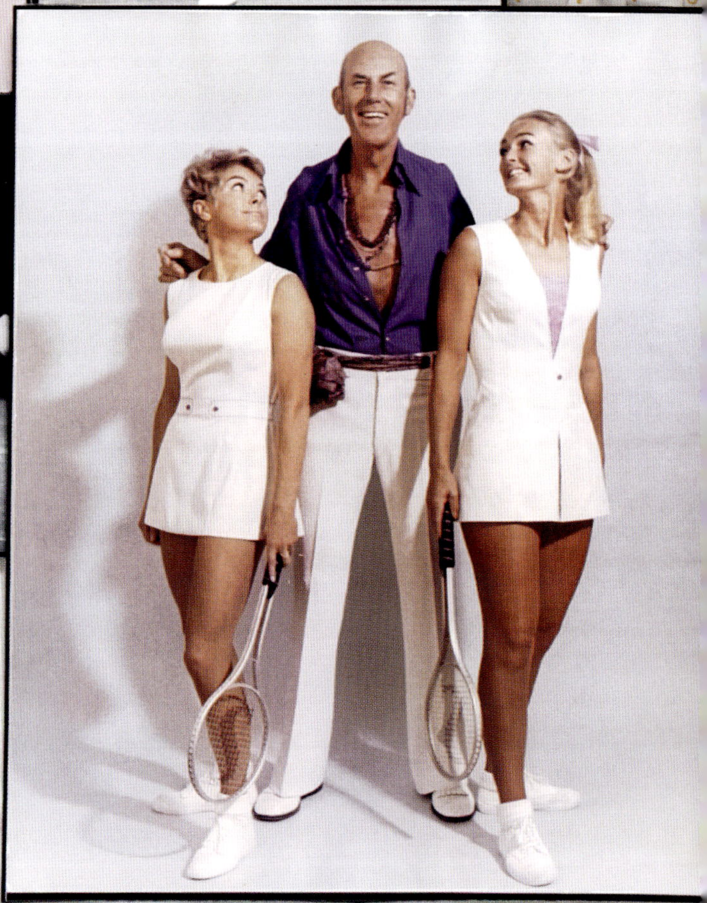

Ted Tingling

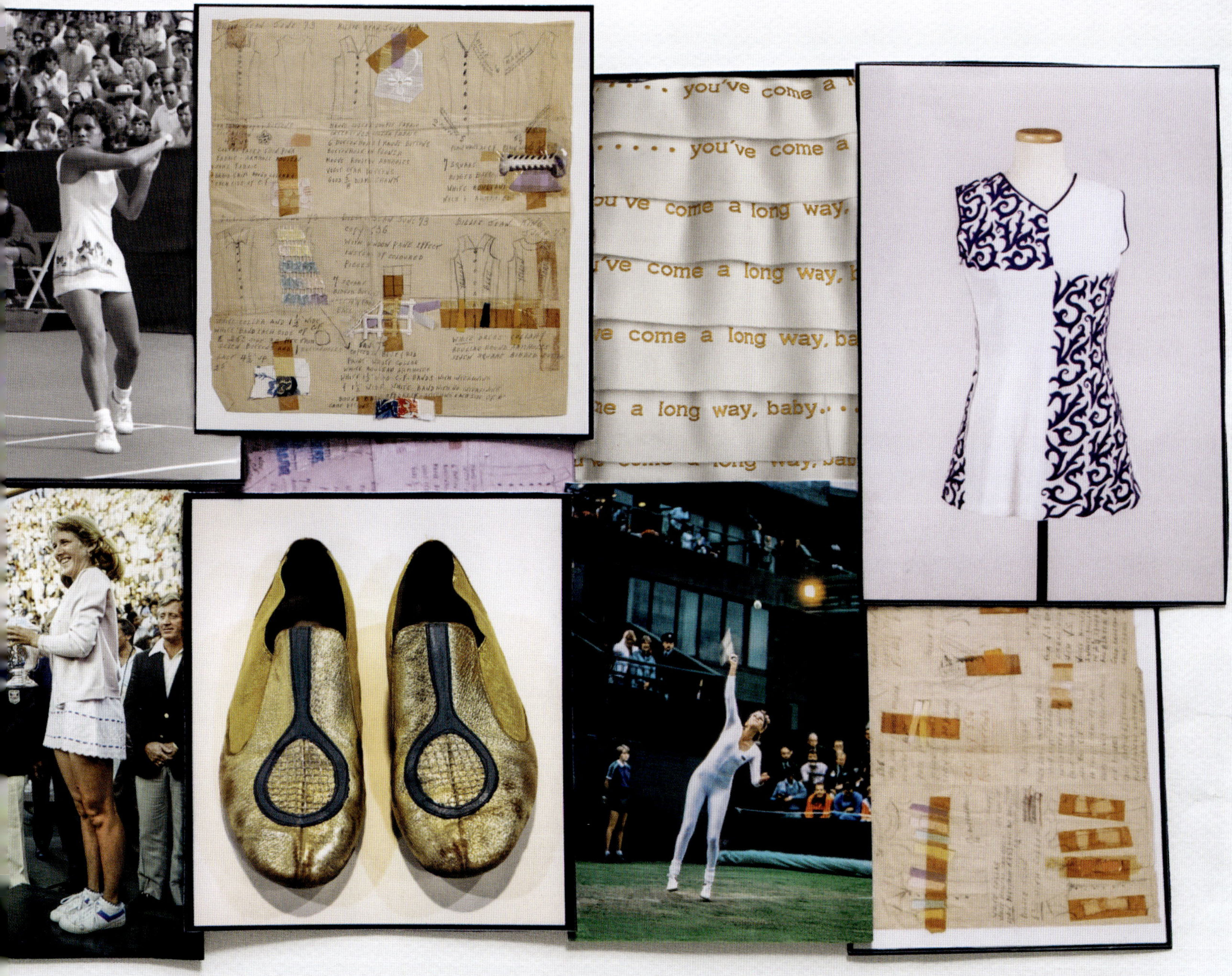
you've come a
you've come a
ou've come a long way,
've come a long way,
e come a long way, ba
me a long way, baby

Multiple Wimbledon bans were imposed on Tinling's designs. The first was in 1949 for Gussie Moran's lace-trimmed undershorts, which had red-faced officials claiming that he had drawn attention to her "sexual area," and he was expelled as a member. The second infraction was another knicker incident: Maria Bueno's dress with matching underwear that featured a sunburst with pink diamond-shaped petals. It was too much sun for the establishment, and they consequently blacklisted all color.

Ban or no ban, Tinling was winning in the design stakes: From 1940 to 1980, 75 percent of women who competed at Wimbledon wore his dresses. In his first decade of designing, he felt "very sensitive" to sports officials' degrading comments that none of his girls had "won," comparing them to mere models. He later set that record straight, and from 1959 to 1970, twelve out of twenty champions lifted the Venus Rosewater Dish wearing one of Tinling's styles.

In 1968, tennis entered the "Open era": Professionals and amateurs were allowed to compete together for the first time in Grand Slam tournaments. Three of the four events changed their names to reflect this shift—the US, French, and Australian to the US Open, and so on. There was prize money to be won—not equal for both sexes, but it was there. This disparity sparked the Virginia Slims Tour launched by Gladys Heldman, with financial backing and nine bold players (including Billie Jean King and Rosie Casals) who risked Grand Slam bans to compete for real earnings. Tinling's designs added the necessary razzmatazz and glamour to attract the crowds.

His Battle of the Sexes design for Billie Jean King was a career highlight. The original dress, made of an opalescent cellophane, was cancelled at the last fitting by King, who felt that the texture of the fabric would be a distraction. Tinling's backup was a recreation of her Wimbledon win dress from that year, made in a different color: mint green, with a royal blue insert on the bodice that matched the shade of her adidas tennis shoes. He stitched over two hundred rhinestones and sequins onto the bodice pre-match, noting that in a venue that large, it needed a good dose of Tinling bling. BJK won against Bobby Riggs, who had challenged that, even as an older male player, he could easily beat any leading female player. (He could not.)

Commercial success followed Tinling in America as his dresses were sold in department stores. He championed every pro he dressed, from Althea Gibson to Tracy Austin, a teenage phenomenon.

Player, fashion designer, commentator, umpire, spy, revolutionary, bridal couturier, player liaison, writer, and dandy—Ted Tinling scored a win every time. He later reminisced about Lenglen's advice to him: "In tennis, there is a beauty of movement, dramatic color, feminine individuality, sexual appeal, technical achievement, the woman's strokes, but it's her clothing which must be conceived to flatter all these attributes." He conceived, birthed, and reared the ultra-feminine tennis form so that when the player stepped out on court, she belonged to no gaze but her own.

"I DIDN'T HAVE MANY TENNIS OUTFITS GROWING UP, SO WHEN TED STARTED MAKING DRESSES FOR ME, HE WOULD SAY 'OH, MADAM SUPERSTAR, HERE'S TEN DRESSES.' I WAS IN HEAVEN. HE APPRECIATED HOW ACTIVE WE WERE, STRETCHING OUR BODIES IN EVERY DIRECTION. HE MADE IT SO THAT WE FELT FREE. WHEN IT FITS GREAT, YOU PLAY BETTER; YOU CAN TRULY BE AND EXPRESS YOURSELF. HE ACTUALLY MADE THE DRESSES AN INCH AND A HALF BIGGER SO THAT WE COULD MOVE. HE THOUGHT OF EVERYTHING. IT WAS HIS LOVE OF DETAILS THAT MADE HIM A GREAT."

—BILLIE JEAN KING

"HE WROTE ON A NAPKIN AT A FANCY DINNER, CAN I MAKE YOUR WEDDING DRESS? AND I SAID YES, SO HE SENT ME A LITTLE SWATCH. THAT'S HOW WE DID IT IN THOSE DAYS. I SWEAR TO GOD, IT WAS THIS BIG SWATCH. AND HE GOES, DO YOU LIKE THIS MATERIAL? I SAID, YES, I LOVE IT. AND HE MADE IT LIKE THAT. I LOVE HIM. HE WAS AHEAD OF HIS TIME, YOU KNOW? HE WAS SO UNIQUE, AND HE WAS SO CREATIVE, AND HE DESIGNED THE DRESSES FOR THE TOP WOMEN IN THOSE DAYS."

—CHRIS EVERT

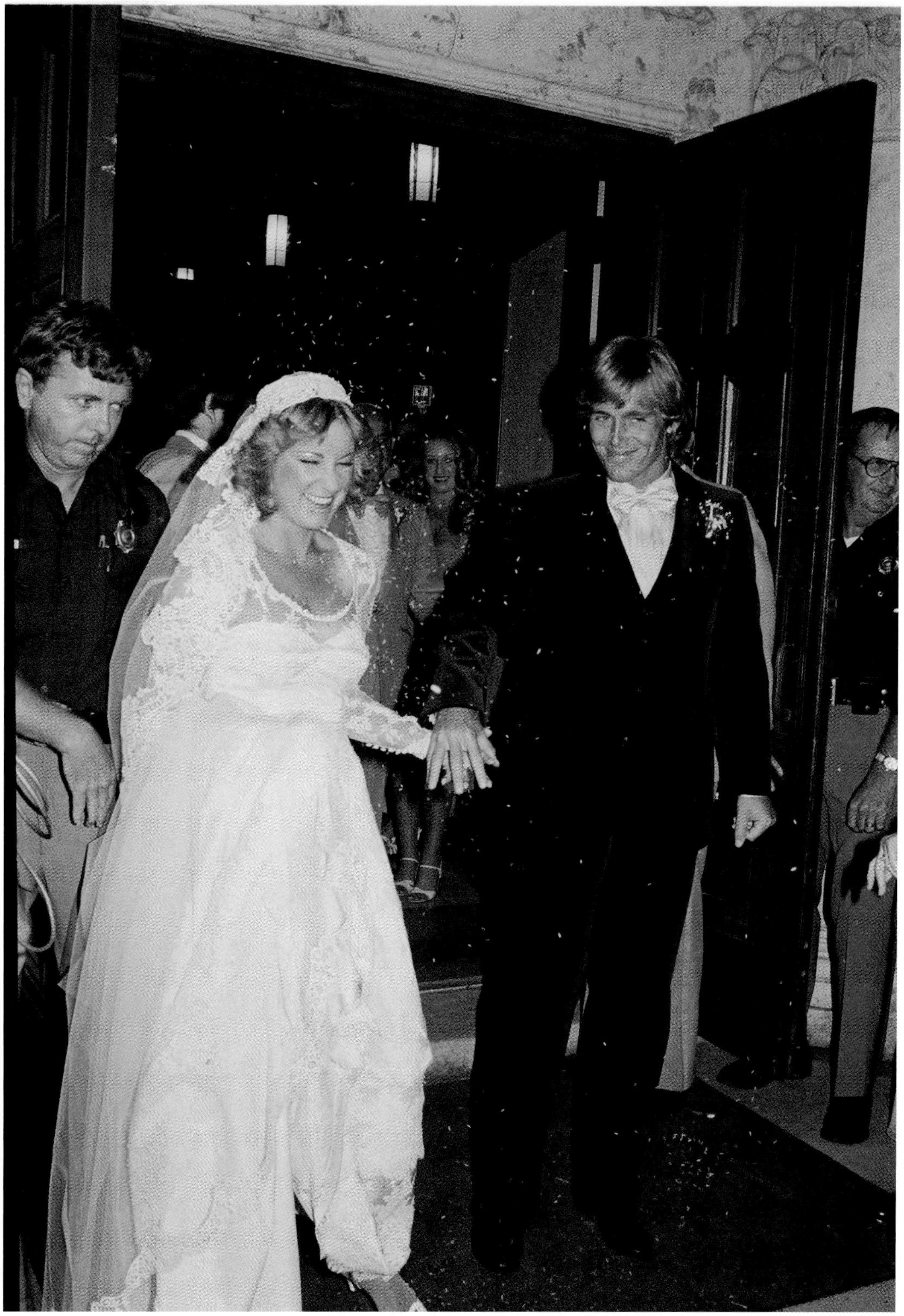

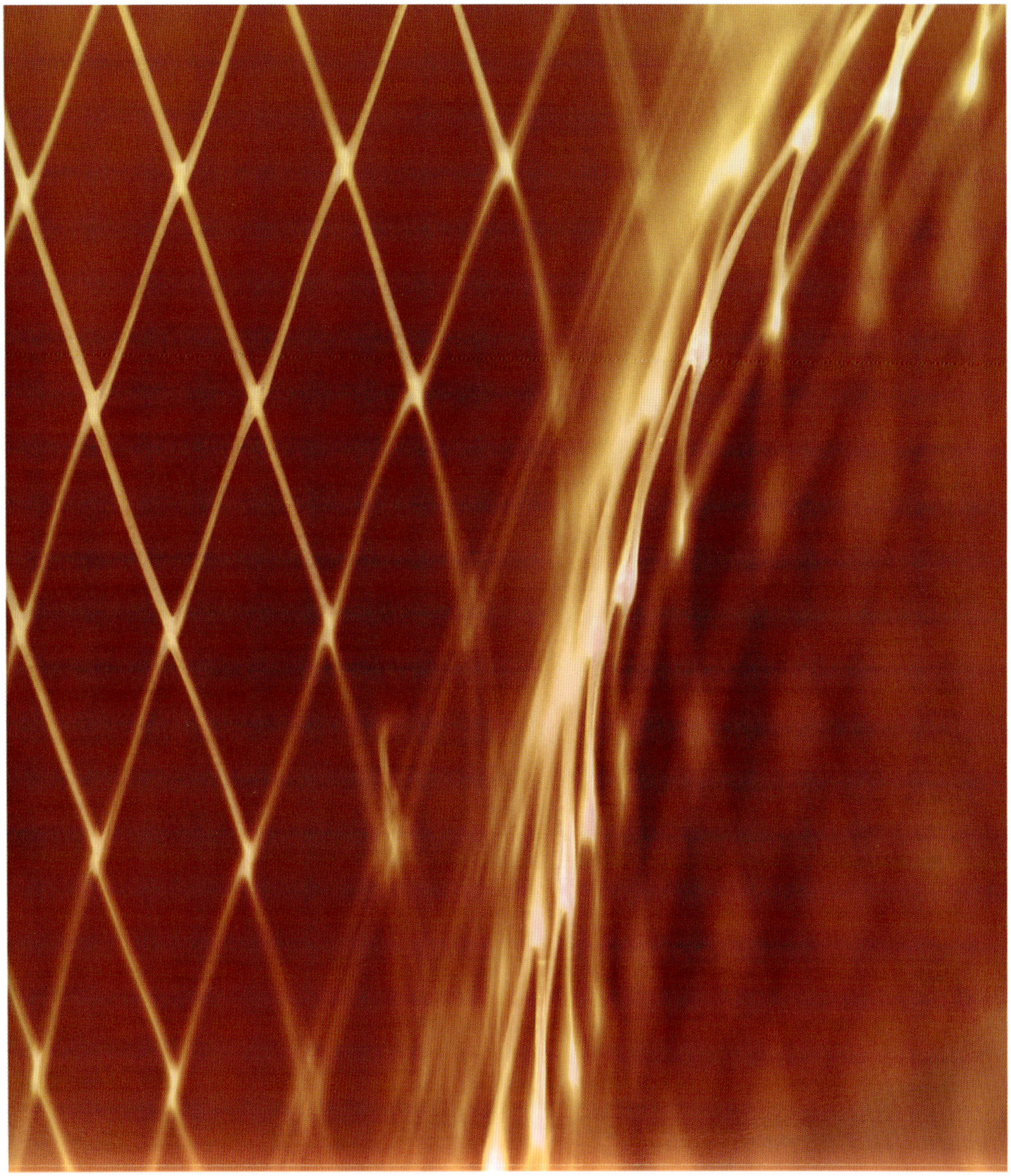

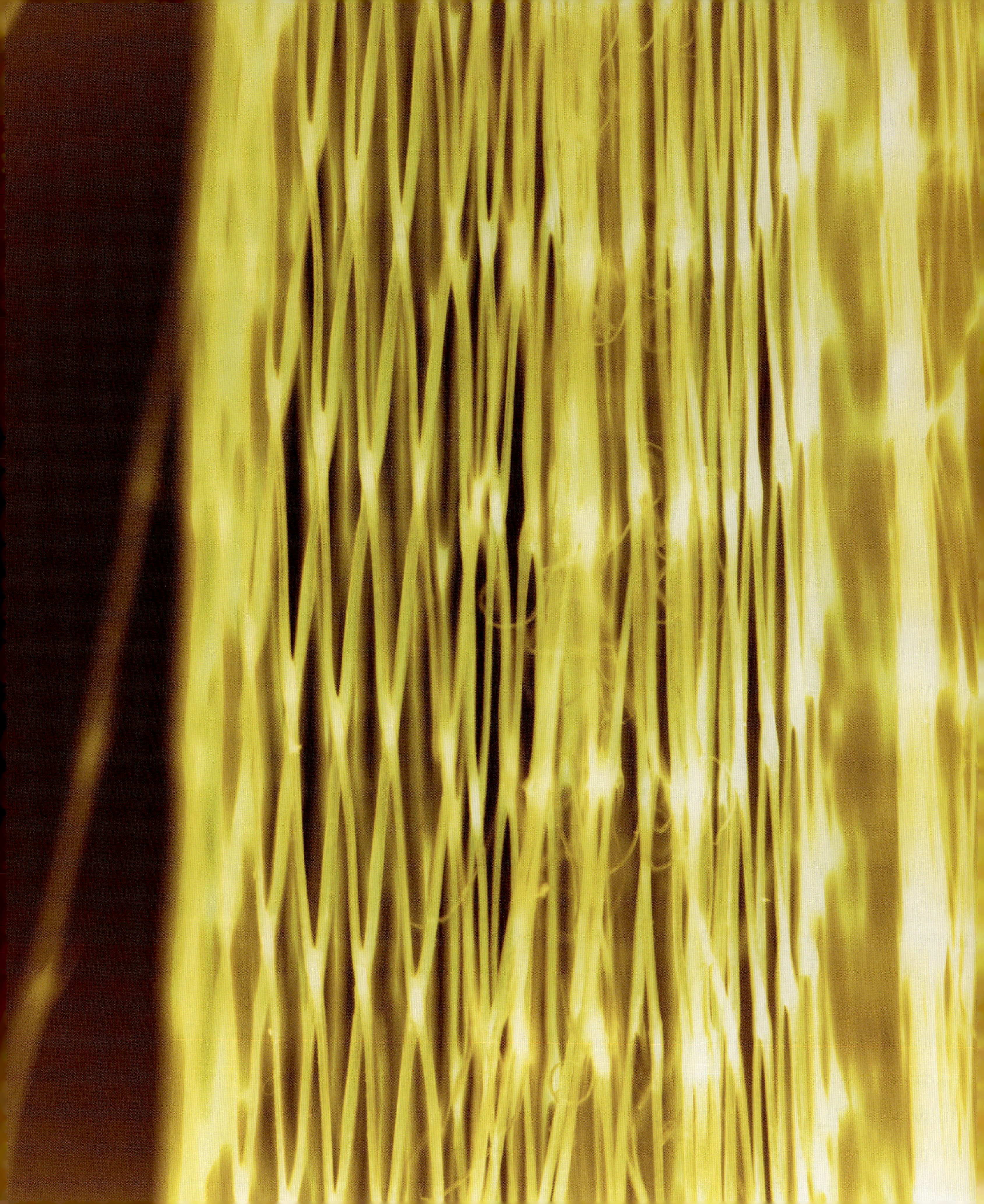

VIJAY AMRITRAJ

SPORTS COMMENTATOR VIJAY AMRITRAJ WAS A SERVE-AND-VOLLEY PLAYER, TACTICALLY ON POINT, WHO MADE THE QUARTERFINALS AT WIMBLEDON AND THE US OPEN.

SKN: What was your understanding of global tennis growing up in Chennai, India, in the 1960s?

VA: Television was nonexistent. Newspapers you could look at, if [there was any news] at all. If you went to a movie in India, during the last bit, there would be a news division film clip, and in that segment they would have sports, sometimes they would have tennis. So I saw the great Pancho Gonzales for maybe a minute.

SKN: Why tennis?

VA: I spent a lot of time in and out of hospital, because my lungs were very poor. The doctors said, He needs to play an outdoor sport to get his lungs better.

My mother was a decent tennis player in college. I got good fairly quickly. By my fourteenth birthday, I ended up winning two major college tournaments. By fifteen, I made my first visit to London; by eighteen, I became India's number 1 and Asia's number 1; and then by nineteen, I was in the world's top ten. When I played the quarterfinal at Wimbledon, at the age of nineteen, the other two players were Jimmy Connors and Björn Borg.

SKN: Yeah, I know their names well!

VA: We were called the "ABC of tennis" by *Sports Illustrated*.

SKN: During this incredible rise and exposure to the Western world, did you shed your Indian skin a bit to embrace this new world and its style?

VA: First of all, my rackets and the tennis clothing I wore in those days was all Slazenger. I loved the golf shirts as opposed to the tennis ones. They just looked classy and fabulous, with a different print on the front of the collar. I was always Indian and became even more Indian as I traveled the world. I continued to play the Davis Cup for India, irrespective of where I lived.

When I played a tournament, there were eight players in the quarterfinals, and seven of them looked like each other, because here I was, in an all-white sport! The only other person of color who played at that time was the great Arthur Ashe.

SKN: You kept your Indian gold jewelry on, it shimmered with your skin color, a glint of your culture, it seemed to stand out against the elite, plush privileged whiteness of the game. Was that an act of quiet resistance?

VA: The gold chain was something my mother gave to me at eighteen. With a cross on it. It still remains. It's never left me, all these years. It's actually where the wins and losses come from. The first four Ds are basically the desire, determination, discipline, [and] dedication to get you to where you want to be. The fifth D is what you need to actually push you over the edge, and that is divine intervention. I've always looked at the cup as half full—which, in fact, the rest of my entire life has always been. My entire life has been a complete miracle.

SKN: Do you think that your personal style was the reason why you were picked for a James Bond film and for *Star Trek*?

VA: Oh gosh no, I'd like to think it was my looks! Yes, I was picked off the standard code at Wimbledon to do a screen test! I thought, Who can say they worked at Pinewood Studios in the morning and played Wimbledon in the afternoon?

SKN: Not many people, Vijay. I think you've trumped that one for sure.

You have literally lived the American dream. Is it because of your nature, your curiosity? What has driven you to all these different branches of life?

VA: There are two or three things that drive me. The first are challenges. The two most favorite movies [franchises] for me have always been James Bond and *Star Trek*, so to be part of both was unimaginable. For thirty years, I was the only Indian on *The Tonight Show Starring Johnny Carson*. So I did all this as the way I was brought up, which was like an Indian. And then there's a famous line in the Bible that says, "When much is given to you, more is asked of you." It's important to respect that. But what about the kids that didn't have it? When Kofi Annan asked me to be a United Nations Messenger of Peace alongside Muhammad Ali, Luciano Pavarotti, Michael Douglas, and Elie Wiesel, the Nobel laureate, I jumped at it, and served for just under seven years during his term. I then started my Vijay Amritraj Foundation, which has been around now for nineteen years. We serve some of the neediest causes in India.

SKN: Is there anything that you haven't done that you would like to do?

VA: Well, there are some side benefits to all this. I was a judge at the Miss Universe pageant!

SKN: That must have been really hard work!

VA: *[Laughs]* There are lots of things you end up being a part of that you still don't forget who you're representing.

SKN: This book is called *ACE*. What does it mean to you as a player, or personally?

VA: Ace? Wow. The ace is the highest card in a deck of cards. An ace is a service winner. When someone does well in business, Oh, you're an ace—it's like saying you're a star, you're successful. But to me the ace has always been: Are you an ace as a human being? Are you an ace in your daily life? Are you successful internally, as opposed to externally? We all know this as we grow up, because it's very easy to fool adults, but it's very hard to fool a child or an animal. They know love when they see it. And when you are putting it on, they can tell. That's why it's so important to ace your own self. It's the hardest market.

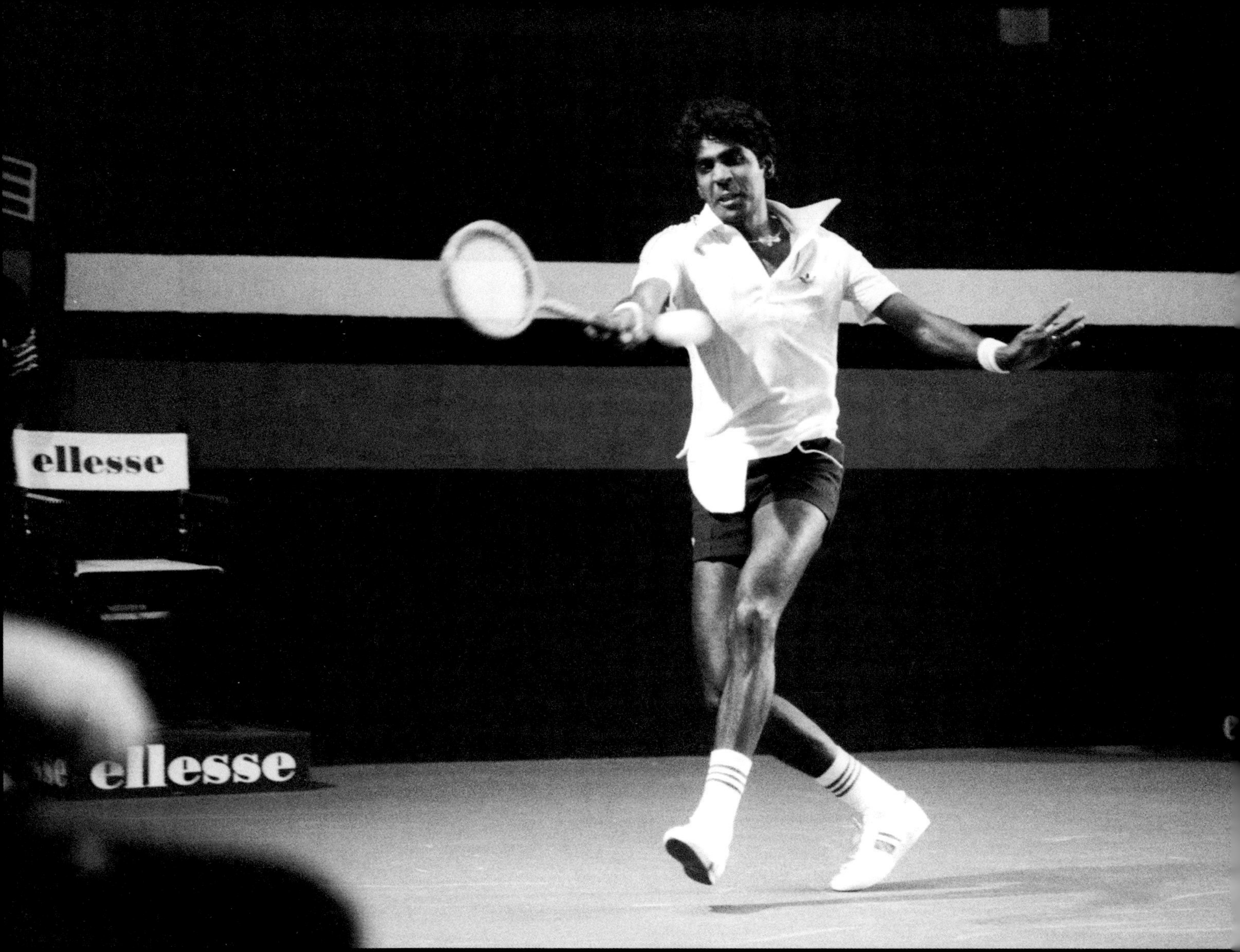
ellesse
ellesse

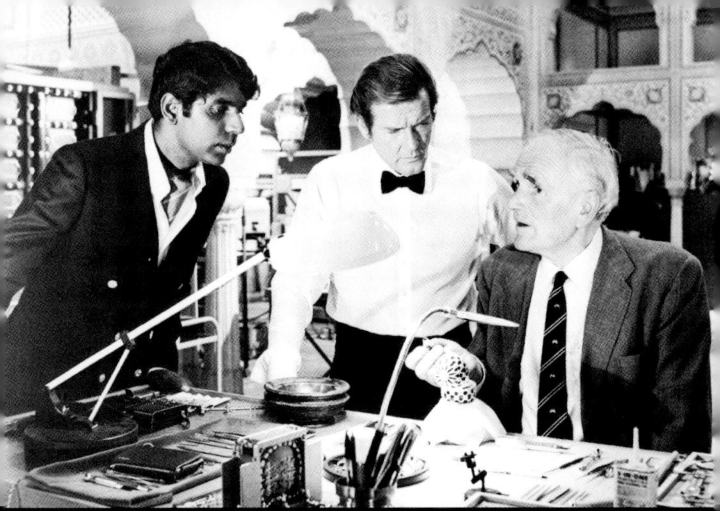

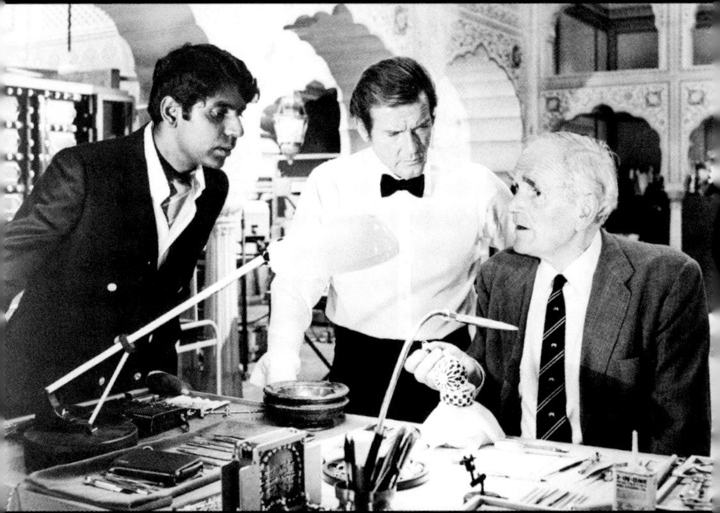

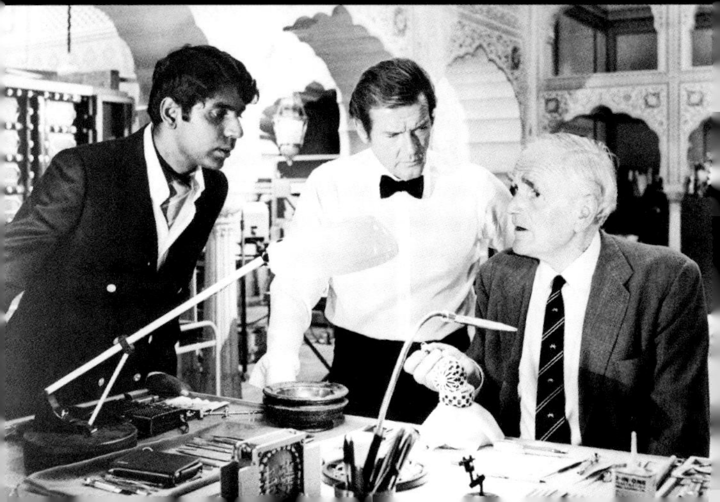

BEN SHELTON

BEN SHELTON IS A RAW, ATHLETIC POWER PLAYER WITH A 150 MPH SERVE.

SKN: You said that you like aggressive hip-hop—especially when going on court. Whose music fuels this mindset?

BS: When I'm walking onto the court, I want to feel locked in, like I'm stepping into a battle. I listen to guys like Lil Baby, Meek Mill, and Future. It's about the energy, something that gets me hyped and puts me in tunnel-vision mode.

SKN: Roger Federer is a fashion icon in his own right; he can easily cross-pollinate, from on court, to the Royal Box at Wimbledon, to the Met Gala. Is he your fashion benchmark? Ten years from now how do you envision your own style journey?

BS: Roger's the blueprint when it comes to elegance and owning every setting, whether it's Centre Court or a red carpet. That versatility is something I definitely admire. But I still want to put my own twist on it—bring some youth, some edge, a little unpredictability. Ten years from now? I see myself still pushing boundaries, whether it's with fashion, the way I play, or what I stand for. Hopefully still repping On, maybe even helping shape the next wave of style-performance crossover.

SKN: Who are your off-court fashion inspirations? Are you into hype drops, low-key street legends?

BS: I like mixing things up. I watch what guys like Shai Gilgeous-Alexander are doing. They are real confident with color and shape. Also love what A$AP Rocky brings, that mix of high fashion with street. And yeah, I keep an eye on what's popping in the hype space brands like Loewe, Aimé Leon Dore, Kith.

SKN: You have already developed a distinct performance apparel style; its usually sleeveless. How do you adapt your on-court outfit to suit your playing style?

BS: The sleeveless look just feels right. I play explosive, aggressive tennis, and the fit has to move with me. I worked with On to find gear that matches that freedom through the shoulders—lightweight, breathable, but still bold.

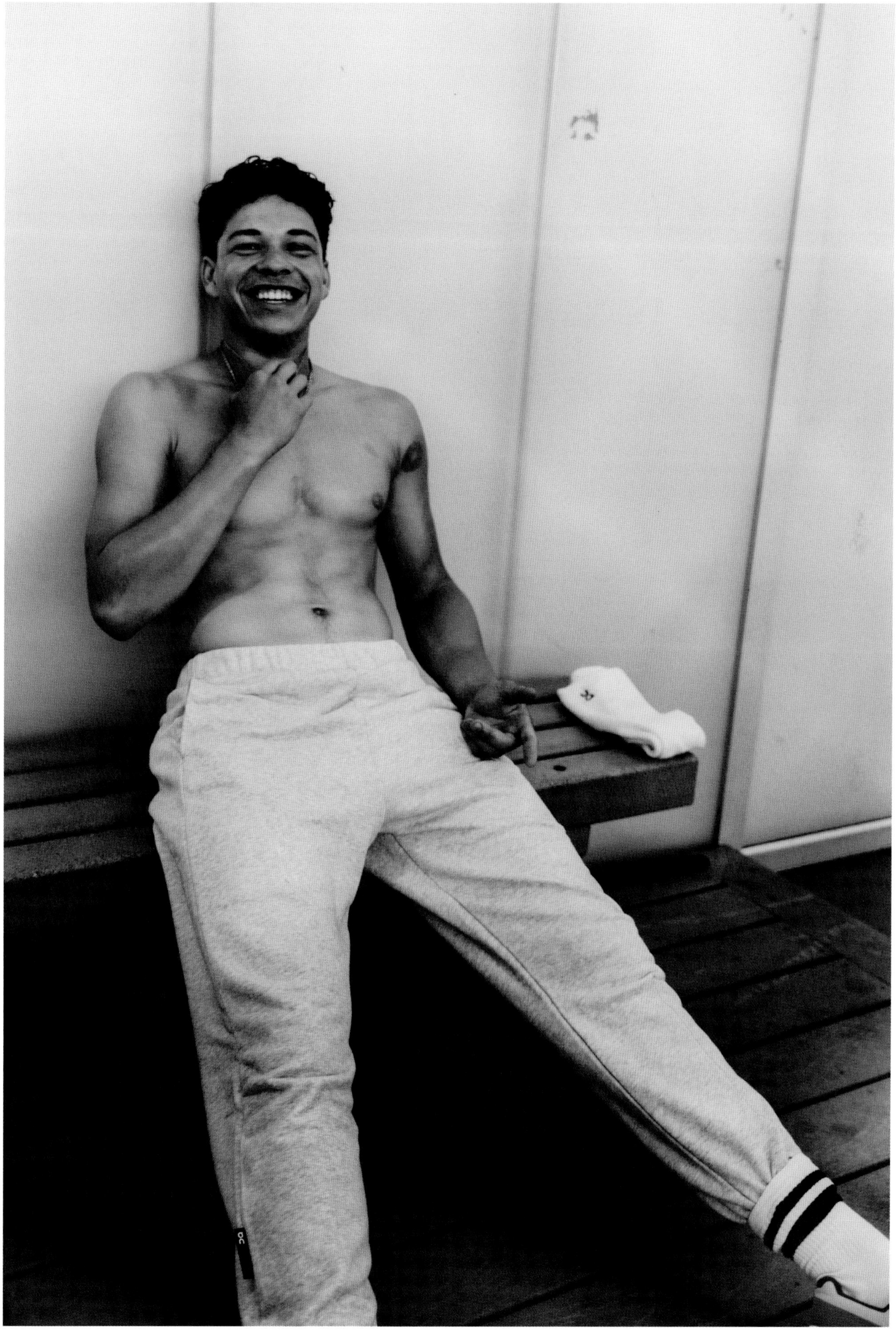

BORIS BECKER

BORIS BECKER IS A SIX-TIME GRAND SLAM CHAMPION. HE COMBINED EXPLOSIVE POWER ON THE TENNIS COURT WITH A DISTINCTLY EUROPEAN SENSE OF STYLE.

Child sports stars orbit seasoned players like streaks of cosmic light. The media intuitively swoops in, knowing that the headlines feed the inner-child spirit in all of us who dreamed of being a superstar in front of our bedroom mirrors. Boris Becker did it in real life. Here he was: *Prodigy! Phenomenon! Wunderkind!* A daredevil performance of rolls, tumbles, and hot-dog winners scraping the baseline, shots that today's players still croon over and replay. Becker's skill and showmanship made him seem infallible—and all this was ablaze at the young age of seventeen.

Becker's perfomance apparel reflected his playing style: bold, with graphic prints and colors and a slim silhouette to match his athletic, youthful build. We all remember Becker winning Wimbledon at seventeen, whether it was before or after our time, and that is the thing about young stars: They are forever etched in our minds as that teen—the court is at their command, and their image and style is dazzled by celebrity.

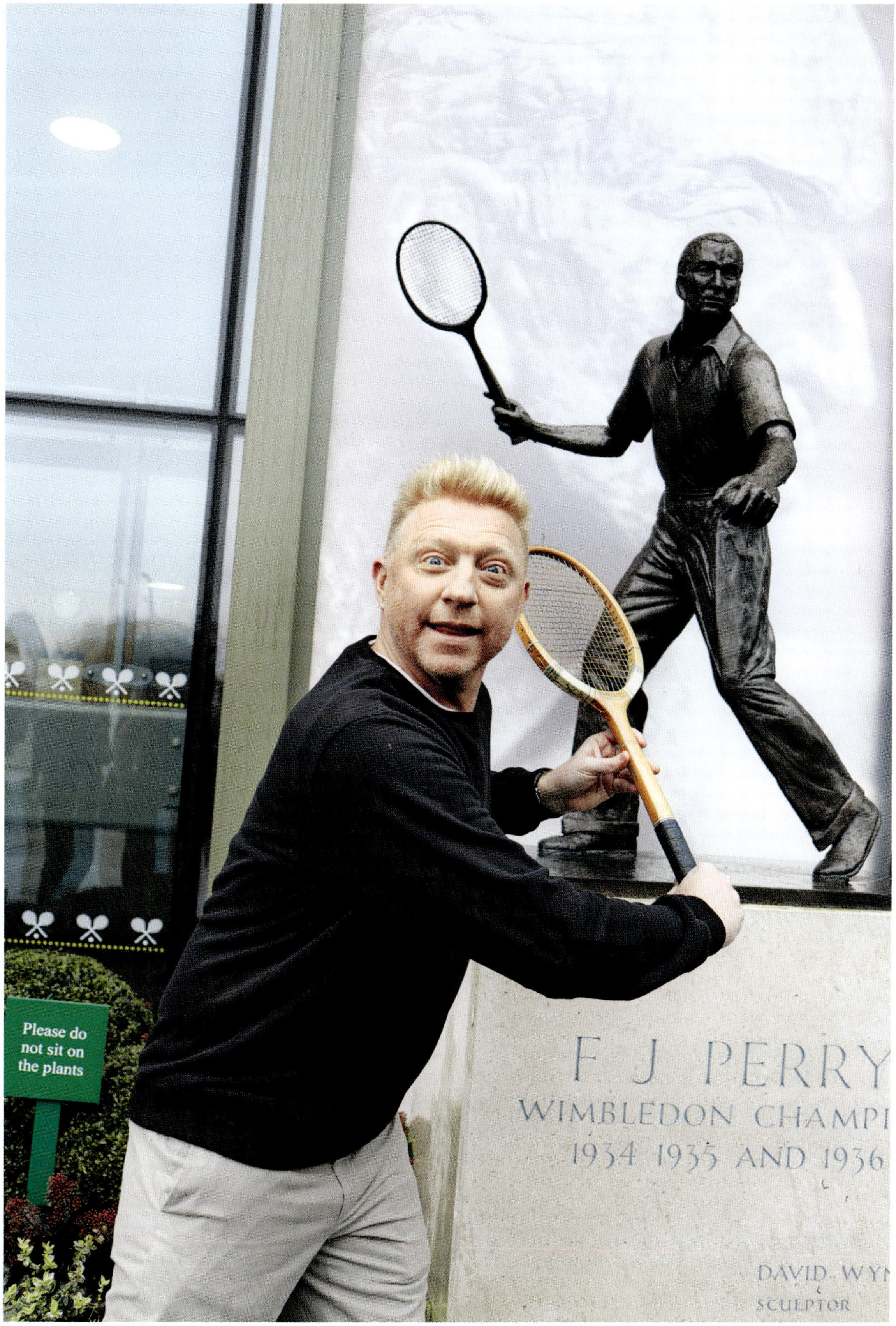
Please do
not sit on
the plants
F J PERRY
WIMBLEDON CHAMP
1934 1935 AND 1936
SCULPTOR

SKN: You have cited Björn Borg as your hero. What kind of impression did he make on your image and identity?

BB: He indeed was my hero growing up. The reason I fell in love with Wimbledon was because of him—he won it five consecutive times in the mid-1970s. And I would say Björn was the first pop star in tennis, you know, with his long blond locks, this scruffy beard, the gold chain, and he wore these tight-tight shorts, the tight shirt—it was really a cool look. And then character-wise, he was very stoic, very calm. You could never read him; he kept it all to himself. I would say he was almost godlike on the tennis court in the mid-'70s.

SKN: You mentioned having a "nice time with clothes" and sticking to a routine. What does clothing mean to you—is it ritual, expression, comfort?

BB: I do, and I still have a good relationship with my clothes. First of all, nobody's dressing me. I always choose what I like as a tennis player and as a gentleman now. It's your signature; people judge you first by your clothes. You should always be wearing the clothes; the clothes shouldn't be wearing you. I'm still in decent shape, but when I was an athlete, I always liked to dress so you could see that I was a fit and muscular man.

SKN: Did certain outfits carry meaning to you—are you superstitious about certain clothes? Would you re-wear winning clothes?

BB: I think that all sports men and women are extremely superstitious. In my day, the company you represented would give you three different shirts: The one that you win in, you keep on wearing—obviously after the laundry—but the other two you put aside.

SKN: You had distinctive body language on-court. How important is this on court presence for a player?

BB: Body language is half the victory. If you have broad shoulders, put them up. If you have a large chest, put it out. It's very important in how you keep your head. If you look down too much, it means you're defensive, almost timid. You also cannot be arrogant, but you can look self-determined instead. You have to ooze confidence, particularly on the tennis court. But in everyday life, it's the same. It's your signature if you walk and talk the right way.

SKN: Clothing can serve as a conduit to shape our identity—a way to manage visibility, control perception—do you feel your style choices like the hats and oversized jackets were part of the process for you as a young person navigating fame?

BB: Winning Wimbledon at seventeen, well, everything changed for me. I had a couple of nicknames. One was Boom Boom, because of my power; the other was Wunderkind, because nobody has ever won Wimbledon at seventeen. So obviously, you then get looked at and treated a different way, and you respond to that. Now, I wouldn't say that every clothing trend that I followed suited me, but I wanted to test the waters—in order to find your own style, you have to try many different ones. It was fun and still is fun for me to dress up.

SKN: Did your on-court fashion style reflect your playing style ?

BB: My aggressive playing style I thought was very reflective of my fashion style. I had very muscular legs, so my shorts and shirts were very tight. It was the fashion then in the '80s and '90s. Also, when you change on the court, you are half naked, so you have to feel comfortable in that environment.

SKN: "If you can meet with Triumph and Disaster and treat those two impostors just the same . . .": This line from a Rudyard Kipling poem is set above the player entryway to Wimbledon Centre Court. We all face the two in different intensities as our human life unfolds—perhaps yours more so, because it was so public—but what do you think of the words triumph and disaster now? Are they the same to you?

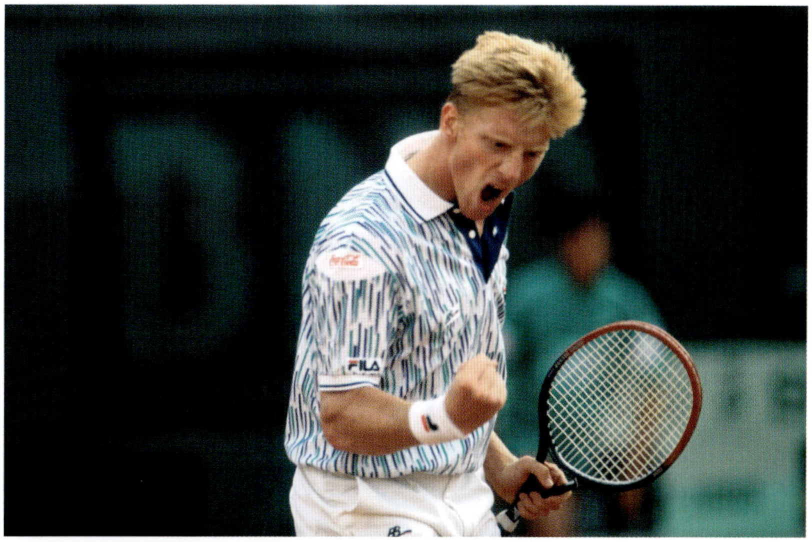

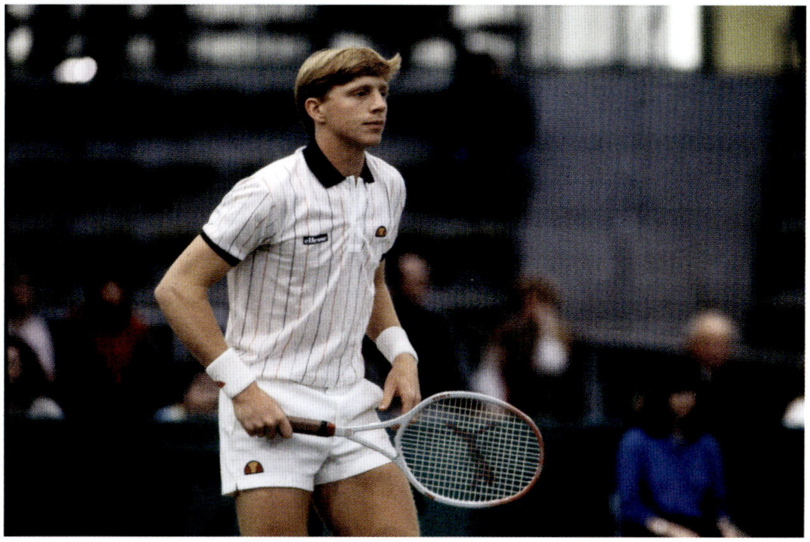

BB: It's probably the most difficult task in life. I certainly had my moment of glory as well as my moment of despair. I had triumph and disaster: a bit of triumph, and dabbled in a bit of disaster. Walking on Wimbledon Centre Court probably a hundred times in my career, I have embedded this poem in my mind, actually, and if you see my life in the last forty years, I very much reflect it. You have to celebrate the wins, the victories, but you also cannot drown in your sorrows when you lose, whether that's on or off the court. It's a wonderful poem, probably the most important for my life.

SKN: Finally, Boris, this book is called *ACE*. What does this word mean to you?

BB: The word **ace** is very fitting. I was the man that served a lot of aces, especially when I was in trouble. An ace was always a fast point, a luxury that I had. But **ace** to me, philosophically, means that you're one of a kind. In poker, ace is the highest card. If you're an ace, you stand out; you're different than the rest. Coming back to tennis, **ace** . . . well, it was my favorite shot.

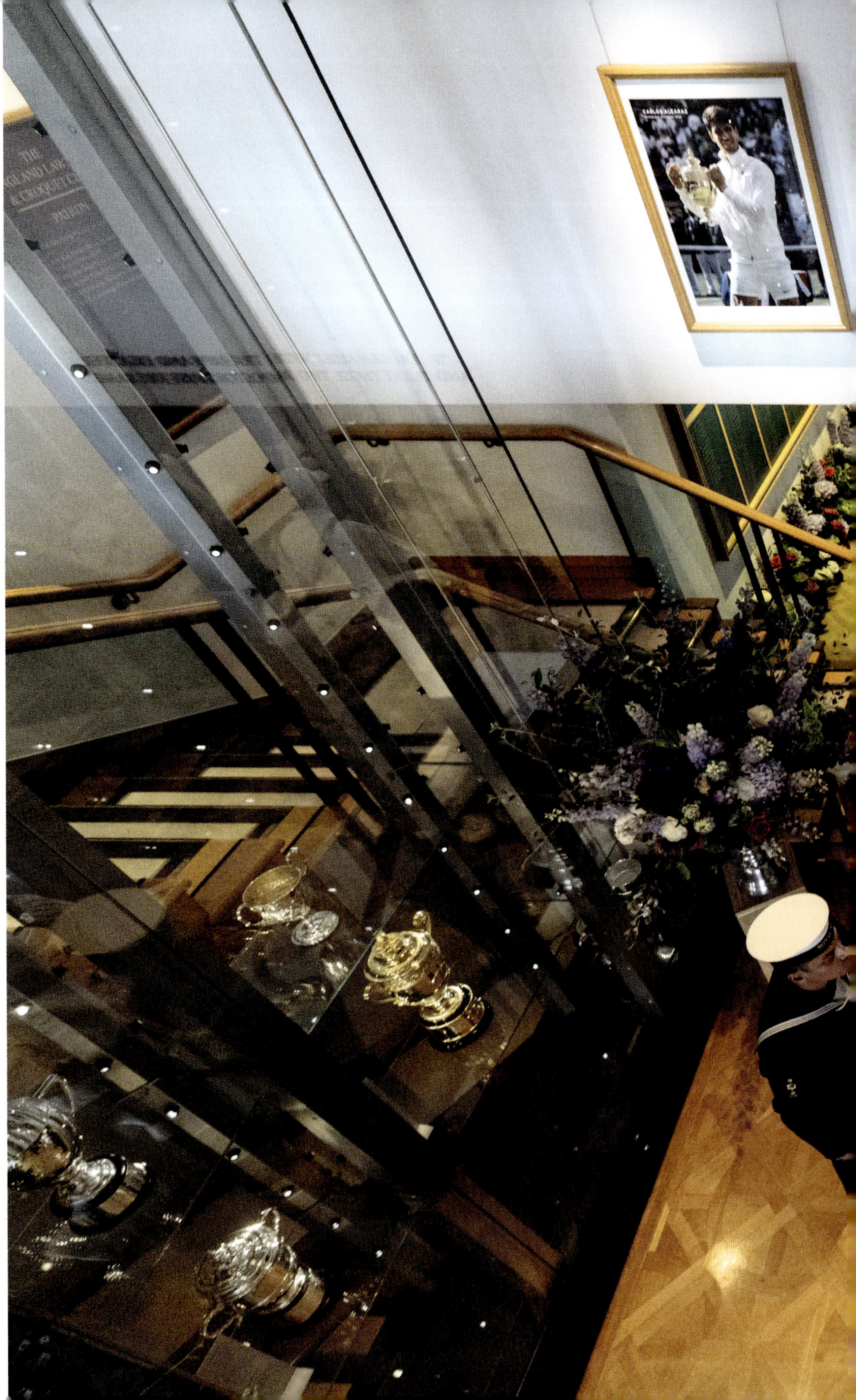

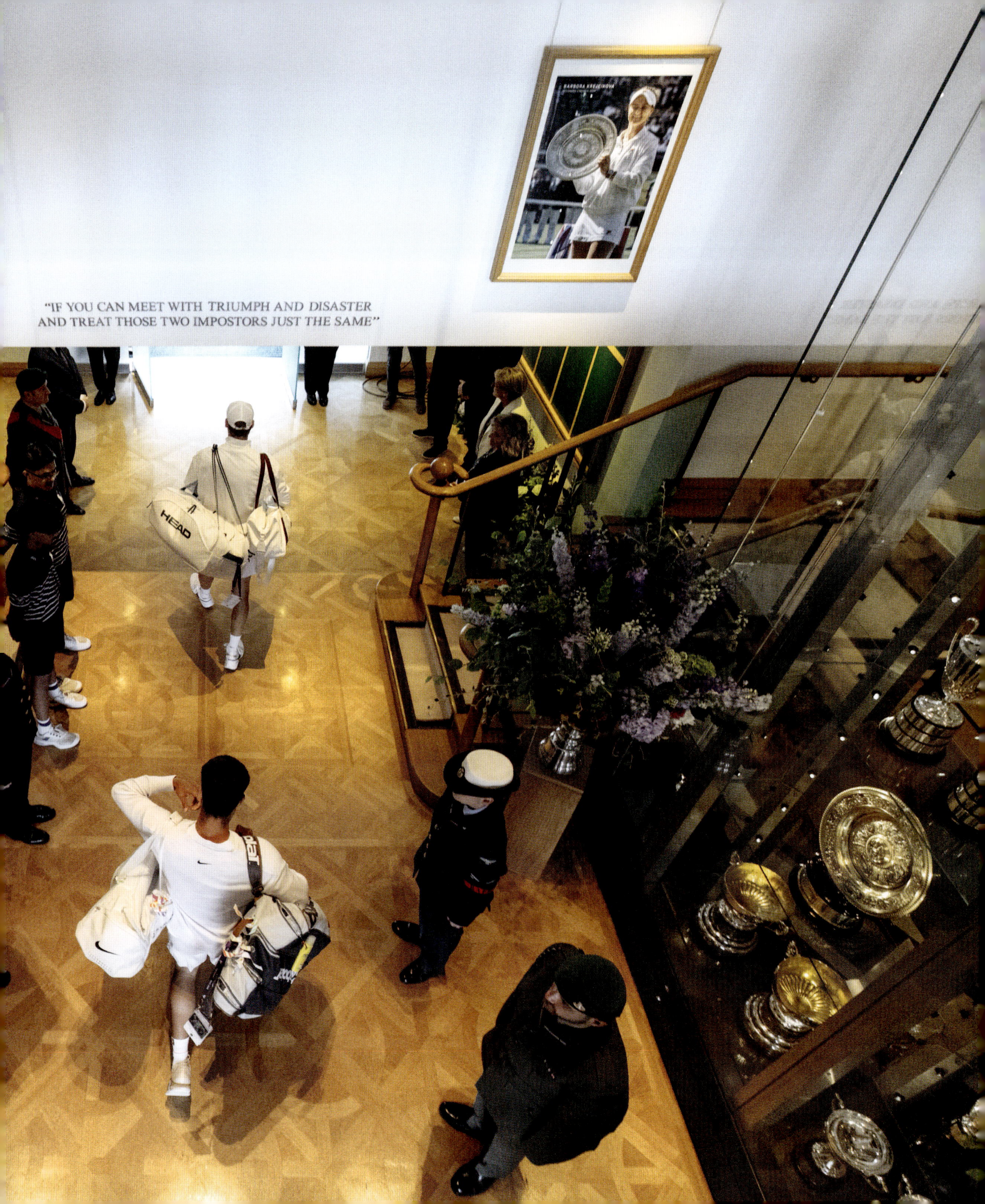
"IF YOU CAN MEET WITH TRIUMPH AND DISASTER
AND TREAT THOSE TWO IMPOSTORS JUST THE SAME"

GUCCI

Read the order of lines on a pitch, track, or court and it will dictate the rules of the game. What the sports person plays within those lines *is* the thing of beauty. The human body has been trained, coerced, and molded into perfection—each flaw persistently erased over time to produce the best game possible.

In fashion, these lines form stripes which convey a sense of motion and speed. For sport brands like adidas or Umbro, implementing this principle for their logo design was a logical alignment. For an established heritage fashion brand like Gucci, adopting the same language was trailblazing. Inspired by an equestrian girth strap made with red and green bands, the Gucci stripe became synonymous with the brand—it appeared on bags, suitcases, and watches. When it was unveiled on a canvas tennis shoe in 1977, a new fashion order was passed: that of the designer sneaker. Balenciaga, Prada, and Dior would all follow suit later, debuting similar token models for either the red carpet or a collectors' shelf, which shifted the sneaker sports concept to designer status. A reissue of the Gucci shoe was launched in 2020 under creative director Alessandro Michele, who also actualized the adidas x Gucci collaboration—a brilliant fusion between high-profile sporting brands and fashion labels that made for super slick cult pieces and mile-long waitlists.

Gucci further embraced tennis with its 2024 ambassador: Italian Jannik Sinner, ranked number one at the time by the Association of Tennis Professionals (ATP). Walking onto Wimbledon turf with his Gucci racket duffel bag—created in collaboration with Head, a leading racket brand—Sinner featured the all-white house monogrammed "GG" leather, a crisp reinterpretation of their artisanal legacy. The parallel stripes on the handle mirrored the geometry of the court and the iconography of Gucci—a quiet reclamation that this is where Sinner conducts his business: with precision, and in style.

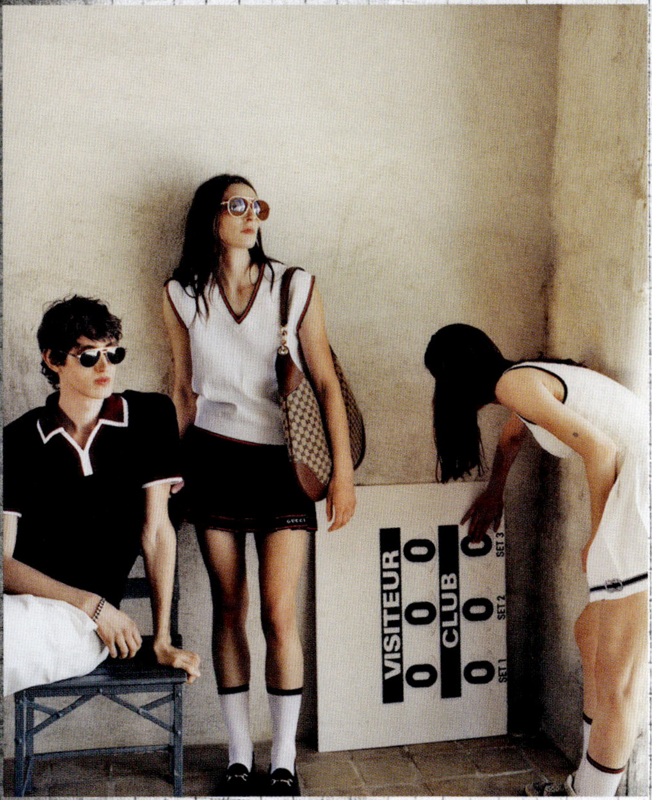

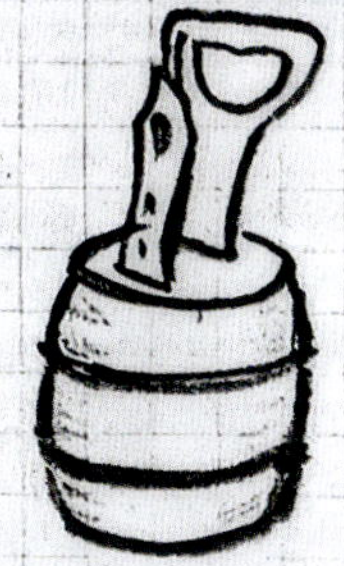

1064
Cavatappi

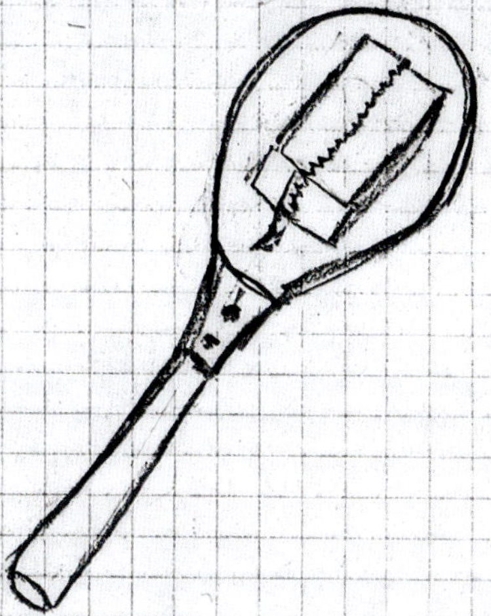

1065
P. racchetta

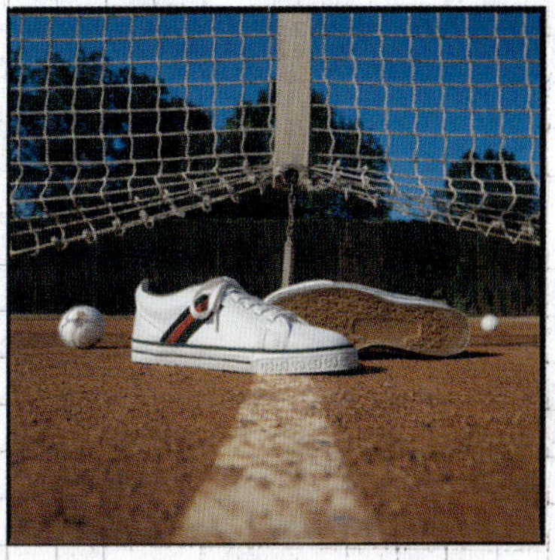

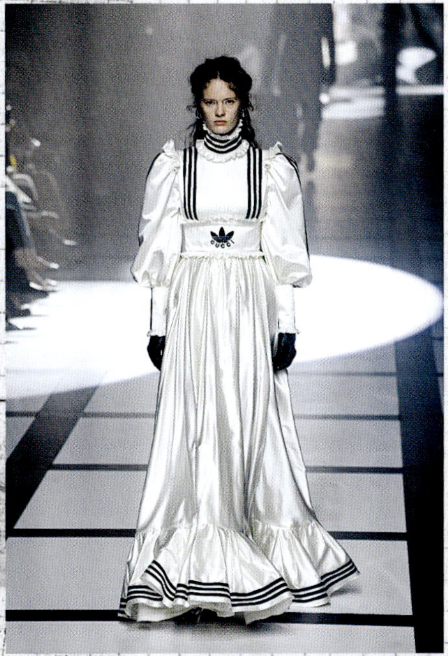

1066
P. pinne-bar

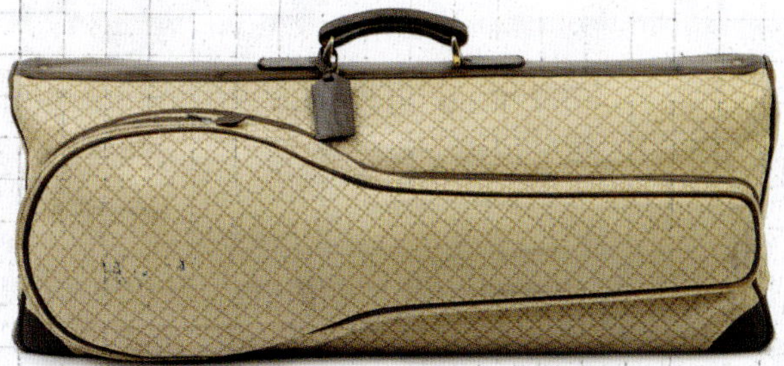

SINNER X GUCCI X NIKE

JANNIK SINNER IS A POWERFUL AND TECHNICALLY PRECISE ALL-ROUNDER WITH FOUR GRAND SLAM WINS.

SKN: If you could sum up your design and fashion ideas for when you are on court and then off, what would they be?

JS: I like to be classy and elegant, but always with a modern twist. I'm only twenty-three years old. I'm lucky to be working with great brands like Gucci and Nike. They know me well and always suggest outfits I really like, respecting my input and my preferences both for colors and materials. On court, the garment is key in order to feel well when performing in different climates and conditions.

SKN: You have become the prize of Italy, an established fashion center known for its effortless sprezzatura. What have you learned since gaining a high profile, style-wise?

JS: In Italy, we are lucky to have a lot of history in fashion. Italians are very proud of the fashion heritage of the country. I was in Milan during Fashion Week, and it is very impressive how the whole city and people in the street dress up for that week. I had the pleasure to attend the Gucci show in February together with Anna Wintour, and it was very interesting to hear her comments and explanations.

SKN: Are there any players or designers you admire?

JS: Obviously Roger Federer has always been extremely classy, both on and off the court. Nike has designed a lot of amazing outfits for him throughout his long career. He is not only a sports icon but also someone I look up to when it comes to fashion. My friends at Gucci have told me a lot of great things about Demna, who will start as their creative director this summer. I'm curious to see his work and influence.

SKN: Finally, this book is called *ACE*—what does that word mean to you?

JS: Great name! I like aces obviously. It's always a good feeling when you hit an ace.

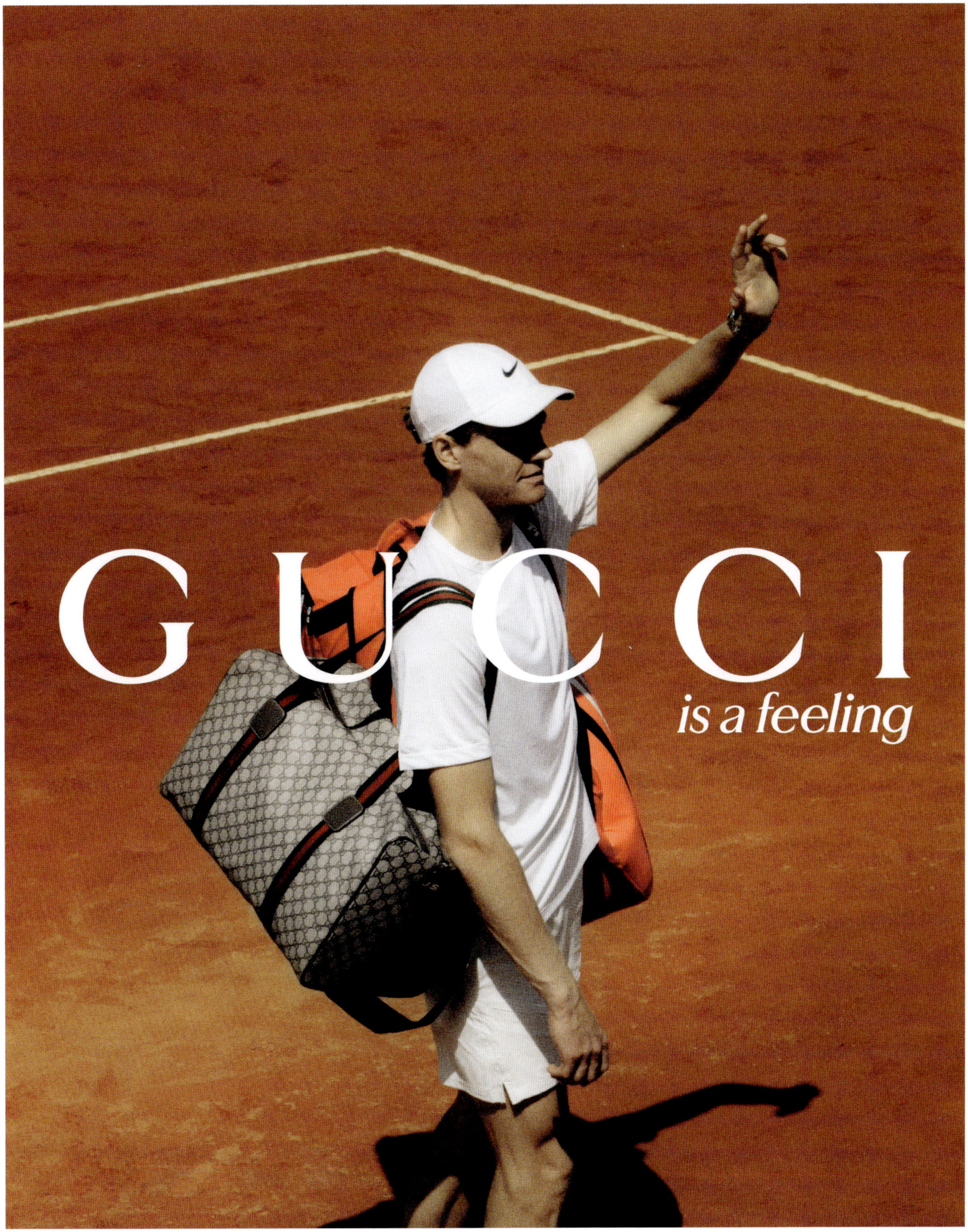
GUCCI
is a feeling

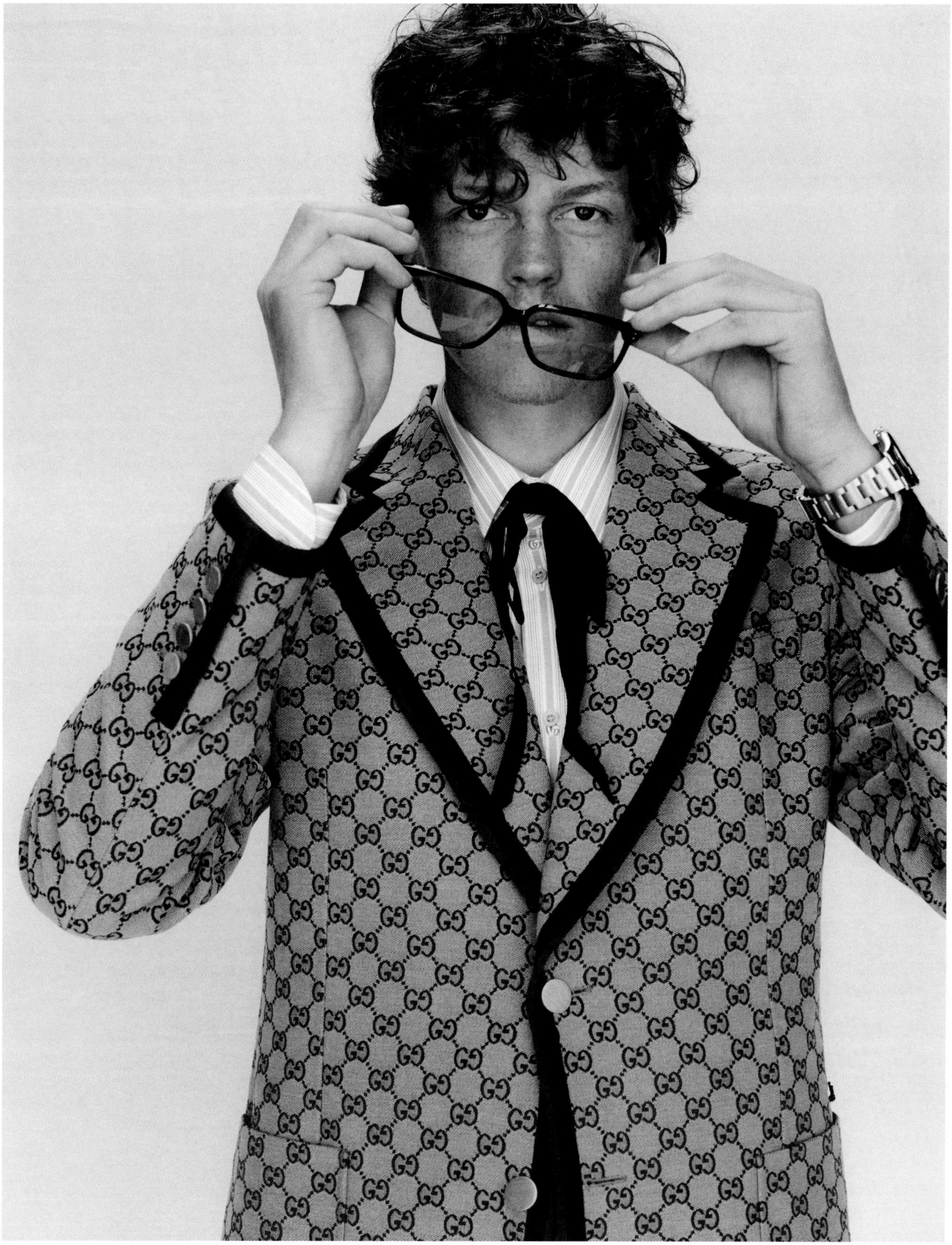

"WE WORE THEM [BEADS] BECAUSE THEY WERE PART OF OUR HERITAGE."

—VENUS WILLIAMS

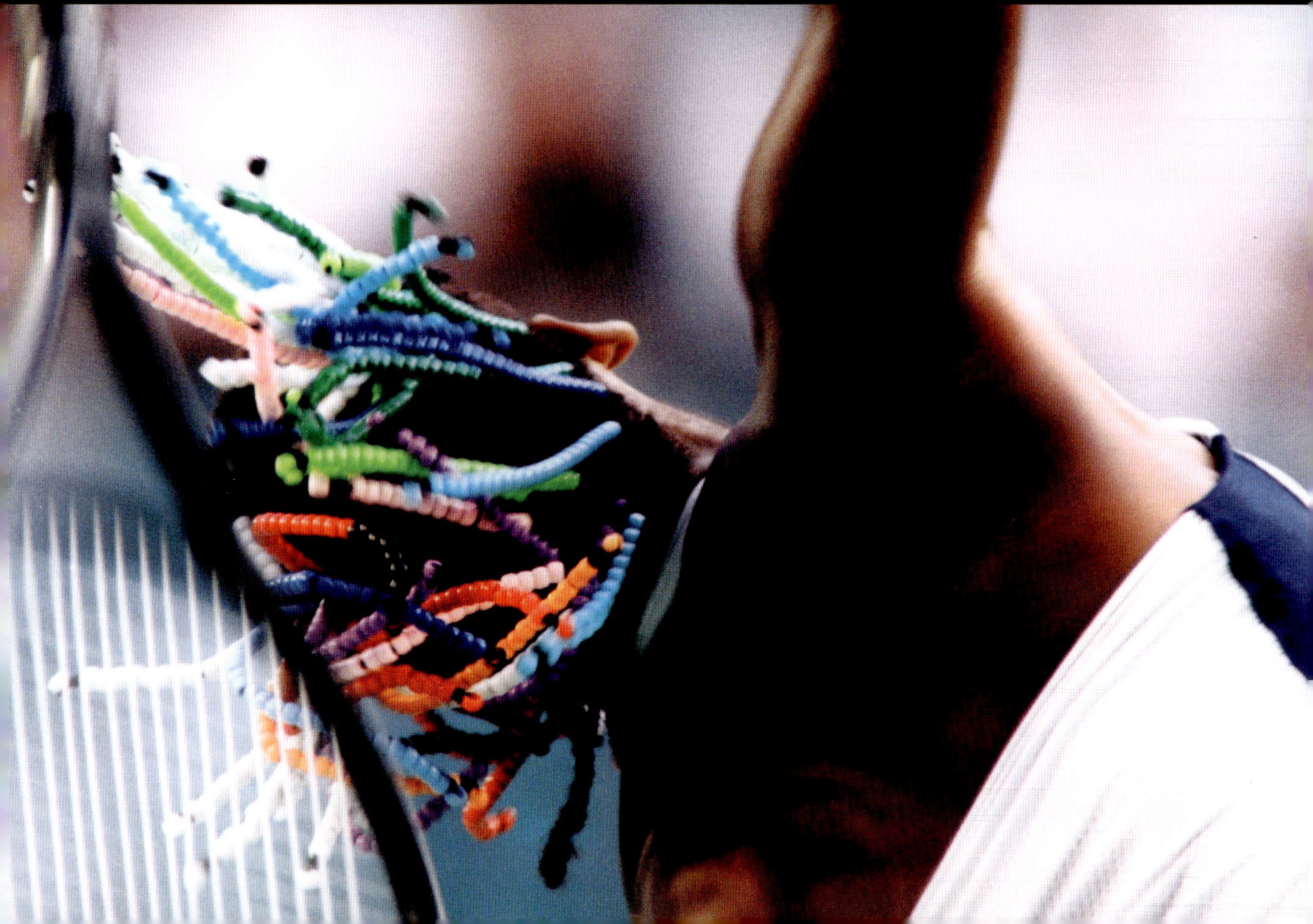

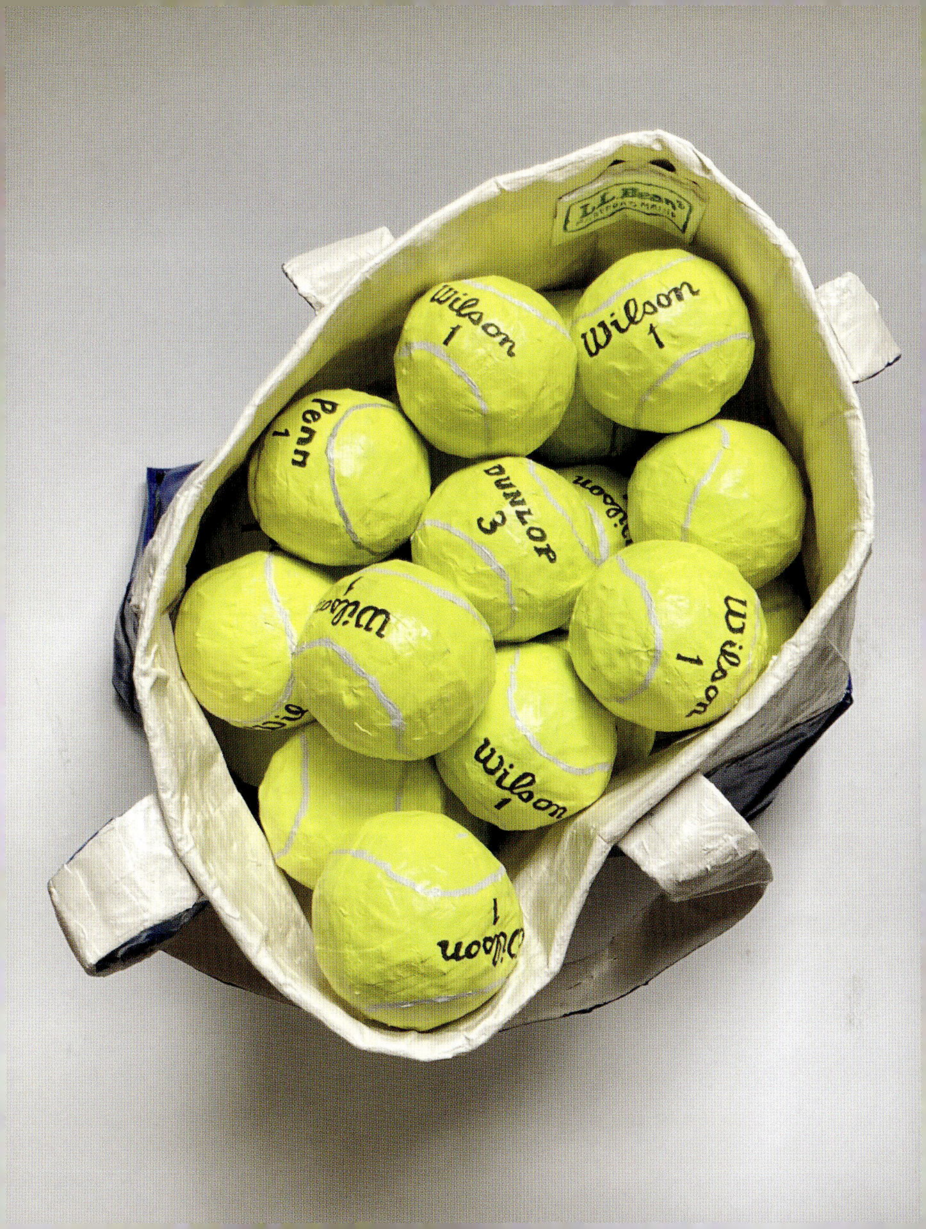
Wilson
1
Wilson
1
Penn
1
DUNLOP
3
Wilson
1
Wilson
1
Wilson
1

NIKE

SPEAKERS

WS: WILSON W. SMITH III,
Design Director, Nike Tennis Footwear

SKN: You have used inspirational references like jazz music or the engineering specs of an Aston Martin for some of the original Air Jordan design prototypes. How did you apply the same thinking techniques to designing tennis shoes?

WS: The game was changing, from the [John] McEnroe serve-and-volley with wooden rackets to a game with metal rackets, so you could hit the ball with all this power. Serena, Agassi, could all return the ball from the baseline more powerfully and at a greater speed than their serve. The game was getting so much more aggressive and expressive, and so our product design was reflecting that.

The creative team from Nike were also inspired from new sources. There were four of us who came from architectural backgrounds, and the inspiration of architecture is that "form follows function." So that is how we thought about our performance products, like we were responding to the function of the game. A lot of the time we would say at Nike to design for the body in motion, because you are capturing the athlete's *energy* and *movement*.

When you look at the dynamics of the game of tennis—say the change of direction with their feet before they even get to the ball—for each surface, they are responding to it differently. On clay, they slide from side to side and pivot like crazy, then on hard courts there needs to be a lot of durability around the toe and inside parts of the shoes. Elsewhere, there needs to be support and protection, because they use their feet like rudders. These are all the factors that make or dictate our design decisions. So we'd add different performance details on the shoes and apparel, like materials that open up breathability or durability.

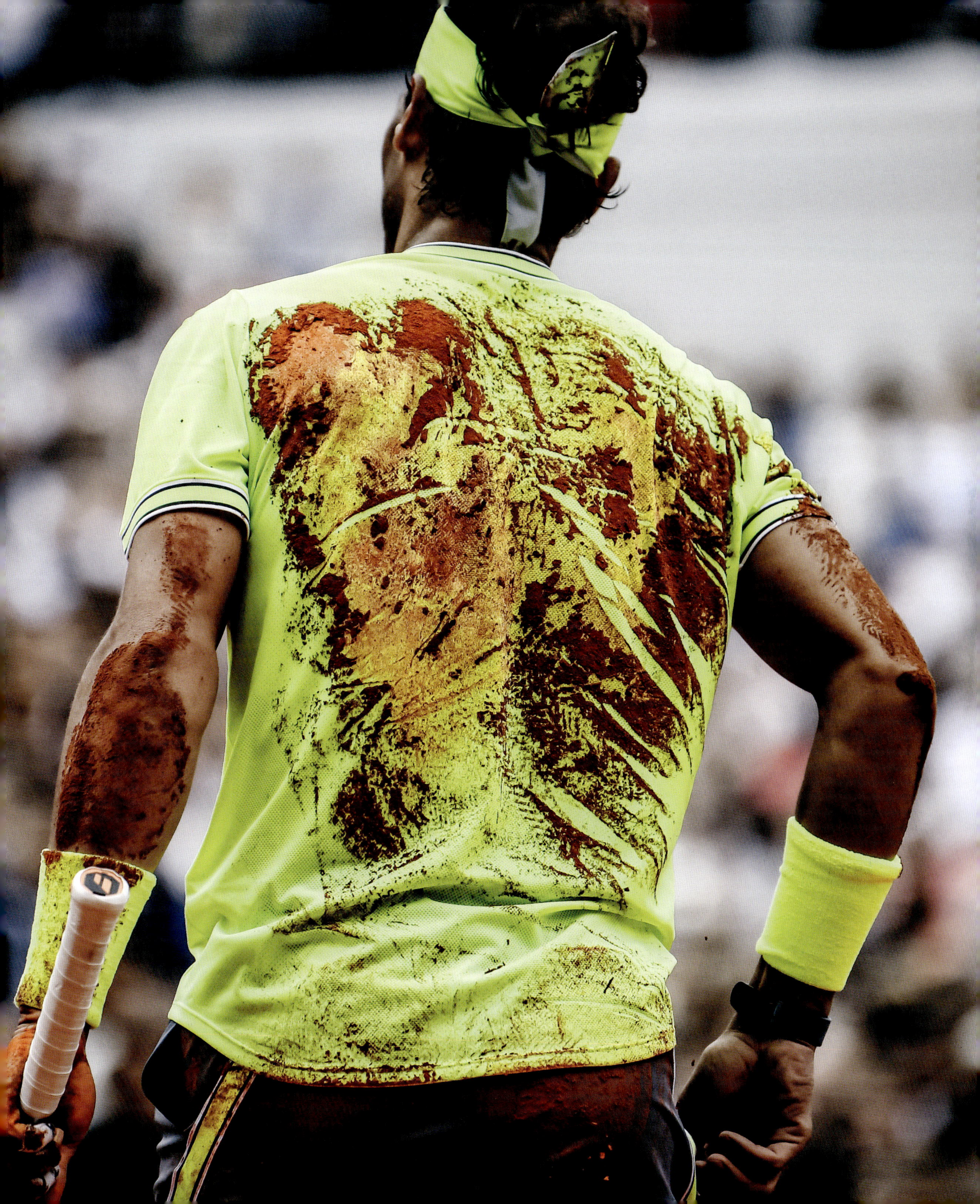

"AS A YOUNG PERSON, I WAS STRIVING TO UNDERSTAND MY OWN IDENTITY. MY PROCESS WAS ALWAYS ORGANIC AND AUTHENTIC. HUMAN BEINGS ARE INSPIRED WHEN THEY ARE CHALLENGED WITH SOMETHING THAT TAKES THEM TO ANOTHER LEVEL. IF IT'S NOT REAL, PEOPLE DON'T BUY INTO IT."

—ANDRE AGASSI

ON AGASSI

WS: Agassi's favorite looks were his jean shorts, and the "hot lava" spandex under denim shorts with the matching sneakers. He told the president of the French Tennis Federation who was considering a dress code that he was a "bozo."

Our design ethos for him was "waking up the country club," and there was this "irreverence justified" motto that was used for him. His story started in 1990, when he was playing in the US Open. He lost to Pete Sampras in the final. There were some central design moments. The first was, there was this whole thing about him not playing at Wimbledon—because of the white rule—and then he did, and they all thought that we were going to buck the system, but we made his whole look so clean and light, which was super expressive.

WS: I was inspired one time watching Agassi play as I was designing his signature shoe. There was this way that he did his wheelhouse forehand return that was up and over; it looked quite explosive. The line of that movement was expressed on the shoe. On another design we made the Swoosh backward, which was also translated by his game. Initially we generated his whole hyper-crisp neon color and pattern story, which was a response to the grunge culture of the time, like Nirvana, and this very mismatched look worked well with him. From a style expression, we used the neon colors and culture often; it worked well in tennis. Agassi would totally get the designs.

Toward the end of the 1990s, we changed Agassi's designs. He said that he didn't want to be so expressive and do brights anymore, he wanted to be more stealth. He didn't even want to be seen in the peripheral vision of his opponents, because he was trying to get every little advantage in his play. From 1999 to 2003, he won five out of his eight Grand Slam championships.

ON THE REMAINING NIKE PLAYERS

WS: We have these personality contrasts of like Andre and Pete [Sampras], then Rafael [Nadal] and Roger [Federer]. The lineage is in the same places—we could say of maybe [Carlos] Alcaraz and [Jannik] Sinner that it reflects the contrast in their personalities. Roger's inspiration came from James Bond, sharks; he was this North Star of sophistication. With Rafa, he was this James Dean character, with the bull and its power to destroy. When I was working with Roger and crafting his story, we would look at his play on different court surfaces. The amazing thing was when Roger moved on clay, his shoes were completely clean, because he had this fluidity of movement on the tennis court surface. But in contrast you look at Rafa's shoes, and his would be all covered in red clay. We designed the Rafa Bull Logo with him, same with Roger and Serena Williams, signature athletes had their own logo.

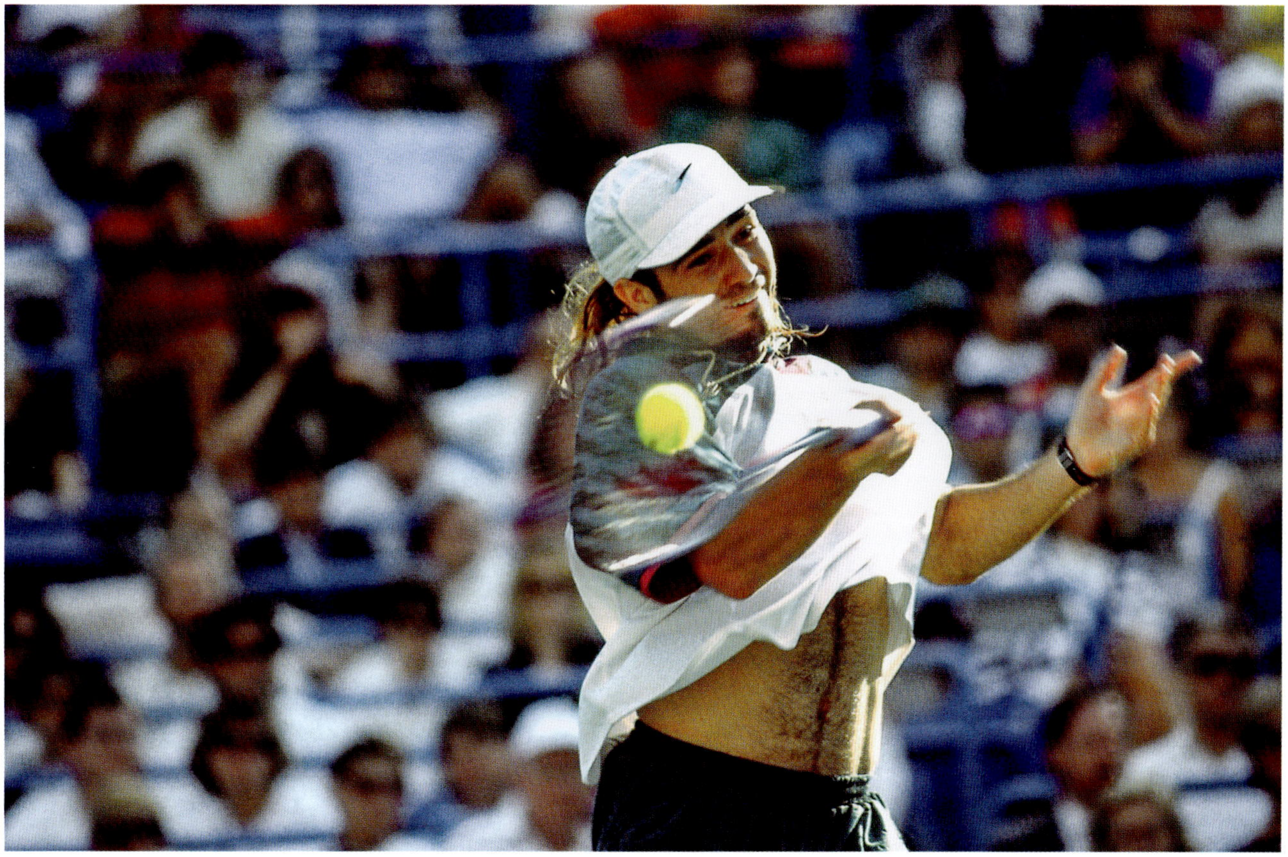

WheeLHouse foReHand

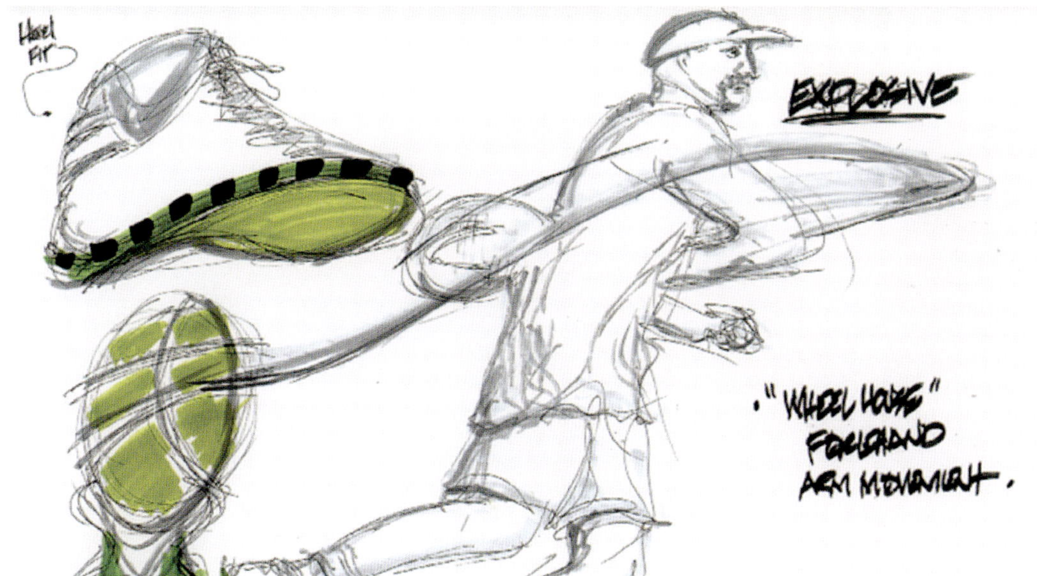

up & oveR

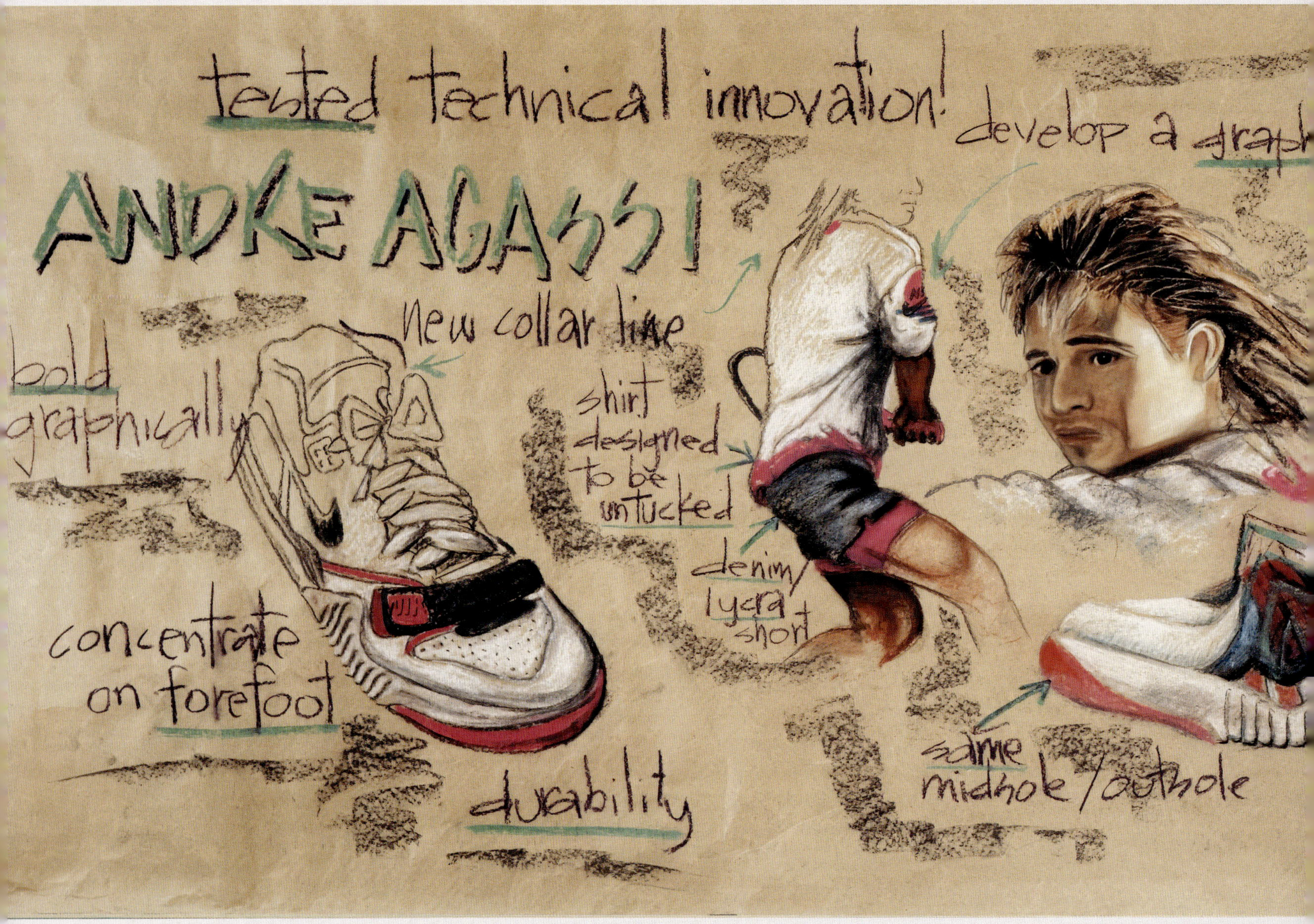
tested technical innovation!
develop a graph
ANDRE AGASSI
new collar line
bold graphically
shirt designed to be untucked
denim/lycra short
concentrate on forefoot
durability
same midsole/outsole

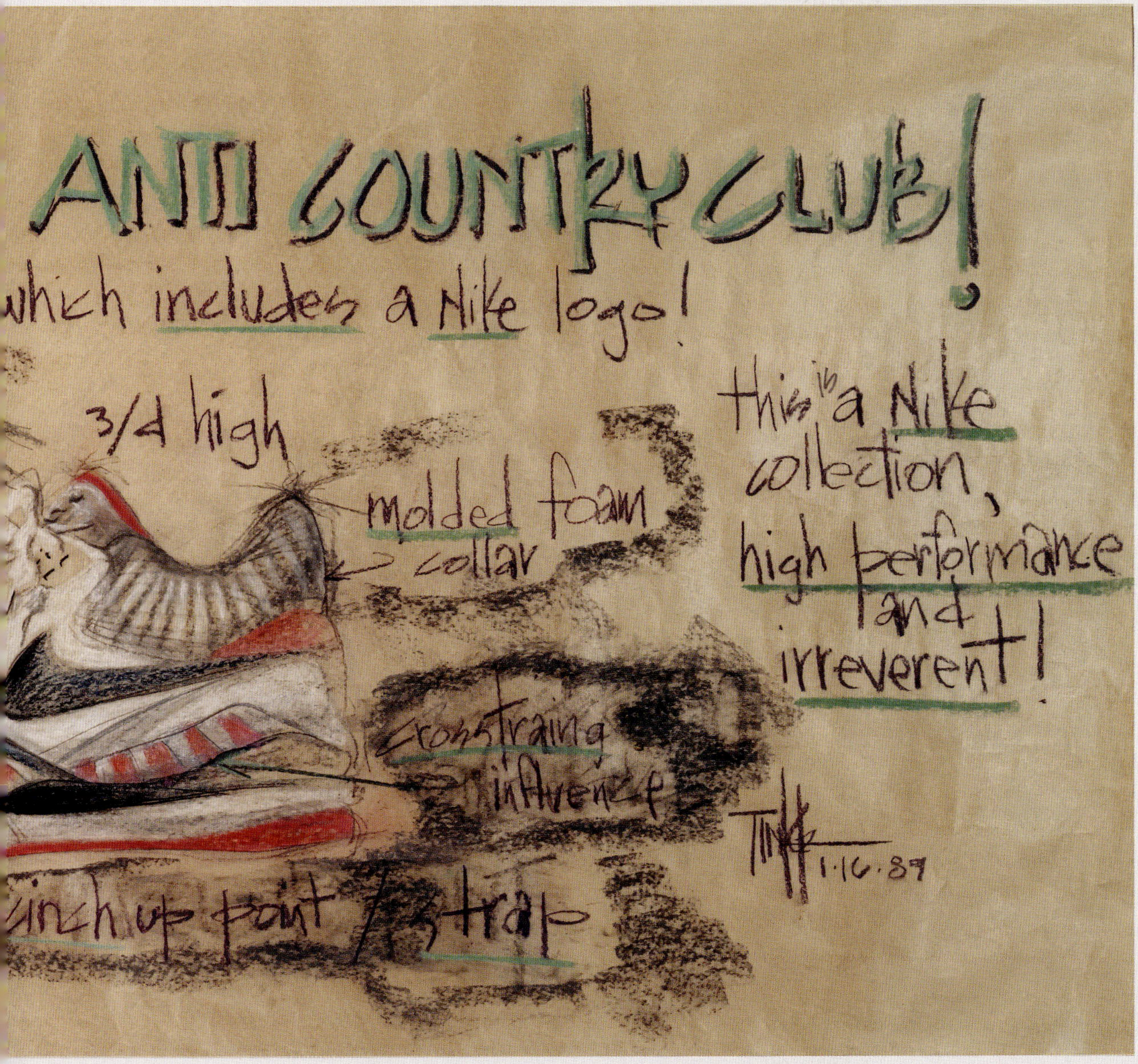
ANTI COUNTRY CLUB!
which includes a Nike logo!
3/4 high
molded foam collar
this is a Nike collection, high performance and irreverent!
Crosstraing influence
inch up point / strap
1.16.89

agassi nike history

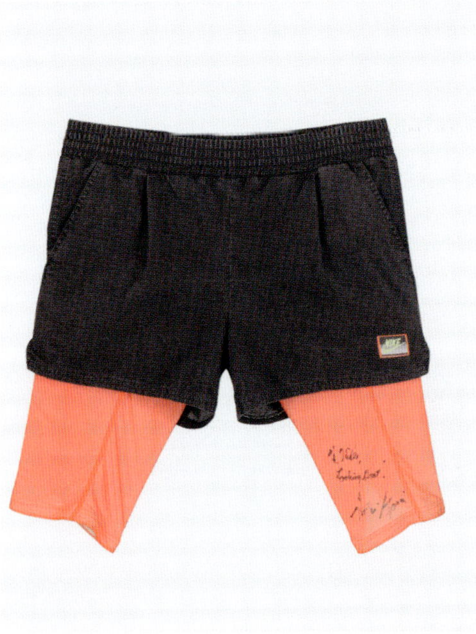
001

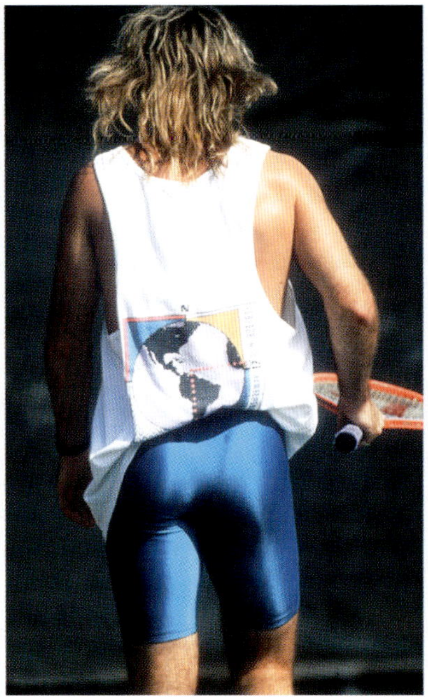
002

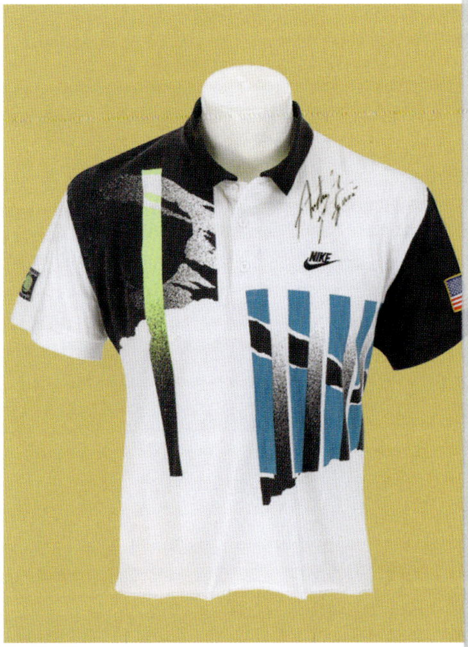

003

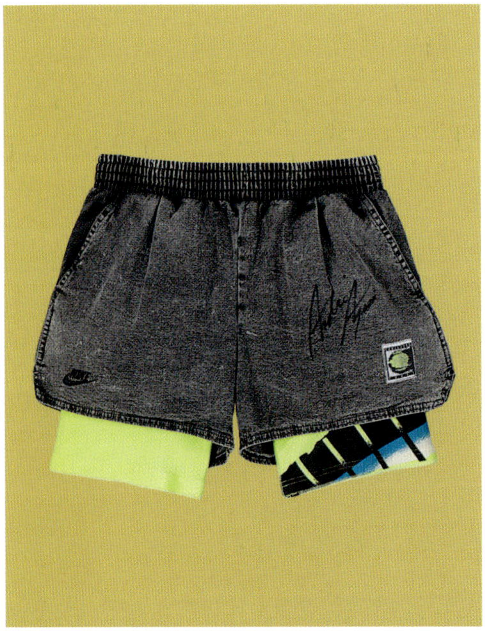
004

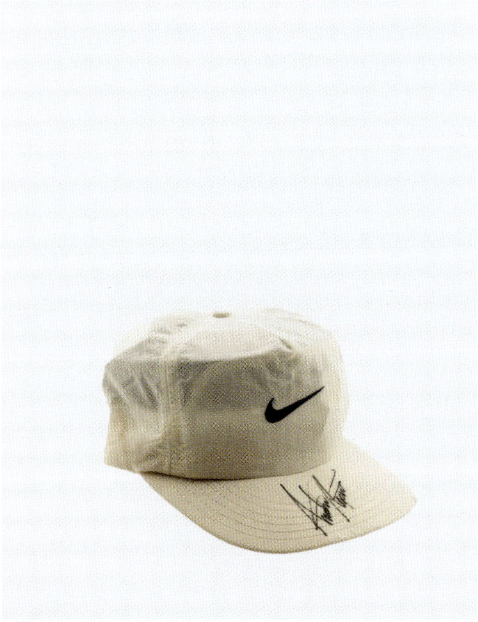
005

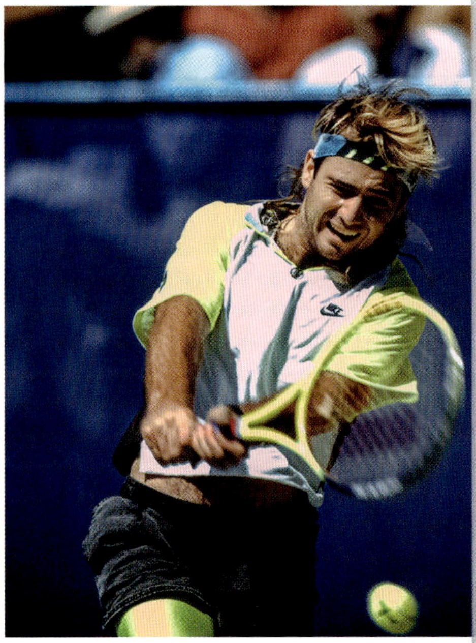
006

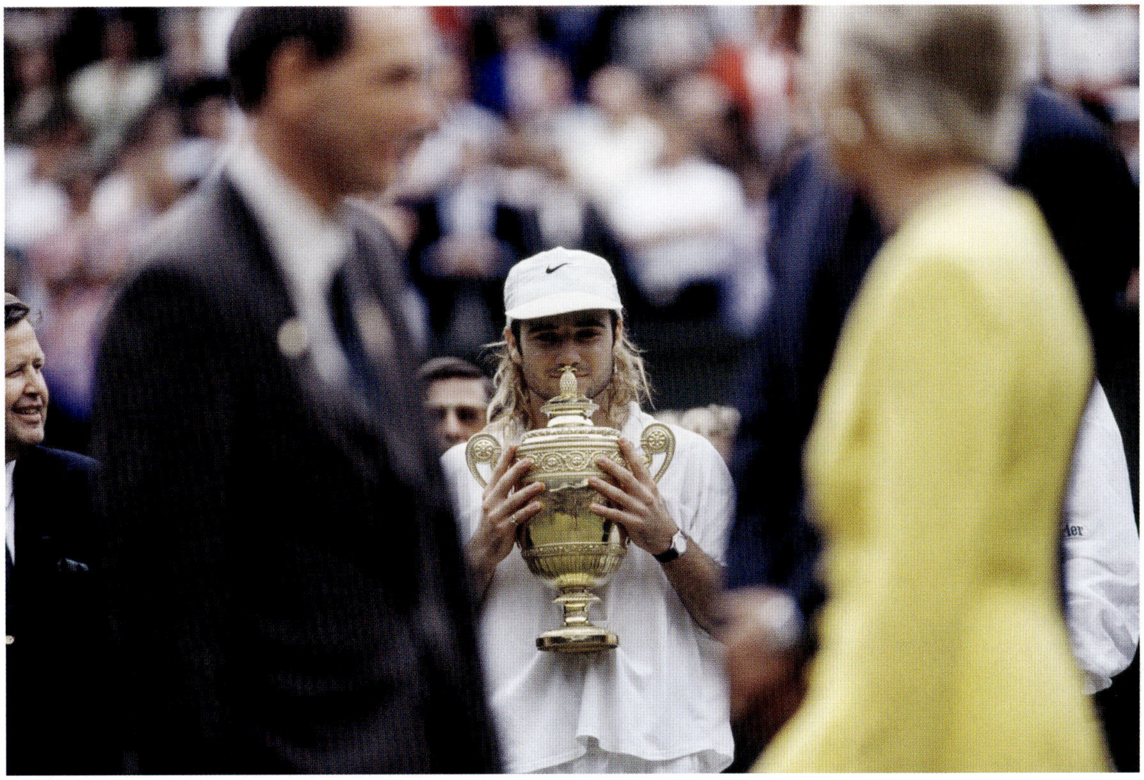

"This look was a moment in Nike history, because it was the first time the swoosh was just embroidered on the hat without the word Nike next to it. We did it to follow Wimbledon rules. Andre wins Wimbledon, and then you have this swoosh hat that he wears with the trophy, and that becomes the identity of the company rather than the name. Our athletes often lead the story."
-Wilson W. Smith III

001: FRENCH OPEN STATEMENT LINER SHORTS, 1990

002: SIGNATURE NEON LYCRA, 1991

003: STATEMENT COURT POLO, 1991

004: STATEMENT LINER SHORTS, 1991

005: SWOOSH HAT, 1992

006: 1991 US OPEN

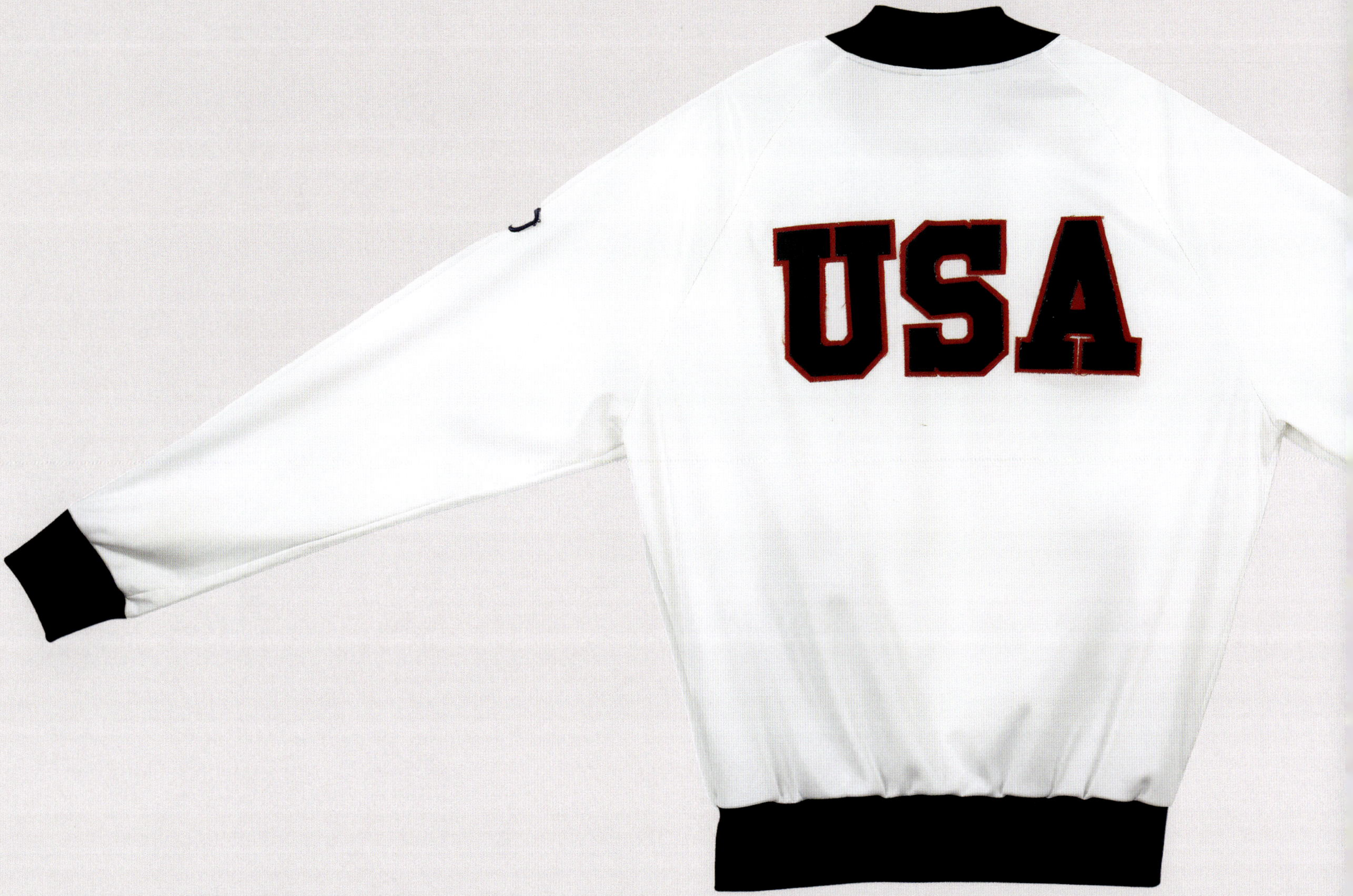
USA

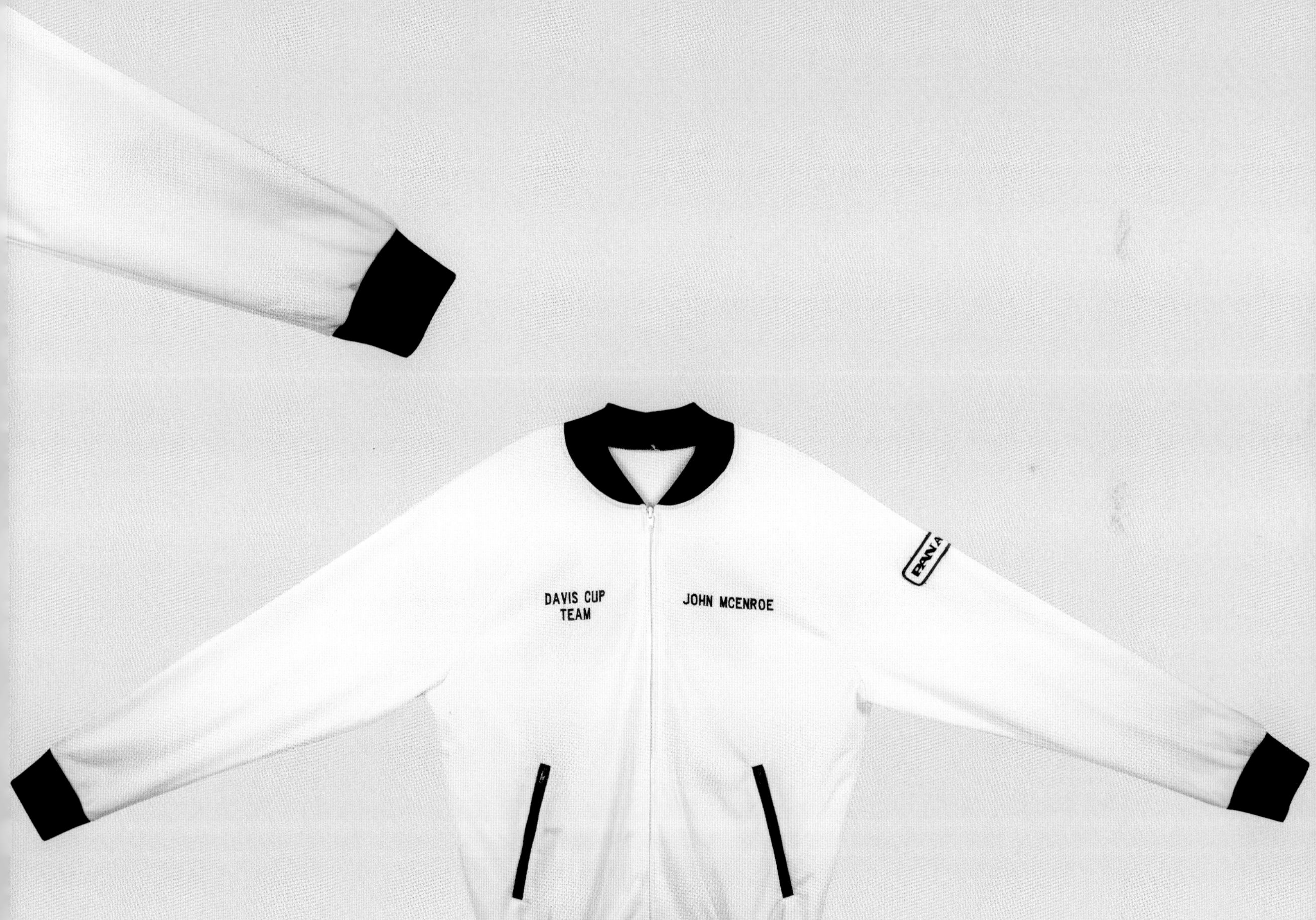
DAVIS CUP
TEAM
JOHN MCENROE

NAOMI OSAKA

NAOMI OSAKA IS A HEAVY-HITTING BASELINER WITH FOUR GRAND SLAM WINS.

SKN: Naomi, you've said that much like writing, fashion allows you to express sides of yourself that aren't always visible on court. How has fashion helped you tell that story—and in turn, how do you feel you've helped shape fashion?

NO: I love the opportunity for storytelling through fashion. I'm so lucky that Nike allows me so much creative freedom with my on-court looks. This year, we created a flower storyline that tied together my grand slam looks, starting with sunflowers at the Australian Open, then cherry blossoms at Roland-Garros, and ending with roses at the US Open. Tennis can be so serious at times, so it's nice to add playful elements where we can.

SKN: The Labubu seemed to bring this joy and playfulness to your look, and it felt like you carried this in your game. Are these extensions of you as a mother?

NO: I'd like to think that joy and playfulness are traits that I apply to being a mother. The Labubus were a ton of fun this year. I'm so glad that everyone seemed to enjoy it as much as I did.

SKN: You've been open about struggles, and your recent honesty about postpartum felt rare in a world where athletes are often expected to project only stoicism. *ACE* looks at how style in tennis has mirrored women's fight for freedom—of movement, identity, and voice—from restrictive dress codes to athletes challenging today's stigmas. How does your path as a player and a mother connect to that larger story?

NO: I like to think of the tennis court as a stage, and we are entertainers. Sure, we are entertaining by playing tennis, but I also enjoy being creative with all of the other details that I can control, whether it be my hair, my outfit, accessories, etcetera. I think that people all over the world utilize their style and fashion to express how they feel or even help channel a particular feeling. When I have a great outfit on, I feel my strongest and most confident, which I think directly correlates with me playing my best tennis.

SKN: This book is called *ACE*. What does the word mean to you?

NO: Obviously an ace in tennis is the best serve you can hit. I sort of try to apply that mantra in everything I do—whether it's the way I dress, or the way I parent, or anything else I'm working on. I always want to put forward the best possible version of whatever I'm doing. I always want to ace it.

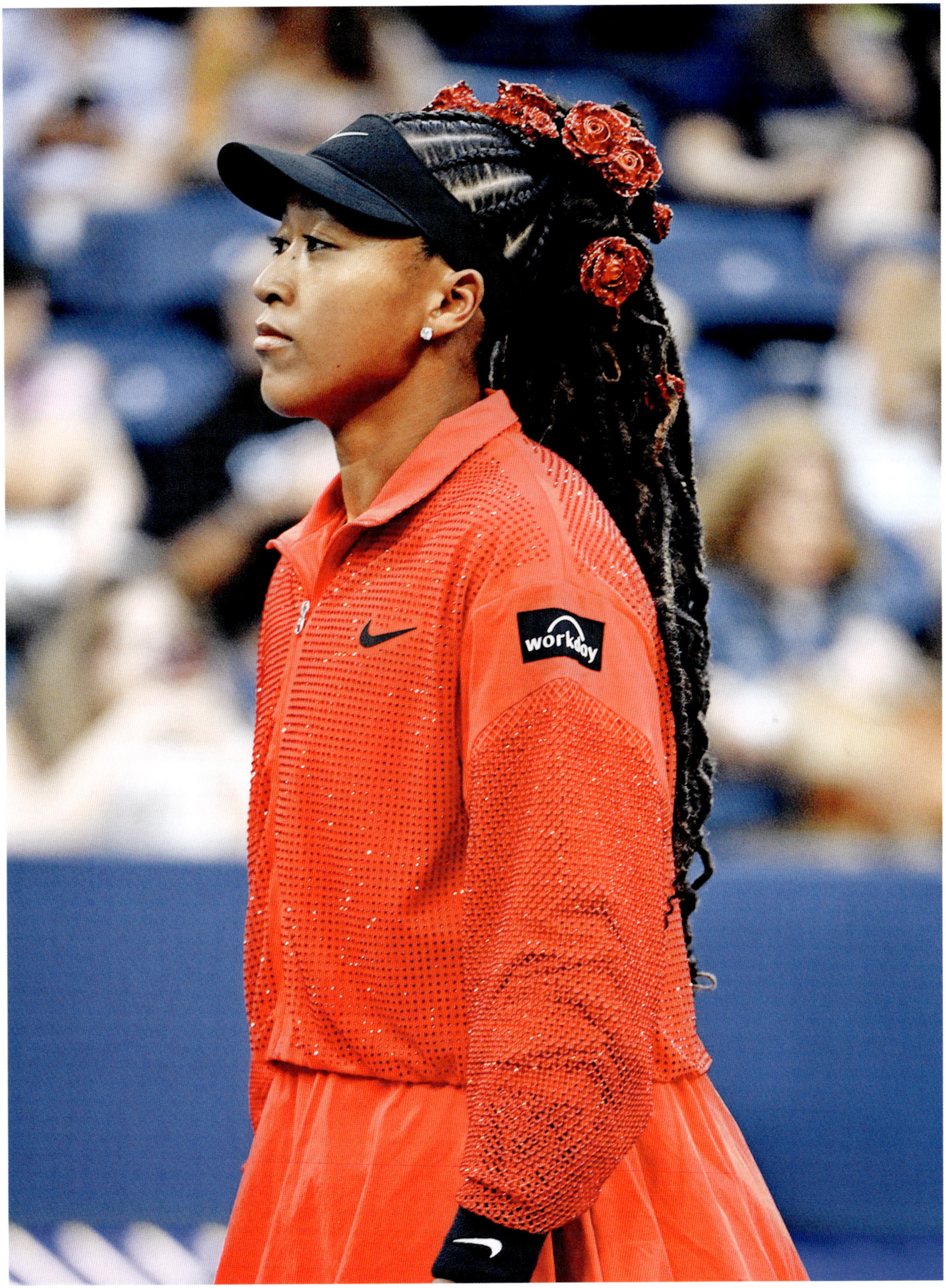
workday

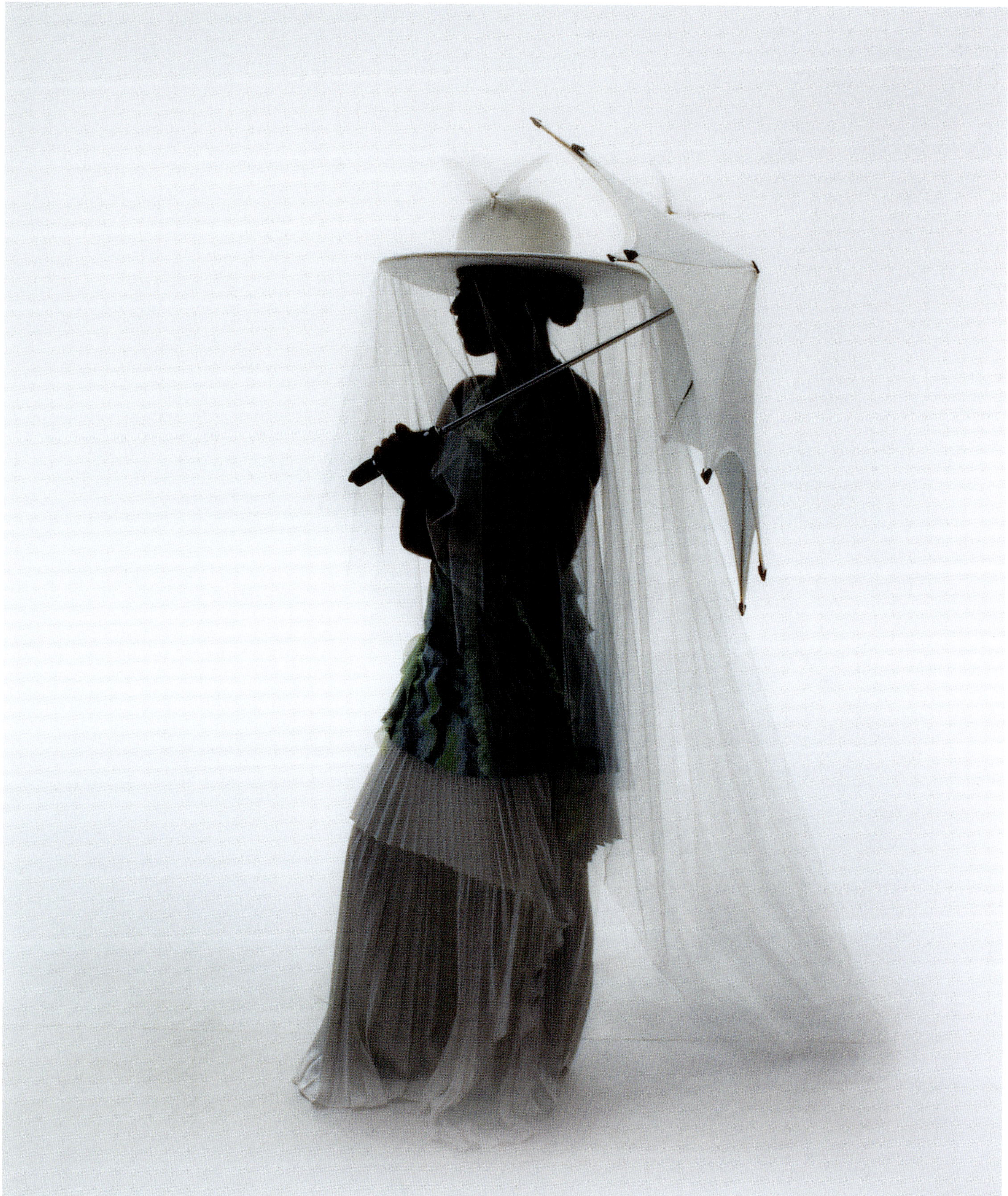

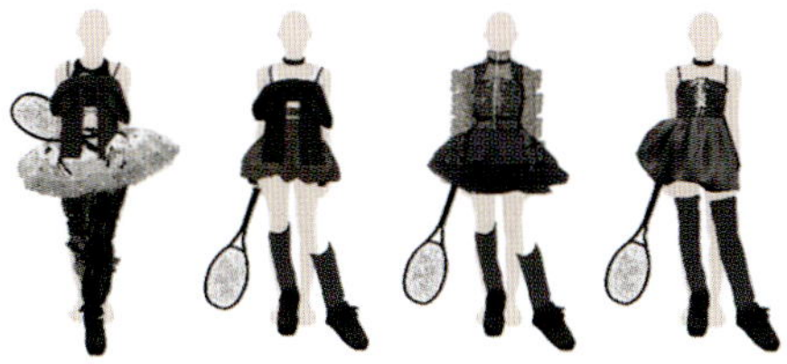

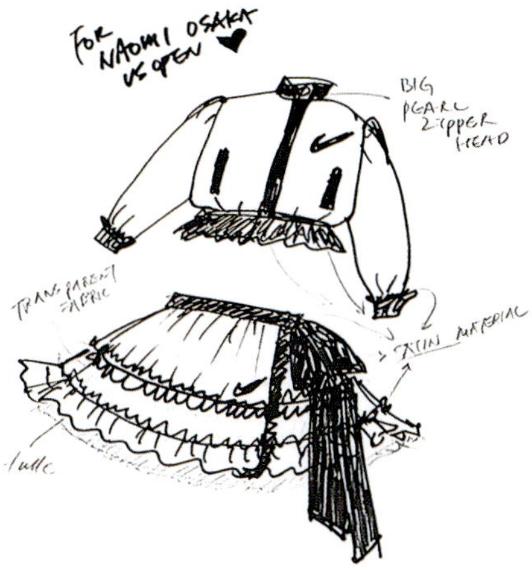

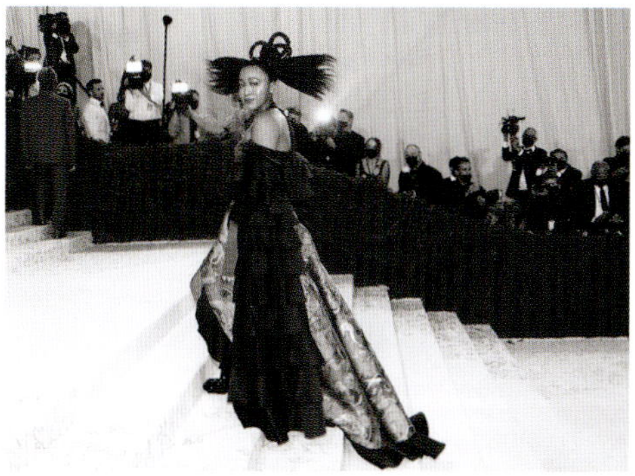

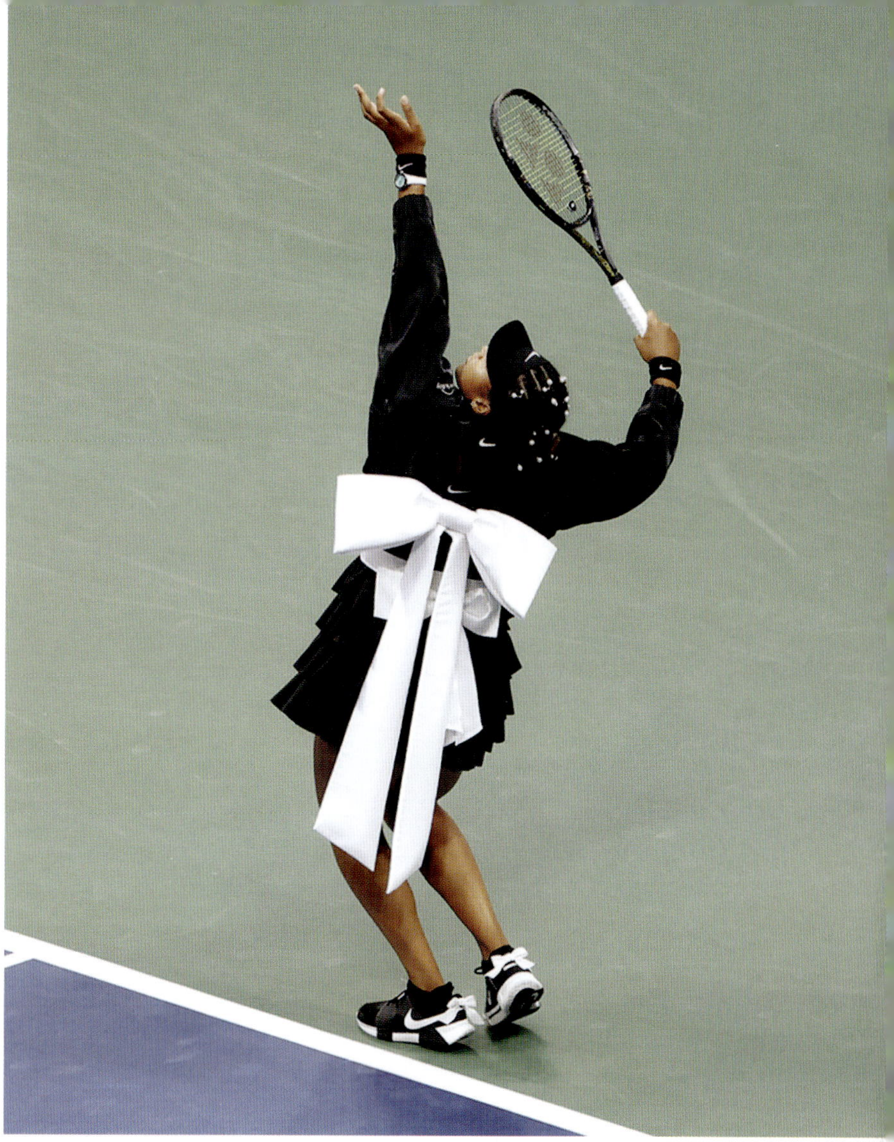

"I FEEL LIKE BEING ABLE TO BE A PART OF MY TENNIS OUTFITS GIVES ME . . . A DIFFERENT STRENGTH, LIKE A SUPER SUIT, SO I TRY TO CHANNEL THAT."

—NAOMI OSAKA

THE HIDDEN OMENS THAT SIGNAL A PLAYER'S LUCK CAN OFTEN INSPIRE DESIGNERS TO INTERLACE THEIR WORK WITH THESE ELUSIVE CHARMS. A BUTTERFLY PEACEFULLY LANDING ON OSAKA'S FACE MAY HAVE BEEN NOTHING MORE THAN JUST THAT—OR PERHAPS, A PREMONITION OF HER AUSTRALIAN OPEN VICTORY IN 2021. COUTURIER ROBERT WUN DREW ON THIS SIGN FOR THE DESIGN OF HER 2026 AO KIT, PINNING A SILK BUTTERFLY TO OSAKA'S PARASOL AND WIDE-BRIMMED VEILED HAT. HIS PALAZZO PANTS OSCILLATED WITH A SUBTLE FLUIDITY AS SHE WALKED ON COURT, AND HER NIKE TURQUOISE-DYED TOP ECHOED THE SAME, BOTH CHANNELING THE BUOYANCY OF A JELLYFISH. THE FULL SILHOUETTE READ LIKE EDWARDIAN-ERA GARDEN PARTY ATTIRE, THE VERY GARMENTS SPORTSWOMEN ONCE SOUGHT AND FOUGHT TO FREE THEMSELVES FROM IN THE 1920S. BUT A CENTURY LATER, OSAKA RECONTEXTUALIZES THE LOOK IN HER OWN TERMS, WITH THE CRAFT OF BOTH A COUTURIER AND SPORTSWEAR GIANT—A TRIBUTE TO THOSE WHO MADE HER CHOICE POSSIBLE.

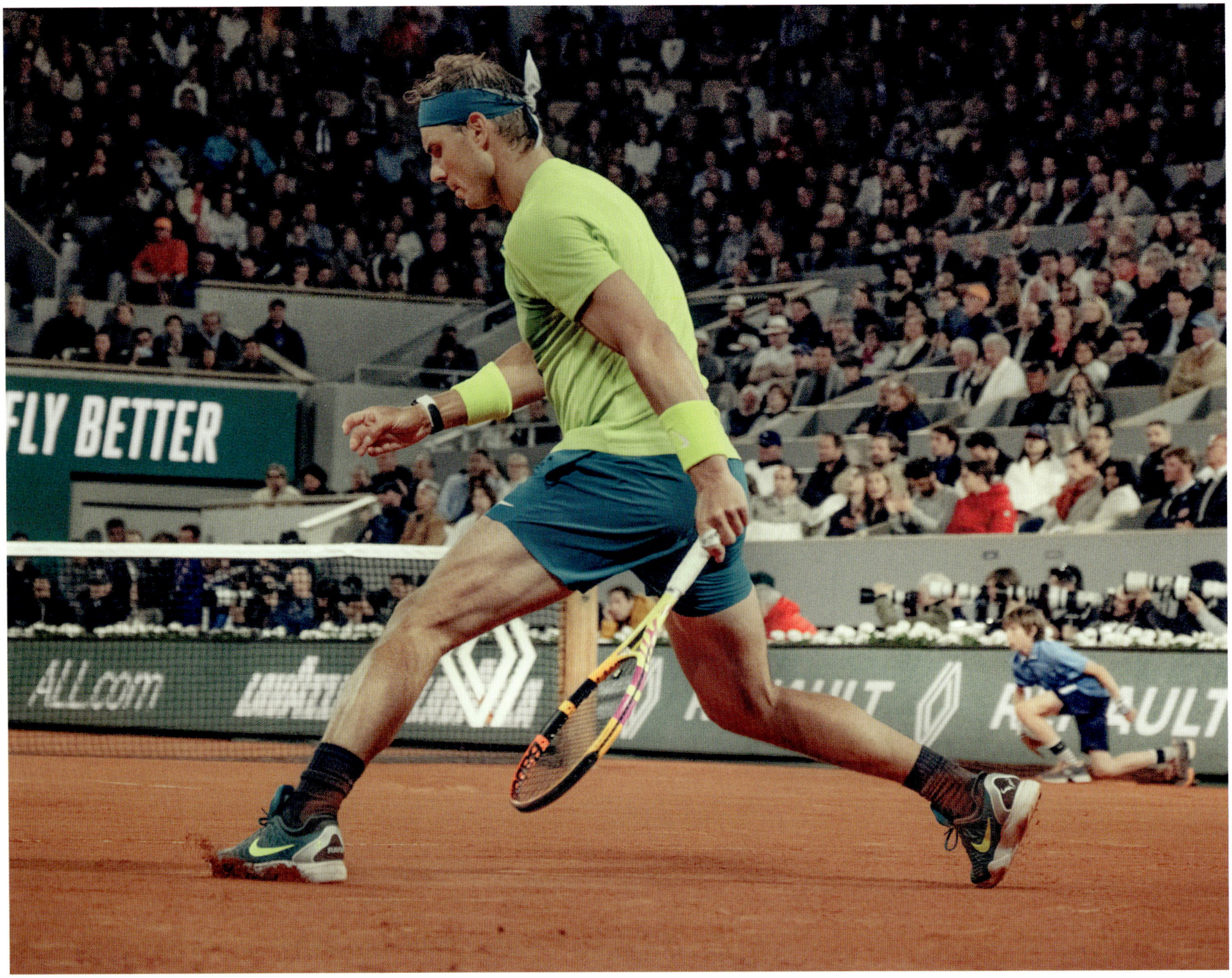
FLY BETTER
ALL.com

RAFAEL NADAL

RAFAEL NADAL IS A LEFT-HANDED BASELINE PLAYER WITH EXPLOSIVE TOPSIN. HE HAS TWENTY-TWO GRAND SLAM WINS AND ONE OLYMPIC GOLD MEDAL.

Repel or attract—the colorway of a flower, insect, or animal can either signal danger to a predator or broadcast health, virility, and dominance. In sport, the effect is arguably the same. Bright colors can serve as a psychological cue, reminding opponents of a player's prowess—certain hues carry scientific weight—or they create a halo effect, turning the athlete into a visual magnet for the masses. Rafael Nadal embraced color—the bolder, the better. And even when clad in black, his neon emblem of a stylized raging bull would ignite the design. Some palettes were subtler, echoing the soft hues of the Majorcan sunrise of his home. But always, his play mirrored the energy of the colors he wore: electric, defiant, unmistakably his. Like the innate toreador Rafa is, he left crowds roaring his name.

"I FEEL GOOD WHEN I SEE FANS WEAR MY LOGOS, BECAUSE THEY ARE SUPPORTING ME."

—RAFAEL NADAL

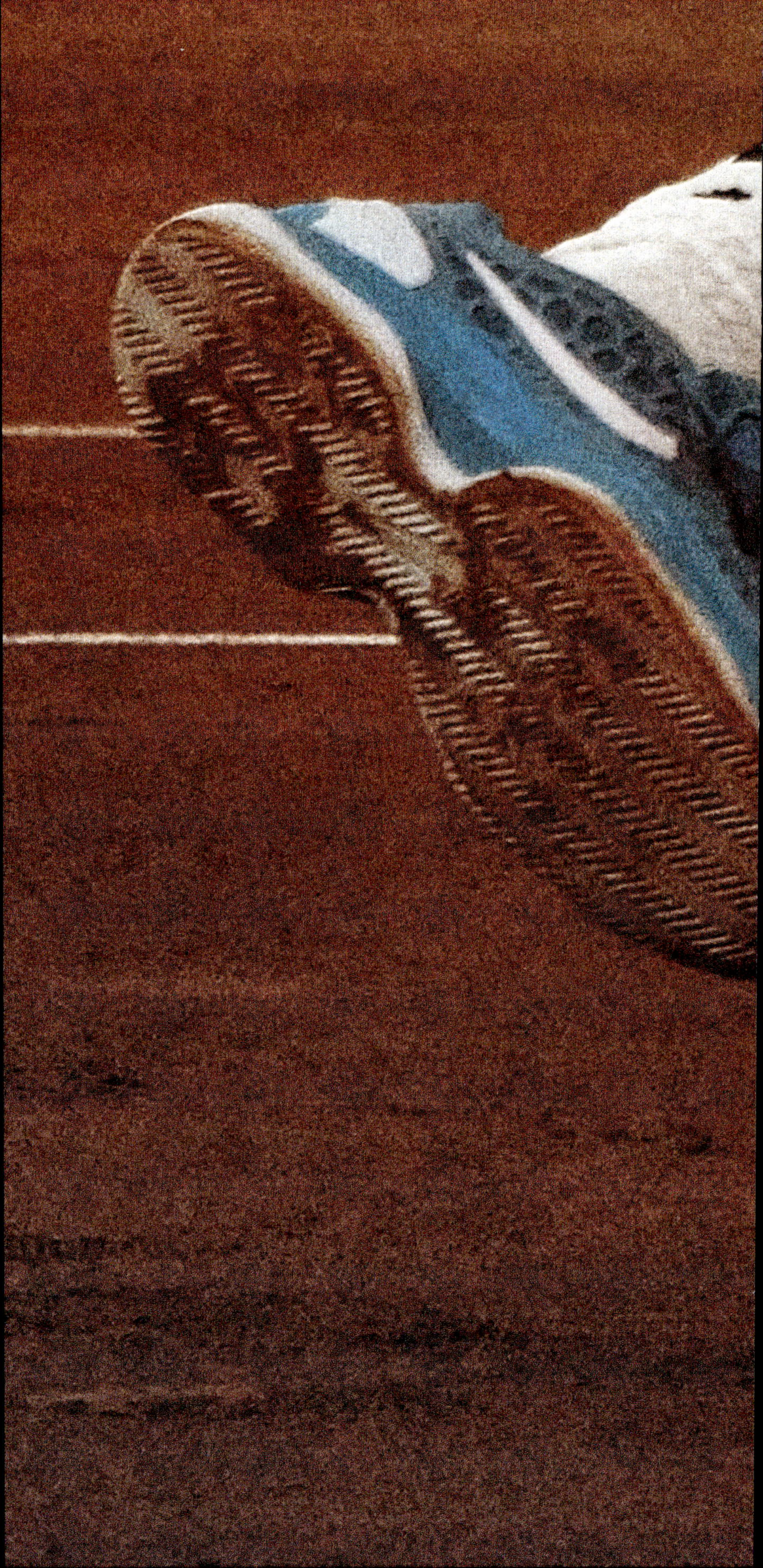

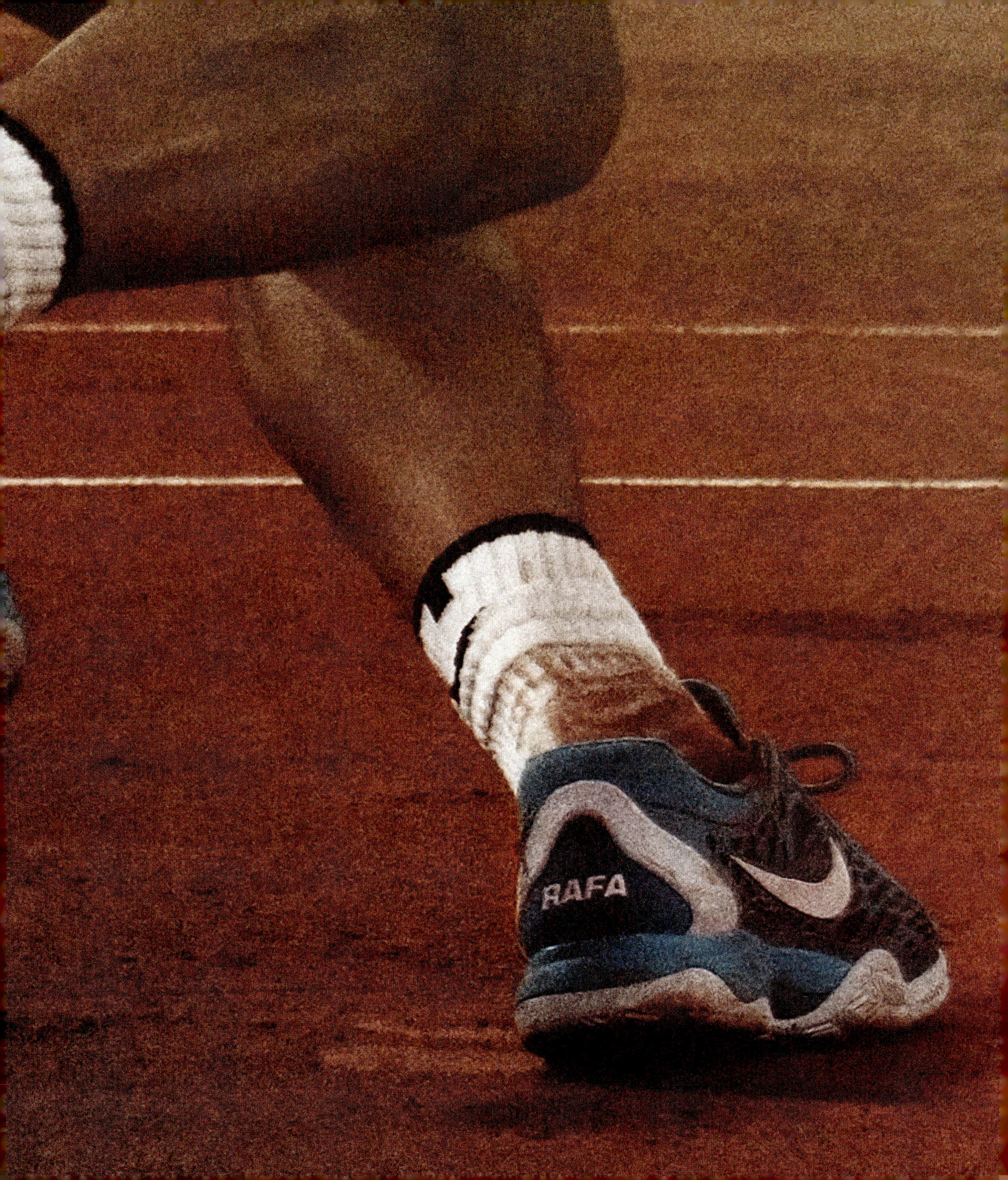
RAFA

SERENA WILLIAMS

SERENA WILLIAMS PLAYS AN ALL-ROUND, TECHNICALLY FORMIDABLE GAME AND HAS WON TWENTY-THREE GRAND SLAMS AND ONE OLYMPIC GOLD MEDAL.

SPEAKERS

WS: WILSON W. SMITH III,
Design Director, Nike Tennis Footwear

ON SERENA WILLIAMS

WS: I was with the Jordan brand for six years when I came back to tennis. I was so excited to work with Serena. We signed her in 2003. At the time, Nike was not intent on making fashion as a lead, but Serena was more fashion-driven. We were excited to listen to her voice.

Nike's [then] CEO Mark Parker, who was also a former designer, had advised me to let her sense of fashion and style lead the innovation, which was a new way of approaching the designs we had created. At Nike, we listen to the voice of the athlete and their different style thoughts. Michael Jordan was a strong visionary and curator when it came to design thinking, whereas Andre Agassi appreciated and understood the design with his cool perspective. And then Serena Williams studied fashion, so she is actually a lead designer in the process. But as designers, we are always articulating an athlete's vision, expressing or reinterpreting it.

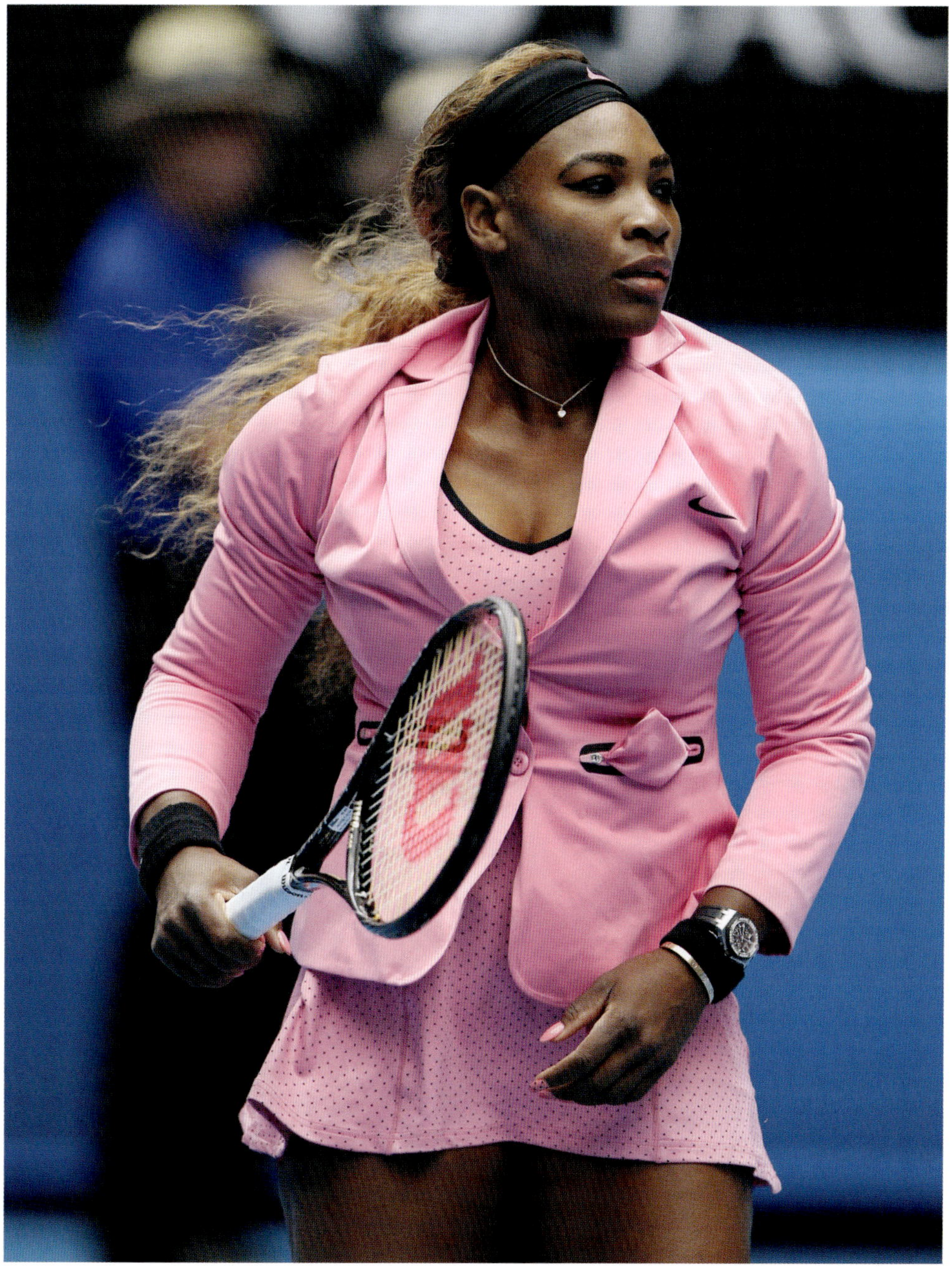

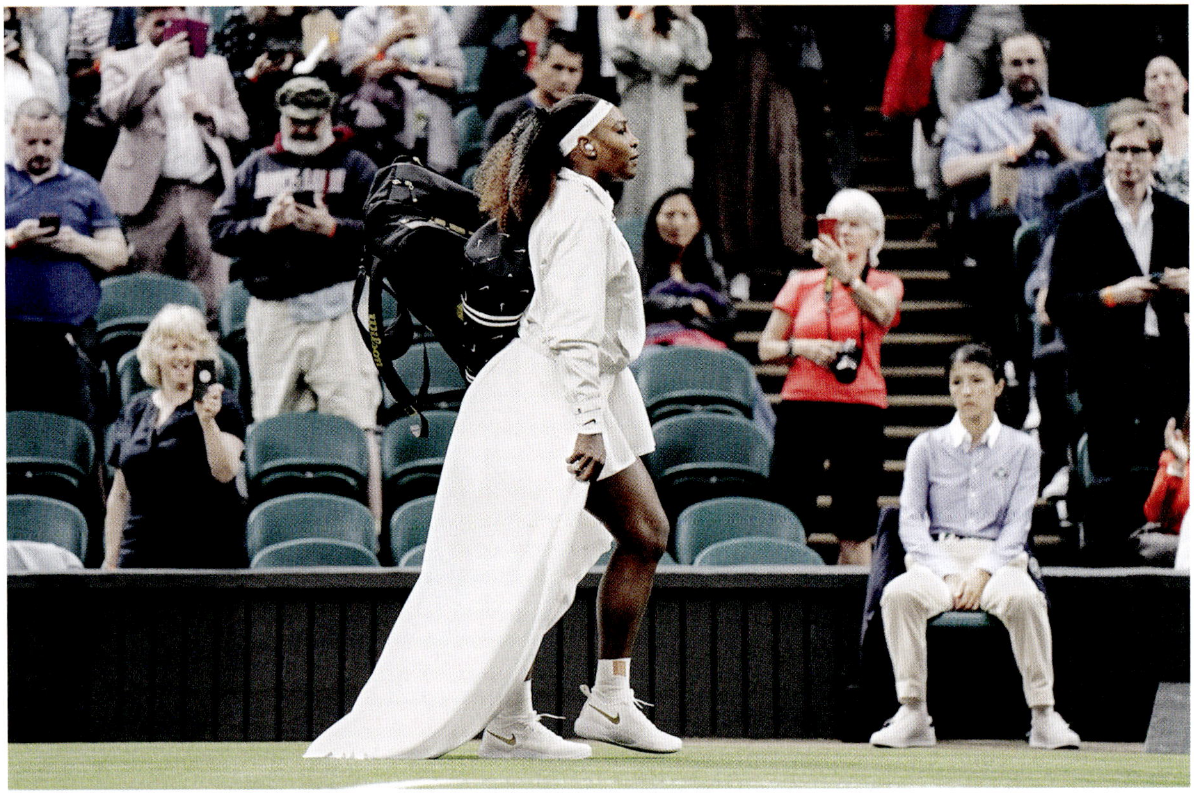

ON DESIGNING THE TENNIS BOOT

WS: In 2003–2004, there were words that we used to describe Serena—**sleek**, **strappy**, **sexy**, **stunning**—that were inspiring my work. At the time, we had ten months to debut the shoe and apparel for the 2004 US Open. For **sleek** and **strappy**, we were inspired around support and stability but with higher-end couture design expressions. **Sexy** was about me thinking of her comfort. I always saw her wearing boots, so that got me thinking, how about a tennis shoe that turns into two different things? A boot—but zip it off, and it is a shoe underneath. And then when I was thinking of the **stunning** part, I wanted to add details. Serena loved Dolce & Gabbana and flowers, so we added that as a version to our concept. Overall, we were looking at a reinforced sock, like a spat. I asked Nike innovation, what do you think of a tennis boot? And they said, well, what if you design it like a compression sock, that could help warm her up to prevent cramping? So that became the performance insight. The whole look became urban style.

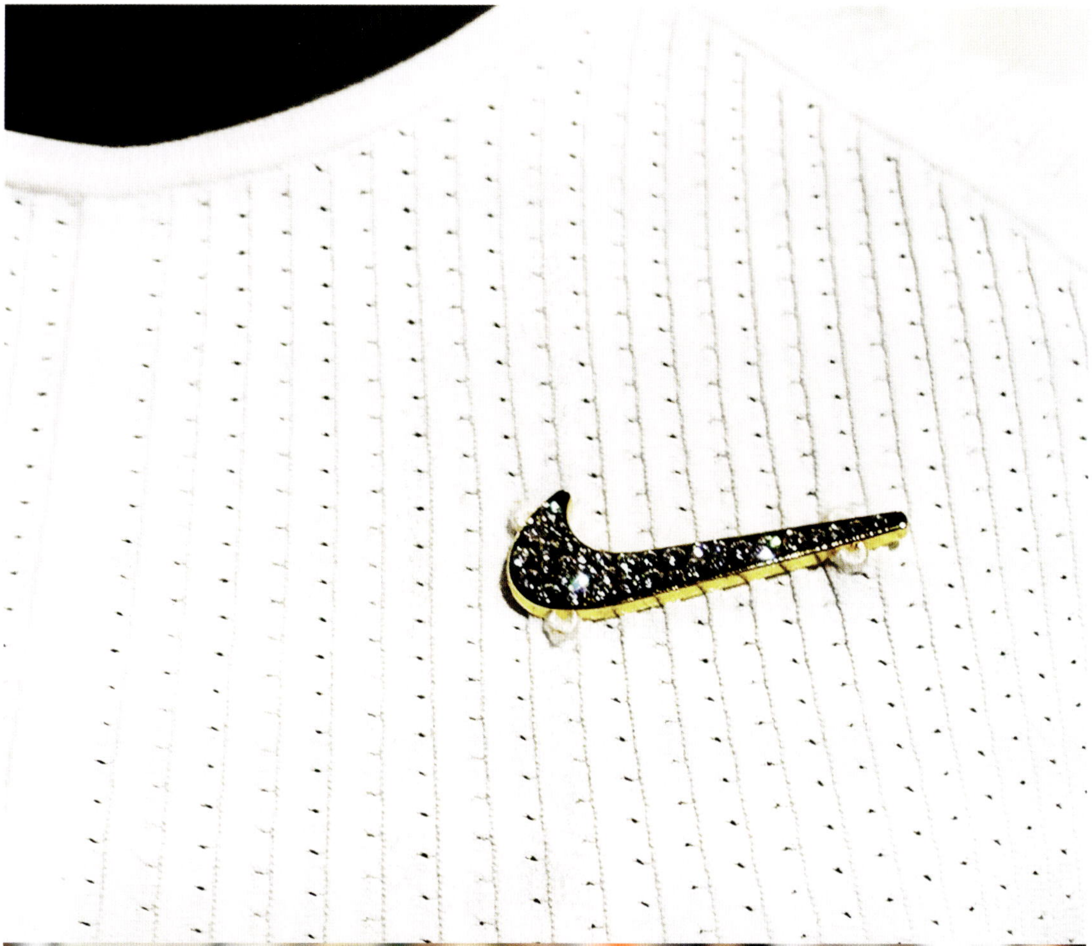

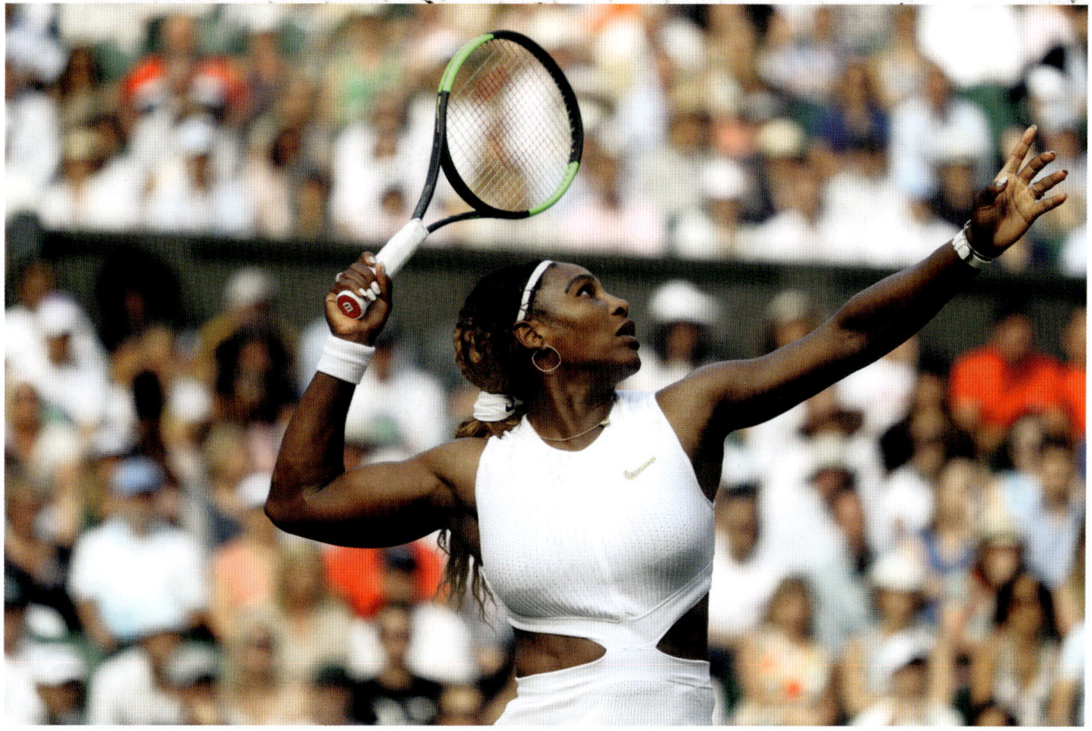

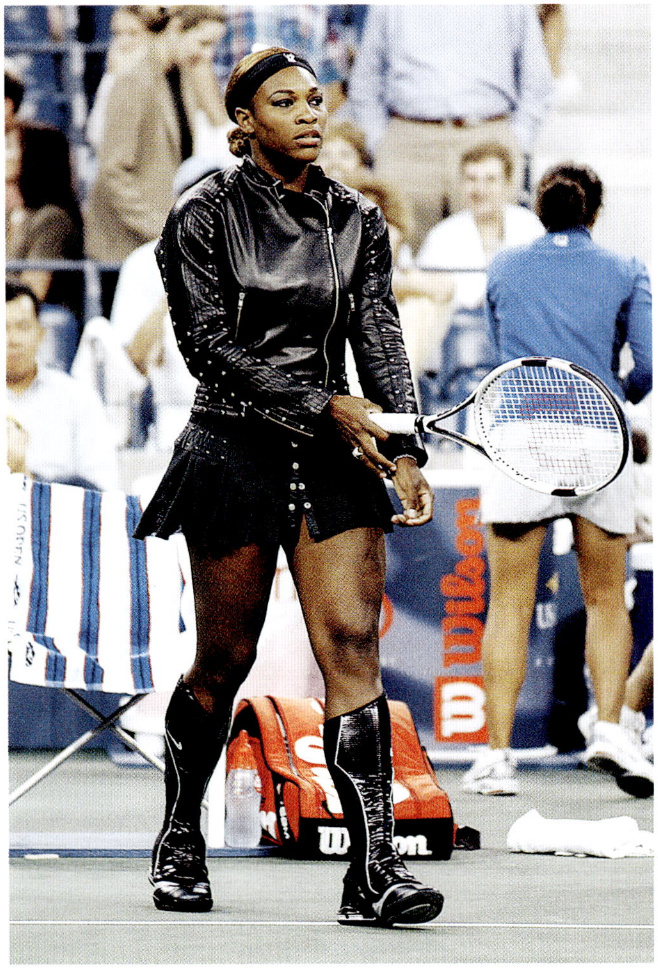

"THE DAY I STOP FIGHTING FOR EQUALITY IS THE DAY I WILL BE IN MY GRAVE."

—SERENA WILLIAMS

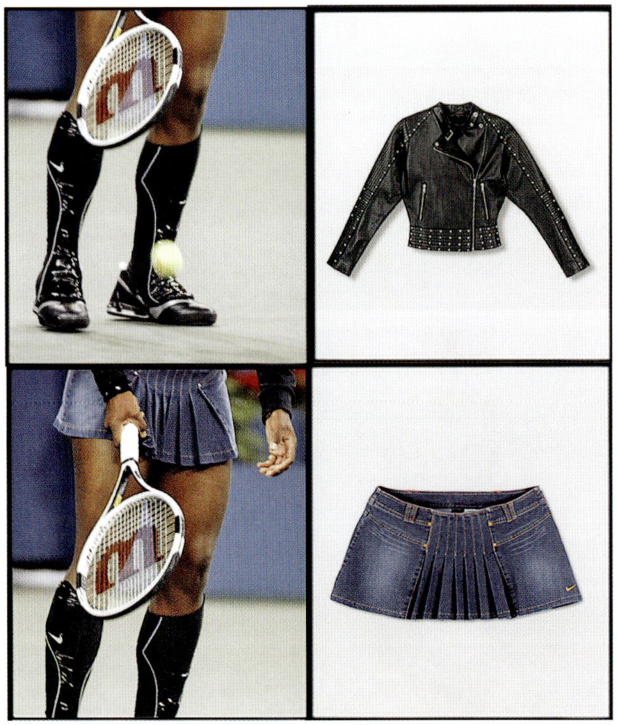

"I HAD JUST MOVED TO NIKE. I WANTED MORE PIZAZZ IN MY OUTFITS, AND I LOVED WHAT ANDRE AGASSI WORE, LIKE THOSE JEAN SHORTS. I WANTED A JEAN SKIRT, WHICH WAS THIS VERY LIGHT FABRIC, AND THEN I WORE THESE AMAZING BOOTS BY WILSON—HE DESIGNED THE BEST SHOES I HAD EVER WORN IN MY LIFE, AND FROM THAT DAY ON I WAS SEALED AS A FASHION ICON IN TENNIS, SINCE THAT DAY THEY WERE LIKE, 'WHAT IS SERENA WEARING ON COURT?'"

—SERENA WILLIAMS

SKN: Why hasn't there been an Air Jordan moment in the tennis world? I would say Serena has the same attraction value as Michael Jordan.

WS: That's a really good question—I think it lined up best with Agassi in the early '90s. That was a pretty strong story not unlike the Air Jordans. A couple of factors: This was before the cross-training shoe for aerobics and running became the casual shoe of choice. People looked at tennis shoes as being the "street shoe of choice" before trainers. The Air Jordan was so aligned with communities that were alpha consumers; Michael Jordan becomes the hope and inspiration for a young black person. The aspirations for my culture and the heroes in our community were different in my time. Like owning a nice car, for example, which meant you made it in life. Then suddenly Michael Jordan hands out an accessible transportation item—a dream of making it, of being part of a bigger cultural story, being a hero in your community—with a pair of shoes. It just worked.

SKN: Do you also think it hasn't happened because the majority of tennis club women were and are from a specific social set, where there is little diversity?

WS: There is a cultural connection to tennis, and so far it isn't as connected to diverse communities. Serena is amazing, but there was a disconnect, and maybe the ladies on the tennis court didn't identify with her. For me, I have always wanted to represent the diversity in design for future generations.

Serena has this energy—she knows that her celebrity is beyond tennis, that it needs to have an impact in a lot of settings. I became the mentor and lead of the Serena Williams design crew for the last five years, and each year we focused on a different cohort of designers across America. Nike has since hired seven to ten new design apprentices for that crew each year. It's helping to diversify the design force.

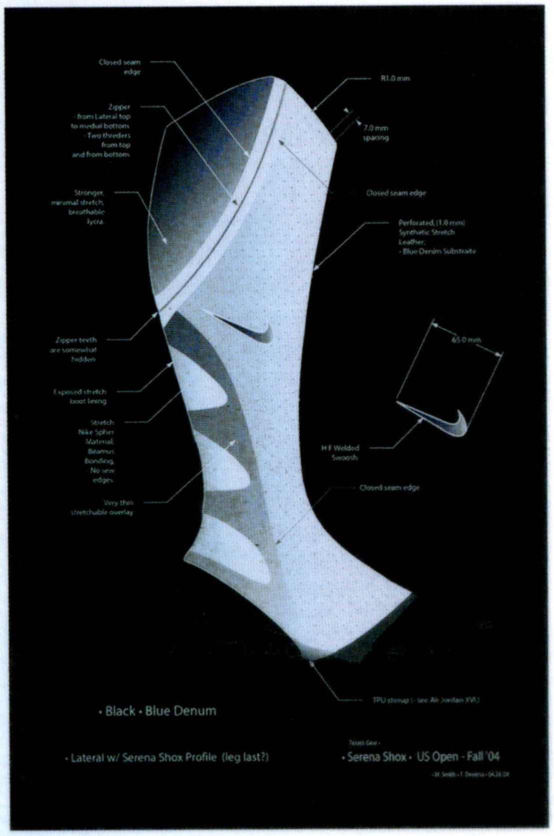

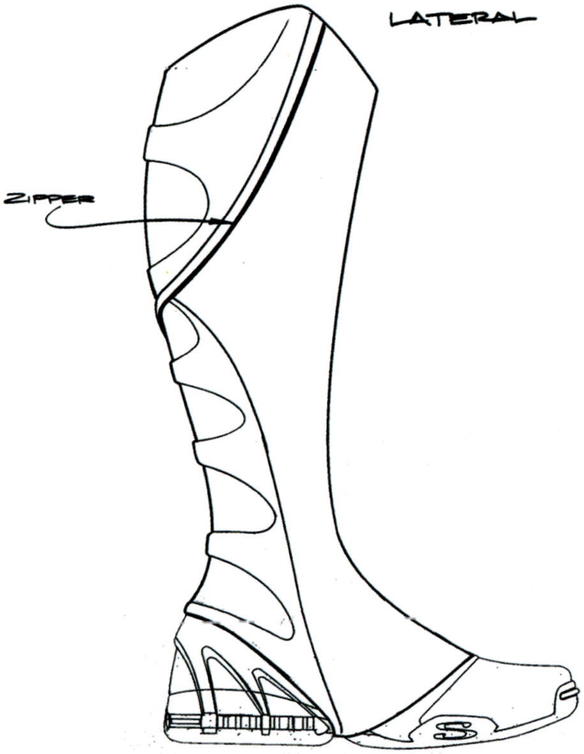

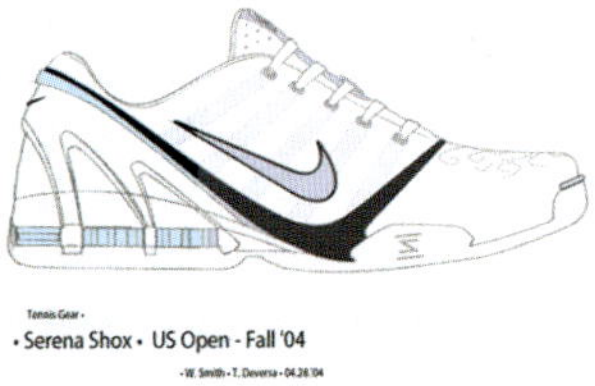

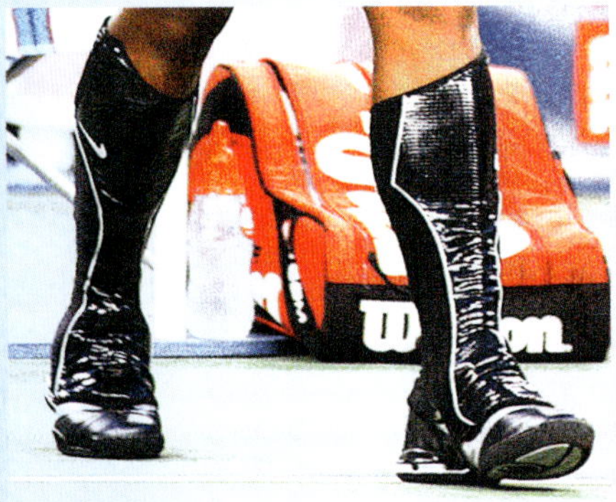

"It was a night match with cameras flashing, and Serena walks on court with them—it feels like she's on a Paris or New York runway. We get to the warm-up moment, and she is wearing the boots, and the US Open officials thought the boots a little too much. So she only warms up in them, and then she zips them off. She is a wearing a denim skirt and a black vest with studs on it. ESPN's SportsCenter showcases Serena in her boots even though she didn't play in them. It felt like a very big influencer moment, because she pushed beyond the game into fashion. It was a style story that became way bigger than her actual game that day. It was one of the highest fashion sports stories of that year. At that point, she was our biggest top-tier female athlete, right alongside LeBron James and Michael Jordan. For us, it was pretty cool to tell this tennis story on US ground too, because tennis was bigger in Europe than it was in America at the time, so this was great for the sport—especially for America."

—Wilson W. Smith III, Design Director, Nike Tennis Footwear

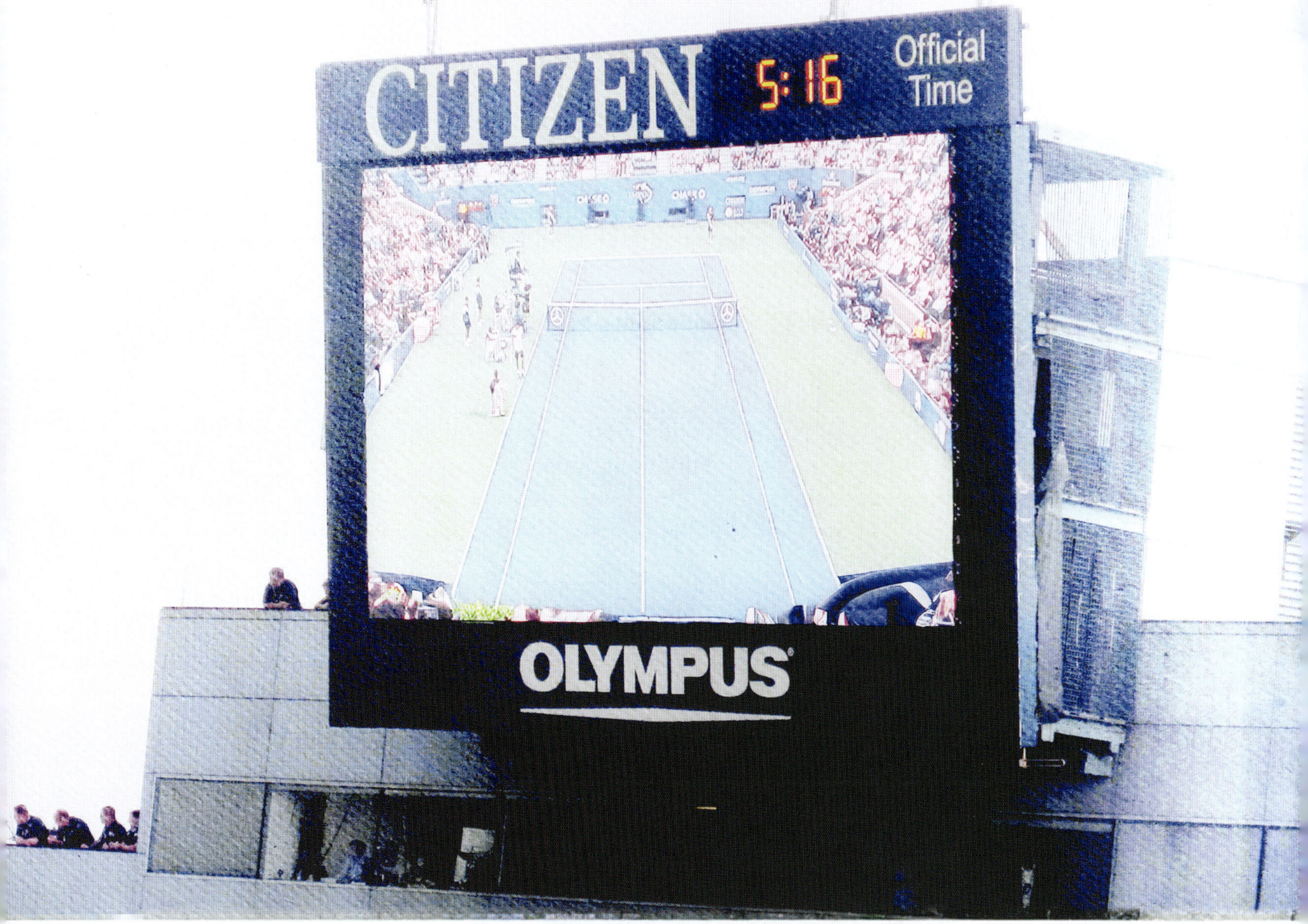
CITIZEN
5:16
Official Time
OLYMPUS

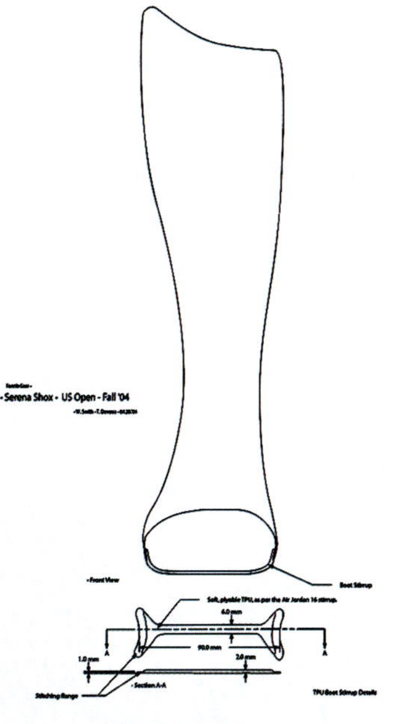
• Serena Shox • US Open - Fall '04
• Front View
Boot Stirrup
Soft, plyable TPU, as per the Air Jordan 16 stirrup.
6.0 mm
90.0 mm
1.0 mm
2.0 mm
A
A
• Section A-A
Stitching Range
TPU Boot Stirrup Details

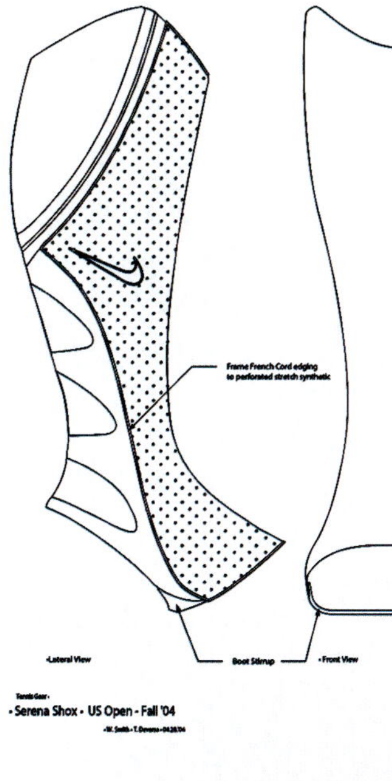
Frame French Cord edging
to perforated stretch synthetic
• Lateral View
Boot Stirrup
• Front View
Tennis Gear •
• Serena Shox • US Open - Fall '04

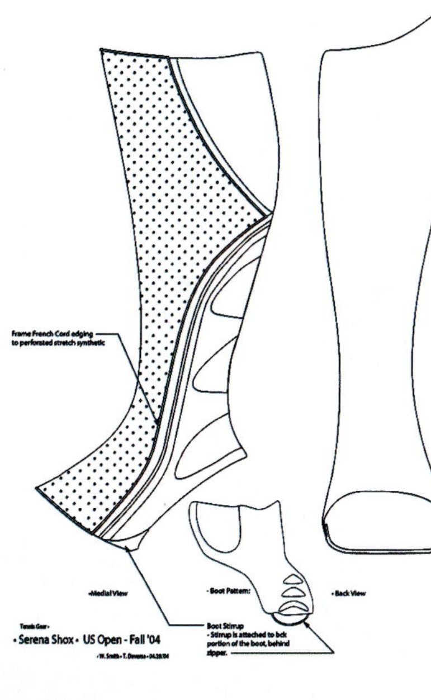
Frame French Cord edging
to perforated stretch synthetic
• Medial View
• Boot Pattern:
• Back View
Tennis Gear •
• Serena Shox • US Open - Fall '04
Boot Stirrup
- Stirrup is attached to bck
portion of the boot, behind
zipper.

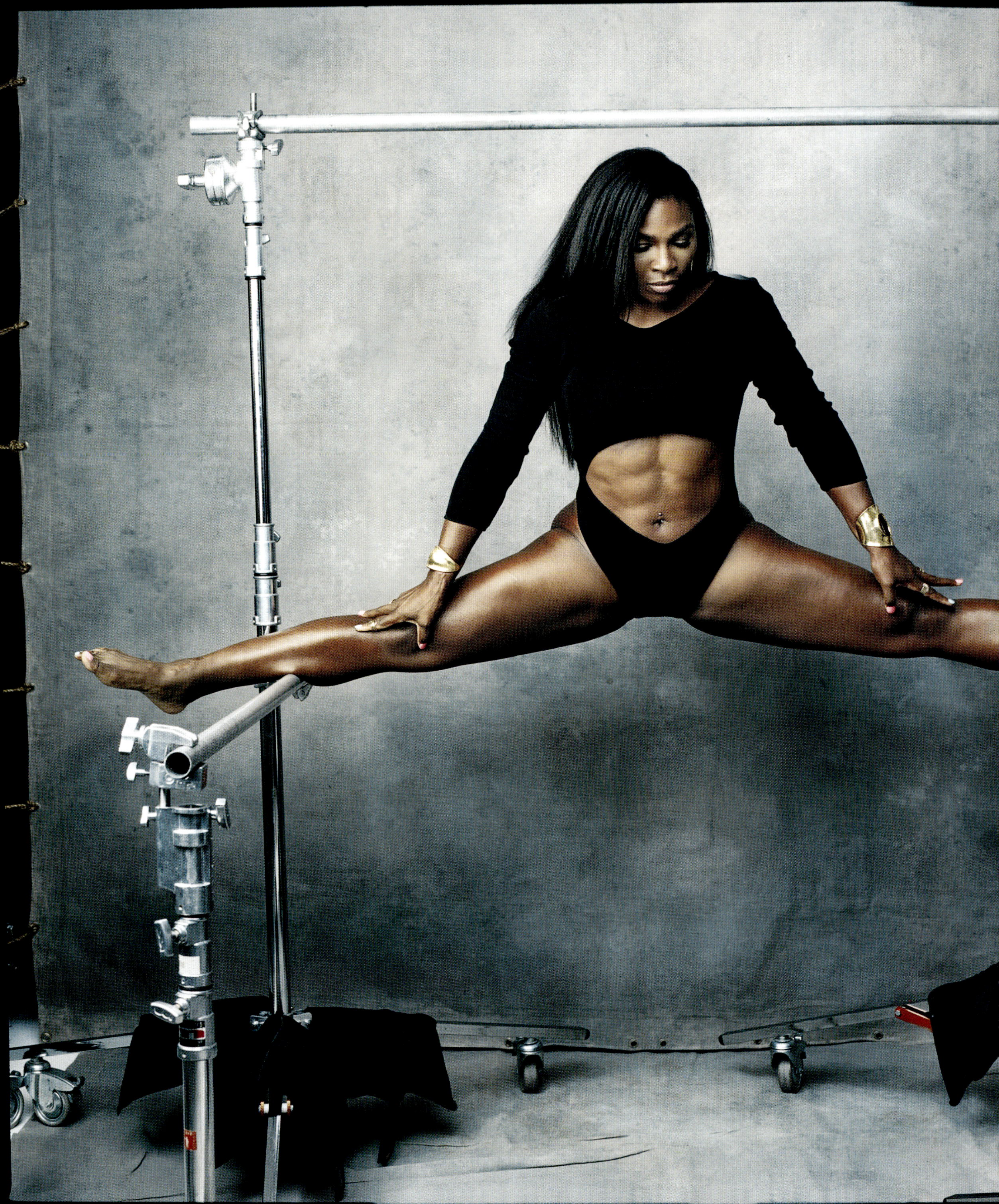

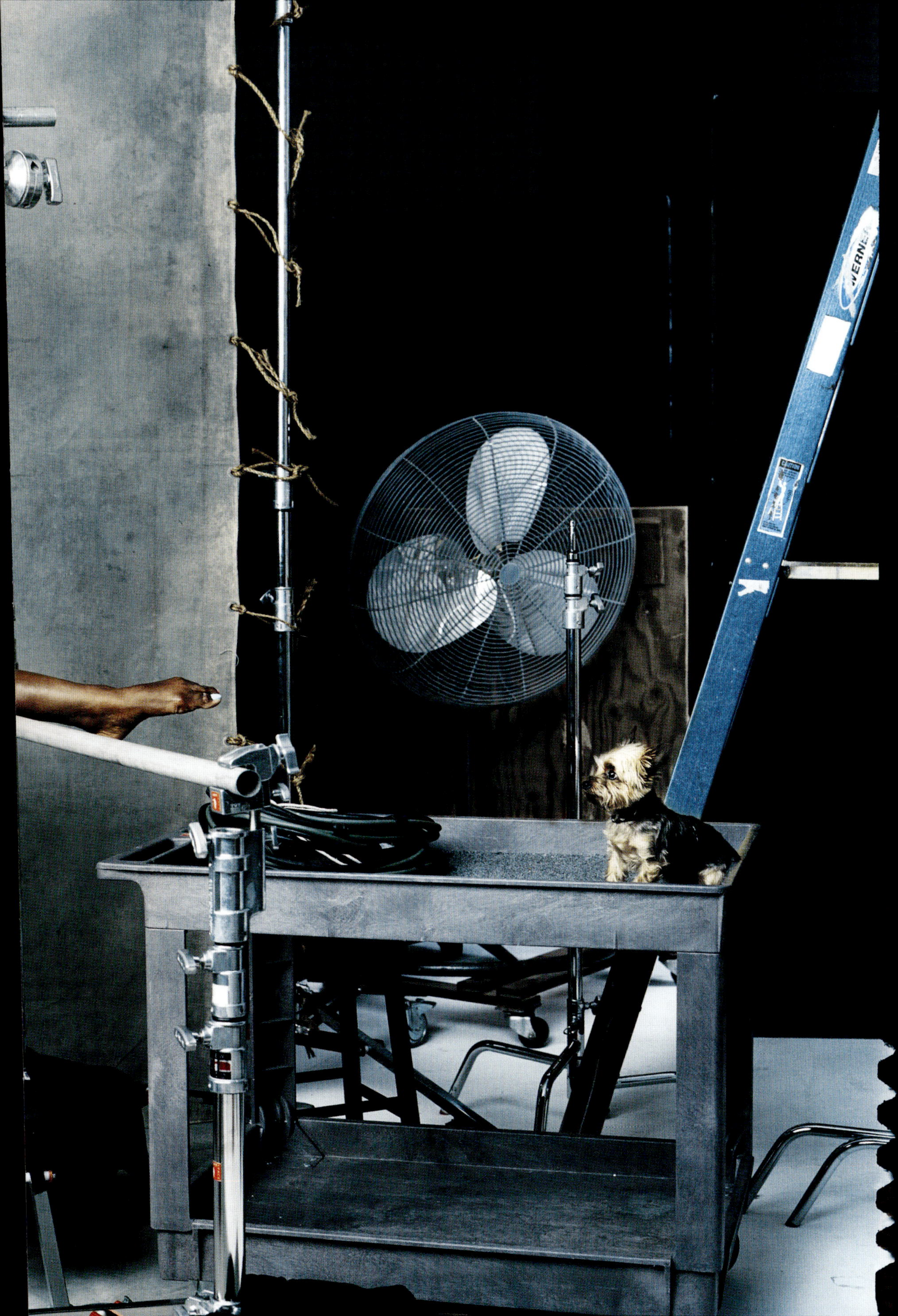

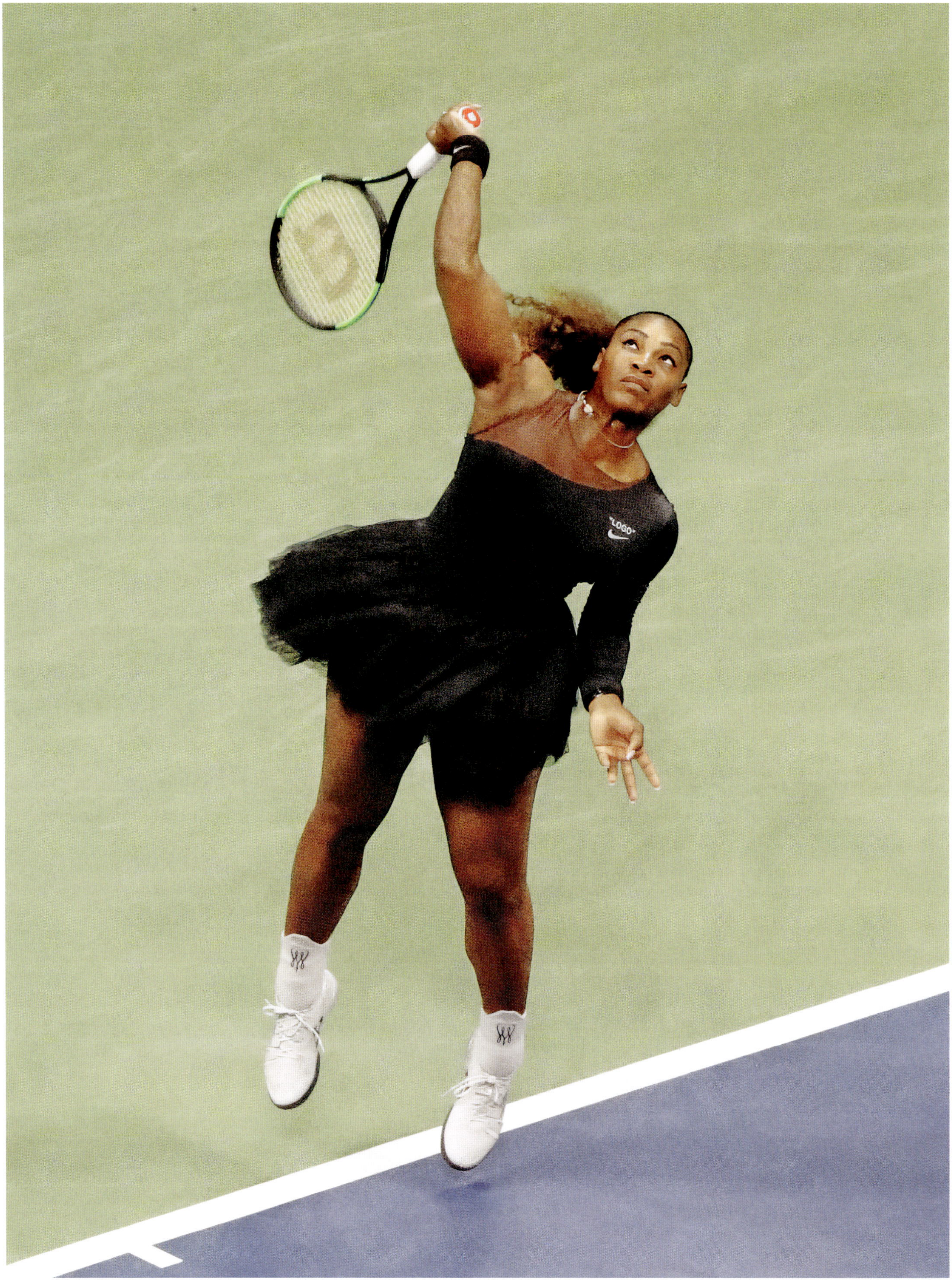
"LOGO"

VIRGIL ABLOH X SERENA WILLIAMS

Maverick moves, serious ones, require a cocreator: a visionary of equal magnitude to you who reflects as you see, creates as you dream. For Serena, it was Virgil Abloh, founder of the street label Off-White and the first African American artistic director of Louis Vuitton menswear, who defied and reshaped conventions within the disciplines of architecture, streetwear, music, industrial design, fashion, and sport. Abloh didn't plug in if it didn't ignite.

"What I love about tennis is the gracefulness. It's an aggressive and powerful game, but it takes touch and finesse," he said. Abloh's social media shows footage of him hitting the ball like a child first given a tennis racket, oversteering as the ball hits an off-center contact point. But he is playing. Abloh's design wizardry lay in his deciphering the tantric mechanics of the game, particularly Serena's, into fashion. Co-inspiring requires mutually beneficial inspiration. Abloh said of Williams, "She is a thought leader, not just a tennis player . . . by existing, she shatters stereotypes." The Nike x Off-White "Queen" collection of 2018 marked the fiftieth year of the US Open being held in Flushing, Queens. The wordplay was intrinsic to the design code. Serena's dress featured a trompe l'oeil effect—the skin tone power mesh shoulder piece supported the illusion—on an asymmetrical black body made of Dri-FIT tech fabric. The word "LOGO" on the chest in a boxy font is archetypal Abloh: ironic, satirical, a lark to test our robotic consciousness and our automotive responses to insignias like Chanel's double *C*. Abloh always thought himself above it: "I would consider myself a *logic*, which would be one tier above a logo." The *real* logo for Abloh? SERENA, which is printed on the back of the full sleeve. The design's call to couture comes within the criterion of the softly draped tutu tulle skirt, with craftsmanship semi-equivalent to a Balenciaga or Dior dress. It was also a reference to Williams's love of ballet and dance—she actually made a little pirouette on court. Abloh was ever clear with his design intention: "to embody Serena's spirit with each swing of the racket," which was "feminine" but honored her "aggression."

Each historic match is immortalized along with its ensembles, with either the play or outfits (sometimes both) hitting the headlines. And so, during her match with Naomi Osaka, Williams was given three code violations—for behavior not dissimilar to her male counterparts in past heated moments, ones that had almost always been overlooked. Williams was naturally upset, and so was the crowd. The citations Williams was given highlighted serious questions about fairness, sexism, and racism within the game. This was design destiny, winning the tie break—her dress and incident are inextricably woven into each other, with neither muse nor designer realizing the potency and message of her dress until after the moment was over.

The French Open 2019 was part deux of their creative partnership. Williams had attended the French Open the year before in an all-black Nike catsuit, a design purposefully engineered to prevent blood clotting; Williams had suffered a near-fatal pulmonary embolism during childbirth eight months before. She was consequently reprimanded by the president of the French Tennis Federation for the catsuit. In a press conference and asked to comment, Williams appeared unusually reticent; she quietly said to the journalists gathered that she had a "great relationship" with French tennis and would not make the faux pas again. Abloh pushed Williams further for her 2019 design. She recalled the original blueprint: "He wanted me to wear this long skirt with a crazy train, and then a cape with the train, and then just walk out on court." She acknowledged a certain regret in declining it later. (Abloh's only response had been "You should have done it.") Following his untimely death in 2021, Williams surmised on Abloh's "greatness"—and still rues not wearing that first option: "I just wasn't brave enough with all the red clay with that train, like the Met Gala at the French Open." She opted instead for three pieces—a crop top, skirt, and cape—in a black-and-white graphic print, the bold stripe arresting like animal hide. Emblazoned on it were the words MOTHER, CHAMPION, QUEEN, GODDESS—in English and crucially also in French: MÈRE, CHAMPIONNE, REINE, DÉESSE.

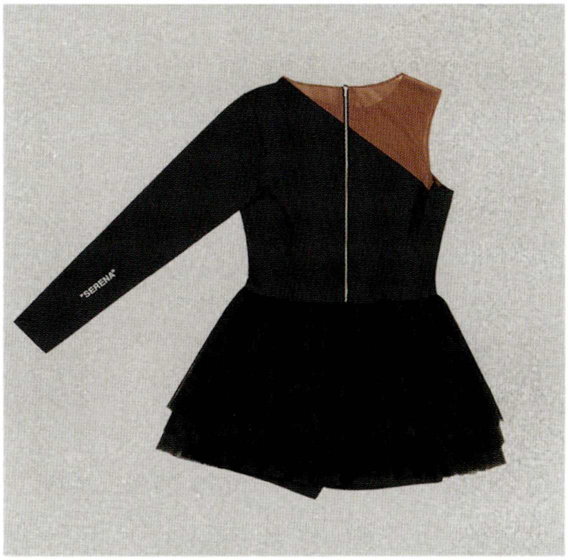
"SERENA"

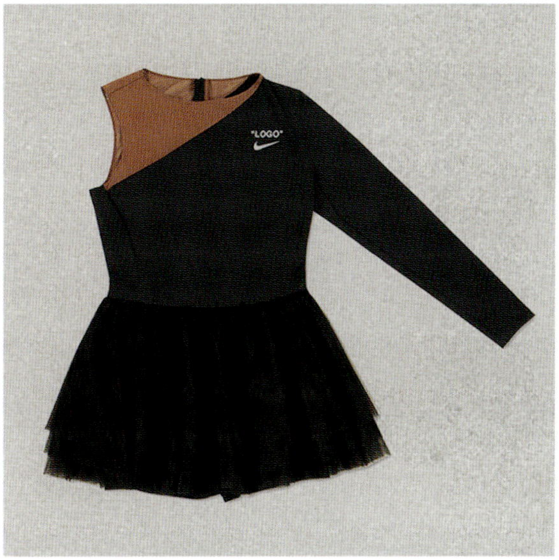
"LOGO"

"SERENA HAS THIS ENERGY- SHE KNOWS THAT HER CELEBRTIY IS BEYOND TENNIS, THAT IT NEEDS TO HAVE AN IMPACT IN A LOT OF SETTINGS." —WILSON W. SMITH III, DESIGN DIRECTOR, NIKE TENNIS FOOTWEAR

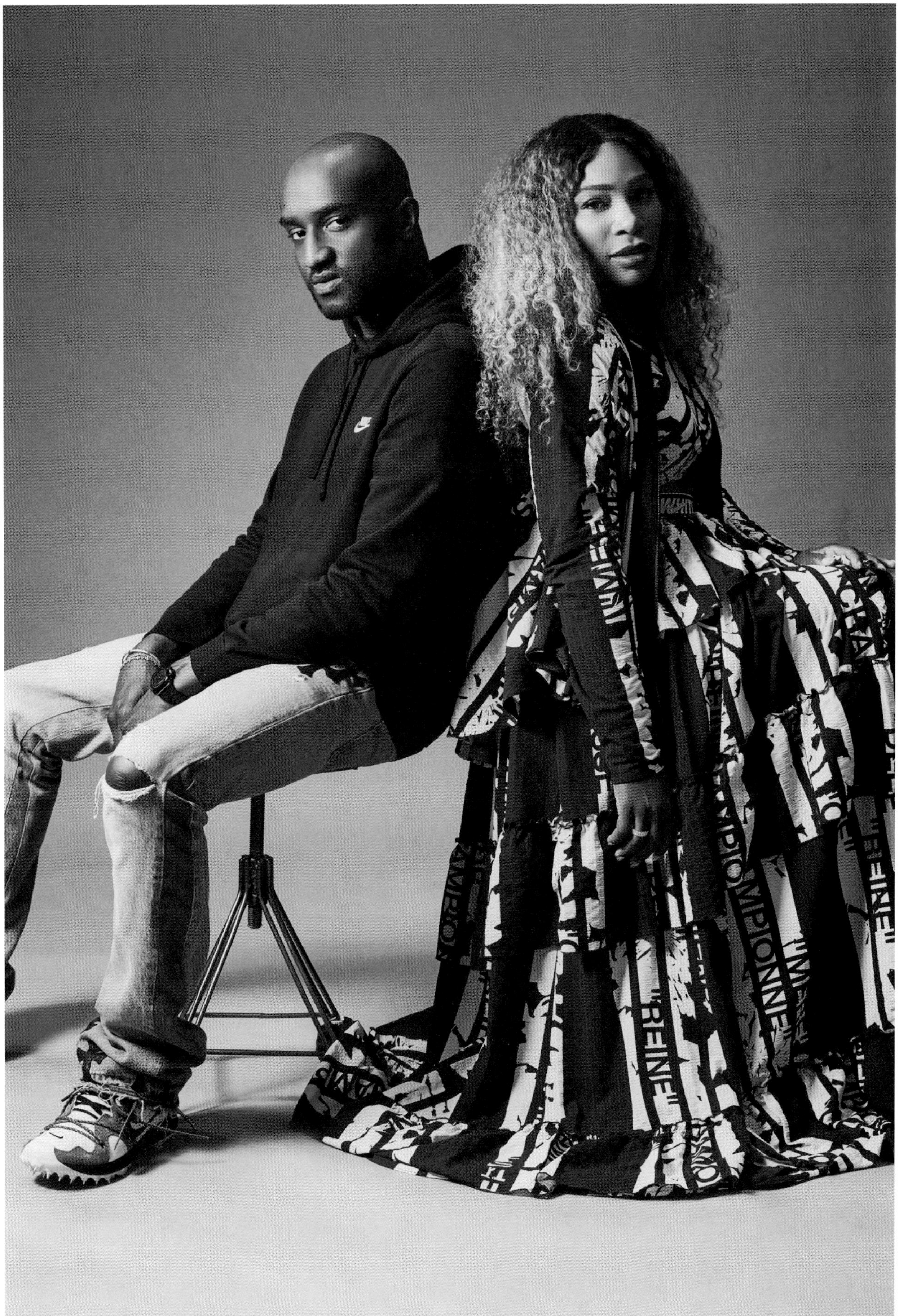

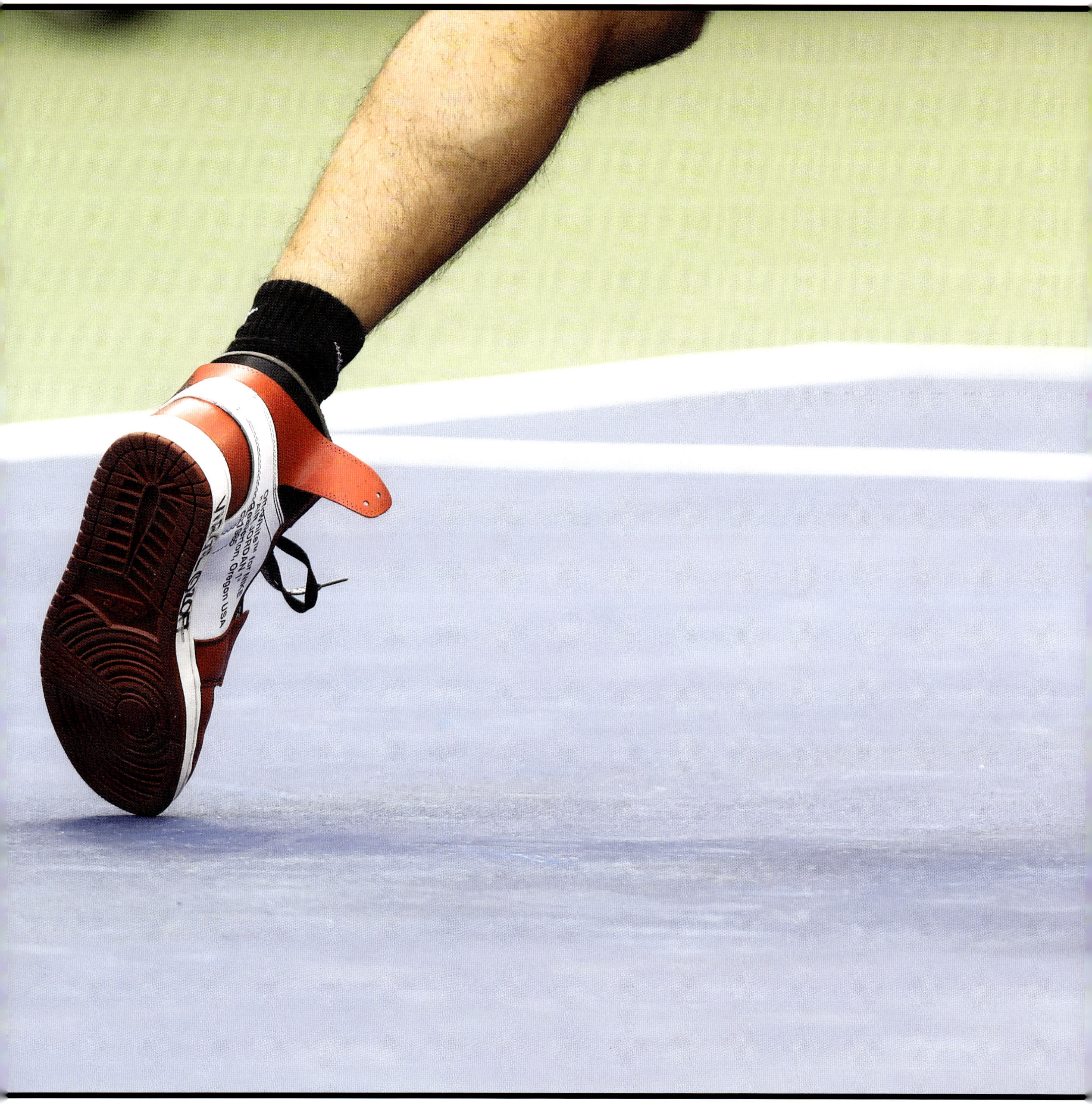
Oregon USA

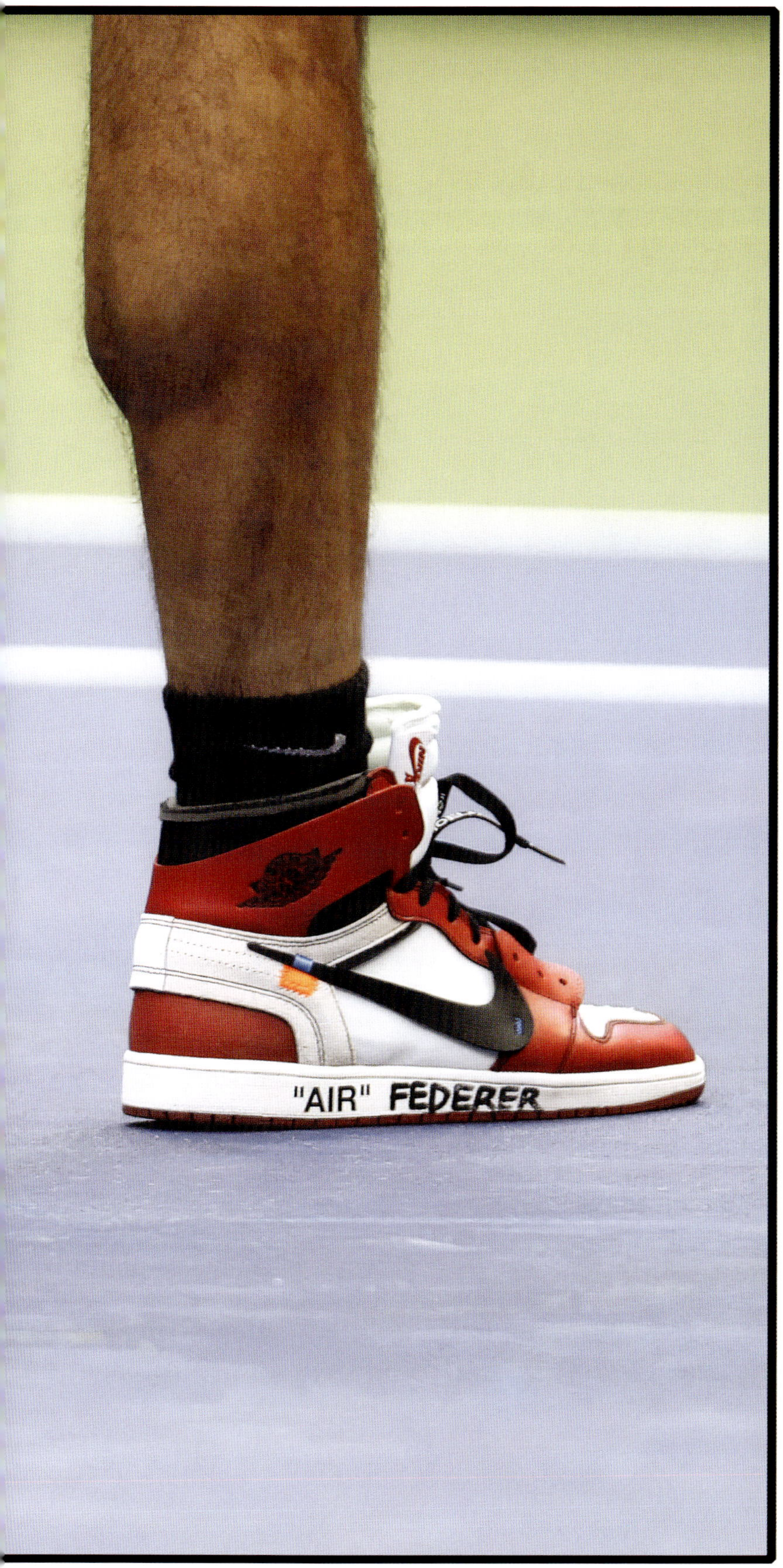

Childhood dreams for Virgil Abloh meant Nike: not to wear them, but to design them. Devotedly submitting design prototypes and swiftly receiving rejection letters were his formative teen memories. Nike had become the first playground for sneakerheads to compare and covet each other's wares. Basketball rookie and phenom Michael Jordan literally took the brand to "flight" in 1985 with his first shoe model: The Air Jordan 1.

Black, red, and white, the Air Jordans were a direct contravention of the NBA uniform and all-white shoe policy. But Jordan kept wearing them, the NBA kept fining him, and Nike kept celebrating this rebel cause. Headlines and better yet, bans, can refuel a brand, turning profit and sometimes making a myth. Hip hop artists like the Beastie Boys and Public Enemy claimed the Air Jordans into their own street vernacular, and film director (and devoted tennis fan) Spike Lee wove the shoes into his film, *Do The Right Thing*, sealing it as a signifier of taste, cool and rebellion.

When Nike came to thirty-six-year-old Abloh in 2016, young boy Virgil must have pinched himself. His brand Off-White had become the calling card of savvy streetstyle and luxury wear. And so just like he did as a child, Abloh took his sharpie and scalpel out. His reworking of classic Nike sneakers like the Air Jordan 1 and the Air Force 1 were decreed to be part of "The Ten." When Roger Federer wore them to play the 2017 US Open, Virgil's lovingly tendered school project could finally be handed in, some twenty years later.

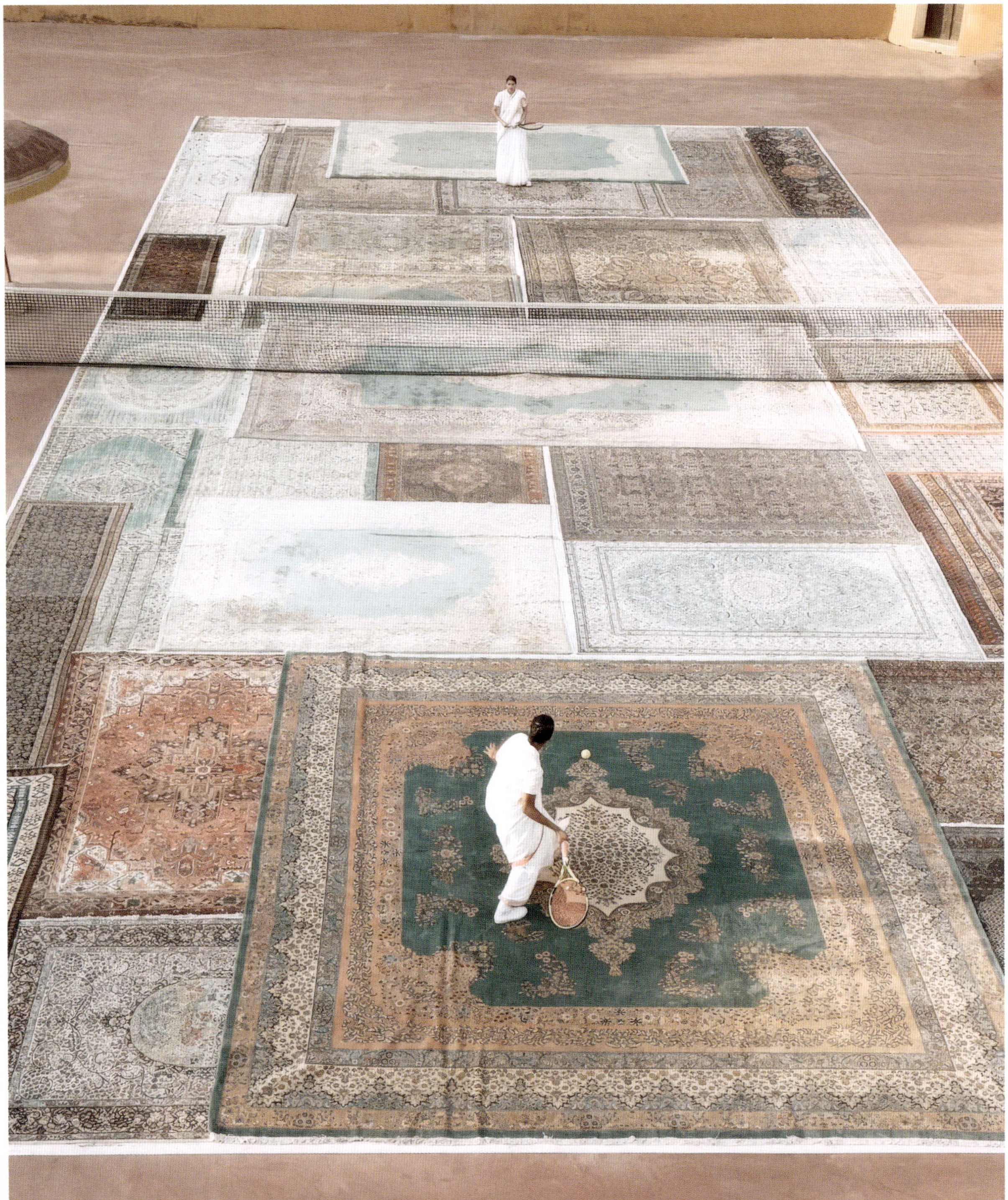

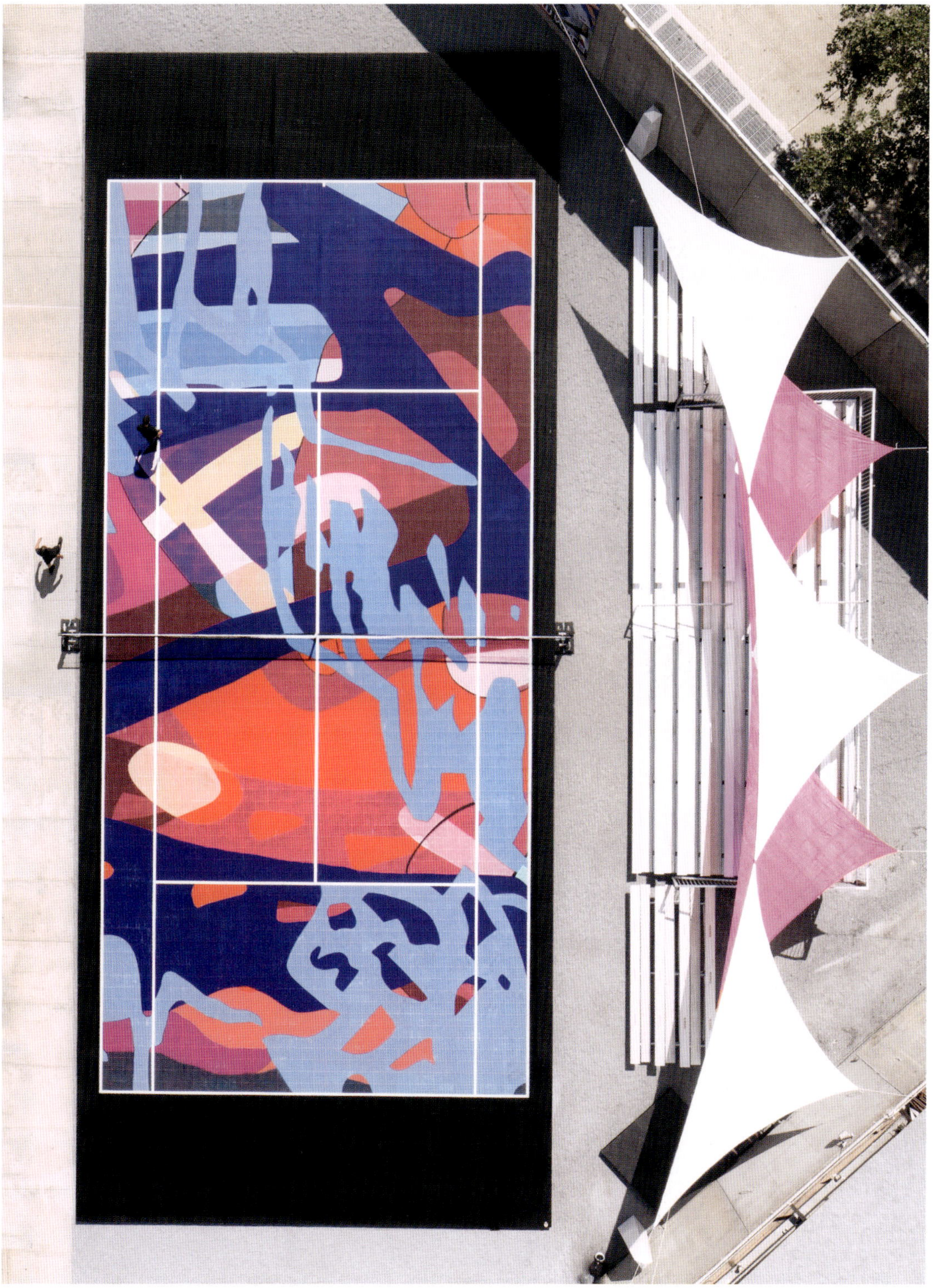

III.

THE COOL

Those who just are—the calm customers who remain timeless, allowing their play and style to speak, as opposed to their personas—fall into the Cool. There is nothing to prove here. Their silence is their sartorial armor. Pop culture immortalizes these players, metastasizing them into a personal canvas for the artists to relay through the medium of film, music, and art. Tennis culture now carries the same breath of cool as any other global sport like football or basketball: The players are their own entities. It was a natural progression for streetwear and for the world of hype to infiltrate tennis apparel. It's a truth or dare to the revered realm of the classics to advocate for a new tennis world—one that is democratized and open.

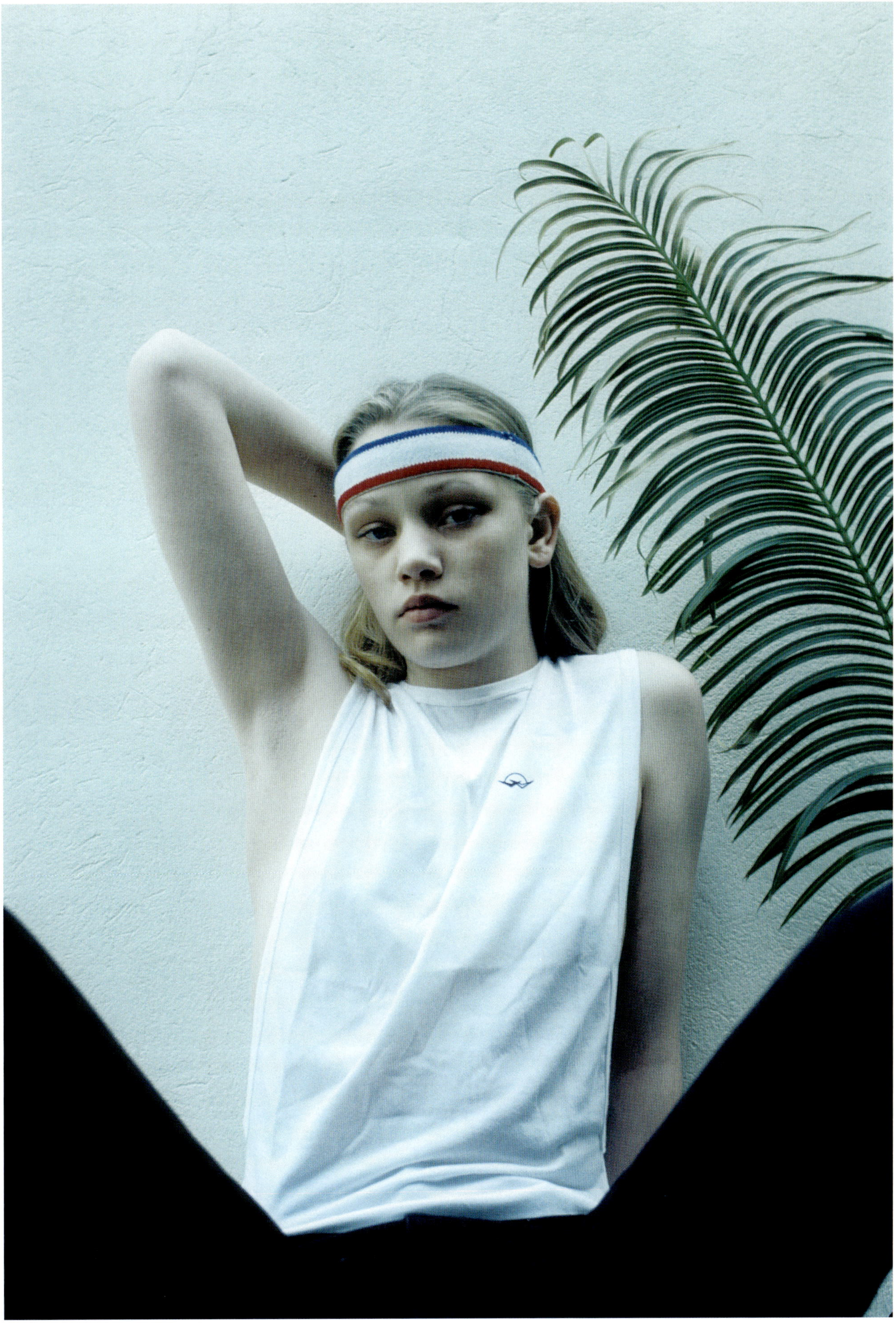

ARTHUR ASHE

THE LEGENDARY ARTHUR ASHE (1943—1993) WAS KNOWN FOR HIS ELEGANT BACKHAND AND POWERFUL SERVE AND HAS THREE GRAND SLAM WINS.

Arthur Ashe served twenty-six aces in his 1968 US Open finals match win. That's some cool. If there was ever a player who successfully intellectualized his persona through his court appearances, it was Ashe. There was simply too much at stake. He was plotting things bigger than Grand Slam wins. He said so himself: "I can make my protest by winning. People don't listen to losers."

An African American man winning in a white, male-dominated game was sensational enough. This was not the time to disrupt, not yet. Schooled by the same mentors as Althea Gibson to be agreeable in etiquette and proper in sportswear, Ashe was a perfect personification of his own collegiate style. He wore an all-white Fred Perry polo shirt with rolled-up sleeves, the AA monogram embroidered below the laurel wreath motif whispering bourgeois charm; matching front-pleated shorts completed the polished veneer. Black boxlike glasses perched on his delicate nose, stayed put. Pristine even post-match, his victory suit was a bomber jacket zipped midway up, just like the Ivy League boys wore it. His message was, well, cool. *LIFE* magazine charted his win with bylines of "icy elegance," assuring the Caucasian American reader that the composed Ashe was one of them. The reportage included sublime pictures taken by John Zimmerman both on and off court that showed a demure Grand Slam champion taking the subway, a sophisticate in his off-court attire: short-sleeved button-down shirt layered with a luxe velour V-necked top, slim fit trousers, black dress socks, and penny loafers. Another shot of Ashe with friends shows him wearing a pinstripe shirt, a day jacket in a mismatched color, a paisley silk cravat with matching handkerchief, and dark trousers. It really was some cool.

Ashe's varsity-prep style on court remained consistently so. In the early '70s, he switched from Fred Perry to Le Coq Sportif, wearing an array of checked shirts and pinstripe shorts. Off court, a love bead necklace betrayed his true bohemian taste, which later bloomed into on-trend wide-collar shirts and patterns clashing on the top and bottom, complete with studded clogs.

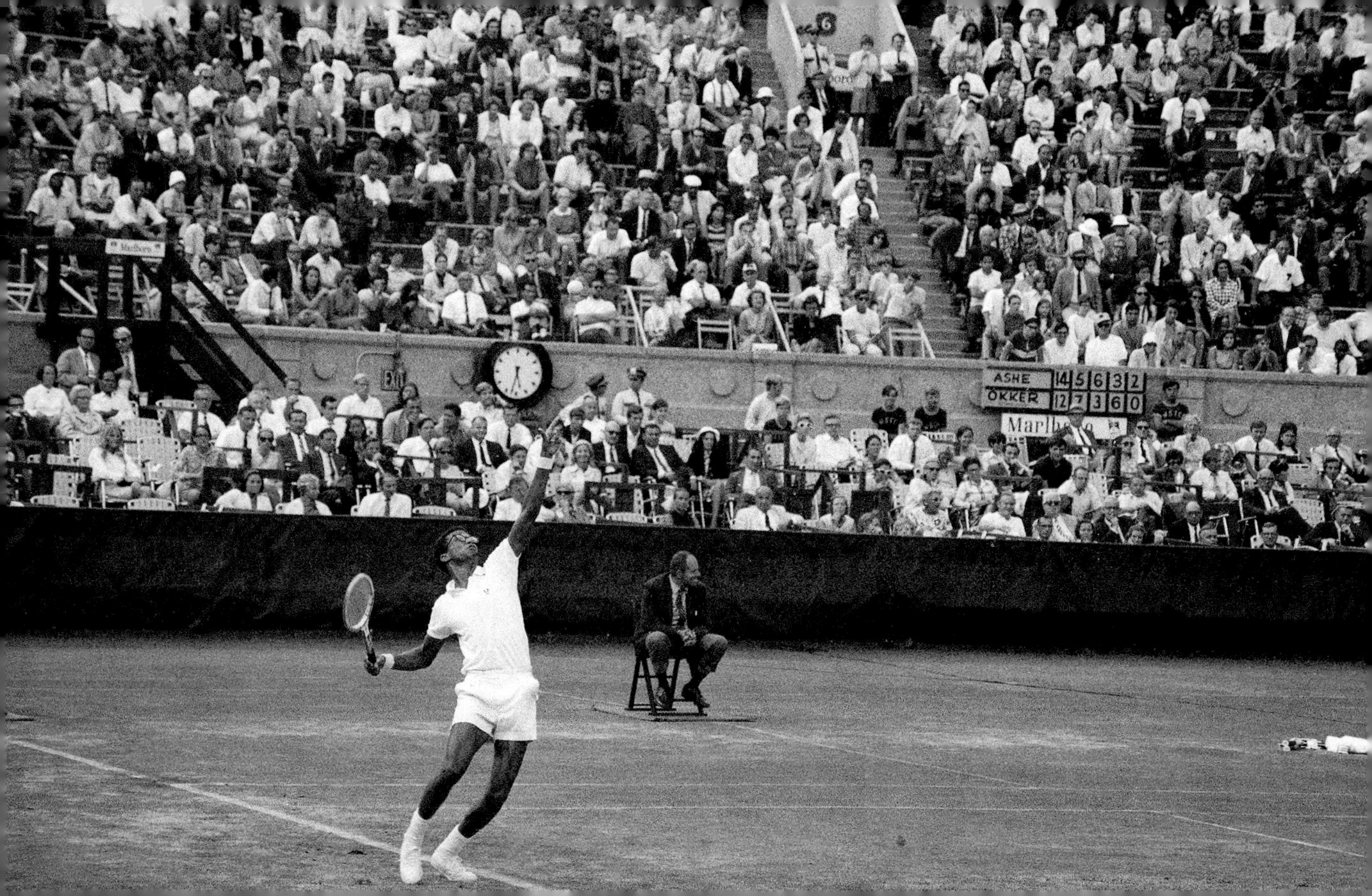
ASHE 14 5 6 3 2
ÖKKER 12 7 3 6 0

Ashe chose to represent his country instead of himself—Jimmy Connors notoriously chose the latter—and captained the Davis Cup from 1963 to 1978, leading the team from 1981 to 1985. His resolute participation in the South African Open in 1973 made him an icon for the anti-apartheid movement: his red shirt with pointed collar and open white placket, racket stretched out to Black South Africans enclosed by a fence. It's the flash of the gold Rolex Daytona on his wrist that relays a message of aspirational freedom and success to the enslaved. It's monumental. Ashe's arrest in Washington, DC, for protesting apartheid highlighted the cause further. After Nelson Mandela was released from prison in 1991, he requested to meet with Ashe.

Ashe contracted HIV during a blood transfusion, but even in sickness, he had work to do. He decided to speak openly about the virus and his impending death during the early years of the AIDS crisis, when the subject was still taboo. "Clothes and manners do not make the man, but when he is made, they greatly improve his appearance," he once said. Ashe unveiled the tools—his skill, style, and voice—all of which he realized for his greater message. To Ashe, serving aces and the oppressed were one and the same.

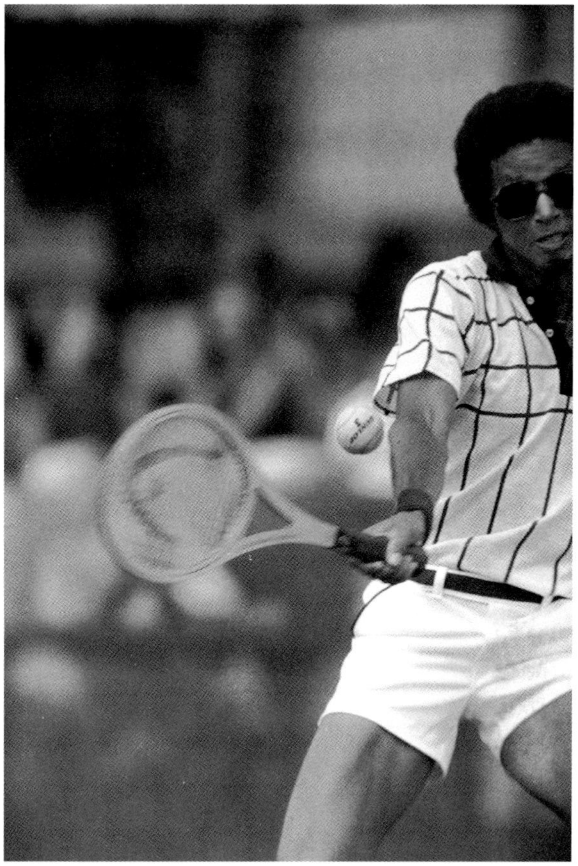

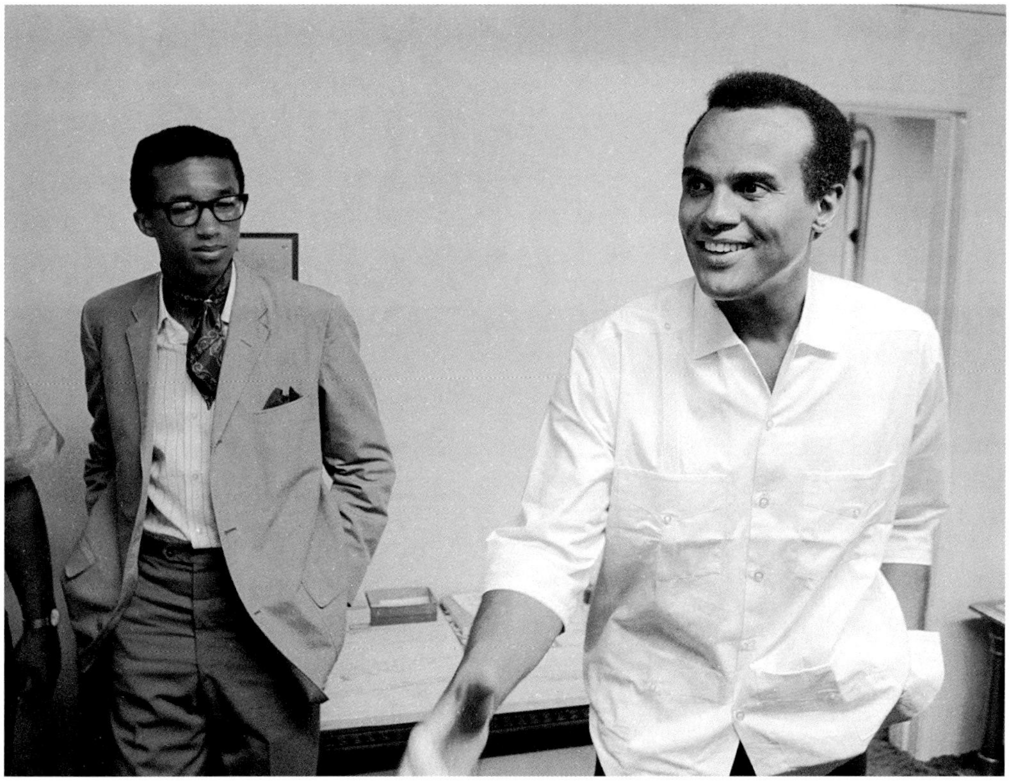

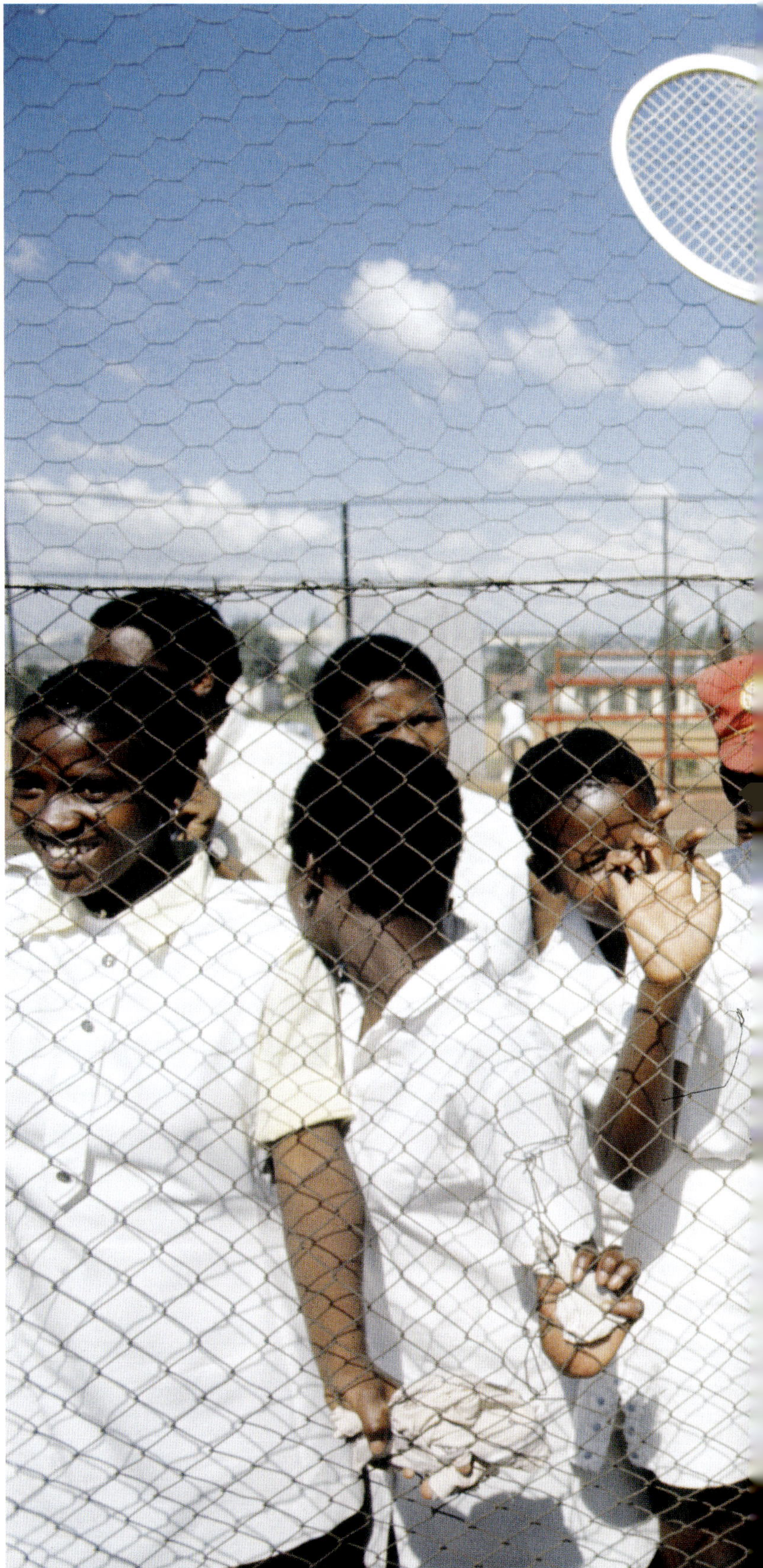

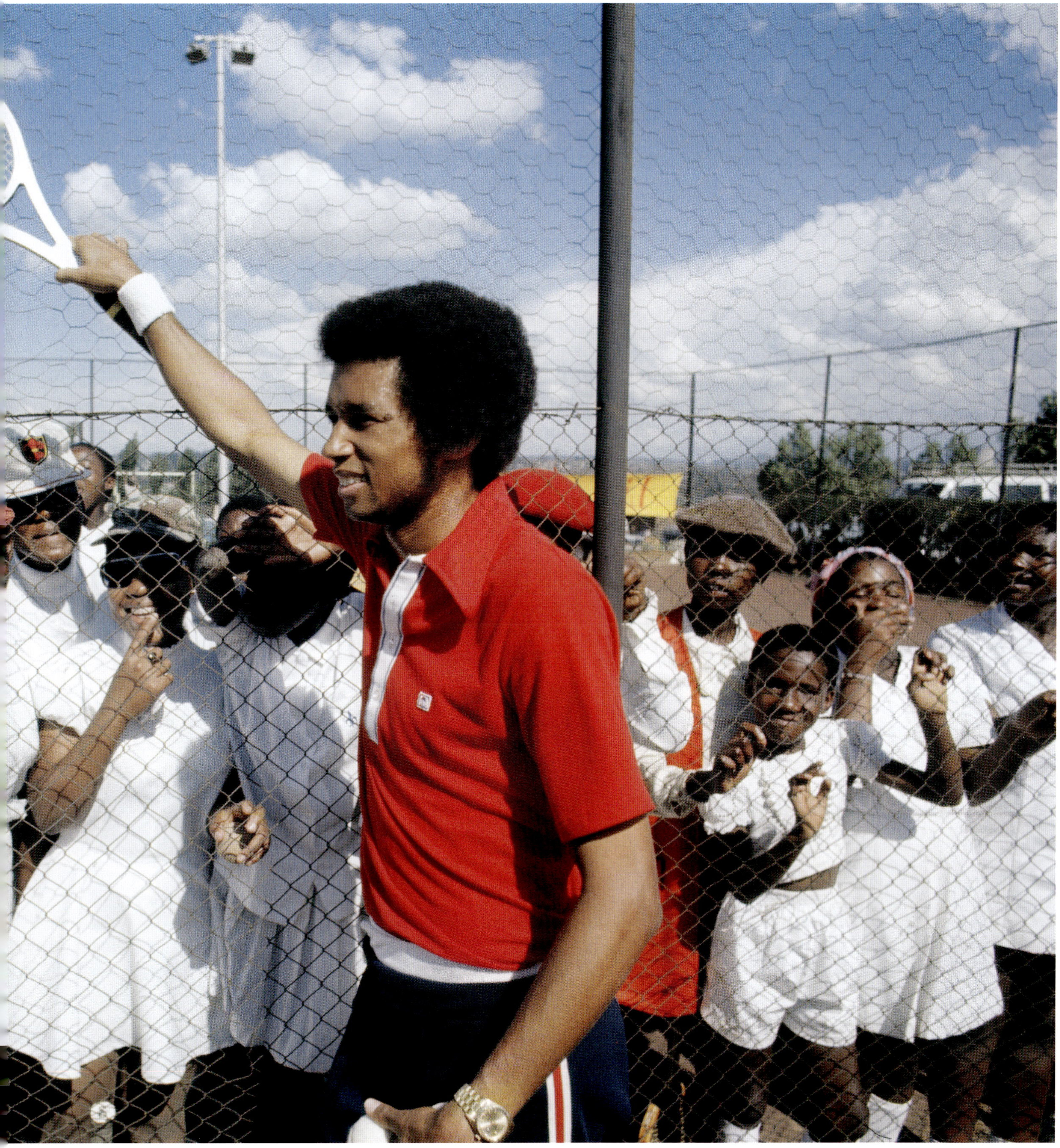

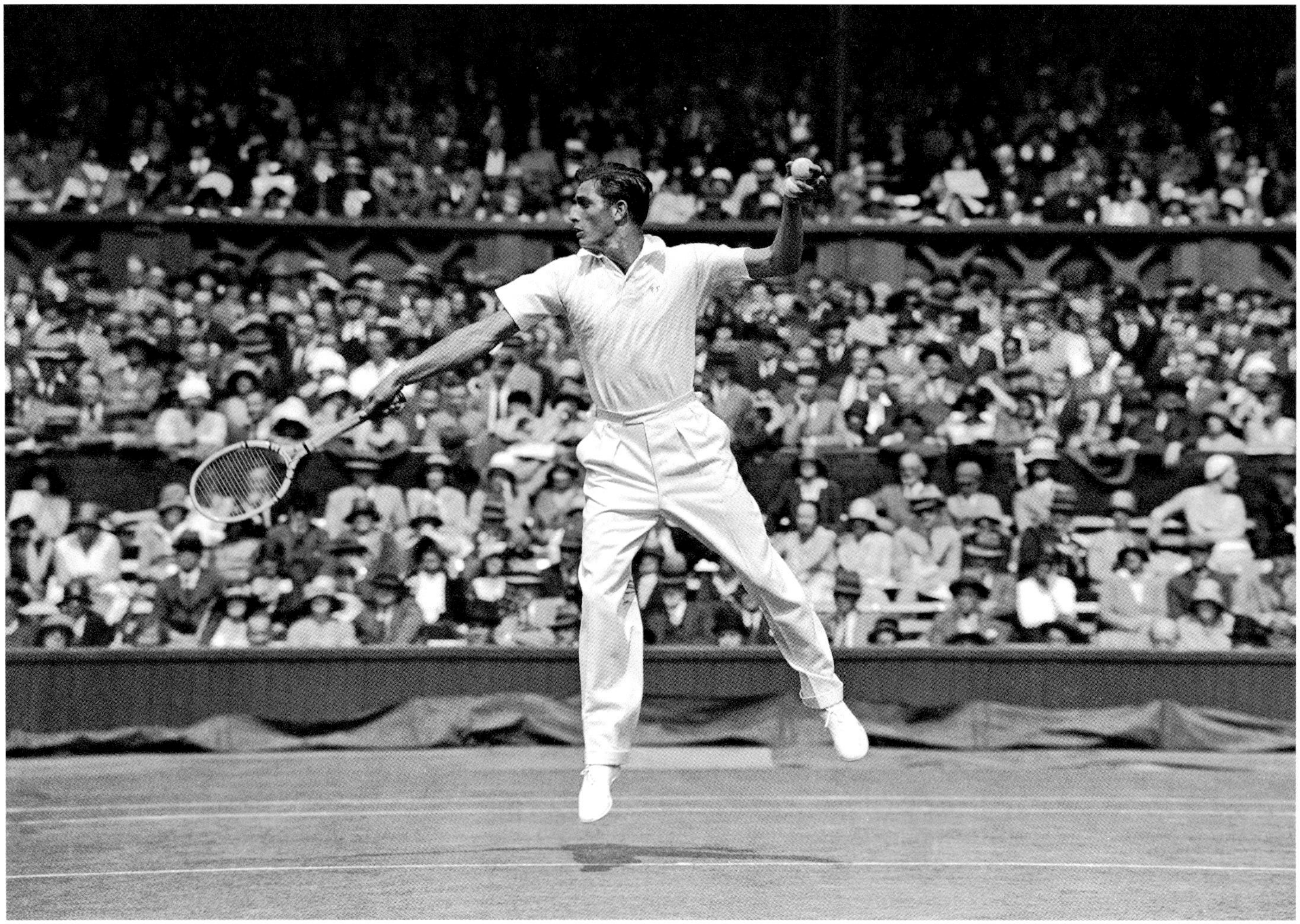

FRED PERRY

FRED PERRY (1909—1995) WAS A QUICK-FOOTED PLAYER WITH AN AGGRESSIVE FOREHAND. HE WON EIGHT GRAND SLAMS.

THE REASON FOR YOUR SHIRT?
ASKED THE QUEEN MOTHER.

"IT'S THE ONLY ONE THAT FITS,
MA'AM," REPLIED FRED PERRY.

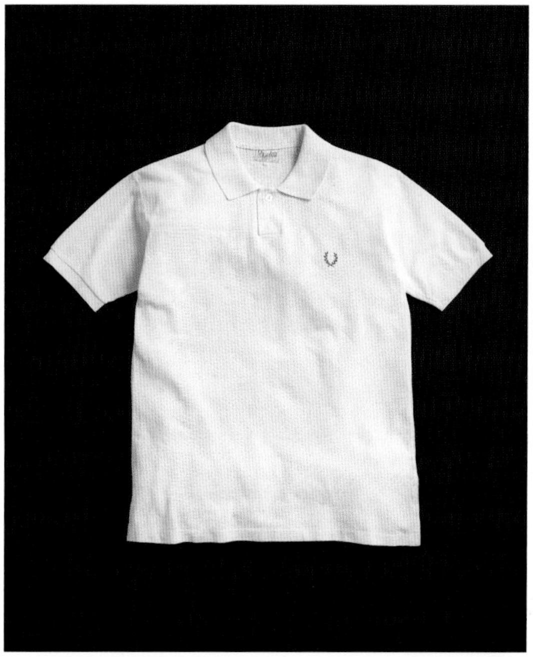

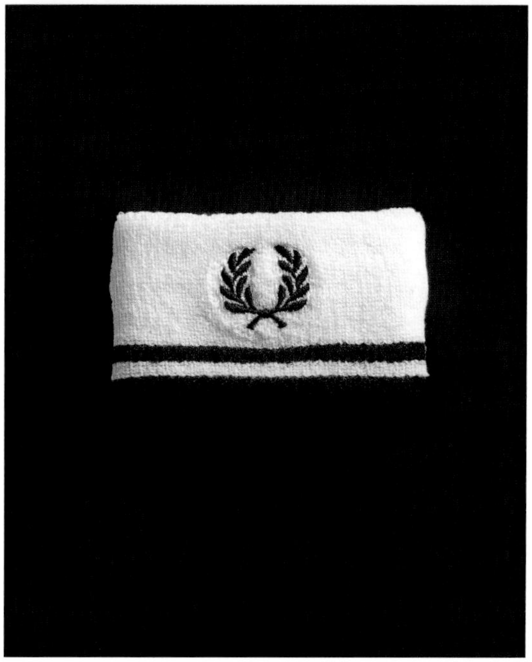

This is the single thread that ran through Fred Perry's life and that of his brand: fit, and fitting in. For where would the son of a cotton factory worker find his pedestal in the paneled pantheon of tennis greats at the AELTC? How would his shirt, designed for tennis performance, burgeon into a subcultural standard-bearer for the social misfits of Britain's working class some thirty years later?

Perry attributed his plebeian Northern England roots "to getting around every door if one seemed closed." Self-taught in table tennis, he became world champion in 1929. When he switched to tennis, he practiced religiously against his garage door and addressed his athleticism by training with footballers at Arsenal FC. The truth was, it didn't matter what he played—his will to win was the skeleton key to every door he encountered.

Soaking in the players' bath at Wimbledon in 1934 after his second Grand Slam, Perry overheard disgruntled committee members loudly proclaim that the best man didn't win. After they left, Perry found his members' tie, the one automatically issued to champions, carelessly strewn on a chair with no presentation, no acknowledgment.

With no family money to back his tennis career, Perry became professional in 1937. He had won Wimbledon in 1934, 1935, and 1936—the unexpected heir to champion neckties—but the club stripped him of his membership. Playing tennis to earn money as a professional was deemed too vulgar. America's freedom appealed to the hardcore Perry: no rules, no class stratification, all access granted. With his impeccably set lacquered hair, Apollonian features, and suave style, his humble roots were slickly combed away, and soon he was courting Hollywood darlings Marlene Dietrich and Jean Harlow.

Tibby Wegner, a footballer and friend, showed Perry a prototype sweatband in 1952. Now retired, Perry was ready for his next adventure, and that was business. He modified the band, choosing an embroidered laurel wreath as the Fred Perry motif—the same used by the AELTC on their victory coins.

The shirt prototype followed. Despite similarities to the Lacoste design—the piqué fabric, buttoned placket, and short sleeves—it was the pioneering fit of the Perry shirt that hit the sweet spot in comparison. The streamlined performance design did not scrunch up; the short sleeves were finished with a soft ribbed cuff to enhance arm mobility during play. The laurel wreath became Perry's insignia; the player's two initials would be embroidered below. (Only two figures other than Perry, who was FJP, were given the honor of three letters: President John F. Kennedy and Billie Jean King.)

Working-class England of the 1960s saw Jamaican immigrants sharing the same council estates as their white counterparts. A youth subculture made a strong brew of music and style: American buzz cuts (copied from astronaut Buzz Aldrin), turned-up jeans, cardigans, Dr. Martens boots, slim-fit suits, V-necked sweaters, white socks, and penny loafers. The girls were in on it too: shaved heads with feathered fringes, two-tone mohair skirts, and more cardigans. The common style currency for both male and female? The Fred Perry shirt.

This new subculture was cool and inclusive. Perry must have been proud of the society outsiders fitting in. When skinheads adopted the shirt, however, wearing it to carry out their acts of racism and hooliganism in the 1970s, it was an unfortunate detour. From the 1980s onward, British musicians like Joy Division, the Cure, Oasis, Blur, and Amy Winehouse carried the twin-tipped collar for a new and welcoming generation.

Fred Perry's gravelly Northern voice is folded into buttery soft Californian tones during an interview with the BBC in 1961. His desired legacy? To be "respected" for his play and achievements. The AELTC finally listened and erected his effigy front and center at the grounds in 1984. He also sought to give back to those who had a far reach to play the sport, as he did. The Fred Perry brand supports young players through extensive grassroots initiatives to this day. It also sponsors the musical subculture it unintentionally inspired. The Amy Winehouse Foundation is one example of a partner with whom the brand has worked closely to provide safe houses—leaving the door wide open for ostracized women in need.

"THANK GOD I AM NOT PLAYING ME TODAY."

—FRED PERRY

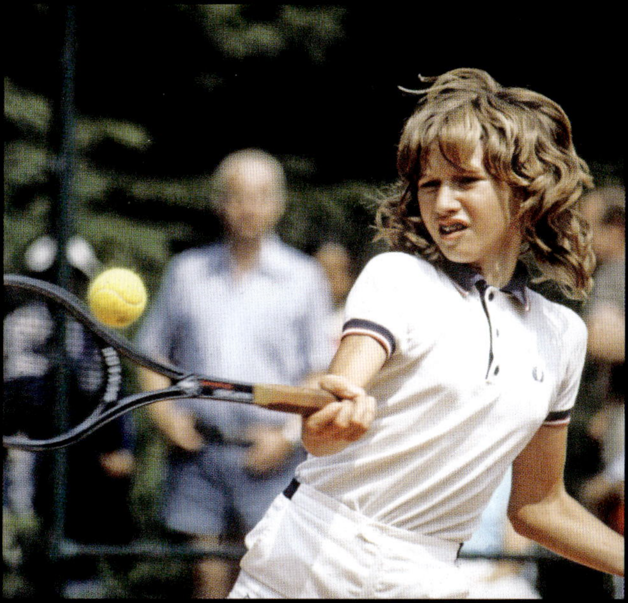

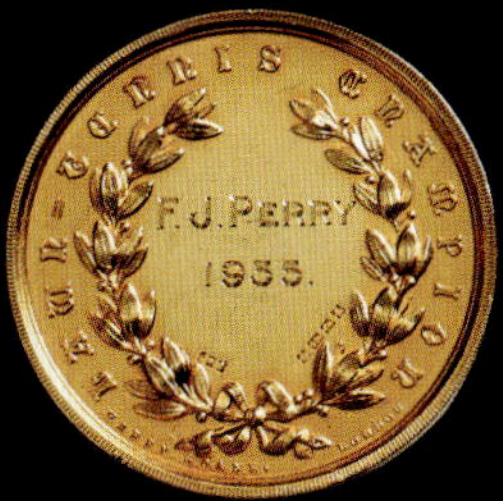

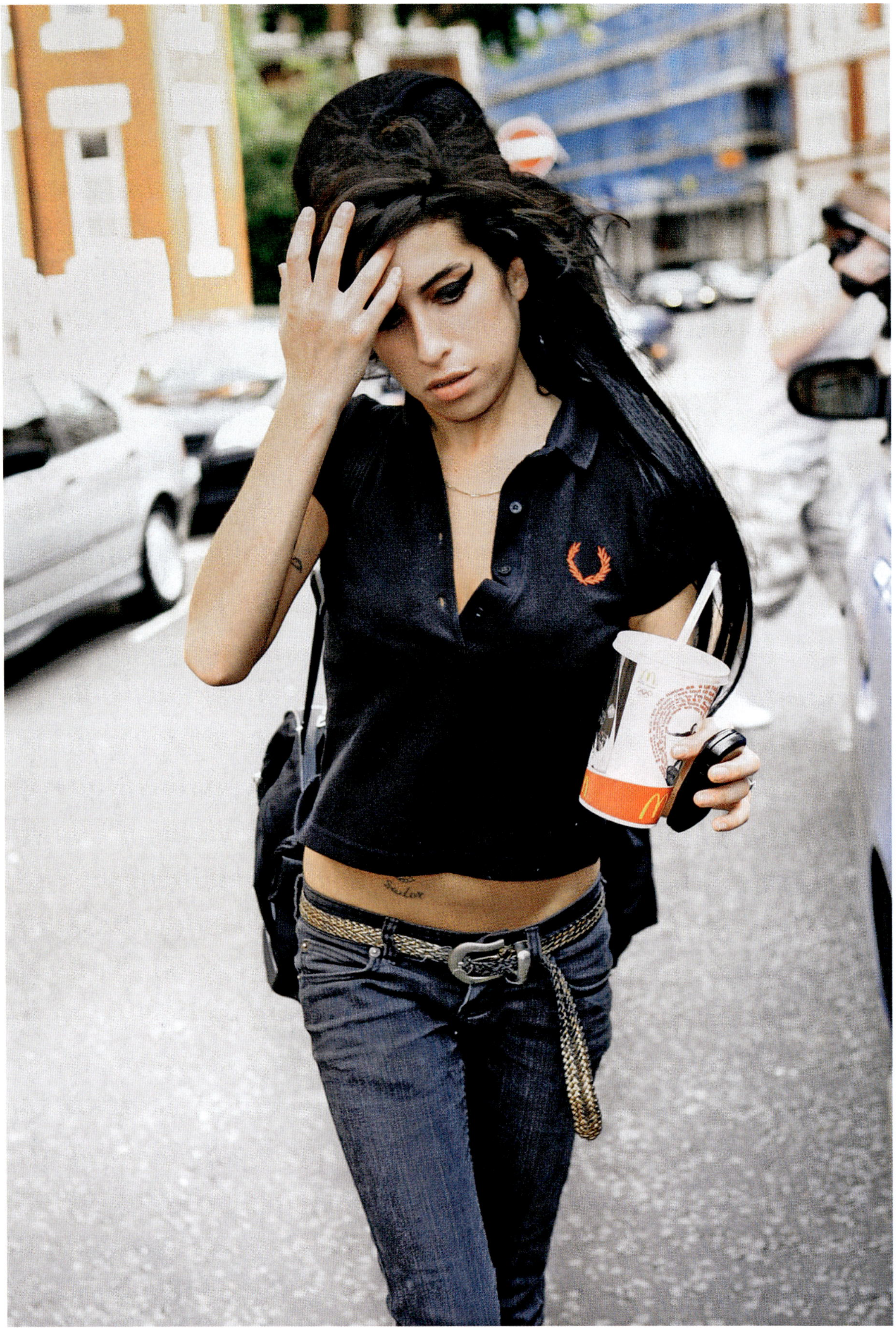

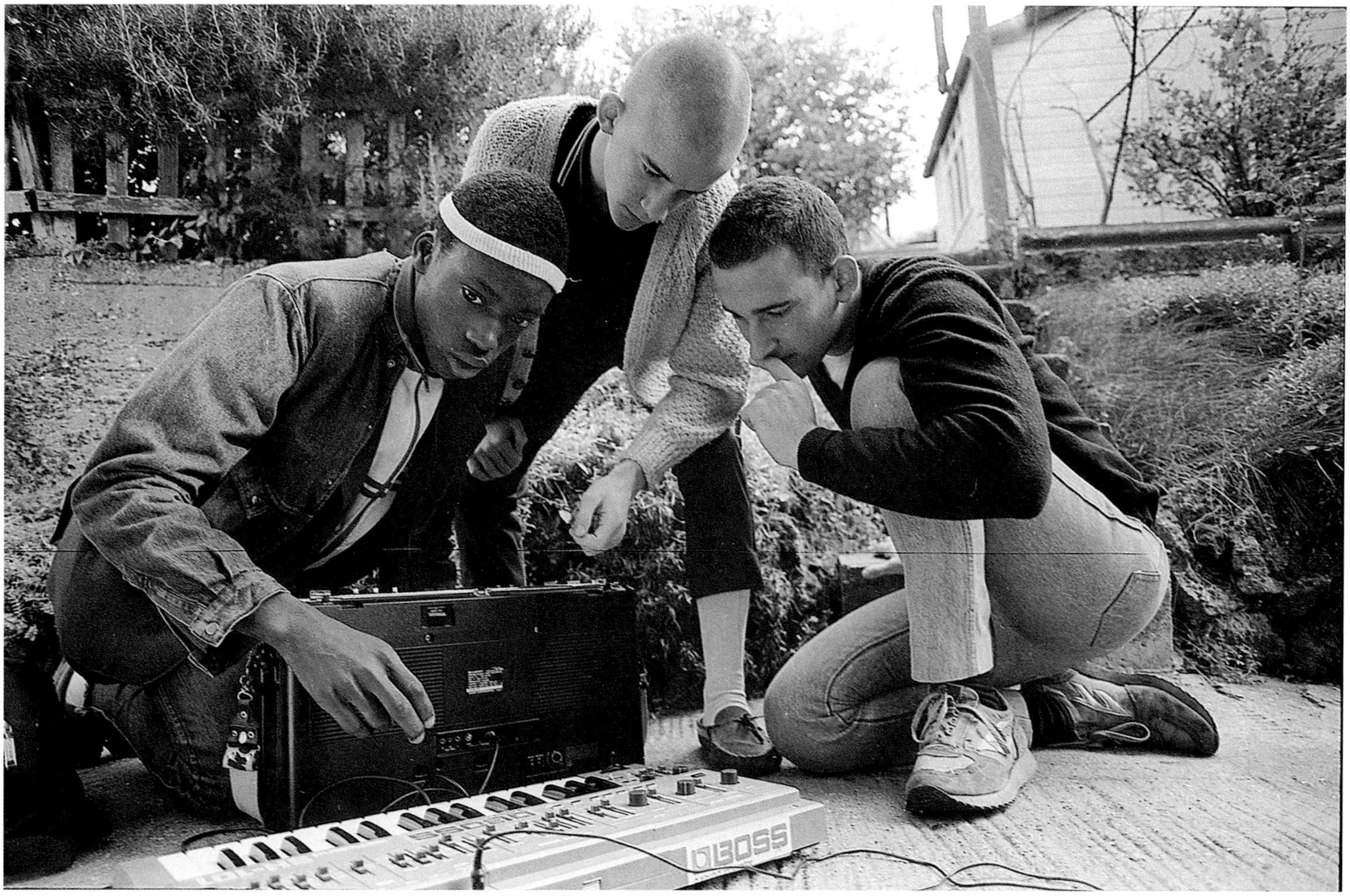
BOSS

FILA X BJÖRN BORG

BJÖRN BORG IS AN ICE-COLD BASELINE PLAYER WITH HEAVY TOPSPIN AND ELEVEN GRAND SLAM WINS, AND IS A FILA AMBASSADOR.

SKN: The 1970s was a transformative year in tennis fashion. What shaped your particular style?

BB: I believe it all started February 1973, when I played a tournament in Philadelphia. I saw three players, Ion Tiriac, Adriano Panatta, and Paolo Bertolucci, at the practice club, with a new Fila collection. It looked so nice, both in style and fashion. All the players said, "WOW, this is something new." We were so impressed with the new styles, and this was what I wanted to wear myself. It was a game changer in tennis fashion, and Fila was the first of all the sports brands (to make it fashionable).

SKN: Was there a deliberate styling on your side?

BB: When I signed my contract with Fila in the mid-1970s, I was very happy because I already liked the design and brand, and it fit me perfectly. This is what people remember about me: playing in perfectly fitted Fila clothing. It was my favorite brand of all time—it still is. I loved the striped polo shirt and track suits.

SKN: Did you collaborate with Pierluigi Rolando from Fila when designing your looks? For example, the Fila red tracksuit top for your Wimbledon win in 1978 was so iconic—were you involved in it?

BB: I never interfered with the design. I trusted them 100 percent because they knew what they were doing. Every year, they came out with new designs and styles. It always looked great, and of course, it fit me perfectly. I always chose different things that I liked to play in. I was so superstitious; I always chose to wear a certain design for Paris and Wimbledon.

SKN: Becker also said that he was very superstitious about his clothes: were you, too?

BB: It's well known that tennis players are superstitious. Every year at Wimbledon, for example, I always had to wear a striped shirt.

SKN: Did you ever see the film *The Royal Tenenbaums* where your Fila looks were clearly referenced? What did you make of that portrayal?

BB: Whenever I see Fila at the movies, on television or anything else, I feel very proud. Recognition of the brand is important for me.

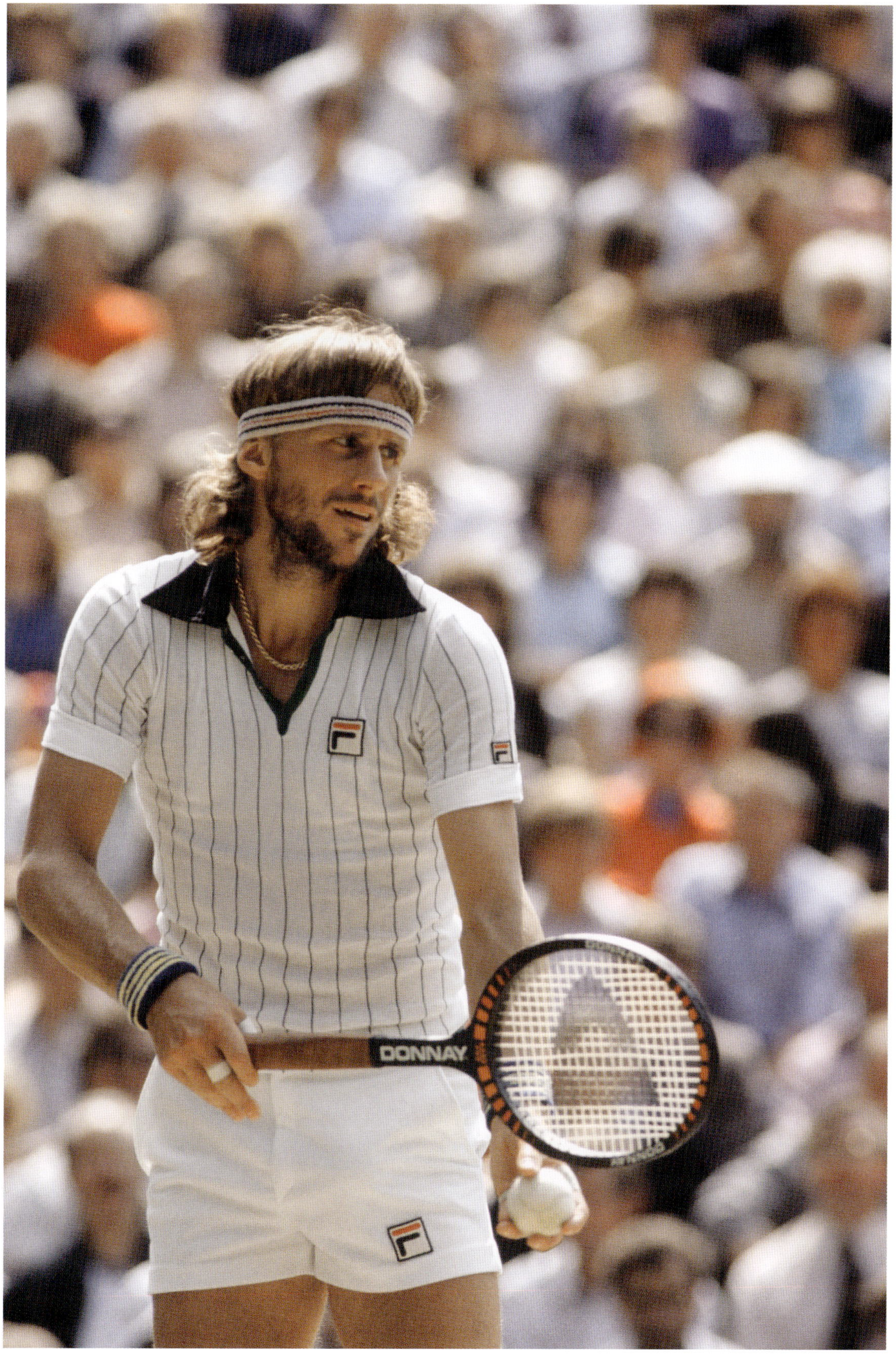
DONNAY

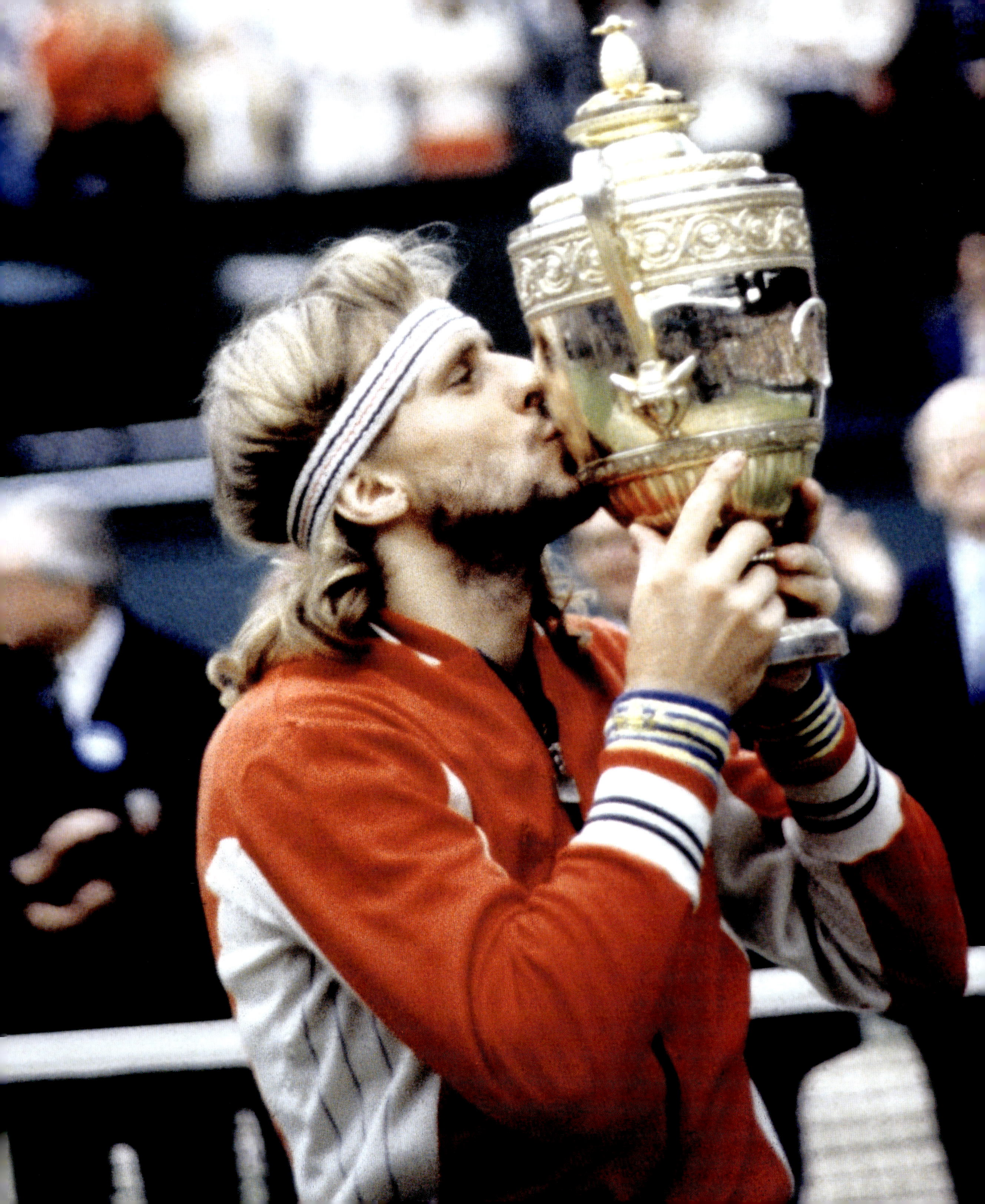

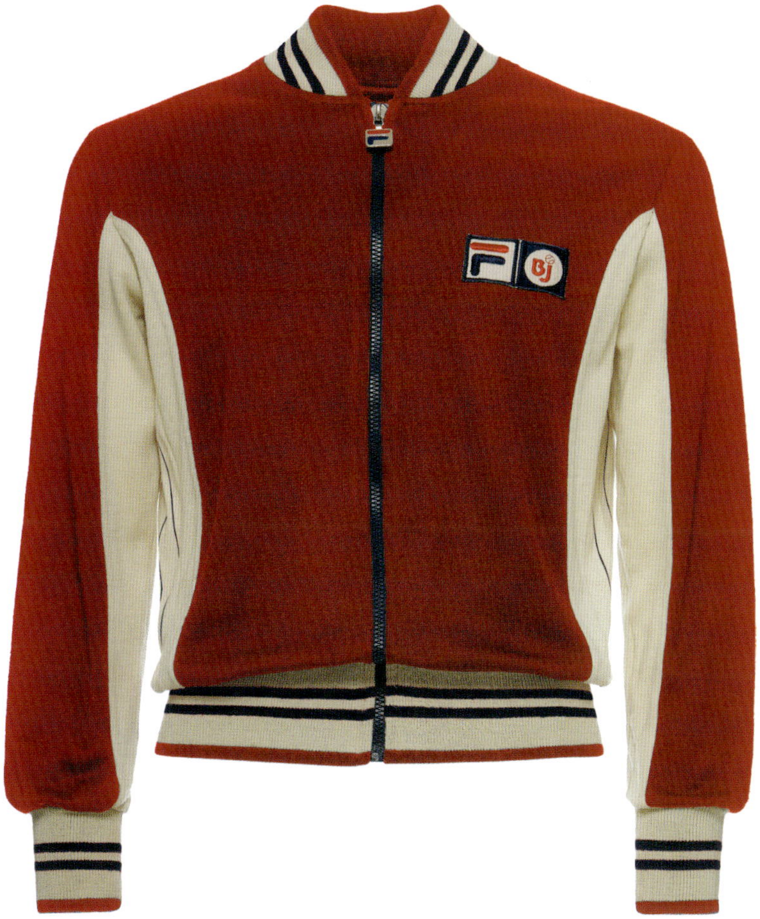

"I AM THE FILA MAN AFTER ALL."

—BJÖRN BORG

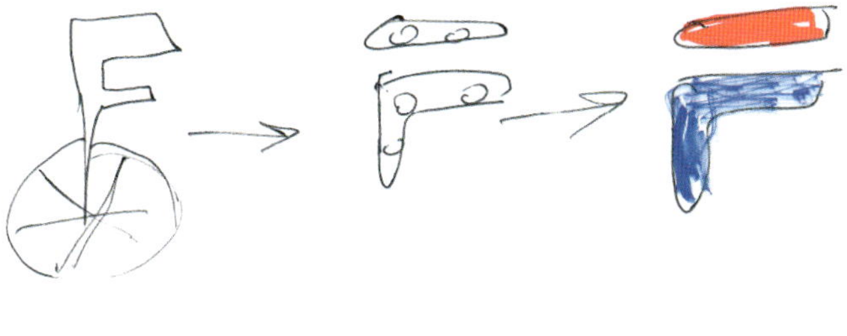

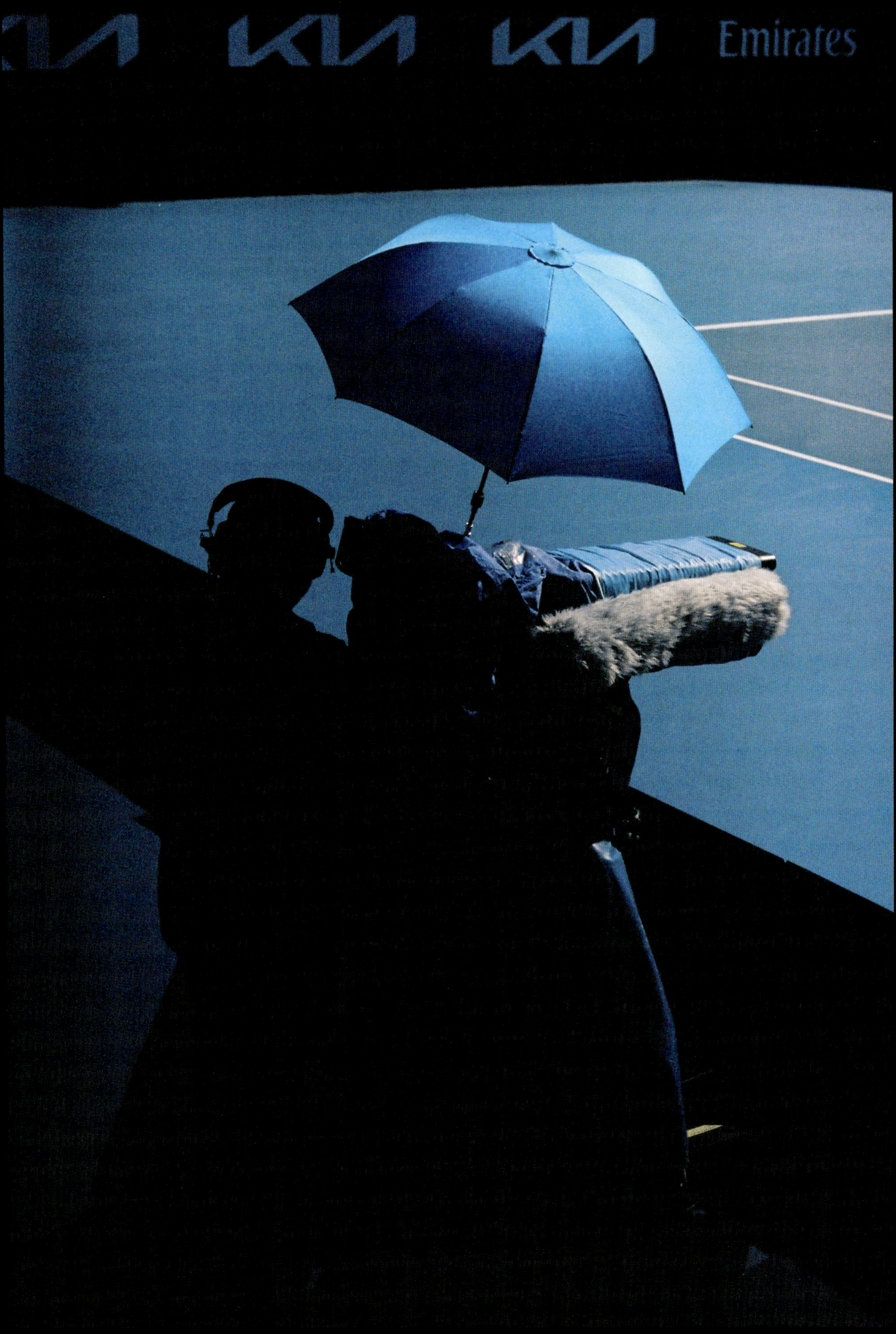
Emirates

GABRIELA SABATINI

GABRIELA SABATINI IS A GRACEFUL BASELINER WITH A HEAVY TOPSPIN, TWO GRAND SLAM WINS, AND ONE OLYMPIC SILVER MEDAL.

I have always liked fashion and design. I believed it was important to feel comfortable with what I was wearing on court, to express my femininity. This is why it was important to have input regarding what I wore. I started at fifteen, and as I became more adult, I was more curious about fashion, perfume, makeup, and I enjoyed these things a lot. As I got more involved in fashion productions, I started my own line of perfumes. I was fascinated with that world. I like flowers, especially the smell. It just means femininity to me. The smell of flowers or perfume can take you to different places, moments, and emotions, so it was a natural move for me to develop my own perfume.

When I think about the word *ace*, it means "I made it."

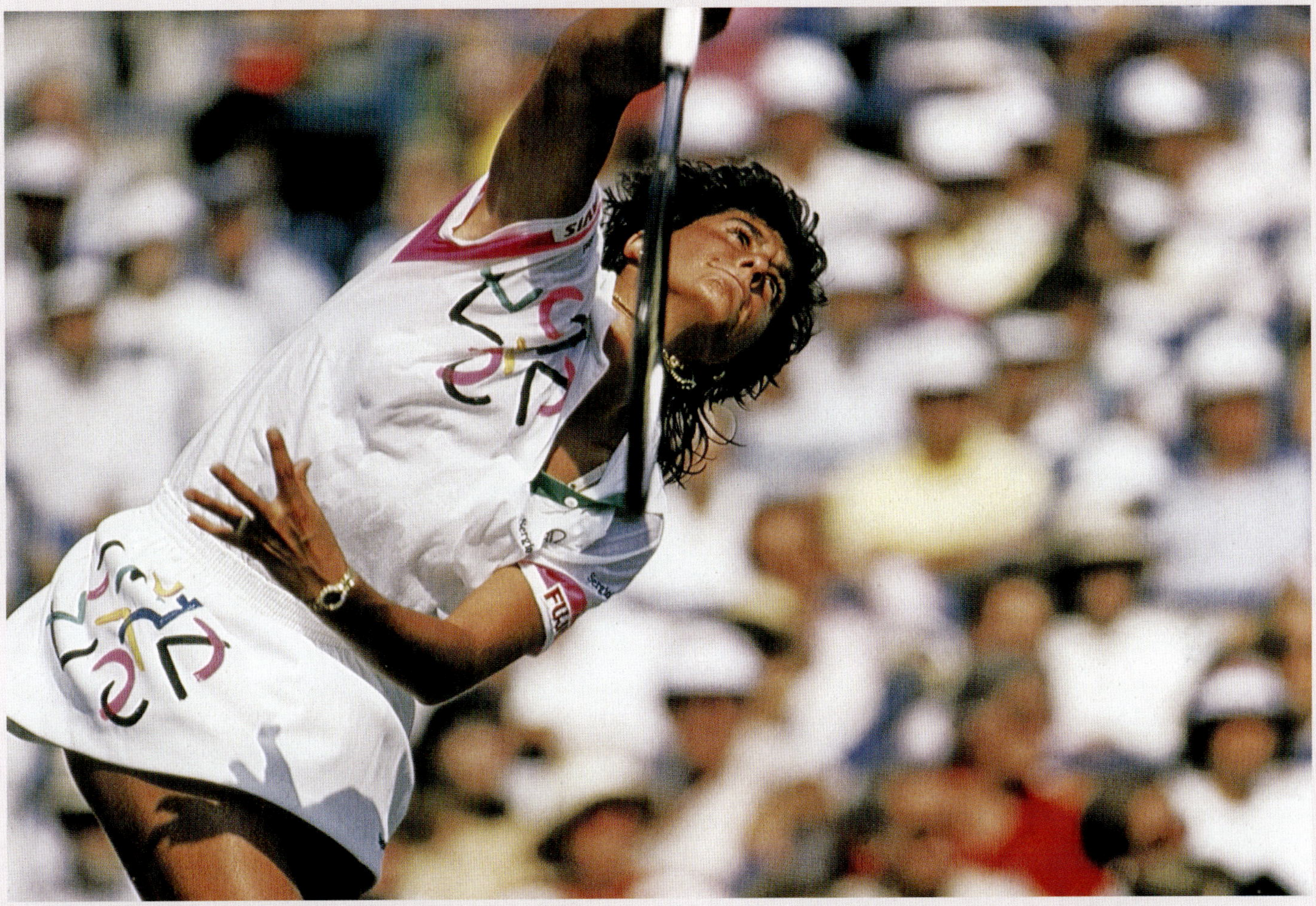

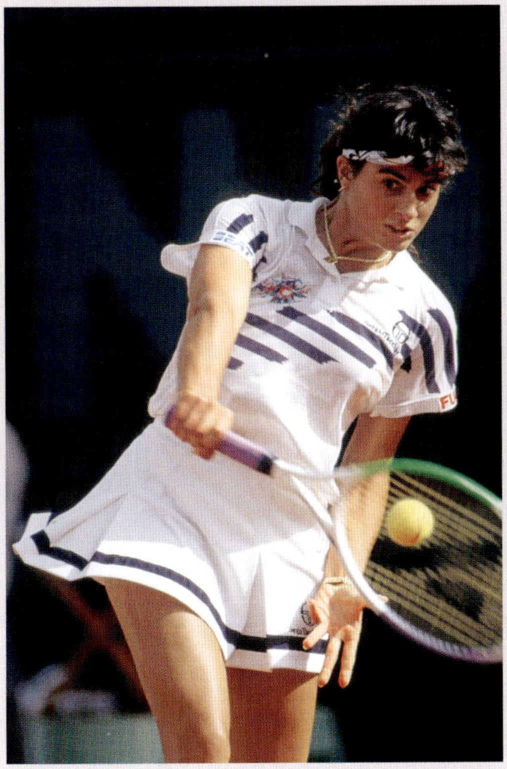

THE TENNIS PARENT

SPEAKERS

JM: JUDY MURRAY,
Andy and Jamie Murray's mother, and Fed Cup women's captain for Great Britain and the national coach of Scotland for ten years.

SKN: Judy, from grassroots to Grand Slams, can you talk to me about your experience as a tennis parent and all the stages you went through?

JM: If your child is exceptional within a team sport, they will at some point be signed by a club—fixtures, training, kit, travel, salary, and bonuses are all taken care of. With juniors, it's very much up to the parents to try to understand that journey as best as they can, and to navigate what can be incredibly choppy waters. I kind of did it in two-year stages. When they were ten, I was looking at what under twelve looks like; when they were twelve, [it was] what does under fourteen look like, and so on. You need to know what's ahead of you so you can plan accordingly. In juniors, there's no prize money, so nothing comes back; you're just paying out the whole time, and as you go up the rungs, costs increase. Financially, it's an enormous challenge, especially if you are a regular family who doesn't come from a wealthy background. So then I was looking for sponsorships, applying for grants.

SKN: Do you think that the press perpetuates an image of you as the archetypal pushy tennis parent?

JM: For sure. When Andy made the third round as a wildcard at eighteen years old, they presented me as the pushy, über-competitive mom, pumping fists in the box and getting excited. You don't see parents sitting in the player box smiling and laughing, because it's completely nerve-racking. I think over the years they've realized what I've done for British tennis, though.

SKN: Has there been any progress since your time in the junior landscape—from the structure to the expectations to the protocol?

JM: I don't think it's changed. In fact, I still think it's a massive advantage if you either have wealth in your family or if you find a wealthy sponsor at a young age, and those are not easy to find, because generally sponsors don't want to invest in potential. If you come from a country that has a wealthy tennis federation or if you're coming from a Grand Slam nation, you are off to a good start, because they can give you access to facilities, events, and expertise.

SKN: In what way would you like to see the parent journey change across the board for the next generation?

JM: I don't think there's a culture of tennis in the UK the same way that there is in France, Spain, Italy, or Germany, and a lot of that has to do with the weather, and also the perception of tennis being difficult to access, difficult to do, and expensive. When my kids were growing up, the tennis club was a place where you could almost spend all day there, and it's about hitting the ball and having fun. So I'd love to see more clubs with open doors and more kids playing the game, more opportunity to compete at a recreational level. A lot of our tennis is geared toward the performer. It's all delivered by ratings and rankings at a very young age, and it should be just about fun, to keep more kids in the game for longer. And that would increase the staying numbers.

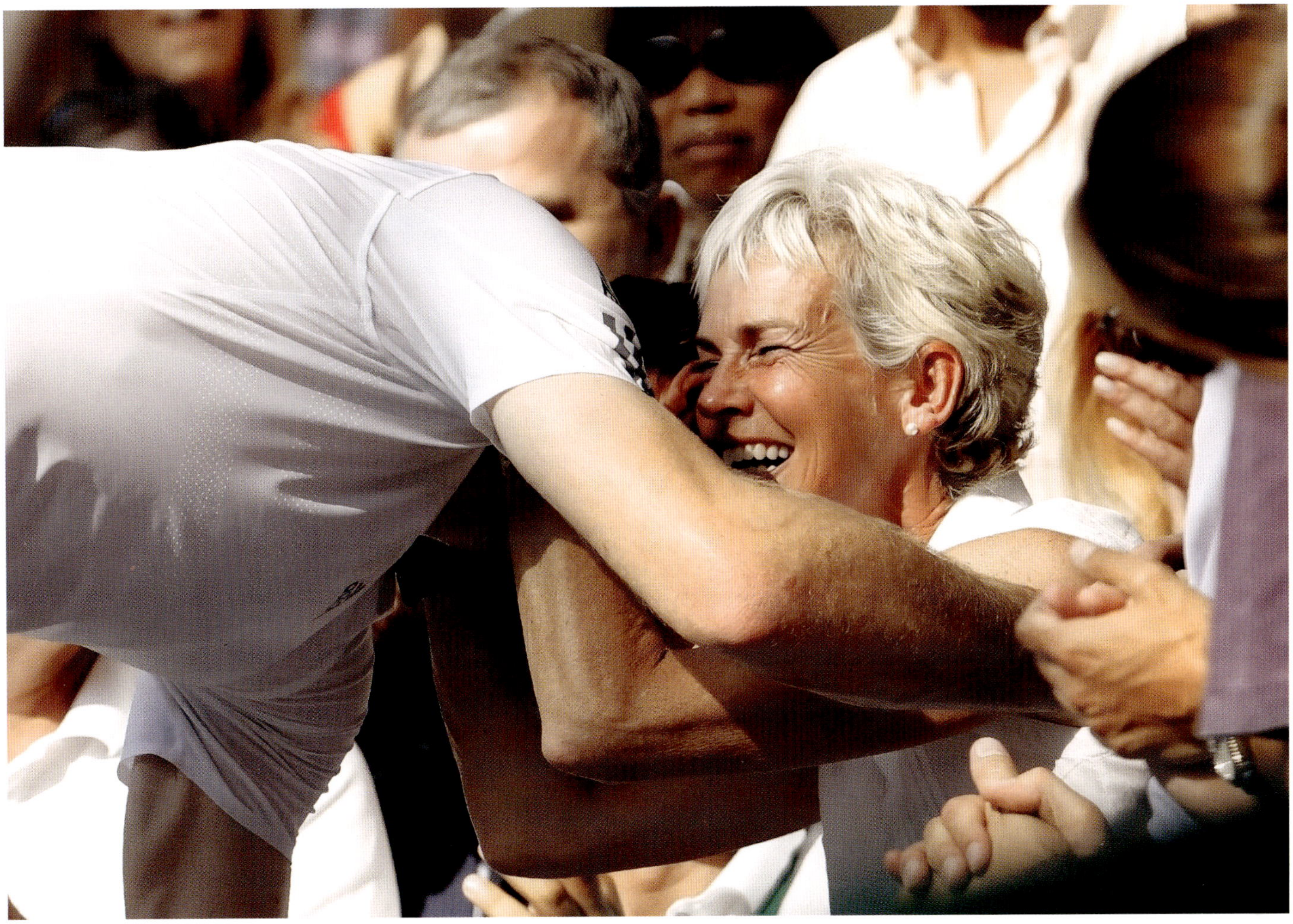

ANDY MURRAY

ANDY MURRAY IS A GRITTY ALL-ROUND COUNTER PUNCHER WITH THREE GRAND SLAM WINS AND TWO OLYMPIC GOLD MEDALS.

I'm sure that a lot of people find it difficult to understand, but my mum knows me very well. I came to tennis thanks to her. She knows when to speak to me, when to be positive, when to tell me off and explain things to me. I don't think that I have ever had an argument with my mum—she's the only person who gets me, who understands me really well. When I speak to her about tennis especially, it is when I need some help from her, some ideas. I suppose I am a bit of a feminist because I have always been surrounded by women, close to Mum and my two grandmothers. I find it easier to talk and open up to them. It's a crying shame that there aren't more female coaches.

HOLLYWOOD

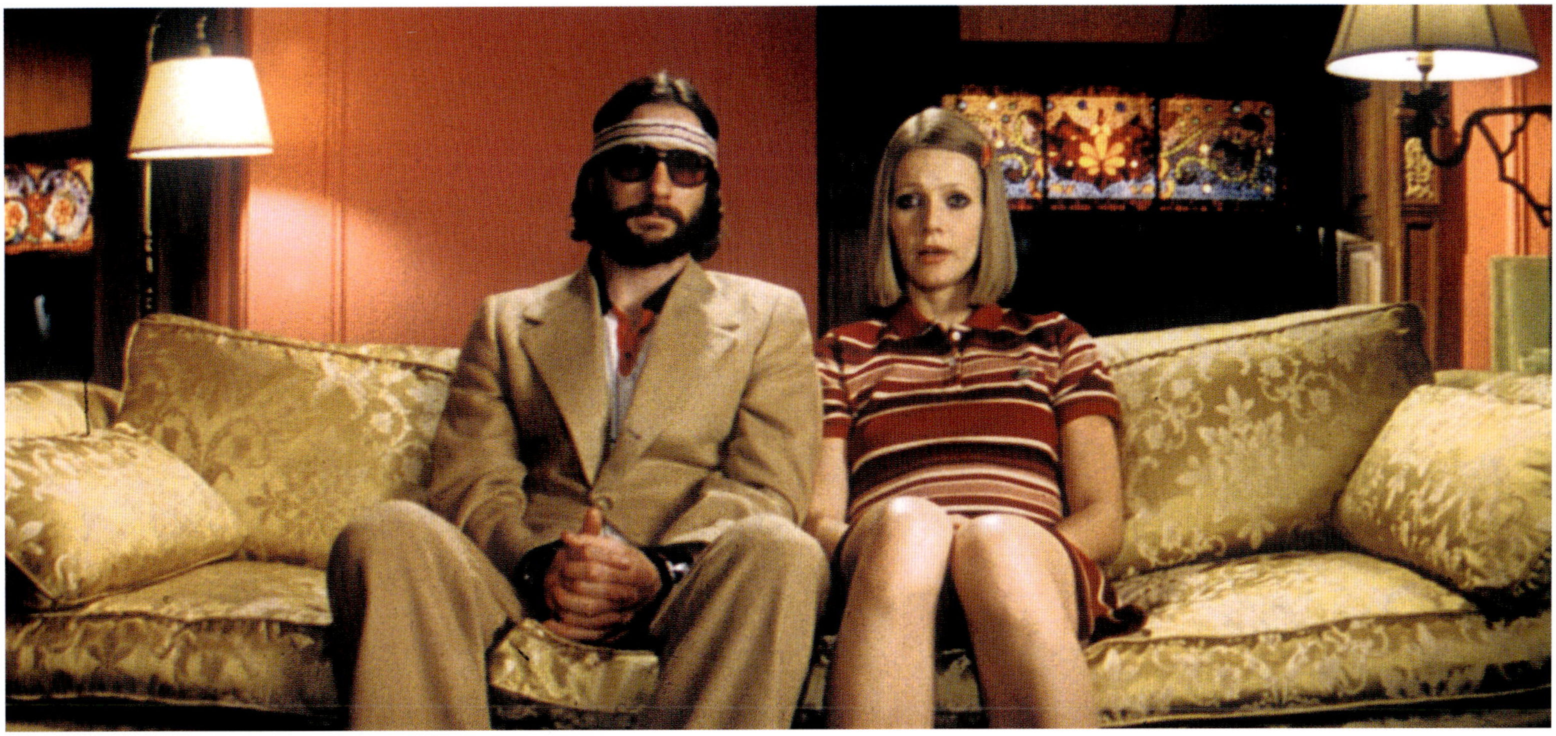

Who would dare pair a Lacoste tennis dress with a $10,000 toffee-color Fendi fur coat? Or a striped knit Fila shirt with a luxe camel double-cashmere two-piece suit and matching Fila striped headband? This is the wistfully weird world of director Wes Anderson and his film *The Royal Tenenbaums*. The movie became a reference point in the fashion lexicon of delinquent dressing. All three central characters—Margot, Chas, and Richie, onetime child prodigies as a playwright, financial whiz, and tennis pro, respectively—are groping through adulthood. Their adult clothes are the exterior badges of their childhood trauma.

Margot's Lacoste tennis dresses ran in a profusion of tricolor stripes, finished with white piqué cap sleeves and collars, a visual breather to this flatline pattern of restrained rebellion. The barrette in her hair and G.H. Bass loafers remain permanently on for inadvertent boarding school chic; the addition of her toast-colored Hermès Birkin and mink Fendi coat gives high luxury plus sportswear—a genius sampling of old money affectations. Margot can't be bothered with the world; the repetitive fatigue of her clothes, her bored aura, monotone voice, all point to this. Her stepbrother Richie "the Baumer" Tenenbaum is the failed tennis pro. He carries his losses sartorially, unable to take off his Björn Borg–inspired sweatband and Fila top, ever ready to replay the match that destroyed his tennis career.

Margot and Richie's visual language of wealthy eccentrics was the crux of Gucci's Autumn/Winter 2015 and Spring/Summer 2017 ready-to-wear shows and became the alphabet of insouciant style for the house under creative director Alessandro Michele. The third adult child, Chas, wore a fire-engine red adidas Beckenbauer tracksuit throughout the film, a leisured spin on the work suit. The style was introduced by adidas in the 1970s; the bold colors and the three stripes on the top and sides of the jacket and pants suggested continuous motion, like a running track, whether the wearer was moving or not. The Trefoil motif was an addition suggested by adidas founder Adolf Dassler's wife, Käthe. *The Royal Tenenbaums* deftly included three sports brands, and for the three leads, diffidently crossbred them with iconic legacy luxury brands—one happy, dysfunctional family.

“YOU PROBABLY HAD ANOTHER GOOD TWO OR THREE YEARS OF COMPETITIVE PLAY IN YOU,” ROYAL SAID.

“PROBABLY,” REPLIED RICHIE.

“I HAD A LOT RIDING ON THAT MATCH, YOU KNOW. FINANCIALLY AND PERSONALLY. WHY DID YOU CHOKE OUT THERE THAT DAY, BAUMER? I KIND OF DISAPPEARED AFTER THAT, DIDN’T I?”

“I UNDERSTOOD. YOU’RE NOT VERY GOOD WITH DISAPPOINTMENT,” SAID RICHIE.

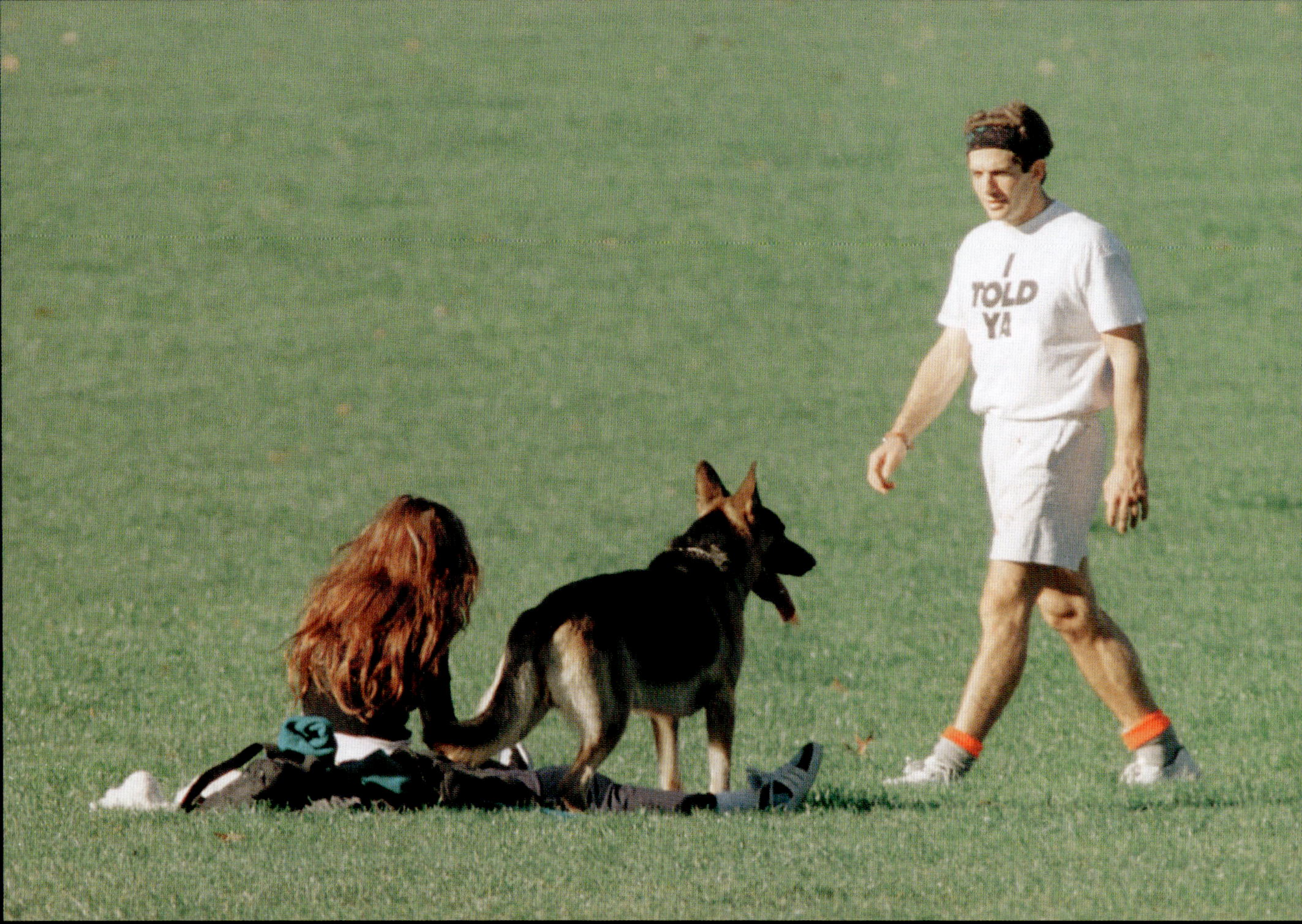
I
TOLD
YA

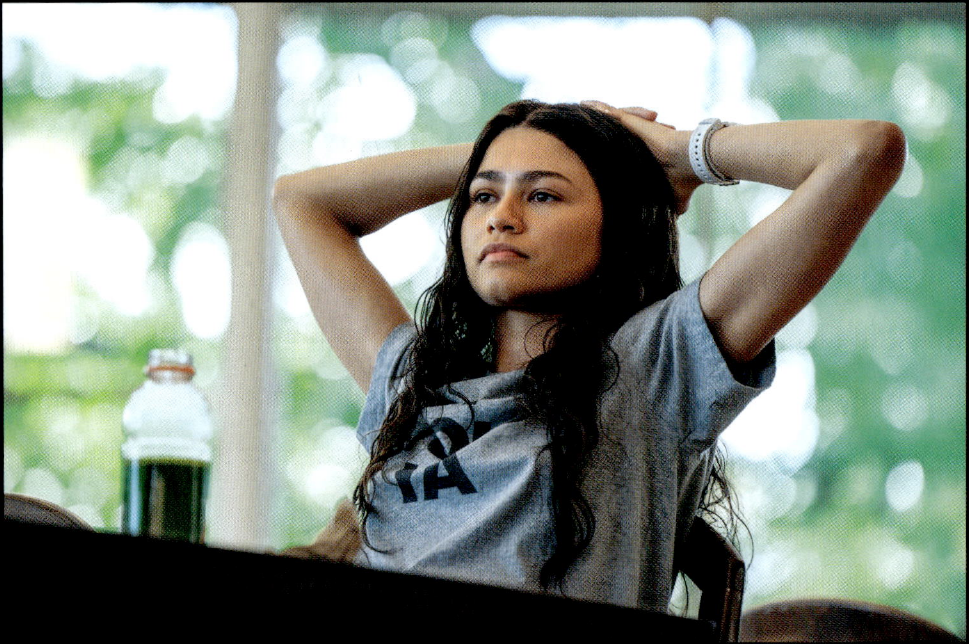

"I KNOW WHEN YOU LOOK AT SPORTS TODAY, IT'S ABOUT THE LOGO—THE AMERICAN DREAM OF A BRAND. THE WALLPAPER AROUND US IS MADE UP OF BRANDS. I HAVE DESIGNED FOR FEDERER AND UNIQLO, BUT TO WORK ON IT IN A 360 [DEGREE] RANGE WITH CHALLENGERS WAS A LITTLE DIFFERENT. I WAS OBSESSED BY JFK JR., HIS T-SHIRTS IN ATHLEISURE AND CENTRAL PARK: JOSH WAS BASED ON HIM. WHEN I DESIGN, IT HAS TO COME FROM SOME FORM OF ART, BECAUSE FROM THERE YOU CAN SEE HOW COLORS INTERACT WITH EACH OTHER. WHEN I THINK ABOUT TENNIS IN PARTICULAR, I THINK OF IT AS INCREDIBLY GRAPHIC—IT'S ONE OF THOSE SPORTS WHERE YOU GET THESE SINGLE INCREDIBLE IMAGES OF PLAYERS AND THEIR STYLE."

—JONATHAN ANDERSON

ROBERT F. KENNEDY TOURNAMENT

KERRY KENNEDY, DAUGHTER OF ETHEL AND FORMER SENATOR ROBERT F. KENNEDY, IS A DEDICATED HUMAN RIGHTS ACTIVIST AND LAWYER CONTINUING HER FAMILY'S LEGACY OF SOCIAL JUSTICE.

The Robert F. Kennedy Memorial was founded by my mother Ethel Kennedy in 1968 as an action-focused, non-profit organization to continue my father's legacy and address the social justice issues that he cared about so deeply. To fund the activities of the organization, the RFK Pro-Celebrity Tennis Tournament was launched in 1971. Farrah Fawcett, Clint Eastwood, Stan Smith, Billie Jean King, and many more, attended and played; it was a microcosm of 70s culture.

My mother used tennis to increase awareness about social justice causes while raising money to support these issues. My father believed that "What is learned on the athletic field is not forgotten, nor are the lessons of character that are forged there ever lost."

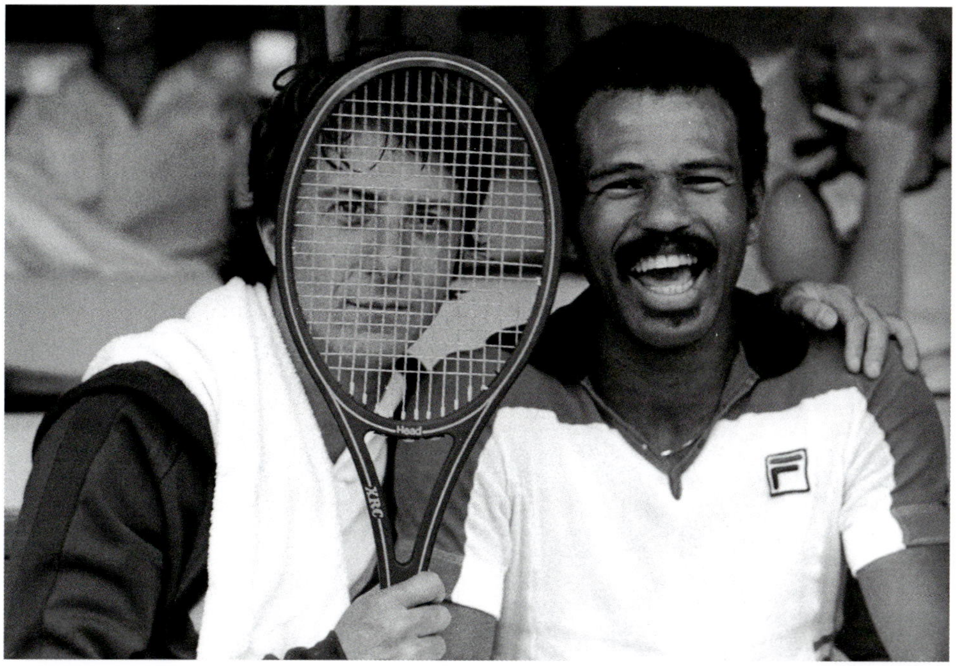

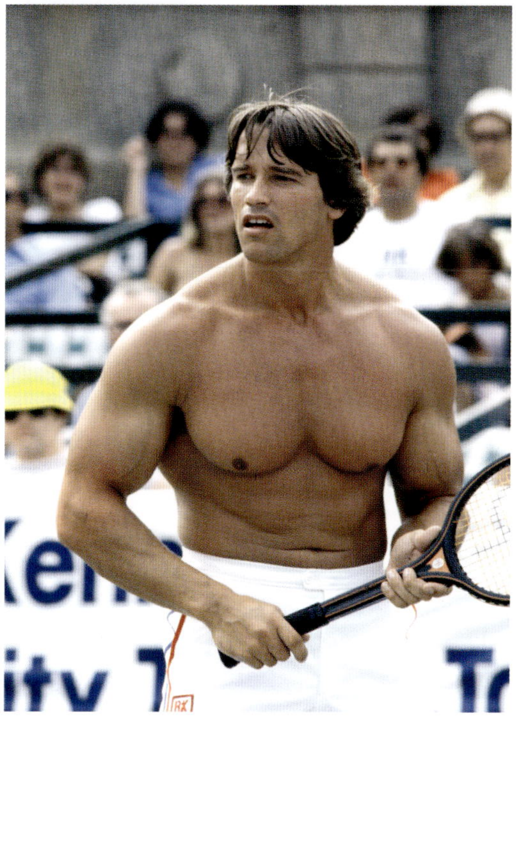

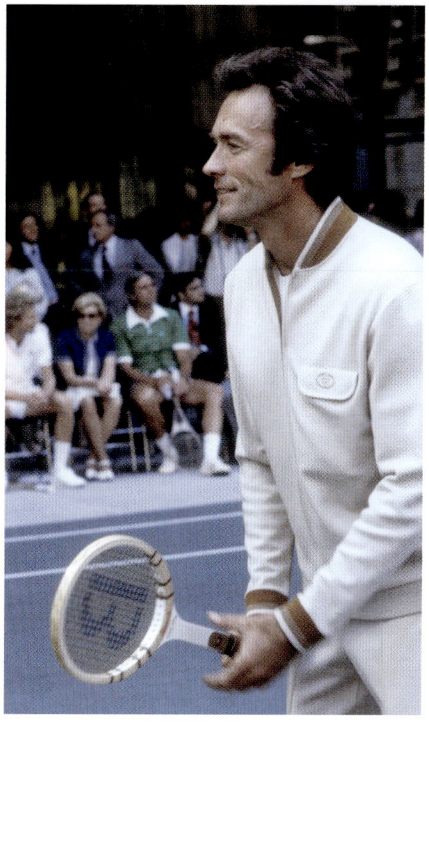

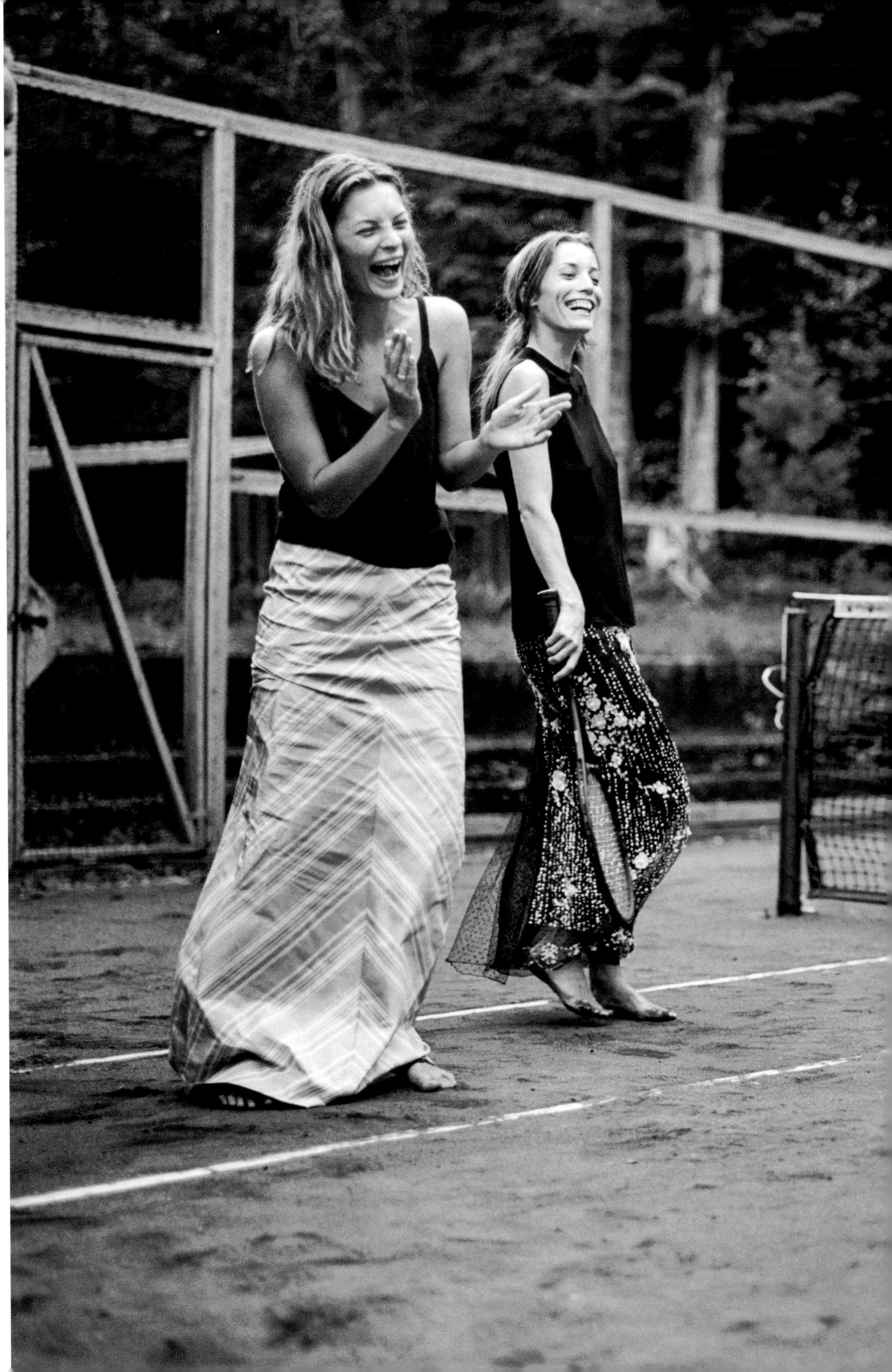

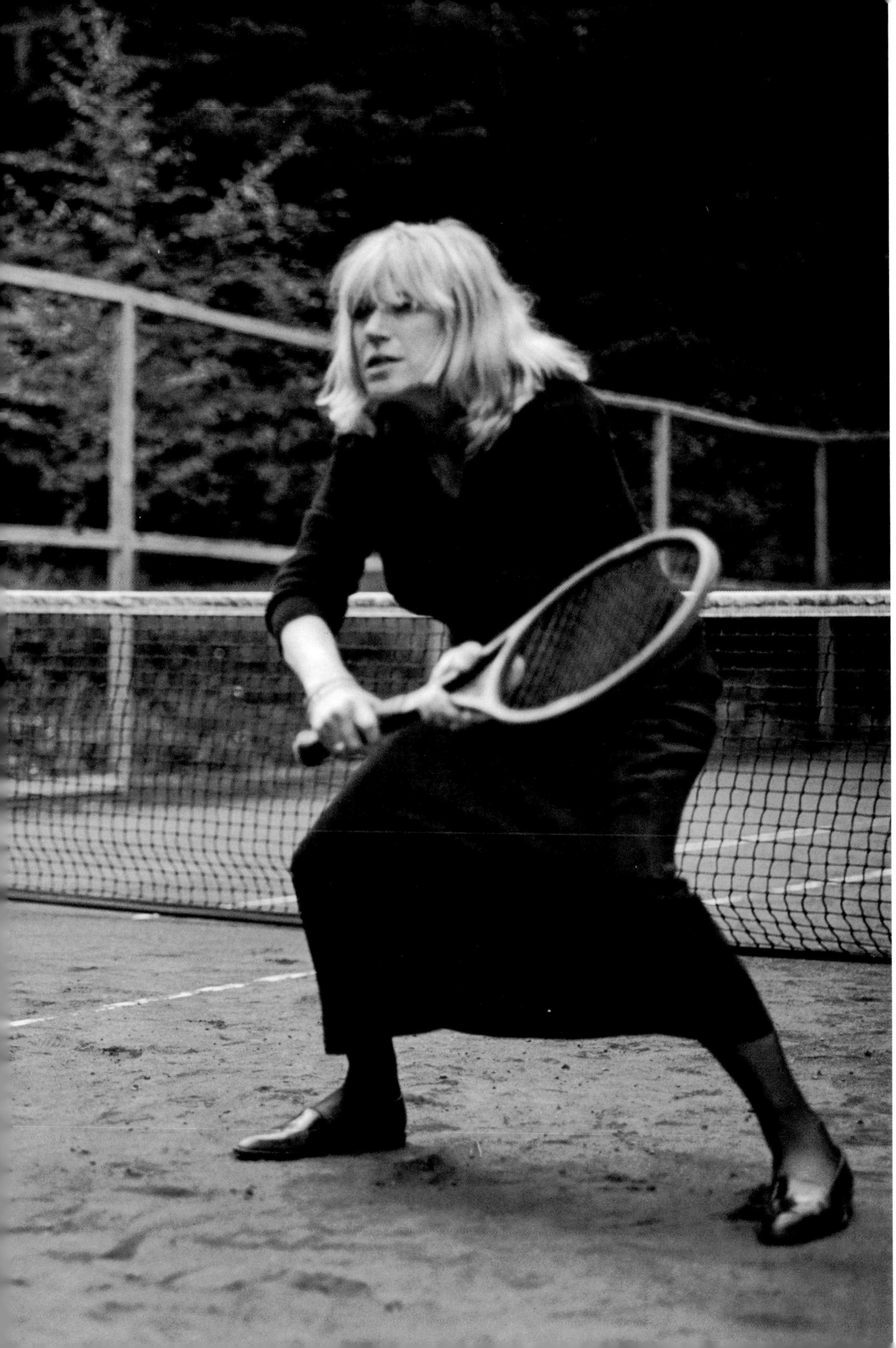

ADIDAS

SPEAKERS

BH: BEN HERATH,
vice president of design, specialist sports

DESIGN

BH: When we started to design for this year, it seemed like it was a very noisy world out there, where we were dialing everything up to the maximum. We wanted to reset and focus again on our sport and core principles, and the key principle was simplicity. We believe that we're at our best when we're beautifully simple, and it takes a lot of work and effort to get us there. It takes confidence and courage to remove and not add things from our designs. This allows us to focus on materials, constructions, how something feels. My design question is: How do they feel when they put adidas on? Do they feel empowered? Confident that they can perform at their best? We obsess over everything, down to the last millimeter, like the weights of the fabric, the breathability, the performance testing—it all comes into play.

In tennis, we want to capture the magic of the movement, but there's a real science behind movement, and the innovation lab is vital for us. What are the movements that the design decisions are based on from, let's say, the serve? Which is a reach to a lunge—so it's the angled pockets to allow ease of entry, or it's a little embroidery to lock the ball in place, or it's the split as they crouch, the track around the arms and the seams as they reach. For the women players, we have learned about uninhibited movement. What adidas is always looking at is performance evolution: What can we do to adjust this? What material would be better? We work closely with the athletes on this, and we've got years of research, data about the body and sweat zones, so we look at airflow, the silhouettes, the buttons, new contouring, and also the colors as a sporting brand. It's about bringing freshness and newness to all our designs. We pick these moments of when do we want to be bold and when do we want to turn things down.

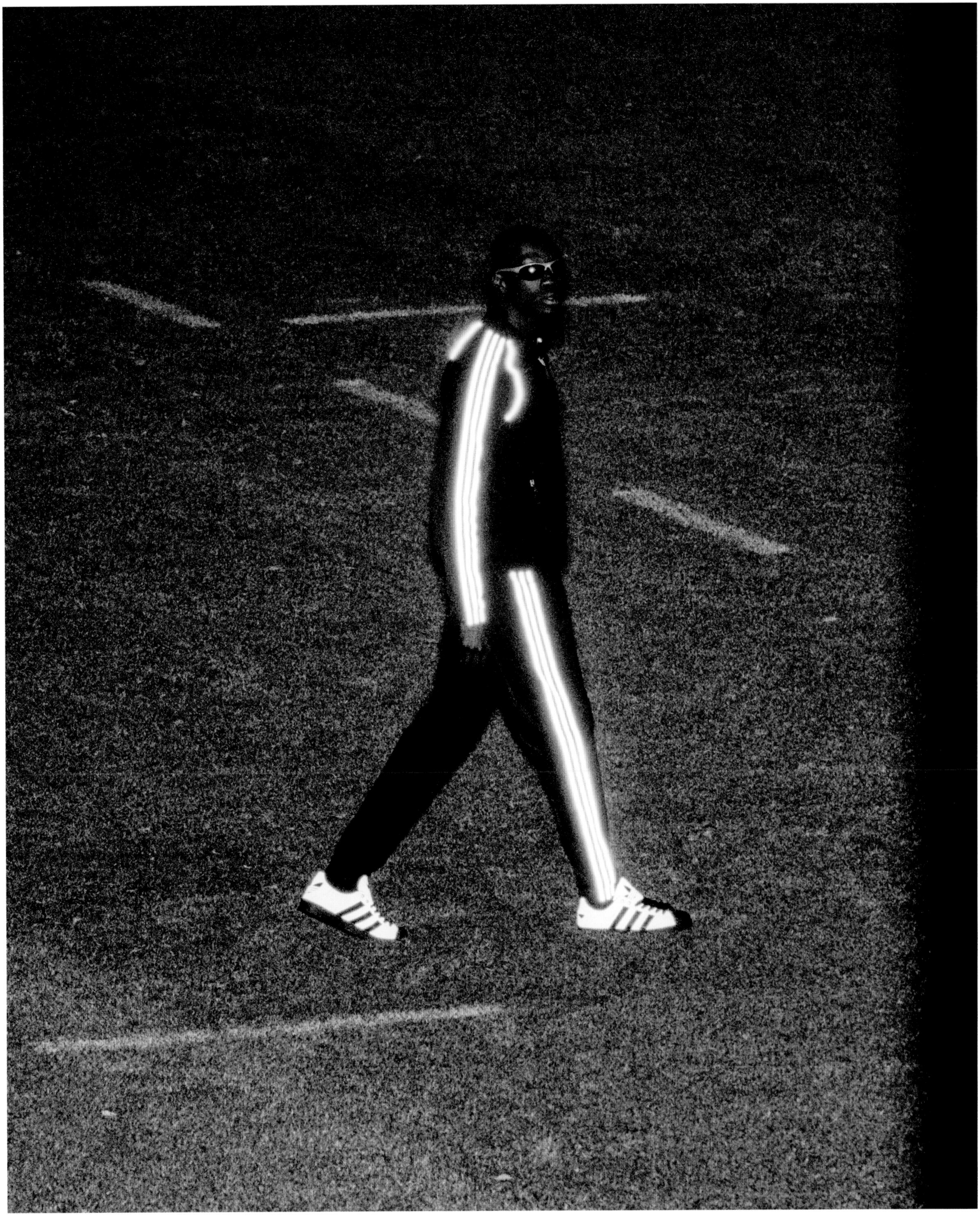

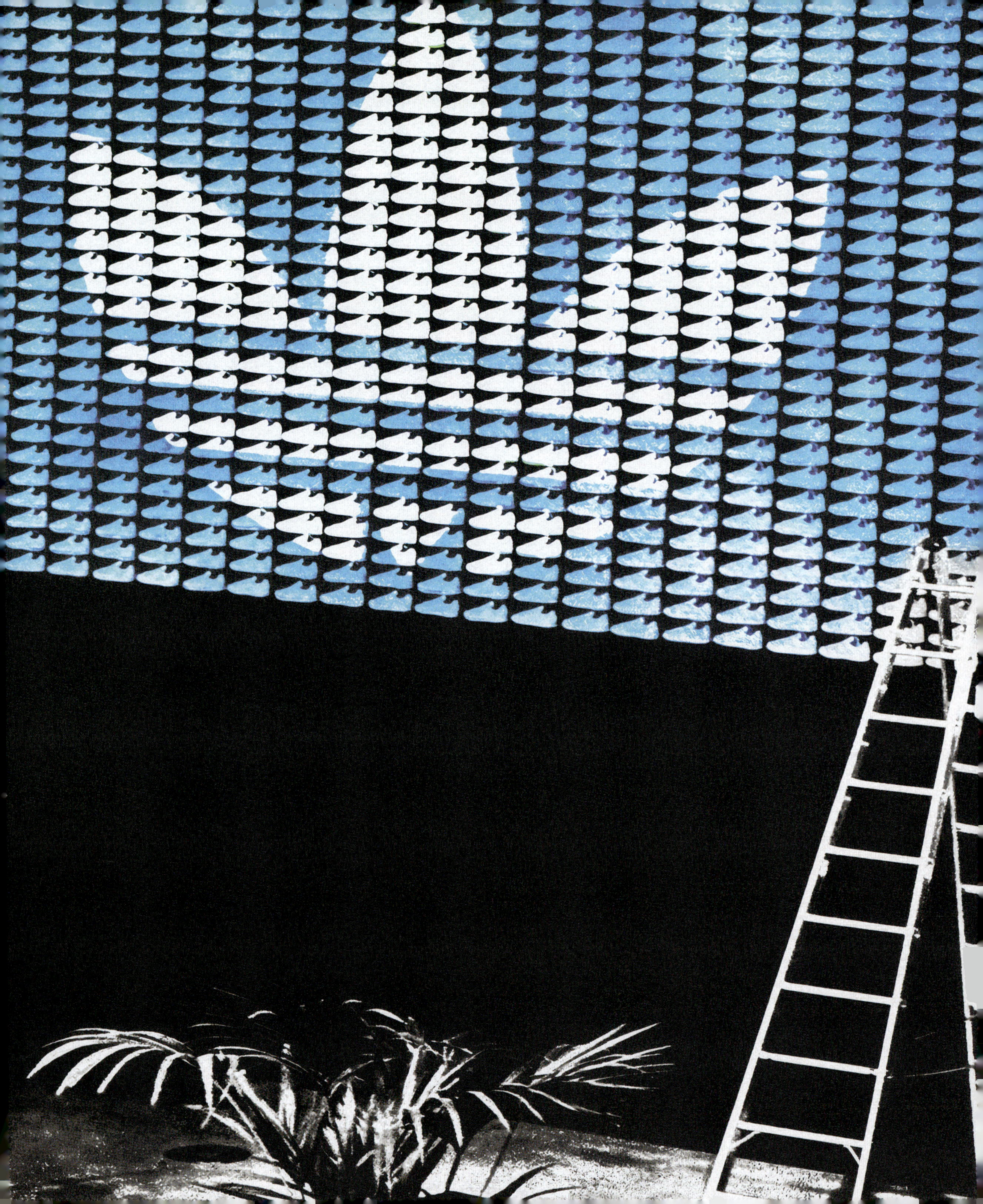

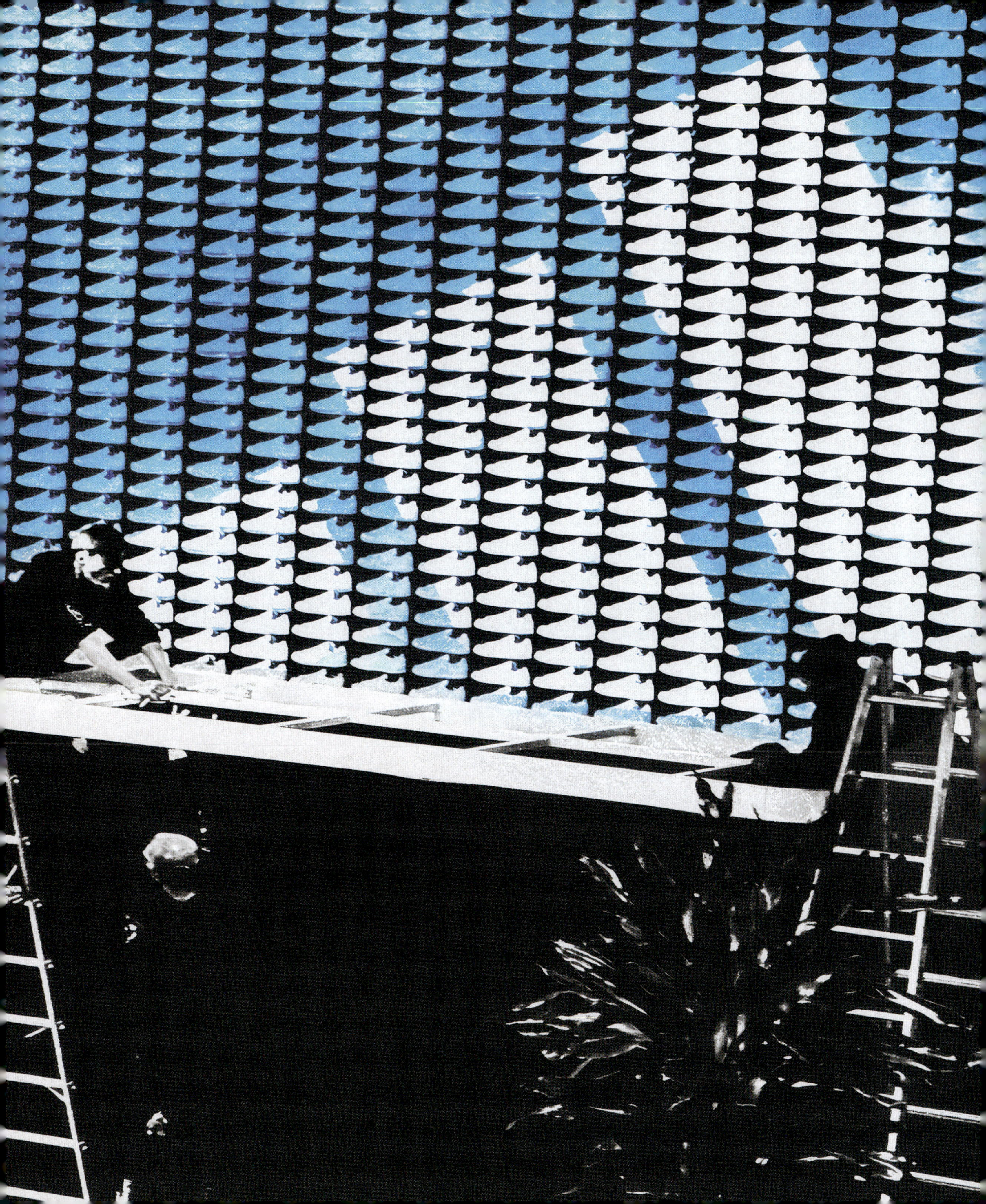

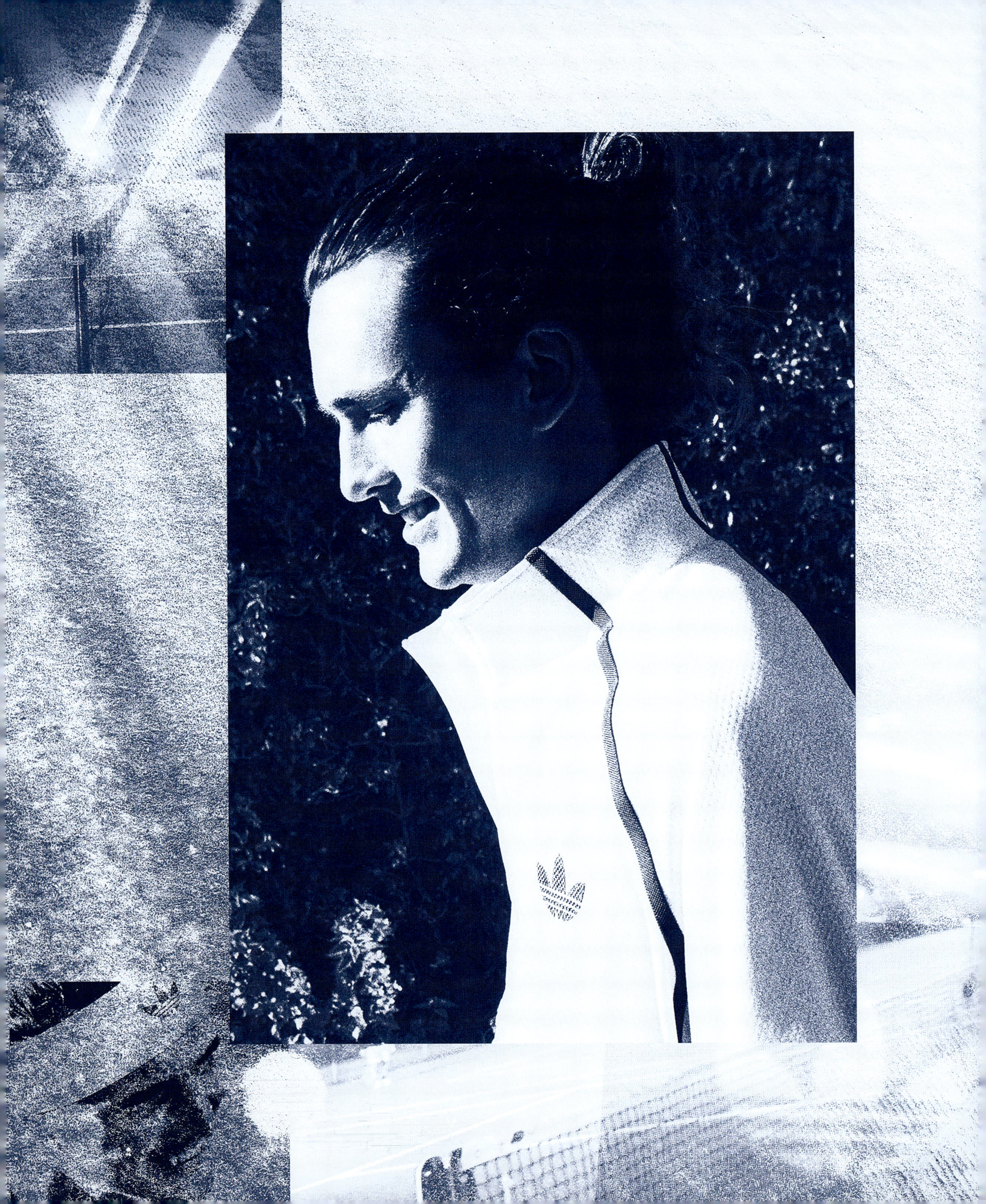

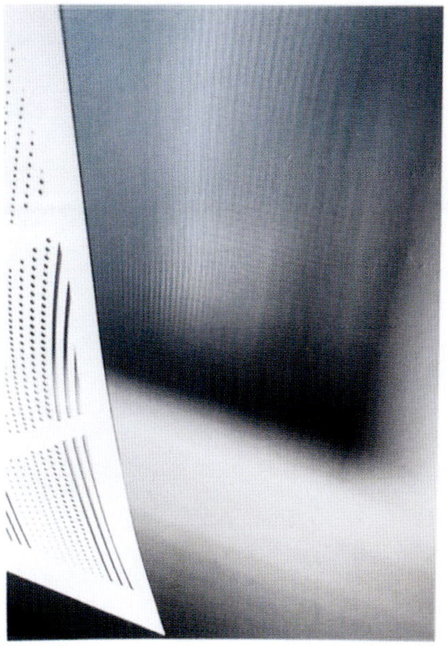

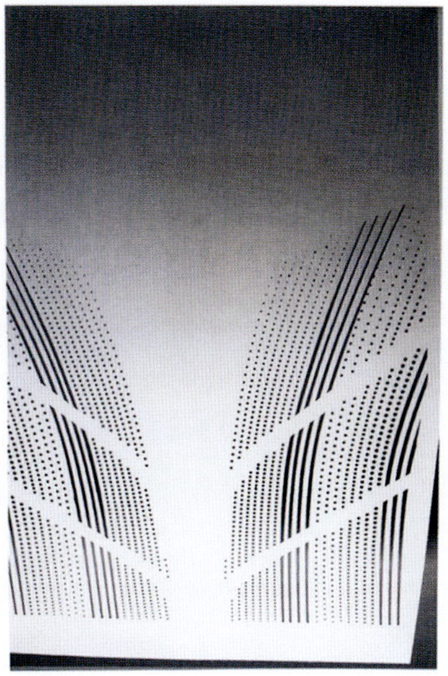

LasER cuT creates the sHaft of light fabric

“WE DID A WHOLE SERIES OF BREATHABILITY STUDIES. IT'S A HAPPY SLAM [AUSTRALIAN OPEN]—THE START OF THE YEAR. WE TOOK THE SCIENCE BETWEEN HEAT MAPPING AND WHERE THE BODY NEEDS VENTILATION AND FOCUSED ON THE MAGIC OF LIGHT AND SHADOW. WE PROJECTED LIGHT THROUGH THIS LASER CUT PATTERN THAT IS EFFECTIVELY A HEAT MAP. IF YOU SEE BEHIND THE SHADOWS, THERE ARE PATTERNS THAT ARE CREATED, WHERE THE LIGHT GOES THROUGH, SO WE TOOK SCIENTIFIC ELEMENTS AND MADE THEM ARTISTIC.”

-BEN HERATH, VICE PRESIDENT OF DESIGN AT ADIDAS, SPECIALIST SPORTS

WIMBLEDON

The culture that is wrapped around the sport is important, and this is part of Wimbledon. There is a huge appetite for the look of tennis right now; whereas before we might have been focused purely on the athlete, now we are looking at what there is beyond the sport—what's trending? What are people buying? What are they repurposing, and how are they styling '70s, '80s, and '90s fashion? We landed on three areas: simple layering, proportion, and styling. It's not just about the T-shirt that you wear on the court, but how do the pieces work together? This research is consumer-led. We started with styling sessions, where we photographed it (the tennis look) in the photo studio with samples coming from the archives of different eras or from the company, to help us make decisions on the overall look. This process is the opposite of a performance-driven process, where we're looking at something that's working and how we incrementally improve. It's the reverse of performance engineering; it's looking at how something looks in our culture. And this is essentially what *ACE* is about, Sunita—fusing these two worlds.

One of the key trends that we saw in tennis was argyle, so we looked at different executions, but with a lifestyle and engineering lens, like the piping that we worked with highlighted seaming, or the way the piqué on the sleeves and collar is super soft, or tennis pulls on the zip. We wanted to keep the whole collection connected to a reference of the past, but also to modernize it, so we engineered argyle as a fabric. We then added the Trefoil, which comes from Originals, and the logo finish, because this is referencing the lifestyle moment. I would say this collection is an important mark for adidas tennis because it's a celebration of sport and culture. There are certain points in the seventy-six years of adidas history where we ask: Where does it make sense to see the Trefoil on performance wear and on court? Where are we merging these two worlds? It's something we do intentionally and strategically. We see this as an important moment in sportswear history, where we as a brand have brought a lot of energy into tennis and lifestyle.

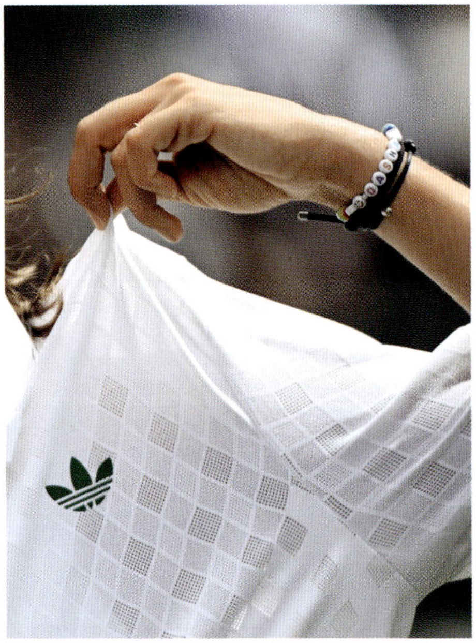

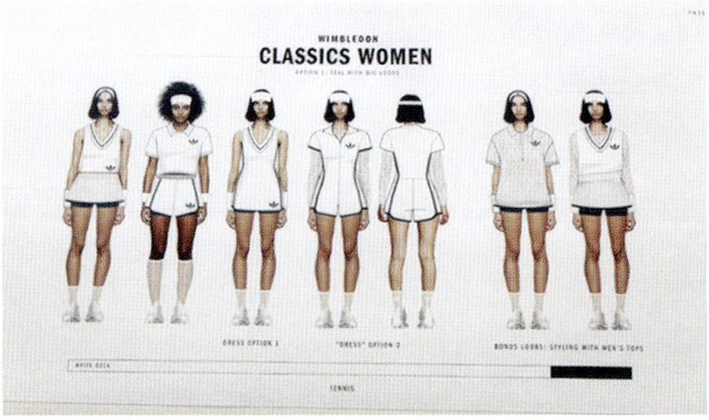

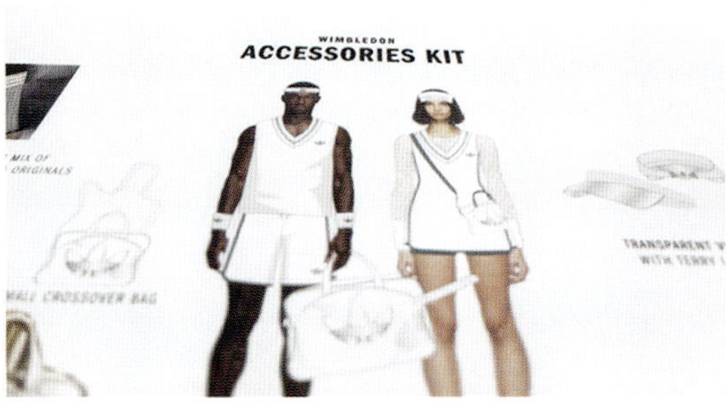

The London Originals Collections

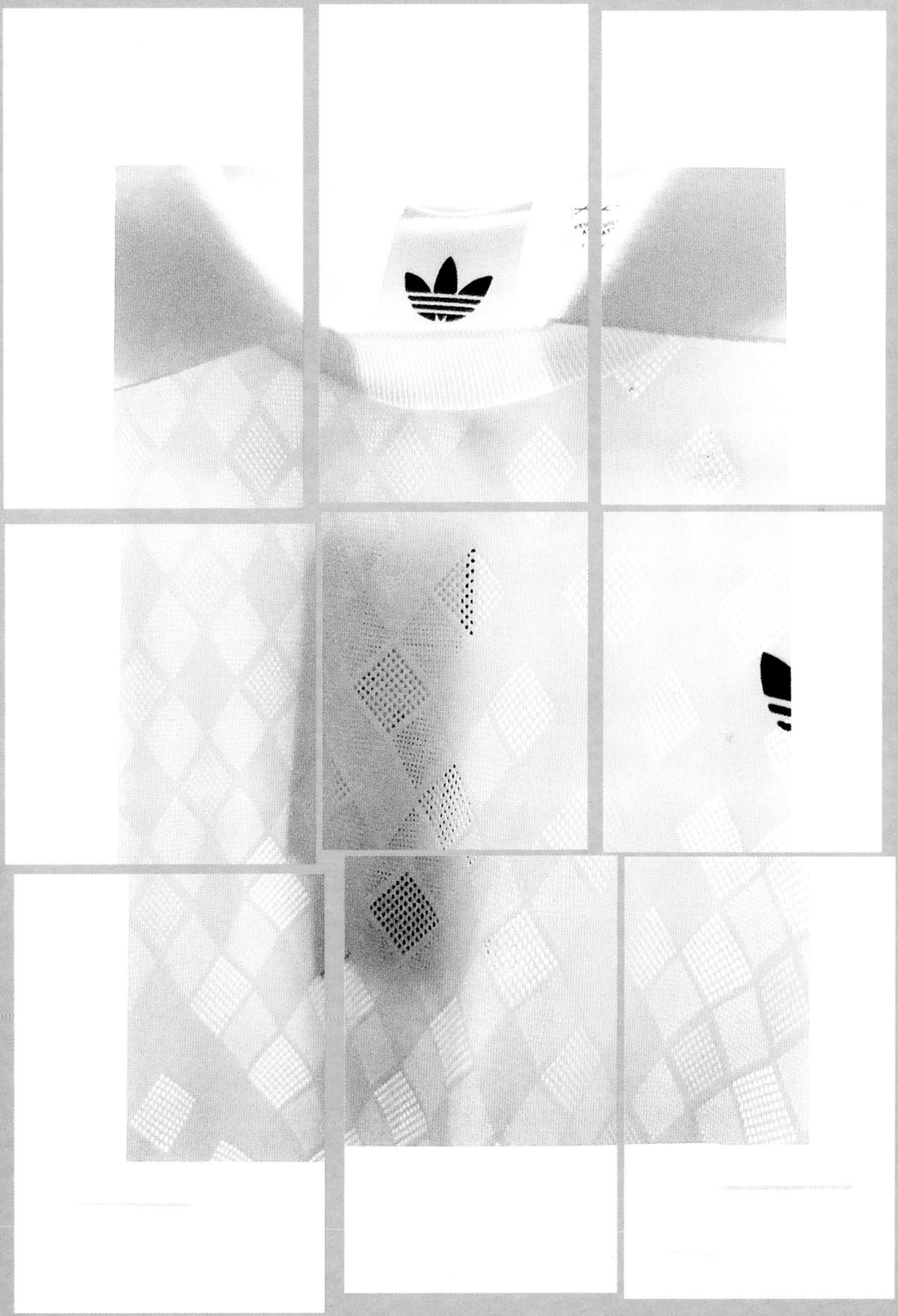

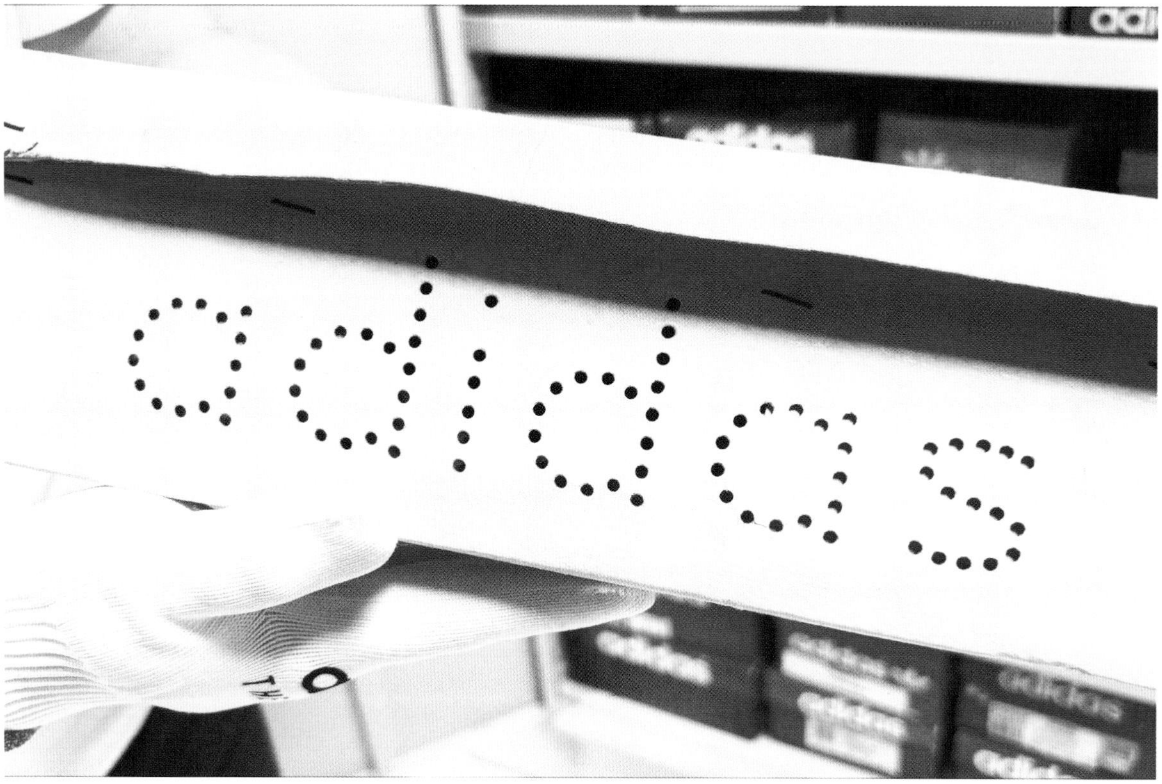

It's the biggest, boldest, most confident, loudest experience of all [US Open], and we wanted to match that level of enthusiasm and energy—Yohji and his team are always excited about working with us. There are aspects that we hold true: the artistry, the craft, the beauty of fabrication and draping materials. What was a real aha moment between the two teams was talking about tennis as poetry, to slow down the player's movements. So poetry became a connection point where we would even do poetry evenings to get inspired.

Wimbledon was referencing the past a little. This Y-3 collection will be looking at the future, at this rebellious spirit. There were certain areas where we felt that we could challenge certain colors, codes, construction, and material. Where we started was looking at the line—the perfection and symmetry of it, the storyline, the line of courts, the lines of garments—and we looked at how we could incorporate that in the draping of materials. We asked where we conceal and reveal the body, where do we need cutouts for breathability and arm movement, and where do we need to cover and flatter the body. There is a challenge of symmetry and asymmetry as well as an idea of energy—captured, contained, and moving in this design with Y-3. We want to challenge how tennis might be typically seen and how we style and script the athletes—but through the Yohji Yamamoto lens.

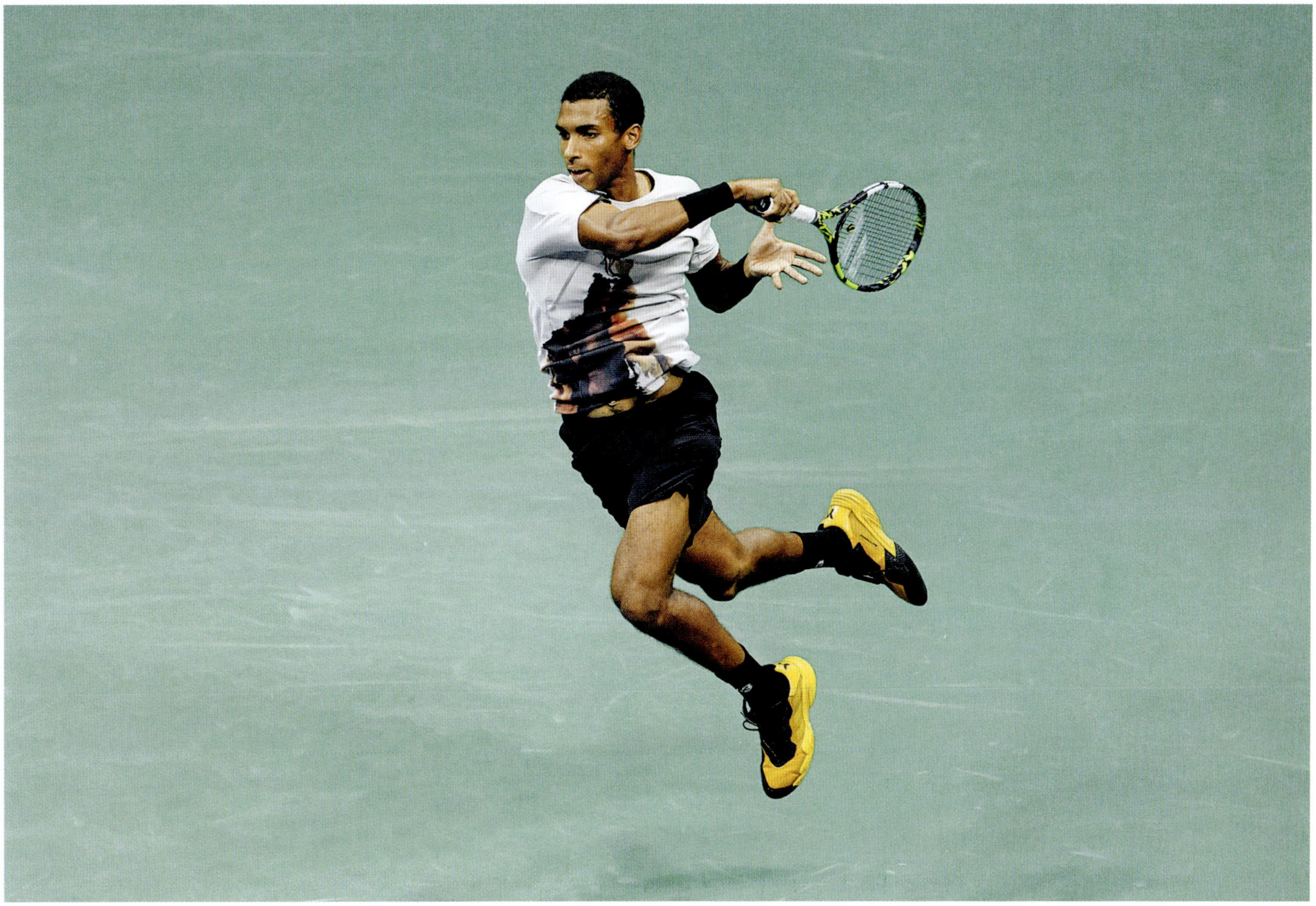

ADIDAS X YOHJI YAMAMOTO

YOHJI YAMAMOTO IS A FASHION DESIGNER.

When I look back at human history, women have always been treated lower than men. Today, I see women, rising—leaders, believers, something. To me, they are powerful and alluring, especially in Japan. My intuition says that the younger generation of women are stronger than young men. In the ordinary world, can men be weak?

One aspect of FEMININITY is the power of a woman to create a baby—humankind. It is the greatest power, and I respect it. Women are born biologically weaker (when comparing their body shape and muscles) than men, but when women train for sports, they grow 50 percent logically and 50 percent innately. Whatever the sport—tennis, golf, soccer—women are more interesting to me than men, because they train so hard.

I love working on women's sporting apparel, so that they can feel even more powerful and alluring while moving naturally. Women have always known how to move, how to maneuver using their hands and feet. When they play, they look like they are trying to win, not like the men, who maybe take their strength for granted.

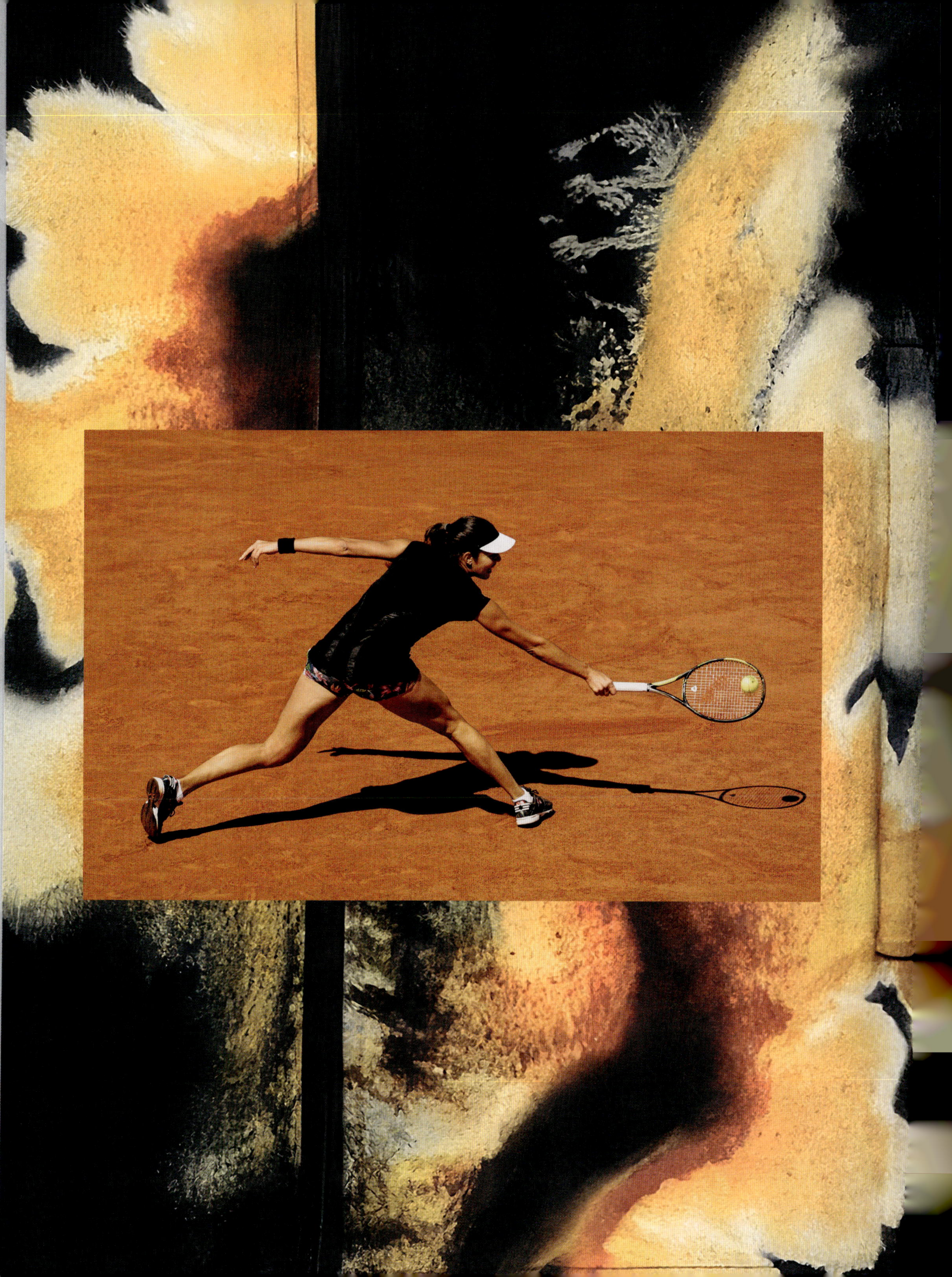

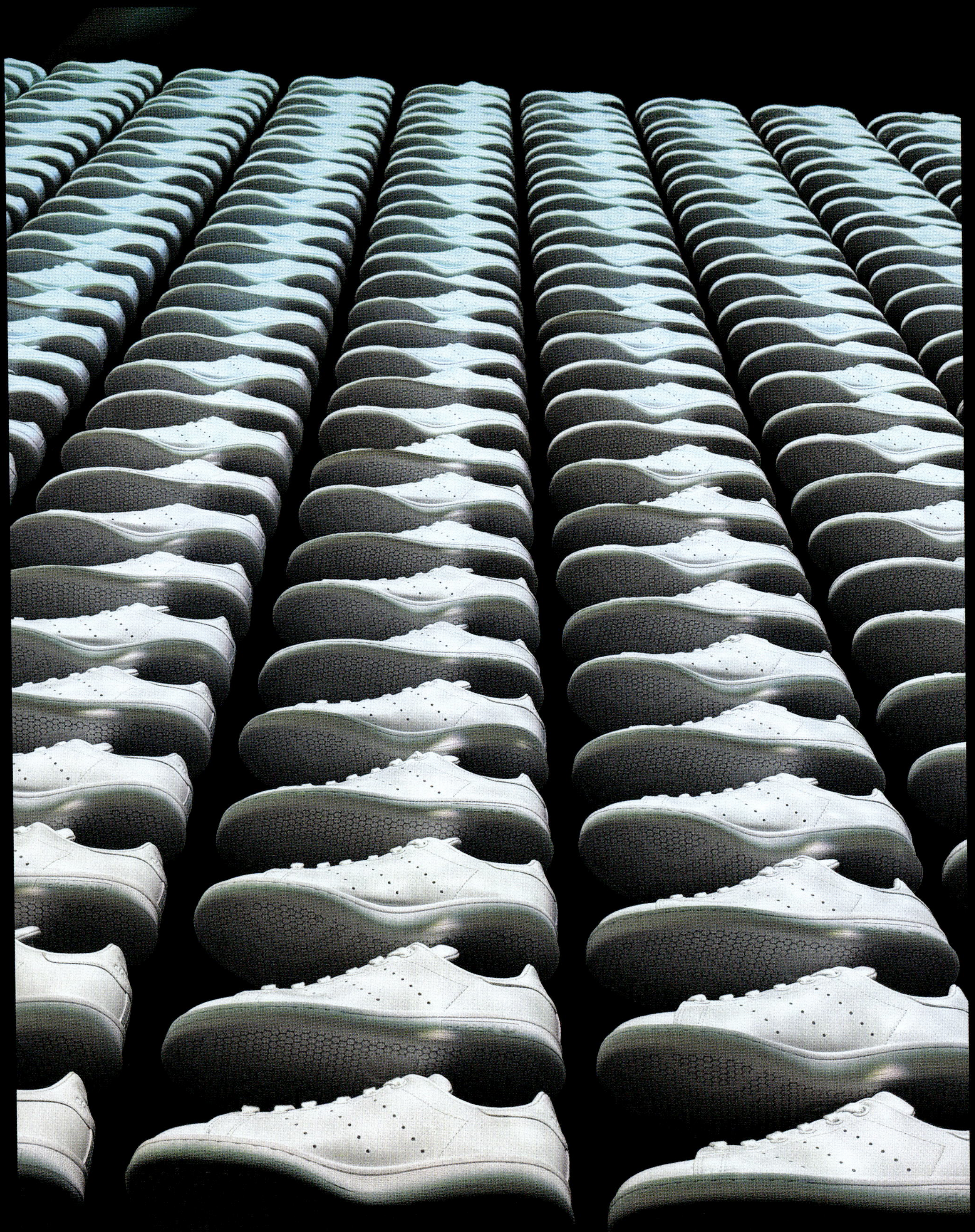

STAN SMITH

SPEAKER

BH: BEN HERATH,
vice president of design, specialist sports

SKN: Let's talk about the Stan Smith, seeing the first tennis shoe in the adidas archives. It started off as performance and then became lifestyle. I noted that your new CEO seriously wants to bring the performance factor back to adidas.

BH: There is something magical about a performance product that is right and then starts connecting with people. It's hard to intentionally do something like that—when you speak to a larger audience off court. If you design performance authentically with purpose in mind and put simplicity into a product, it gives it a chance to live beyond [itself]. The Stan Smith shoe is so minimal; it's just three pieces, when you look at it. But it performed in its day. The speed of adoption happens quickly, and there isn't a formula to guarantee for that to happen. As a performance designer, I think about simplicity. I question: Is that what people want to wear, on court and off court? But I always address the athlete first. When you go beyond the sport, like Stan Smith's shoe, it's amazing to see it repurposed into culture. Sneaker culture is so vibrant and alive and it fuels design, color, material choices. Sport is always our heart, but when it connects to the culture around the sport, it allows a speedier transition into culture. The Stan Smith is loved by generations. It's extraordinary.

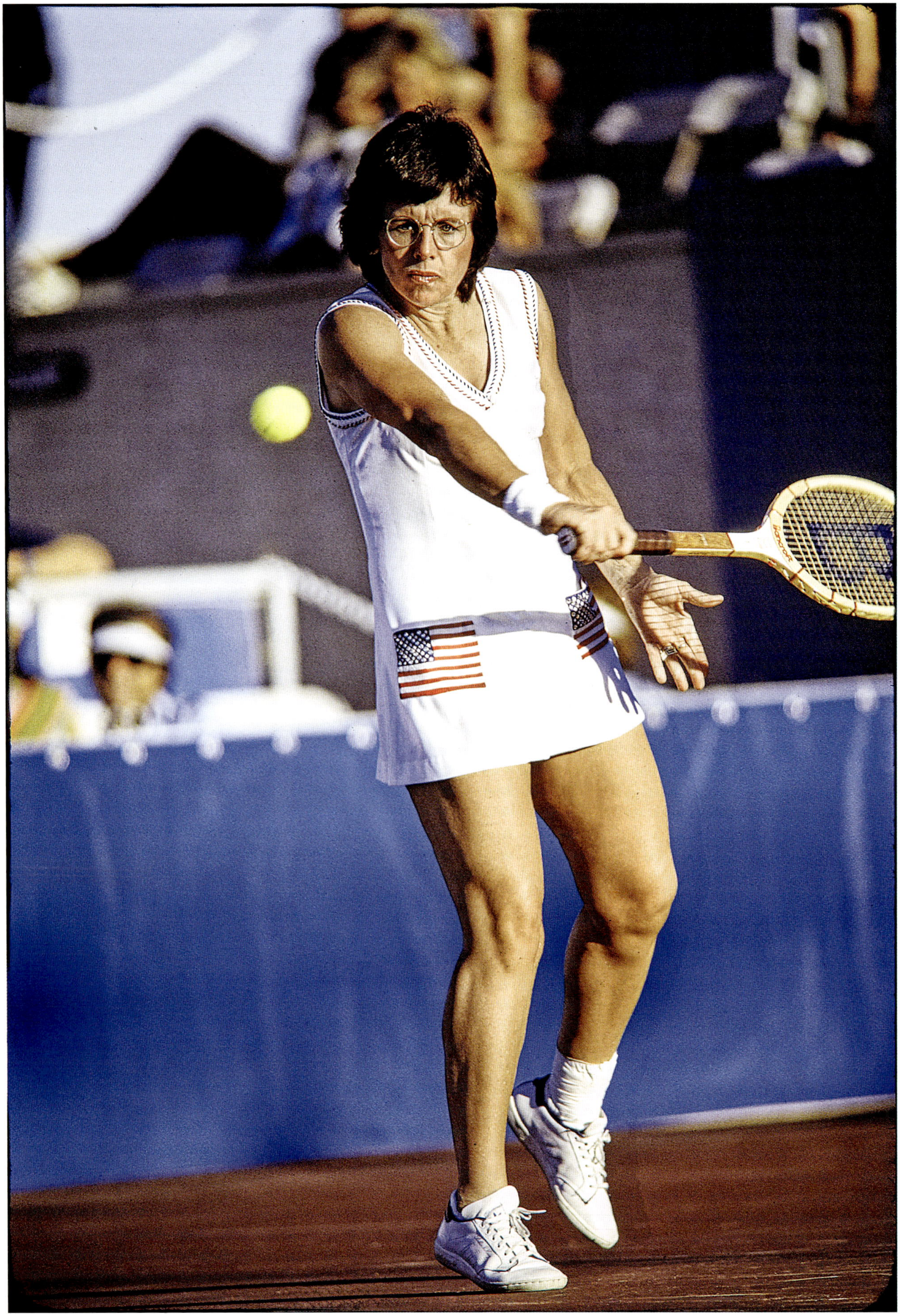

BILLIE JEAN KING

BILLIE JEAN KING IS A FIERCE SERVE AND VOLLEYER WITH TWELVE GRAND SLAM WINS.

ON TENNIS

Tennis to me is art and science together. The game started for both men and women. But women had to wear corsets, hide their bodies, and couldn't let their ankles or their wrists show. It really was a reflection of where women were at, the lack of freedom. Everything is a microcosm of society, but fashion tells you where you're at.

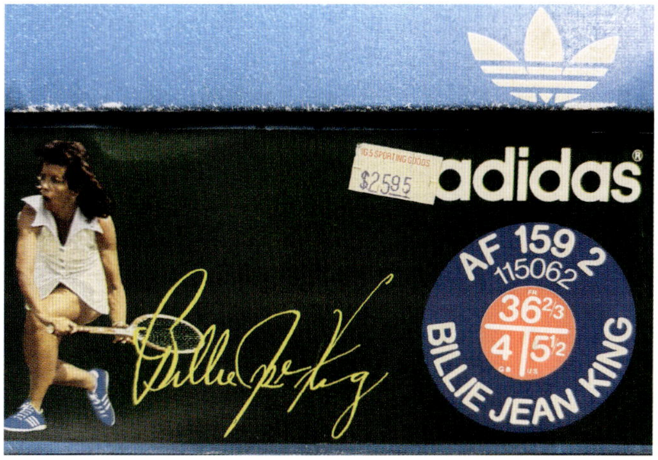

SKN: What collabs have stood the test of adidas time?

BH: Tennis as a sport has a great history of collabs. Each team brings something new to adidas that we are proud of, that shows the dimensions of tennis on and off court. Let's look at Y-3, which is actually sport and street and advancing the future. The Pharrell collab was amazing. He worked on several sport categories: football, running, and the US Open. The Palace collab was another standout. Who would put tennis and skate together, and at the oldest Grand Slam at Wimbledon? There is also tennis and fashion, which is a runway. Stella [McCartney] brought a spotlight to the importance of woman athletes and built an identity where she could bring her sense of how to complement a woman's body with the right seaming, color, graphics. She elevated the needs of performance, but with her fashion eye, it's a different viewpoint. We are very good as a brand at bringing opposites together. It's also about bringing people together that have diverse experience and learning from that.

STEFANOS TSITSIPAS

STEFANOS TSITSIPAS IS AN AGGRESSIVE ALL-COURT PLAYER AND TWO-TIME GRAND SLAM FINALIST.

SKN: Fashion seems to play an important role in the way you present yourself. What's your style?

ST: Yes, fashion is something that I enjoy. Ever since I was a kid, it has always been a way that I express myself—it's not a matter of being trendy, it's a matter of telling the world who I am. It's a balance of relaxed elegance and low-key confidence. It's about keeping it simple and timeless, while also not being afraid to play around when it feels right.

SKN: What fashion brands do you gravitate to and why?

ST: There are several that I admire. I appreciate brands with a strong identity: Y-3, Loro Piana, Fear of God, Loewe. It's nice when fashion becomes poetic and, in a way, a story is being told through it.

SKN: You've spoken about art and creativity as well—how does that influence you and your style?

ST: Art encompasses it all for me—it's the way one moves, the manner in which the light hits a wall, or even the silence when one is journaling or photographing. So it naturally makes its way to how one gets dressed. Clothing is a visual language to me. What you are wearing can express something and not have to say a word. It's the link of art, creativity, and style—they are all intertwined.

SKN: Are you involved in the creative direction of your designs at adidas? Does your vision find its way to the final design?

ST: Absolutely. Throughout the entire time I have worked with adidas, I have always had the sense that I am a true collaborator. They actually do listen and they do value my input, which means a great deal to me. Whether it's tweaking a fit, providing input on a new shoe, or assisting in molding the appearance of a kit, we keep lines of communication open. That bond makes a big difference, both in regard to performing and being comfortable on the court.

SKN: Of all the collections with adidas, which has resonated with you the most and why?

ST: There have been a few in my time, but the Australian Open ranges always resonate. Melbourne is a city that is so close to my heart—the Greek people there are amazing, and my favorite place to play, always, is in front of them. And I must say the adidas Y-3 x Palace collaboration in 2018—that was a fun crossover. I'm a huge Wimbledon fan, and skate culture is always something I loved, so the two coming together was something that really resonated with me. I also had a particular liking for the Thebe Magugu collection during the US Open. It was definitely something very unique!

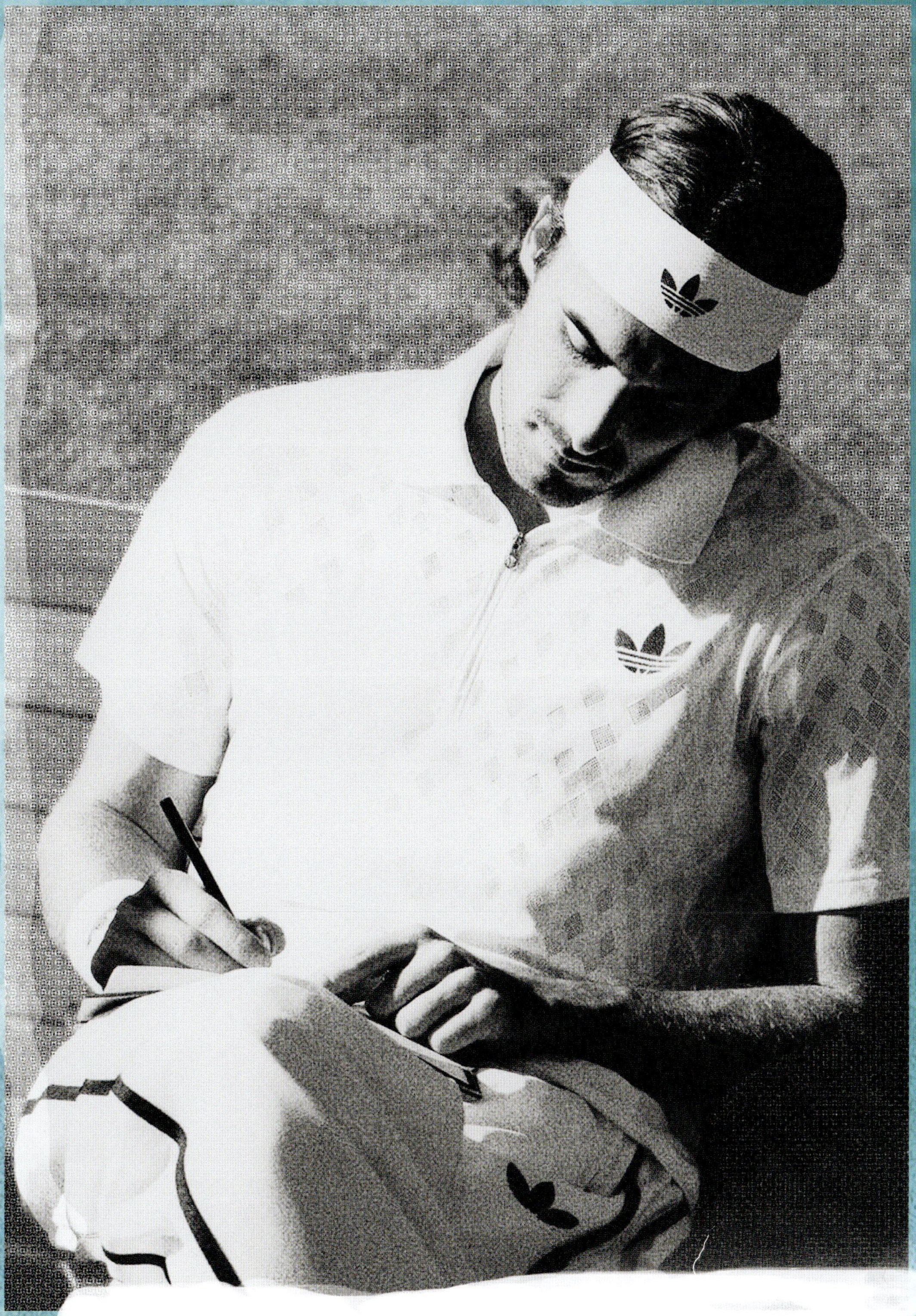

"Art encompasses it all for me—it's the way one moves, the manner in which the light hits a wall, or even the silence when one is journaling or photographing."

—Stefanos Tsitsipas

X PHARRELL

PHARRELL WILLIAMS IS THE MEN'S CREATIVE DIRECTOR FOR LOUIS VUITTON AND A LONGTIME ADIDAS DESIGN COLLABORATOR.

"THE SCORING SYSTEM IN TENNIS STARTS WITH 'LOVE,' WHICH I THINK IS AMAZING. SO, I WANTED TO AMPLIFY THAT MESSAGE—ESPECIALLY NOW."

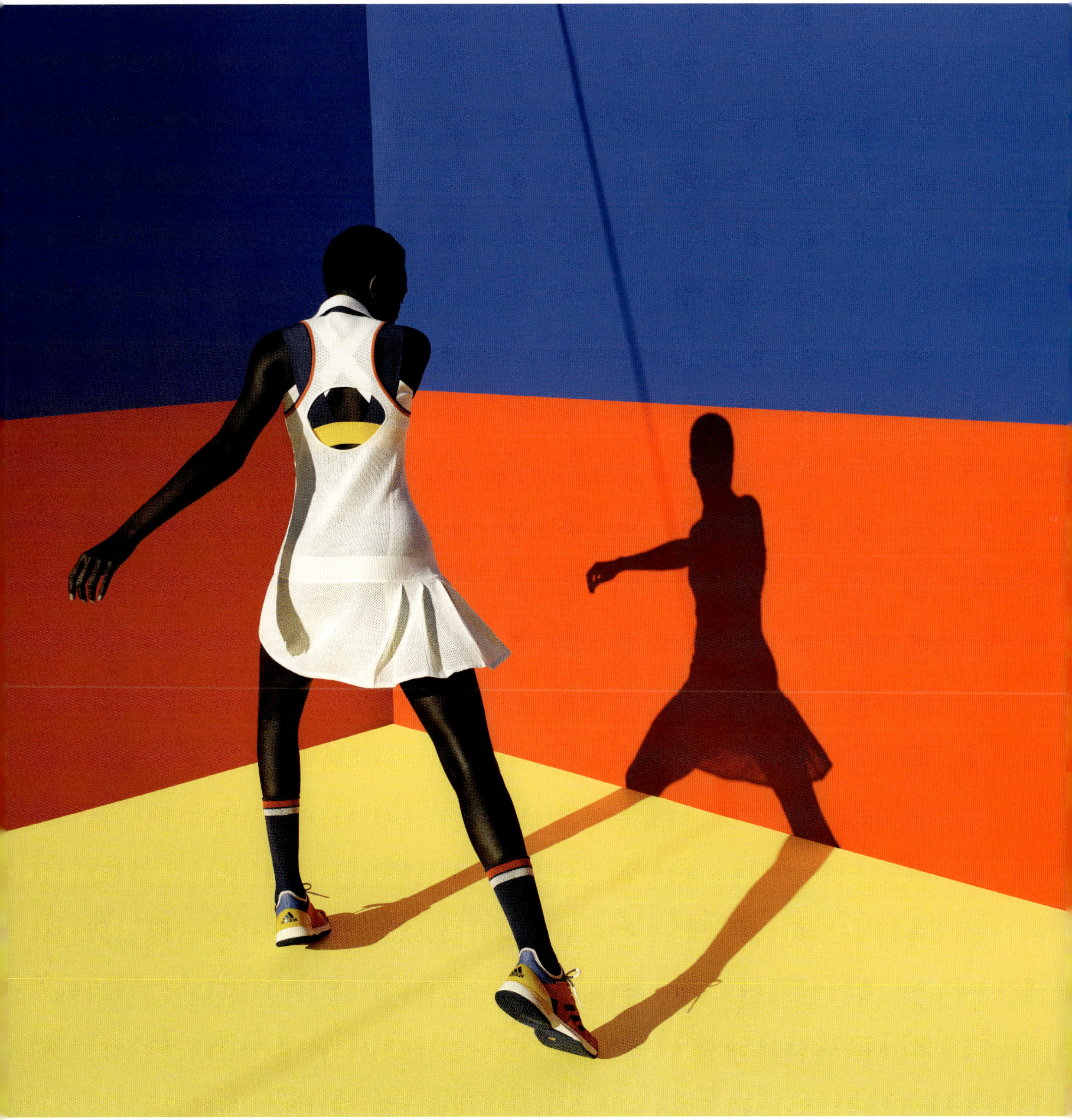

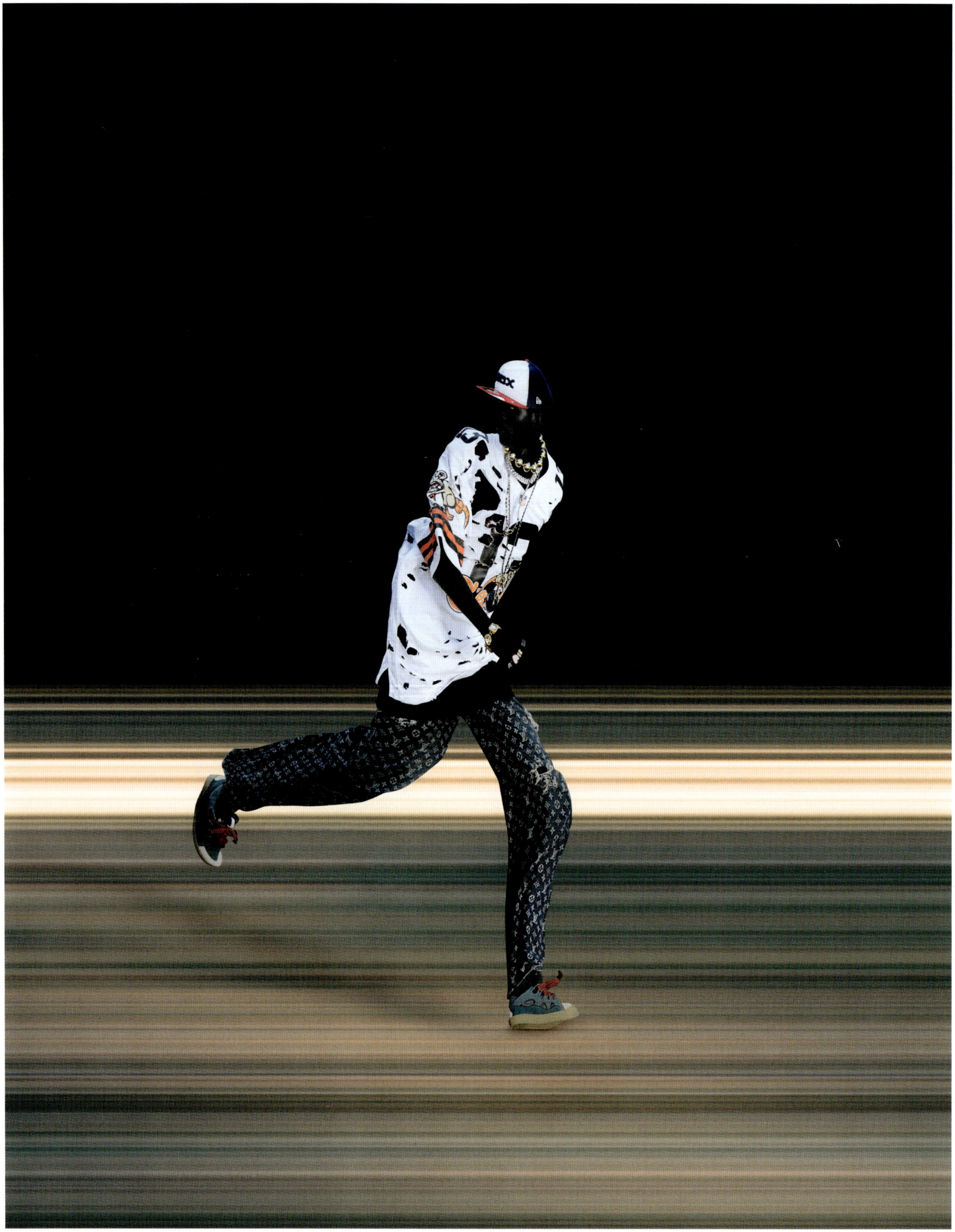

"FASHION AND SPORTS HAVE ALWAYS SHARED A DEEP CONNECTION—BOTH ARE ABOUT SELF-EXPRESSION, PERFORMANCE, AND PUSHING BOUNDARIES. ATHLETES, LIKE DESIGNERS, SHAPE CULTURE THROUGH THEIR STYLE, INFLUENCING HOW WE SEE MOVEMENT, CONFIDENCE, AND IDENTITY. THE CFDA HAS LONG RECOGNIZED THE POWER OF THIS INTERSECTION, WHERE INNOVATION IN MATERIALS, DESIGN, AND STORYTELLING ELEVATES BOTH FIELDS. WHETHER ON THE RUNWAY OR THE PLAYING FIELD, STYLE IS A STATEMENT OF AMBITION, CREATIVITY, AND INDIVIDUALITY."

—STEVEN KOLB,
CHIEF EXECUTIVE, COUNCIL OF FASHION DESIGNERS OF AMERICA (CFDA)

HYPE & PALACE

The sum parts that equal *hype* are classical sportswear—the polo shirt, crewneck sweater, sport coat—and streetwear staples, like hoodies, T-shirts, track pants, and sneakers. Hip-hop, sports, skateboarding, and the surf scenes shaped the silhouette; hype was born from the underground archetypal cities of Los Angeles, Tokyo, and New York before evolving into a full-scale fashion commodity. Once relegated to the back of the closet, streetwear was repositioned front and center under the transformative touch of hype.

Supreme, Palace, and A Bathing Ape used skate culture as a savvy entry point into a multi-hyphenate world where art, music, and fashion began to converge. The hype for *hype* circled around limited editions, timed drops, high price tags, and coveted collaborations with legacy houses like Louis Vuitton, Dior, and Balenciaga, which propelled an insatiable desire among groupies to hunt the prized assets down. Palace, founded in South London, tapped into irreverent British youth culture, the same subversive spirit that once gave brands like Fred Perry, Fila, and Lacoste a cult following. In 2014, the label debuted its first mainstream sports foray with adidas Originals, and in 2016, it delivered their lauded tennis collaboration. Two seemingly discordant sports—skateboarding, rooted in rebellion and rawness, and tennis, preened and pruned with history and tradition—joined forces. It was one of the most successful hype drops in the course of tennis fashion history. Lev Tanju, the founder of Palace, proffered: "We're not trained designers. We like weird stuff; we don't want to be normal. It's just clothes we wanted to make."

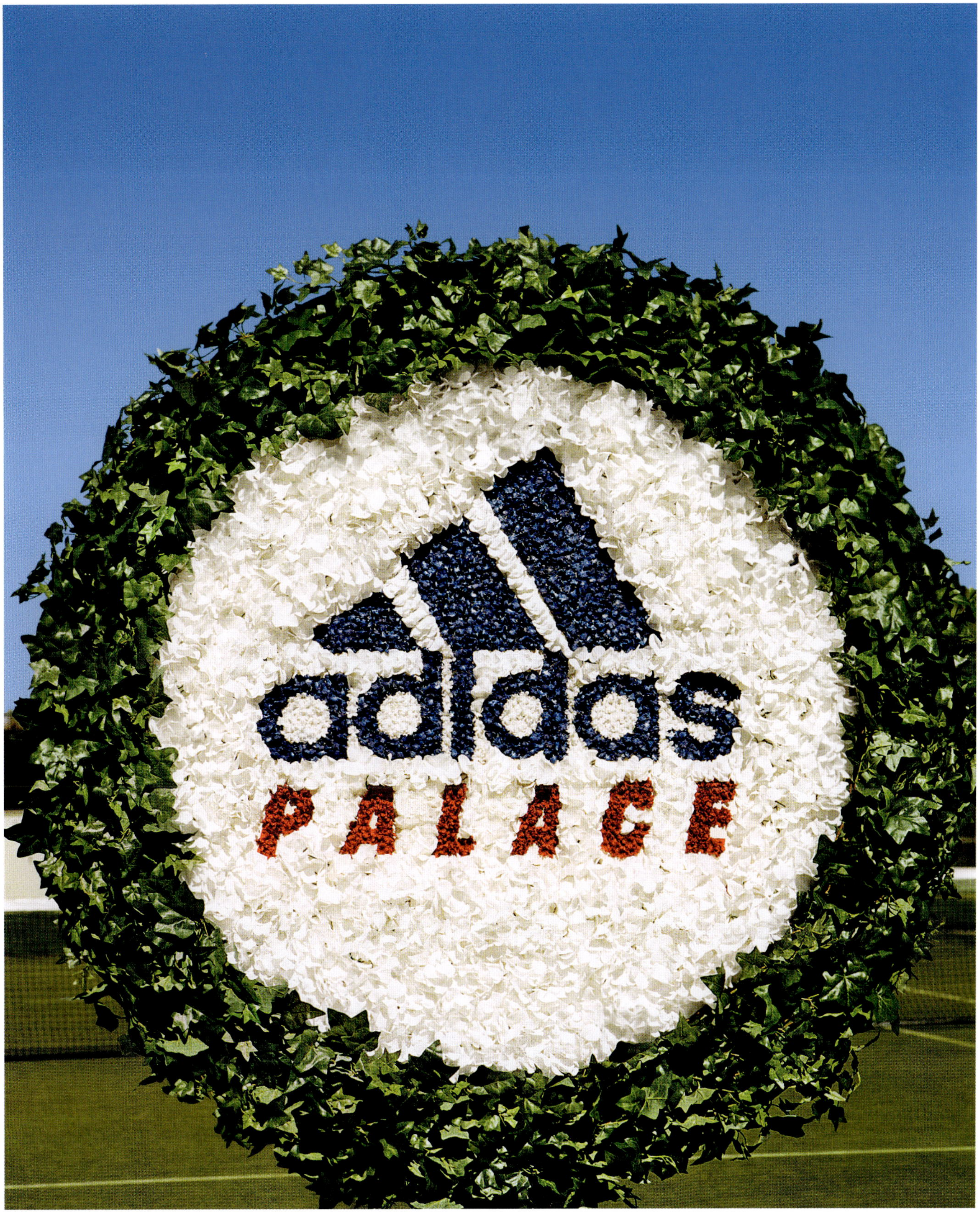
adidas
PALACE

THOM BETTRIDGE

THOM BETTRIDGE IS THE EDITOR IN CHIEF AND CHIEF BRANDING OFFICER OF i-D.

SKN: How does the convergence of sports, fashion, and hype culture reflect deeper shifts in how we construct identity and desire today?

TB: I don't love using the word hype, because I feel like it limits the dynamic that is larger and falls under the "hype umbrella." There was a turn that happened in fashion twelve years ago, where brands needed to live online and cooperate within the attention economy. These brands that fell under the umbrella of hype were the early movers in understanding this attention economy: using social media to tell stories, drive demand, then create scarcity and mythology around the product, creating a secondary market. But the reason why I hesitate to use the word hype is that a lot of those logics have now become part of fashion, and their marketing for everyone. You see it in collaborations—even Dunkin' Donuts is doing one with Sabrina Carpenter. They have to make sense and enhance each other. When that first started, it was only the Supremes of the world who were really doing it in a big way. So in a way, that logic is now permitted in all of our consumer culture. And now we're figuring out what's next.

SKN: So you see it more holistically now?

TB: Exactly. Look at Audemars Piguet, an ultra-luxury brand—they do drops, collabs, there's a waitlist for their products. A lot of the people who were buying A Bathing Ape ten years ago are now buying these watches instead, because they're older and richer now. That's why I like to think of it in the bigger picture, because the things we associate with hype are now almost endemic to fashion. This whole "quiet luxury" thing is almost a reaction to that. It's like a pendulum swing: Brands were really relying on logos, clout, attention, and Instagram, and then there was this saturation point where people became too disenchanted with that. I also feel like the brands themselves realize that, like, *Wow, we're doing huge numbers in terms of brand awareness, but is it actually selling shit? Are we just getting a lot of attention?* There was the shift in focus on an aesthetic level to this idea of quiet luxury. If you look behind the symbolism of it, on an economic level, it's like luxury is focusing on rich people again rather than the aspirational, which is the word we use for non-rich people.

SKN: Is *i-D* covering that part of the world? It has always been top-heavy with pop culture and fashion; will there be a conscious editorial shift? How will sports be recontextualized within the magazine's aesthetic and critical framework?

TB: For me, it's all about anyone who's relevant on a wider cultural level, no matter what area they come from, and who is part of the conversation. We're definitely going to celebrate athletes who are participating in culture and breaking out of the sports world. We live in this time where athletes are very multi-hyphenate, like Serena Williams dancing on the stage at the Super Bowl.

SKN: Are athletes a safe bet for brands in the luxury sector? If we look at their clean living, dedication to their vocation, and so forth, they are often good role models for young people. Do you think that it's a better angle for brands to support, rather than musicians or any other kind of cultural leader?

TB: It's interesting, because when it comes to sports, there are multiple factors that need to align right, because sometimes the person who's best at the sport doesn't necessarily have the charisma or the cultural relevance to carry a brand message. So if you think of the perfect alignment of Michael Jordan, the best basketball player of all time, it was just the force of his personality in such a magnetic way, and that's getting it all right. If you look at tennis, for example, it has suffered a bit from the fact that Djokovic isn't someone that a sixteen-year-old from America will think of as cool. If you look at Agassi, he wasn't the best at tennis necessarily during his time, but he was someone that people could resonate with personality-wise. He had this kind of frenetic energy that was contagious. So that's the challenge of sport: How do you align, be best at it, with all these interpersonal qualities?

SKN: Which brands have done it right?

TB: People give Nike a lot of flak, but in tennis they've done a lot of really smart things, in particular with Serena Williams and Naomi Osaka. They've let those two people flex their personal style in tennis and really embody a sense of creativity beyond sport that has really enriched the presence of both of them. I feel they've done some of the most interesting branding exercises. Let's take Serena doing this Off-White collab—that's one of the most iconic sport and fashion moments ever, but she was doing it for a lot longer, because if you look back fifteen years before, there was that denim outfit, which was cool. The thing about tennis that is unique compared to other sports is that the camera is on one person all the time, and so it really becomes this canvas for showmanship. You're watching someone's face for hours on the TV. I even noticed the jewelry that people were wearing, because the camera is that close-up to them. There's no contact in the sport either, so there's a way to be neutral, and some can lean into that and say something with that attention.

SKN: Well, you mentioned Virgil, so let's talk about the great Virgil Abloh. What do you think is his legacy, in terms of this holistic version of hype and making it reachable back then?

TB: I interviewed him so many times during his lifetime. Something he figured out that other people didn't is that you can take a creative and intellectual approach, and if it's strong and clear enough, you can apply it to pretty much anything. Ideas that may have been too high-concept, too niche in the context of tennis, he was able to hone in on them. He was like, "If Serena dressed like this, this would be cool."

SKN: What was his intellectual approach to his design?

TB: A lot of his work was inspired by '60s and '70s conceptual art. You know, taking a shoe and writing SHOE on it—that comes from a tradition of postwar artwork, this idea of making something by deconstructing it. He would take the design and then would strip things off it, and that was what he was adding to it. He was so very contemporary art strata. Then he famously had this "4 percent" rule, so if you changed something by 4 percent, that's enough to change what it inherently is. I think things like that were what allowed his work to be so widely known and flexible. To enter the world of tennis, he had to create this sort of magnum opus thing; he would just take what's there and mess with it in a way that is impactful.

SKN: Who is our equivalent now? Do you feel like fashion has found that design space that Virgil created, or do you think it was just a unique gift for us—a one-off?

TB: It's really hard to say whether there are people who are in that space now. I also feel like the world is maybe less interested in some of those gestures now. When it comes to designers, people actually now enjoy being part of something niche, rather than being part of something that's a bigger movement or that's very popular en masse.

SKN: What's the thinking behind wanting to withdraw back into niche—is that to feel specialized or unique again?

TB: Fashion is a reflection of personality, and when you're paying a lot for something, you want to feel like it's specific to you and that it aligns to your values. For a lot of brands that are very successful now, they found a very specific customer in a specific community and aesthetic. Whereas I think things were a little bit more open before, in Virgil's time.

SKN: What collabs have you really liked that have crossed into the tennis fashion world seamlessly?

TB: I think that the great tennis collab of the world is yet to happen, actually. I feel like there's untapped potential still.

SKN: Are you going to spill what you think would be the most ideal collab?

TB: I wish I knew, because I would be pitching it to someone. Early on, Ralph Lauren took a really interesting approach to tennis, because of the polo shirt that is so foundational to that business, and he introduced all these interesting ideas. In 1972, he did an all-black tennis collection, when the tradition then was to wear white tennis clothes. That idea of the polo shirt with the big pony on it and the tennis context was super cool. There are interesting ways that people have managed to play with tennis aesthetically. Even though I'm a big fan of Palace, I find it a little less interesting to be like, *Oh, let's take that skater thing and mix it with tennis.* Thinking about it historically, the most important collabs are the ones where both parties leave never being the same again. I don't know if that's necessarily happened in tennis yet.

SKN: Can you name moments that have happened with other brands or other sporting categories where they've left never being the same again?

TB: Michael Jordan wearing branded shoes in the NBA—basketball and Nike were never the same. Supreme and Louis Vuitton collaborating, like Louis Vuitton became the luxury house of that world of streetwear, and Supreme became more than a skateboarding thing and more fashion. Those are examples of moments where they're kind of transformational for both brands. But what's really interesting about tennis is the personalities. They are so central and important, and also the rivalries you have, like Sampras and Agassi, Nadal and Federer . . .

SKN: Yeah, they were kind of legendary. It's funny that it's always the men who duel against each other; it's very musketeer-esque.

TB: It's tricky, because Serena was just so dominant, so when someone beat her, they never really did it again. When tennis is at its best is in men's tennis when there are two titans who are always duking it out. I was a child of the '90s, so I remember Agassi; he was captivating. Same with the Williams sisters with the beads in their hair. There is this peacocking to tennis that I have always found interesting. The most important sports moment was the Nadal versus Federer match; it lasted for six hours or something. It's not even like I really cared that much about tennis at the time, but it was like a Greek tragedy unfolding before your eyes. Stylewise, I find tennis interesting: the codes, the uniform, the suit. This culture of clubs, and then the individualities that just can't be contained, even within these rules.

"I THINK THE GREAT TENNIS COLLAB OF THE WORLD IS YET TO HAPPEN, I FEEL LIKE THERE'S UNTAPPED POTENTIAL STILL."

—THOM BETTRIDGE

EPILOGUE

Tennis has come a long way from where it began—it had to. Freedom, or the sense of it, starts with the human body, our choice to move. The clothes we wear should enable these kinesics, whatever the sport. Tennis isn't team-based; it's individual. The personalities who endure and excel in its physical and mental rigors seamlessly direct and create their stage and story. Fashion was and is a vital conduit to this narrative—an amplifier of the players' style and spirit. The fashion designers and brands who codesign with the athletes have a one-to-four hour window, depending on match duration, to showcase their creations. The player today can savor physical, sartorial, and social liberation in the pursuit of peak performance. This is the style of tennis—but what of the times?

Tournament prize money is now relatively stabilized across both genders, though the critics still argue that match duration, physical endurance, and skill are incomparable between men and women; overall annual earnings remain disparate—still. Women players have remained vocal, speaking out on unfair umpire calls, postpartum struggles, body shaming, racism, ageism, and restrictive dress codes—still. The grassroots of the sport still remain thoroughbred: Working-class kids and minorities who make it as pros are few and far between. Tennis, soccer, and basketball all evolved roughly around the same era, and yet the latter two have grown exponentially in comparison to tennis. Their surge in popularity lies in origin and reach—a field, street, or local park to kick or bounce a ball can organically light a child's first spark of play, which is then commonly nurtured in schools and colleges. That dream then turns into a possible calling for a life like that of sporting titan Kylian Mbappé or legend Michael Jordan—both began with similar playbooks and won. These two athletes prove that identifiable and relatable faces of inspiration and aspiration are key for a sport to become diasporic. Talent scouts from both disciplines also intentionally zero in on lower-income communities to poach raw talent and widen their recruitment pool. Tennis, in contrast, still fails to connect the dots the same way—the path from child player to pro is often solitary and costly.

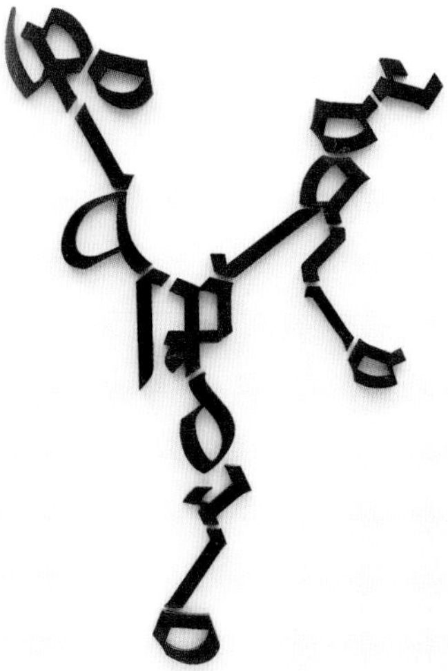

Today, tennis ranks as the fifth-most-popular global sport—a positive signal of systemic shifts slowly developing within the game. Tennis players are gradually emerging from varied worlds, and these pros seem intent on not only shaping their sporting destinies, but making sincere moves to inspire the young to play the game and dream the dream that once was theirs.

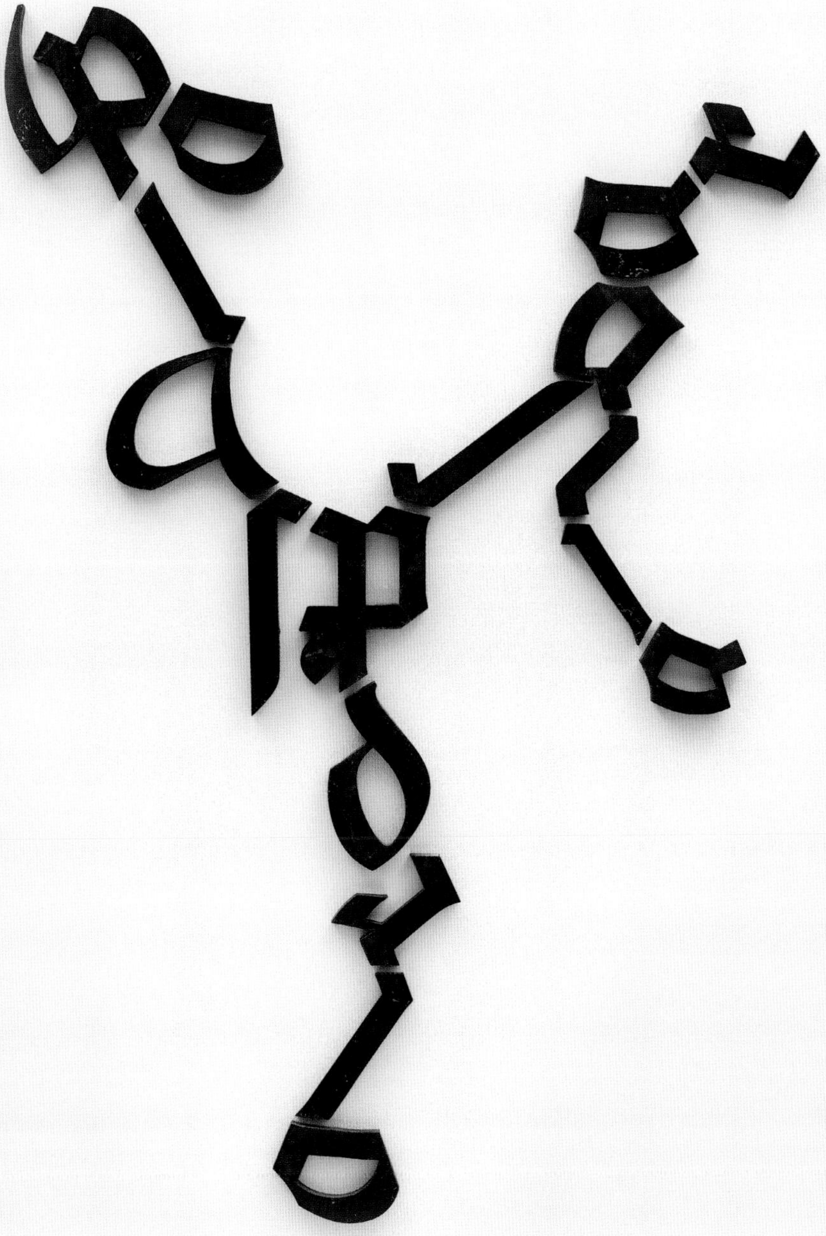

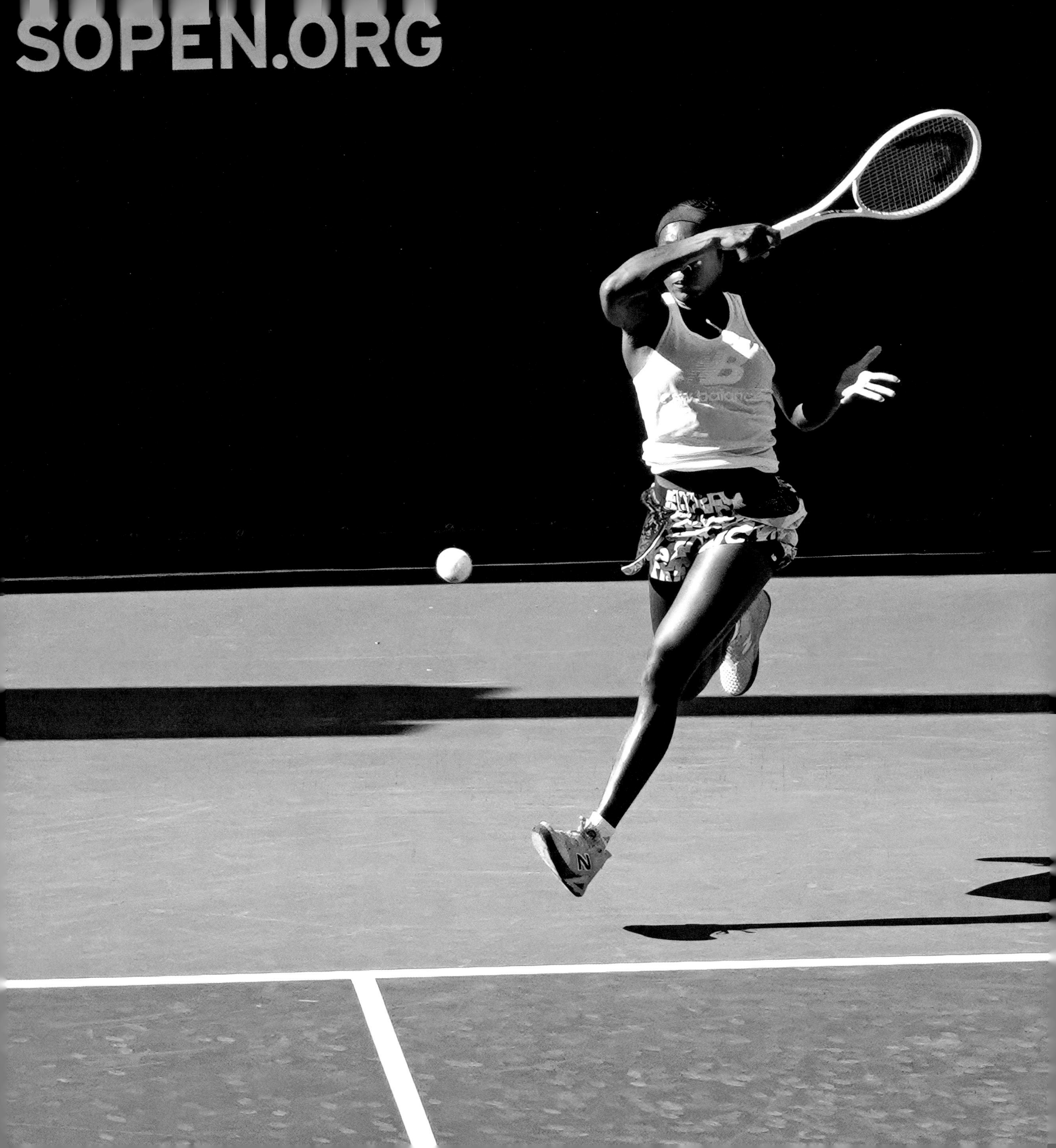
SOPEN.ORG

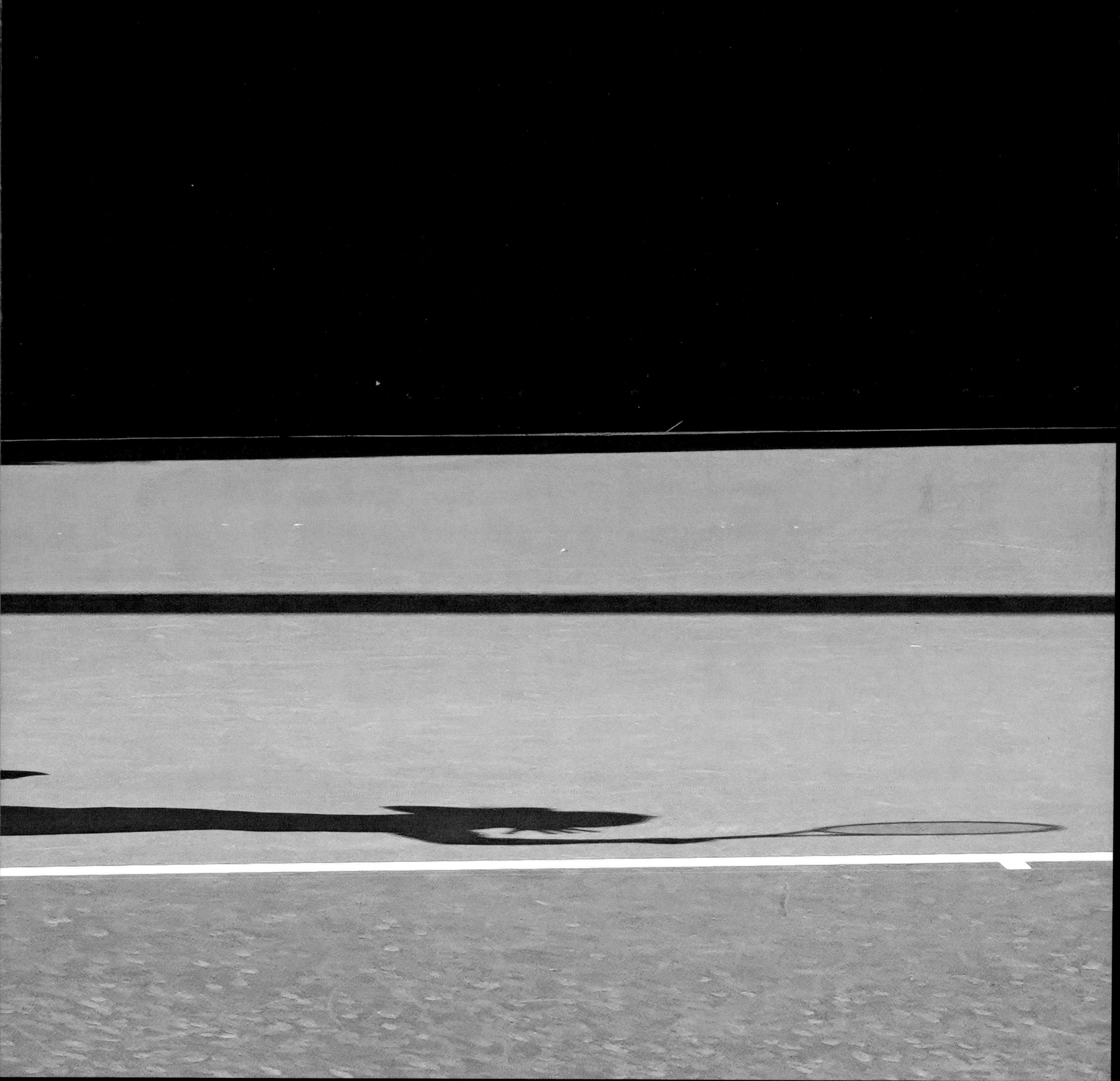

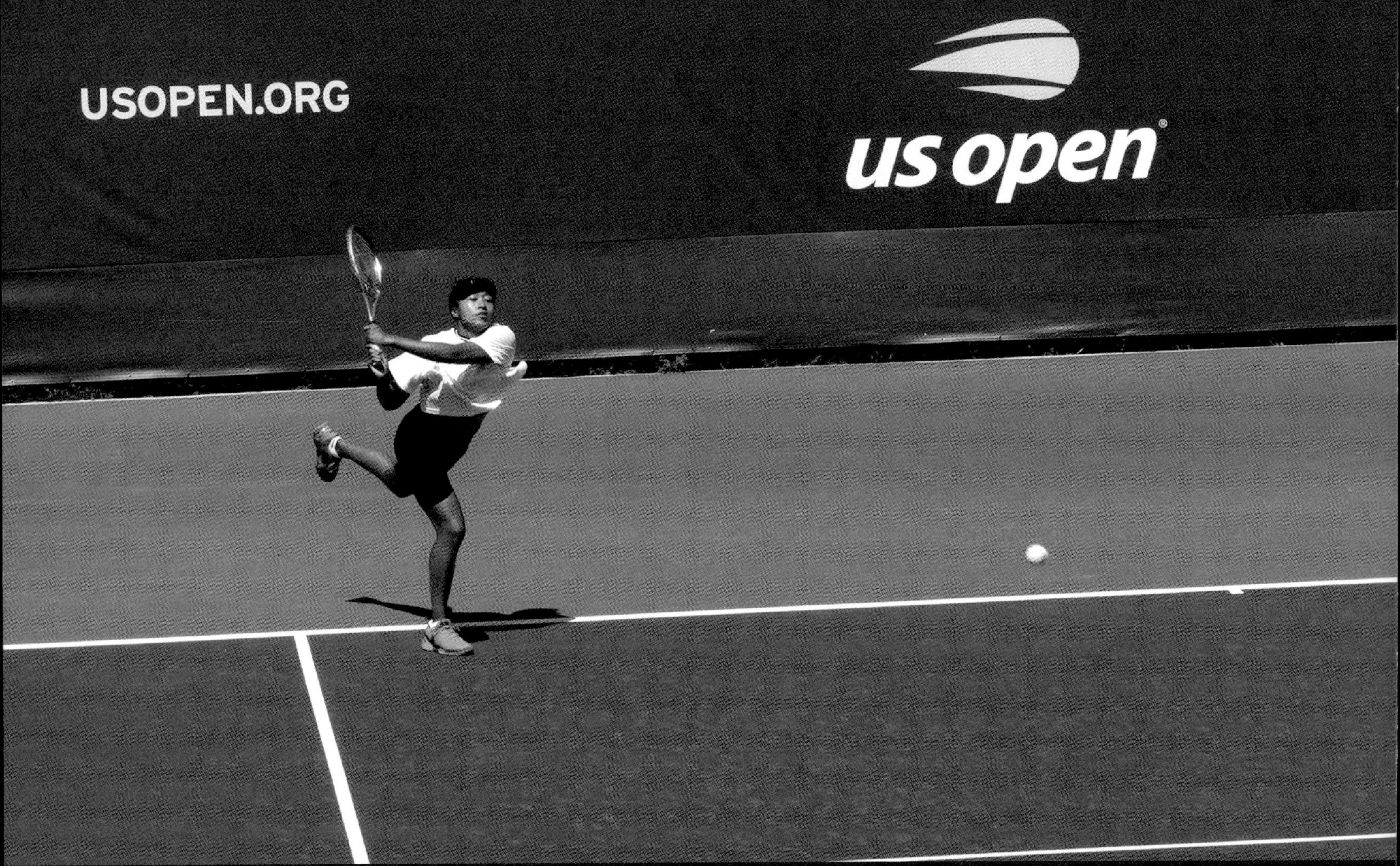
USOPEN.ORG
us open

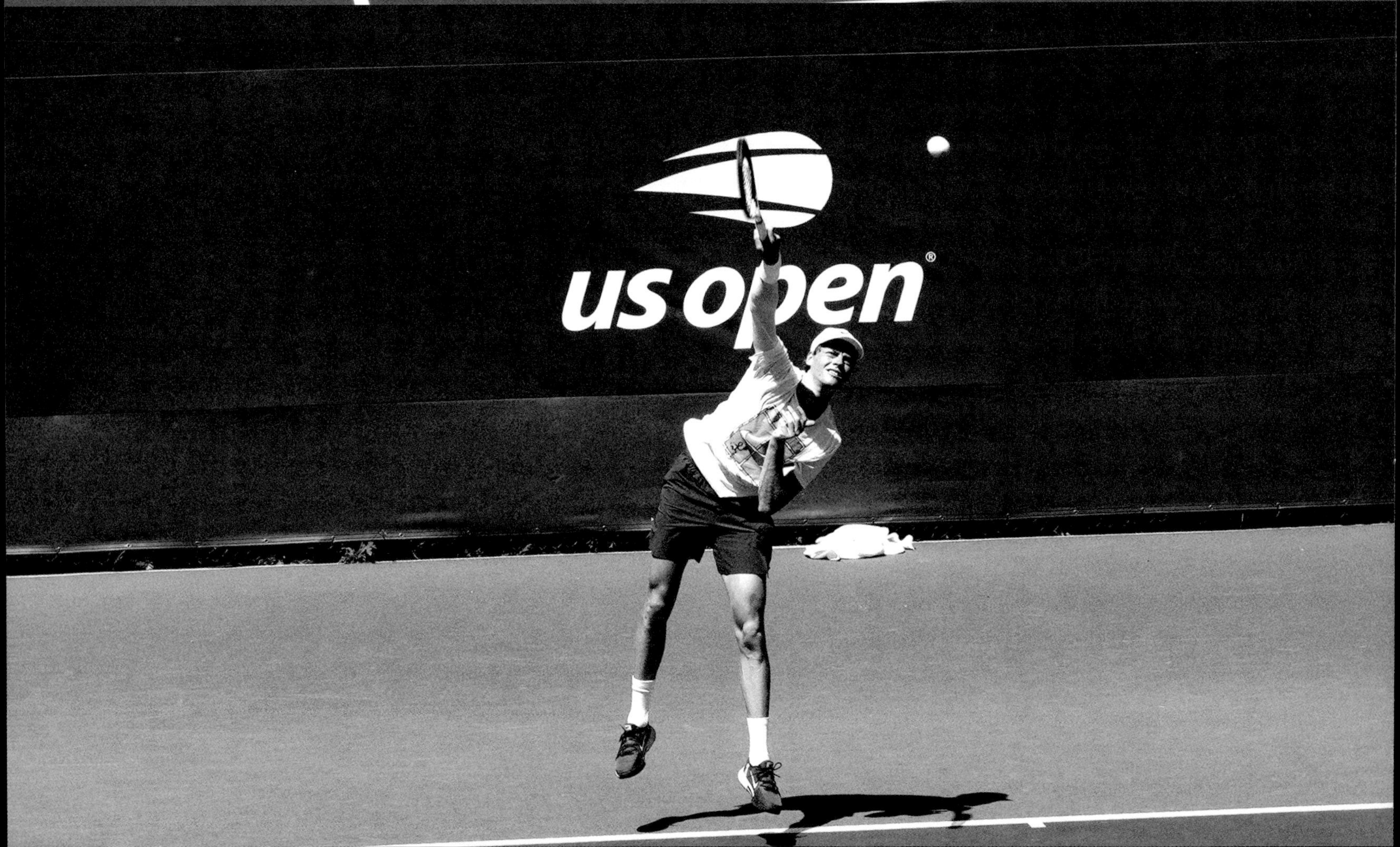
us open

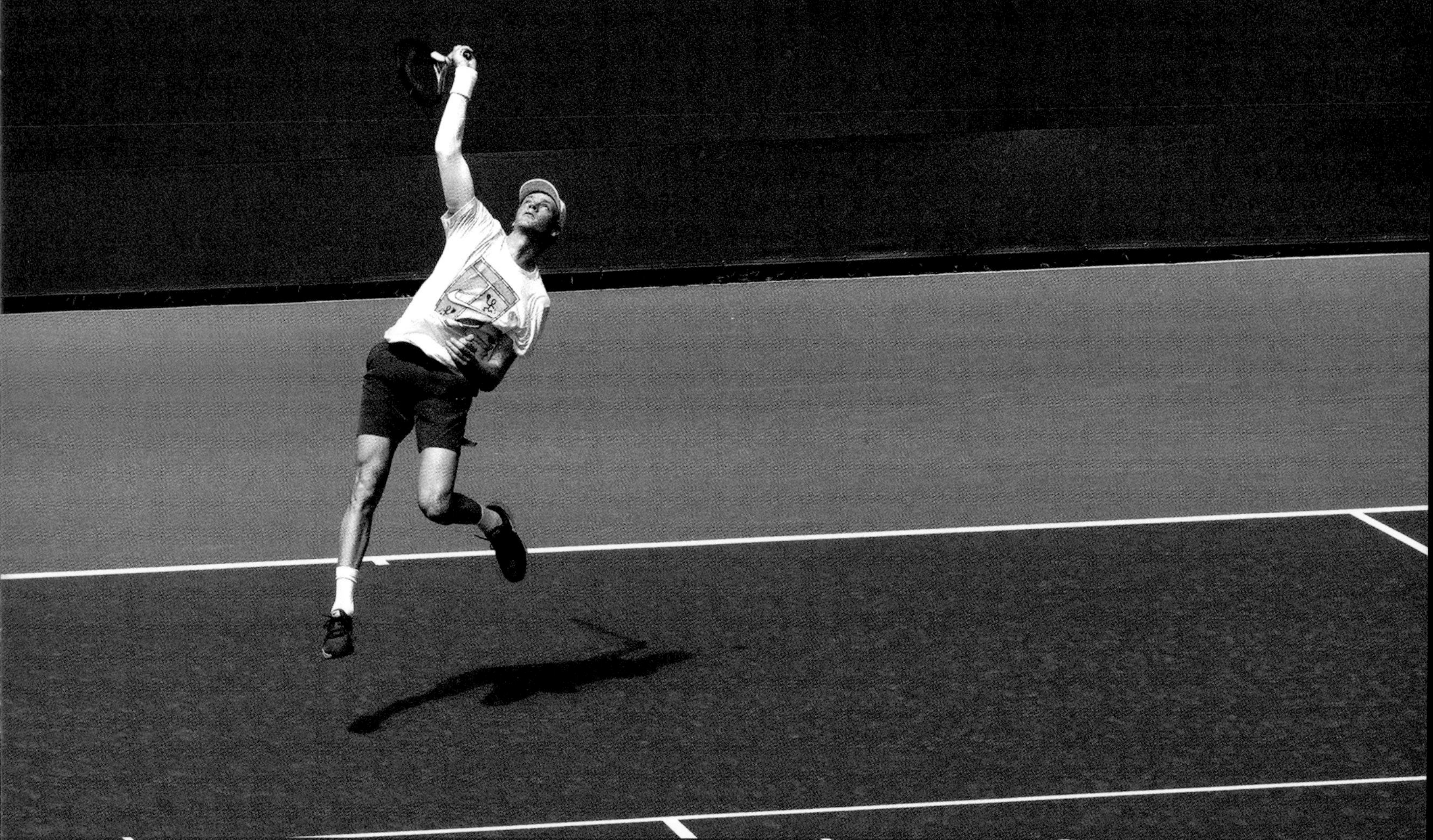
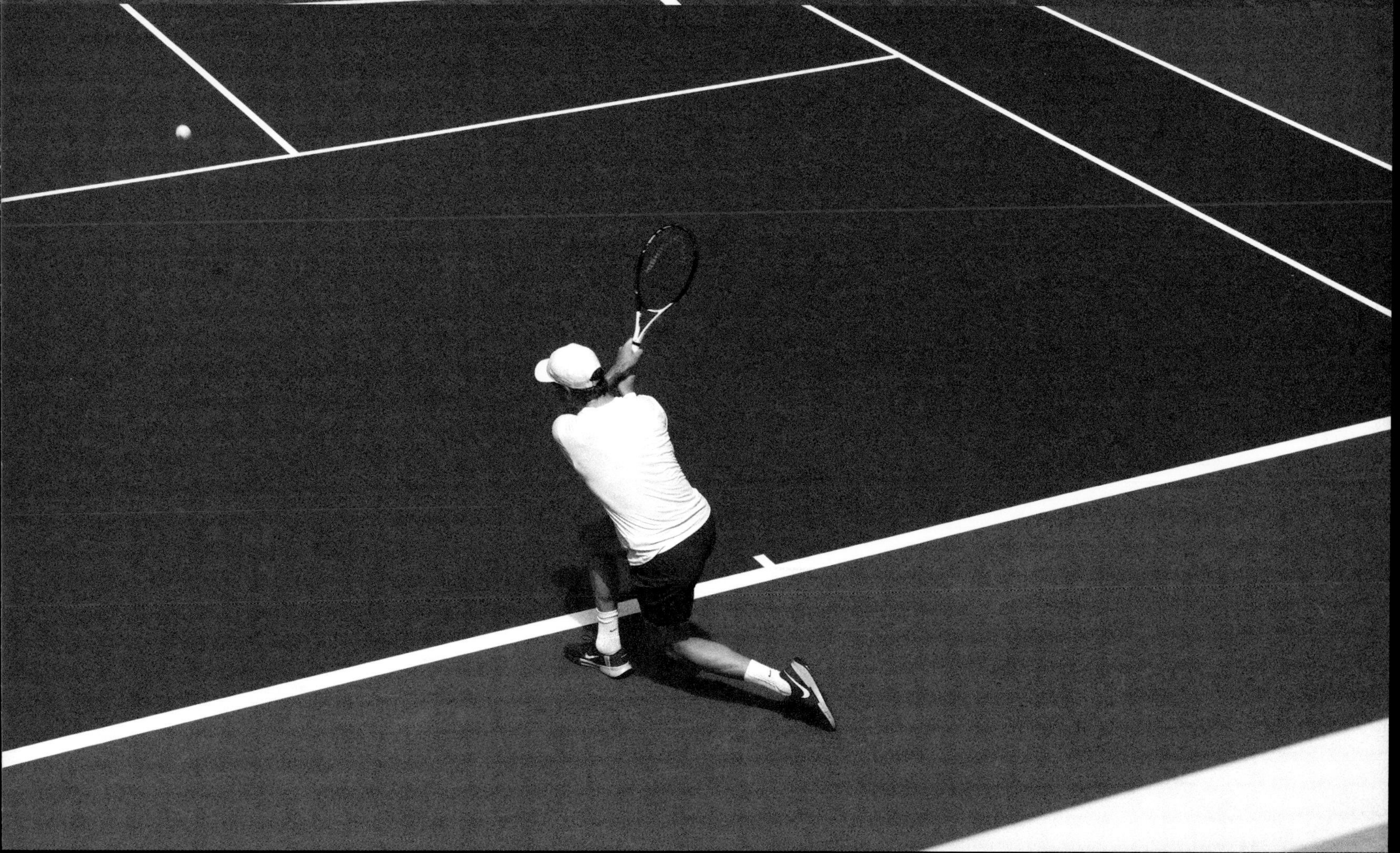

ACKNOWLEDGMENTS

To our son, Millan, we want what you want.

To Chin, for always managing to ace it, especially when I write, my family (Mummy!) & friends—my love and thanks.

To my agent Alexis Hurley, the spine to my books, and editor Rebecca Kaplan, for playing and believing in *ACE*.

To my wingwomen: editorial advisor Georgia Mulvaney Thomerson and designer Alexandra Carr, custodians and interpreters of my vision.

To Gabby Fisher & Abrams, Paul Lerner for the pragmatic advice, Selda Bensusan of New Balance for being a trusted friend and early champion of *ACE*, Julien Farel for his generosity, Holly Ross for that list, and to Ari Marcopoulos, for our US Open shoot day that was all art and little commerce.

To those who make the engine turn at every level of the game, from clubs (CLTC) to Grand Slams: the coaches (especially Dukes Meadows & the Rafa Nadal Academy), physios (Touch Tuina), match officials, and agents who are intrinsic to the sport and its future.

To the contributors and advisors of *ACE* and their teams, my sincere thanks: Steven Kolb; Dame Anna Wintour; HRH Duke of Kent; Lady Helen Taylor; Nicholas Turnbull; the New Balance team, especially Evan Zeder, Mary Lawton, Chris Davis, Brian Lynn, Josh Wilder, and, of course, Coco Gauff; Vijay Amritraj; Maria Sharapova; Victoria & Albert Museum; the House of CHANEL & Archives, especially Cecile Goddet-Dirles; the House of Gucci, the Wimbledon Museum & Library; the Wimbledon team; Marta Kostyuk; Joelle Michaeloff & Wilson; Pelagia Kolotouros & Lacoste; Chris Evert; Monica Rich Kosann; Marion Fasel; Andrea Ferolla; Hugo Vickers; David Lauren & Ralph Lauren, Tory Burch; the Nike team, especially Wilson W. Smith III & Nicholas Schonberger; Jannik Sinner; Boris Becker; Ben Shelton; Alex de Minaur; Naomi Osaka; Candice Marks; Jaipur Rugs; International Tennis Hall of Fame; Kerry Kennedy & the Robert F. Kennedy Memorial; Dominique Fenn & Fred Perry; Björn Borg & Fila; Isabel Mascareñas; Judy and Andy Murray; Gabriela Sabatini; the adidas team, especially Jake Wisdom; Ben Harath; Oliver Junggeburth; Stefanos Tsitsipas; Billie Jean King, Palace; Thom Bettridge; Caroline Fabre; Yohji Yamamoto; Anthony at Trunk Archive; Victoria Gomelsky; Jane Harnick; Susan White; Chiara Marinai; Mary Taylor; Pharis Ahmed; Inès da Silva; Bruce Weber & team; Ezra Petriono; Mel Bles & Webber Represents; Viviane Sassen & We Folk; Juergen Teller; Linder Sterling; Isabelle Wenzel; Lotus L. Kang; Bernie Kaminski; Jack Pierson; KAWS; Giasco Bertoli; Rachael Bos; Gavin Watson; Angèle Châtenet; the John G. Zimmerman Estate; Natalie Candrian; Robin Galiegue; Stas Komarovski; Alasdair McLellan; Robbie Lawrence; Alex Webb; Radka Leitmeritz; and Mark Borthwick.

To the readers and the dreamers of acing it: Sport is a unifier and levels us all—for race, class, and creed will always fall away as we play. So play.

ENDNOTES

19 **It had earned her the right:** *International Herald Tribune*, quoted in Alan Little, *Suzanne Lenglen: Tennis Idol of the Twenties* (Wimbledon Lawn Tennis Museum, 2007), 56.

19 **Compared to a brilliant:** Ted Tinling with Rod Humphries, *Love and Faults: Personalities Who Have Changed the History of Tennis in My Lifetime* (Crown Publishing, 1979), 26.

19 **Crowned "La Divine" by all:** Hannah Jane Parkinson, "Court couture: why tennis fashion owes it all to Suzanne Lenglen," *The Guardian*, June 11, 2023, https://www.theguardian.com/fashion/2023/jun/11/court-couture-why-tennis-fashion-owes-it-all-the-suzanne-lenglen.

19 **Clothes must "free the body":** Anne Matheson, "Teddy Tinling Goes to America," *Australian Women's Weekly*, July 16, 1975, 2.

20 **American *Vogue* reviewed**: "Suzanne Lenglen Shows How to Dress for Tennis," *Vogue*, December 1, 1926.

20 **You should see:** "Court couture: why tennis fashion owes it all to Suzanne Lenglen," *The Guardian*, June 11, 2023.

20 **No less than my own:** Alan Little, *Suzanne Lenglen: Tennis Idol of the Twenties* (Wimbledon Museum, 1988), 134.

22 **Movement of every limb:** Stephen Wagg, "Sacred Turf: The Wimbledon Tennis Championships and the Changing Politics of Englishness," *Sport in Society* 20, no. 3 (October 2015): 398–412 (cited in *The Atlantic*).

24 **It has a classic simplicity:** Helen Wills [Moody], *Tennis* (Charles Scribner's Sons, 1928), 24.

24 **Details of decoration:** Gabrielle Chanel, *The Outlook*, "Woman's World–Tennis," June 4, 1927.

26 **A divided skirt:** *The New York Times*, June 1931.

26 **Trouser skirt:** "The Elegance of Elsa Schiaparelli," *Daily Express*, 1931, n.p.

26 **Should be soundly beaten:** Paul Cocozza, "Kirilenko courts high fashion with her 'cheeky femininity,'" *The Guardian,* June 25, 2006, https://www.theguardian.com/sport/2006/jun/26/wimbledon2006.wimbledon5.

26 **"A tremendous advantage":** Helen Hull Jacobs, *Beyond the Game* (J. B. Lippincott, 1936).

26 **Fashion does not exist:** Paul Morand, *The Allure of Chanel* (Pushkin Press, 1996), 179.

35 **Forgotten your trousers:** Henry Austin, "Bunny," quoted in Bruce Tarran, *Bunny Austin: The Man Who Made Shorts Popular* (Wimbledon Museum Press, 2004), 62.

38 **Helen Wills playing tennis:** Charlie Chaplin, quoted in Larry Engelmann, *The Goddess and the American Girl: The Story of Suzanne Lenglen and Helen Wills* (Oxford University Press, 1988), 71.

38 **Clash of nations:** Boddy, Kasia, "American Girl: The Iconographies of Helen Wills." Historical Social Research 43, no. 2 (2018): 109–128.

48 **I hope it makes me happy:** Althea Gibson, *I Always Wanted to Be Somebody* (Harper & Brothers, 1960), 176.

48 **In her virtual isolation:** Tinling, *Love and Faults*, 45.

48 **You can't eat a crown:** Gibson, *I Always Wanted to Be Somebody*, 35.

51 **The actor on Broadway**: Rod Laver with Bud Collins, *Education of a Tennis Player* (New Chapter Press, 2010; originally 1971).

52 **What should it matter:** Andre Agassi, *Open: An Autobiography* (Alfred A. Knopf, 2009), 166.

52 **We are always checking:** Haresh Ramchandani, "Wimbledon May Change All-White Rule as Billie Jean King and Judy Murray Highlight Anxiety over Menstrual Cycles," *Tennis Majors*, November 8, 2022, https://www.tennismajors.com/wimbledon-news/wimbledon-may-change-all-white-rule-as-billie-jean-king-and-judy-murray-highlight-anxiety-over-menstrual-cycles-634702.html.

58 **Create a concept for the name:** Michael Gross, *Genuine Authentic: The Real Life of Ralph Lauren*. (HarperCollins, 2003), 72.

62 **"Embodied elegance and classicism":** Gross, *Genuine Authentic*, 72.

71 **Elegant, minimal:** Riccardo Tisci, quoted in Steff Yotka, "Maria Sharapova and Riccardo Tisci Talk About Her Swarovski-Studded Tennis Dress," *Vogue*, August 28, 2017.

72 **I was not incredibly talented:** René Lacoste, quoted in Paul Gallico, *Farewell to Sport* (Alfred A. Knopf, 1938).

72 **Soon everyone was wearing them:** René Lacoste, *Lacoste on Tennis* (Vendome Press, 1979), 37.

76 **I like the idea of camouflage:** Novak Djokovic, quoted in "The Colour of What I Wear Is Very Important," *Life Beyond Sport*, n.d.

80 **She is said to imitate the male:** Simone de Beauvoir, *The Second Sex*, trans. H. Parshley (Vintage, 1989; originally 1949), 15.

113 **Emphasizing construction:** Cathy Horyn, "Miuccia Prada: An Intellectual Force in Fashion," *New York Times*, March 9, 1996.

126 **Star runner in peace and calm:** Tinling, *Love and Faults,* 24.

126 **Clothes had to be dramatic:** Tinling, *Love and Faults,* 42.

126 **Person and player can be quite contradictory:** Tinling, *Love and Faults,* 132.

130 **The first was in 1949:** Tinling, *Love and Faults,* 145.

130 **In his first decade of designing:** Ted Tinling, Tinling: *Sixty Years in Tennis* (Sidgwick & Jackson, 1973), 212.

130 **Must be conceived to flatter:** Tinling, *Sixty Years in Tennis*, 210.

154 **Part of our heritage:** Venus Williams (@venuswilliams), "When @serenawilliams and I...," Instagram, November 16, 2021, https://www.instagram.com/p/CWWRCIBjoPq/.

158 **As a young person:** "Andre Agassi: Identity and Authenticity," *Life Beyond Sport*, 2018.

169 **A part of my tennis outfits:** Karl Plume, "Osaka dons tutu 'super suit' in triumphant US open return," *Reuters*, August 28, 2024, https://www.reuters.com/sports/tennis/osaka-dons-tutu-super-suit-triumphant-us-open-return-2024-08-27/.

173 **Because they are supporting me:** "I feel good when I see fans wear my logos, because they are supporting me," *Nike News*, 2010.

178 **The day I stop fighting:** Serena Williams, "The Day I Stop Fighting for Equality Is the Day I Will Be in My Grave," *Harper's Bazaar*, July 9, 2019.

179 **What is Serena wearing:** Serena Williams, "Serena Williams Reflects on Her Life in Looks: From Nike Catsuits to Camp Gucci" interview by *Vogue*, August 8, 2022, https://www.vogue.com/video/watch/life-in-looks-serena-williams.

185 **It takes touch:** Virgil Abloh, quoted in "Serena Williams Will Wear Virgil Abloh at the U.S. Open." *Vanity Fair*, August 13, 2018, https://www.vanityfair.com/style/2018/08/serena-williams-will-wear-virgil-abloh-at-the-us-open?srsltid=AfmBOornwTU2SoPMP1kGTmtr_c2fEumk95X6yAMtDzJk3X_JBEB_b25y.

185 **By existing she shatters stereotypes:** Virgil Abloh quoted in "'She Is a Thought Leader, Not Just a Tennis Player' Virgil Abloh on Creating a Custom Cover Look for Serene Williams," British Vogue, October 5, 2020, https://www.vogue.co.uk/fashion/article/virgil-aboh-serena-williams.

185 **One tier above a logo:** Virgil Abloh, quoted in Dino Bonacic, "Virgil Abloh Designs Serena Williams' US Open Look," *10 Magazine*, August 15, 2018, https://10magazine.com/virgil-abloh-designs-serena-williams-us-open-look/.

186 **But honored her "aggression":** "Virgil Abloh and Nike Celebrate Serena Williams with 'The Queen' Collection," *Nike News*, August 13, 2018.

186 **She had a "great relationship":** USTA, US Open Press Conference, August 26, 2018.

186 **He wanted me to wear this:** Vanessa Friedman, "Serena Williams on Virgil Abloh and the Power of Fashion," *New York Times*, September 3, 2019.

186 **"You should have done it":** Friedman, "Serena Williams on Virgil Abloh."

186 **Met Gala at the French Open:** Friedman, "Serena Williams on Virgil Abloh."

198 **People don't listen to losers:** Arthur Ashe with Arnold Rampersad, *Days of Grace: A Memoir* (Alfred A. Knopf, 1993).

198 **Icy elegance:** "The Icy Elegance of Arthur Ashe," *LIFE,* September 20, 1968.

200 **Clothes and manners do not make:** Ashe, *Days of Grace*, 121.

205 **It's the only one:** Fred Perry, *Fred Perry: An Autobiography* (Stanley Paul, 1984), 56.

205 **To getting around every door:** Mihir Bose, "Fred Perry: The Original Sporting Rebel," *The Guardian*, May 10, 2009, https://www.theguardian.com/sport/2009/may/10/fred-perry-tennis-wimbledon-biography.

207 **Thank God I am not:** Fred Perry,

quoted in Max Robertson, ed., *The Encyclopedia of Tennis* (Allen & Unwin, 1974), 211.

223 **Not very good with disappointment:** *The Royal Tenenbaums: The Screenplay* (Faber & Faber, 2002).

248 **"The scoring system":** Pharrell Williams, quoted in Steff Yotka, "Pharrell Williams and Garbiñe Muguruza Are Bringing Love to the US Open with Retro Adidas Outfits and a Social Campaign," *Vogue*, August 26, 2017.

252 **"We're not trained designers":** Tanju, Lev. Interview by Jake Woolf. *GQ*, September 29, 2014.

PHOTOGRAPHY CREDITS

Page 6: Dukes Meadows / Sunita Kumar Nair

Page 9: Photo by Jean Catuffe / Getty Images

Page 10: Giasco Bertoli

Page 11: Mel Bles

Page 12: Mikael Maria D'Alessandro Tennis Tales / Artwork Alexandra Carr

Page 17: Clive Brunskill / Allsport / Getty Images

Pages 18–19: Photograph by Jacques Henri Lartigue © Ministry of Culture (France), MAP-AAJHL

Page 21: CLOCKWISE FROM LEFT: Chronicle; Photo by Thomas Iannaccone / WWD / Penske Media / Getty Images; Wimbledon Museum & Library

Page 22: Bridgeman Images

Page 23: Ezra Petronio / Art Partner

Page 25: CLOCKWISE FROM TOP LEFT: Patrimoine de CHANEL, Paris © CHANEL; Harri Peccinotti; © Lanvin Heritage; Central Press / Hulton Archive / Getty Images; © Lanvin Heritage; AP Photo / Staff / Len Puttnam

Page 27: Radka Leitmeritz

Page 28: CLOCKWISE FROM TOP LEFT: IMAGO / ABACAPRESS; ABACAPRESS; Sankei Archive via Getty Images

Pages 30–31: Brendan Beirme / Shutterstock

Pages 32–33: Photo by Kirn Vintage Stock / Corbis via Getty Images

Page 35: TOP: Photo by Hudson / Topical Press Agency / Getty Images; BOTTOM: David Saville / Getty Images

Pages 36–37: @Linder Sterling / Courtesy Modern Art, London

Page 39: J. A. Hampton / Stringer

Pages 40–41: Designed by Helen Wills for Stehli Silks Corporation, 1927. The Victoria & Albert Museum, T.87F-1930

Page 43: TOP: PA Images; MIDDLE: Trinity Mirror / Mirrorpix; BOTTOM: Courtesy of Lady Helen Taylor

Page 44: Angèle Châtenet

Page 45: Wimbledon / Courtesy Sunita Kumar Nair

Page 47: IMAGO / United Archives International

Page 49: Carl T. Gossett Jr. / The New York Times / Redux

Page 50: John Patrick Fletcher / Action Plus Sports Images

Page 53: Allstar Picture Library Ltd

Pages 54–55: Viviane Sassen

Page 57: IMAGO / Panoramic by PsnewZ

Page 59: TOP: Photograph by Bruce Weber / Courtesy of Ralph Lauren; BOTTOM: United Artists / Photofest

Pages 60–61: US Open 2025 Ari Marcopoulos

Page 65: Courtesy of NIKE

Page 66: FROM LEFT: IMAGO / Paul Zimmer; Clive Brunskill / Getty Images

Page 67: Steve Parsons / PA Images / Alamy

Page 68: FROM LEFT: IMAGO / ABACAPRESS; Courtesy of NIKE

Page 69: FROM TOP: Courtesy of the Dept of Nike Archives, Courtesy Natalie Candrian, Courtesy of the Dept of Nike Archives

Page 70: CLOCKWISE FROM TOP LEFT: IMAGO / Icon Sportswire; IMAGO / Capital Pictures; Courtesy Natalie Candrian; IMAGO / Shutterstock

Page 73: IMAGO / Bridgeman Images

Page 74: FROM LEFT: Courtesy Sunita Kumar Nair, taken from the book Lacoste by Laurence Benaim; Courtesy Sunita Kumar Nair

Page 77: Radka Leitmeritz

Page 79: Stas Komarovski

Page 81: Rachael Bos

Pages 84–85: Trinity Mirror / Mirrorpix

Page 86: Julien Farel & Alex De Minaur by Ari Marcopoulos, US Open 2025

Page 87: Helen Wills charm bracelet courtesy of Wimbledon Museum

Page 88: Shaun Brooks / Action Plus Sports Images / Alamy Live News

Page 91: Juergen Hasenkopf

Pages 93–94: Courtesy of Wilson

Pages 96–97: Courtesy Tory Burch

Page 99: Robin Galiegue

Page 101: Corinne Dubreuil

Page: 103: TOP: Nippon News; BOTTOM: Courtesy New Balance

Pages 104–116: Courtesy New Balance

Page 108 : Imago / Imagn Images

Page: 112: Andy Cheung

Page: 114: Courtesy of Sunita Kumar Nair

Page 118: LEFT: Courtesy New Balance; RIGHT: Dhairius and @FactoryDowntown

Page 121: Isabelle Wenzel

Page 125: © Pauline Ballet / FFT

Page 127: Courtesy Jaipur Rugs

Pages 128–129: Artwork Alexandra Carr. CLOCKWISE FROM TOP LEFT: Courtesy of the ITHF; ASSOCIATED PRESS; Pedro Marinello, Museo de la Moda, Chile; Courtesy Wimbledon Museum; ITHF Museum Collection, 2011; Associated Press / Alamy

Page 133: Moore / Associated Press

Pages 134–135: Lotus L. Kang, Synapse series, 2024. Courtesy the artist and Franz Kaka, Toronto. Photo: LFdocumentation

Page 138: IMAGO / Pressefoto Baumann

Page 139: © United Artists / Courtesy Everett Collection

Page 141: Alex F. Webb

Page 143: © Juergen Teller, All Rights Reserved

Page 145: TOP: IMAGO / Norbert Schmidt;

BOTTOM: IMAGO / Sportfoto Rudel

Pages 146–147: Courtesy All England Tennis & Croquet Club

Pages 149–151: Courtesy of Gucci (except runway model: IMAGO / Independent Photo Agency Int.)

Page 152: Philip Gay / Art Partner Licensing / Trunk Archive

Page 153: IMAGO / Team 2

Page 154: Bernie Kaminski

Page 157: © Pauline Ballet / FFT

Page 159: TOP: Paul Sutton-PCN; BOTTOM: Courtesy of NIKE

Pages 160-165: Courtesy of the Dept Nike Archives / Getty Images / Professional Sport

Page 167: Media Punch

Page 168: IMAGO / UPI Photo

Page 169: TOP: Courtesy of Naomi Osaka and Nike; MIDDLE: Courtesy of Naomi Osaka; BOTTOM: UPI Photo

Pages 170–172: Radka Leitmeritz

Page 175: Associated Press / Alamy

Page 176: Adam Davy

Page 177: TOP: Courtesy Sunita Kumar Nair; BOTTOM: Associated Press / Alamy

Page 178: TOP: ZUMA Press, Inc.; BOTTOM: BOOTS: IMAGO / ZUMA Press Wire; CLOTHING: Courtesy of the Dept of Nike Archives

Pages 180–181: Courtesy of Sunita Kumar Nair and Dept of Nike Archives

Pages 182–183: Norman Jean Roy / Trunk Archive

Page 184: Xinhua

Page 187: Courtesy of Dept of Nike Archives

Page 189: Mathieu Cesar

Pages 190–191: Photo by Ella Ling / Shutterstock

Page 192: Courtesy Jaipur Rugs

Page 193: Photo courtesy of Alon Sicherman and Demian Neufeld

Page 197: Mark Borthwick

Page 199: Dave Pickoff / Associated Press

Page 201: TOP: Associated Press / Alamy; BOTTOM: Copyright © John G. Zimmerman Archive

Pages 202–203: Gerry Cranham / Offside

Page 204: Associated Press / Alamy

Page 205: Courtesy of Fred Perry

Page 207: LEFT: IMAGO / Horstmüller; RIGHT: Courtesy of Fred Perry

Page 208: IMAGO / Avalon.red

Page 209: Photo by Gavin Watson / Barry, Neville, Gavin. Hawthorn Rd, High Wycombe. 1984

Page 211: Courtesy of Fila

Page 212: IMAGO / TT

Page 213: Courtesy of Fila

Page 214: Radka Leitmeritz

Page 215: Courtesy of Sunita Kumar Nair

Page 217: TOP: Walter Iooss Jr. / Contributor; BOTTOM: Tony Henshaw / Alamy Stock Photo

Page 219: PA Images

Page 221: Buena Vista/Photofest

Page 224: TOP: INSTAR Images; BOTTOM: IMAGO / Capital Pictures

Page 227: All images: Ron Galella / Contributor

Pages 228–229: © Bruce Weber & Marianne Faithfull

Page 231: Thibaut Grevet

Pages 232–233: Courtesy of Sunita Kumar Nair

Page 234: Courtesy of adidas

Page 235: Courtesy of adidas

Page 236: LEFT: Courtesy of adidas; RIGHT: Courtesy of adidas

Page 237: Courtesy of adidas

Page 238: Courtesy of Sunita Kumar Nair

Page 239: Courtesy of adidas

Page 241: BACKGROUND: Courtesy of adidas; artwork by Alexandra Carr. INSERT: IMAGO / Action Plus

Page 242: Courtesy of Sunita Kumar Nair

Page 244: Courtesy of the ITHF / John Russell

Page 245: Courtesy of Sunita Kumar Nair

Page 247: Courtesy of adidas. Artwork: Alexandra Carr

Pages 248–249: Viviane Sassen × Pharrell; photograph by Viviane Sassen and Stevenson

Page 250: Thibaut Grevet

Page 253: Courtesy of adidas and Palace

Pages 258–259: Courtesy of the artist Jack Pierson

Pages 260–263: All photos by Ari Marcopoulos

GLOSSARY

Page 17: Steffi Graf, Australian Open, 1989. Her adidas top featured bold Memphis style graphic motifs, a design influence that defined much of tennis fashion in the 1980s.

Page 19: A Grand Slam competition consists of the four major tennis tournaments held annually in different countries and played on distinct surfaces: the Australian Open (Plexicushion hard court), the French Open (clay), the US Open (Laykold hard court), and Wimbledon (grass).

Page 26: Naomi Osaka. Detail of her micro pleated, triple layered skirt: chiffon, Dri FIT, Lycra (an elastic synthetic fiber known for exceptional stretch, recovery, and resistance to perspiration).

Page 28 (Left): Roger Federer in a Nike cashmere and linen herringbone knit cardigan with his signature RF logo, photographed with Rafael Nadal, Wimbledon, 2012.

Page 28 (Right): Jean Paul Gaultier for Hermès, tennis themed runway show, Spring/Summer 2010.

Page 28 (Center): Crown Prince Akihito and Michiko Shōda in classic tennis attire, Karuizawa Tennis Court, Japan, 1959.

Page 30: Princess Diana leaving the Vanderbilt Racquet Club in her tennis look, London, 1987.

Page 33: Members of a tennis club in full garden attire gather for a group portrait, ca. 1890.

Page 35: Henry Wilfred “Bunny” Austin in his shorts, having a cup of tea after his loss in the Davis Cup, Wimbledon, 1937.

Page 35: Members of the dress reform party, London, 1937.

Page 38: Helen Wills, Wimbledon, 1935 (also called the All England Croquet and Lawn Tennis Club—AELTC), wearing her signature visor and Patou dress. She favored functional, straight, sleeveless shifts crafted from cotton piqué or linen.

Page 43 (Top): The Duke of Kent and Princess Diana, Royal Box, Wimbledon, 1986.

Page 43 (Middle): The Duchess of Kent comforting runner up finalist Jana Novotná, Wimbledon, 1993.

Page 43 (Bottom): Lady Helen Taylor, Wimbledon, 2023.

Page 46: Althea Gibson, Wimbledon, 1957, wearing a Fred Perry polo shirt and a belted, knife pressed pleated skirt.

Page 48: Althea Gibson celebrating with neighborhood children, Harlem, New York, 1957.

Page 50: Detail of Markéta Vondroušová's Nike skirt, Wimbledon, 2023.

Page 53: Roger Federer wearing a Nike military style cotton jacket with embroidered RF logo, Wimbledon, 2009. The look evoked the formal men's playing attire of the 1930s.

Page 59: Diane Keaton and Tony Roberts in Woody Allen's *Annie Hall*, 1977.

Page 60: Ball boy in Ralph Lauren, photographed by Ari Marcopoulos, US Open, 2025.

Page 65: Maria Sharapova in full Nike Atelier, designed by Martin Lotti, 2025.

Page 66: Maria Sharapova, US Open, 2017, wearing a favored dress silhouette featuring a fitted bodice with lattice detailing and an A line skirt, complete with her signature wave. Crafted from Nike Innovation Dri-FIT, a high performance, moisture wicking polyester, the dress supported the body's natural cooling mechanisms. It was constructed using body mapping techniques to allow optimal airflow to high heat zones during play.

Page 66: Maria Sharapova, Wimbledon, 2008, removing her tuxedo jacket to reveal a tuxedo inspired top with tailored shorts. While women players regularly practice in shorts for thermoregulation and unrestricted movement, they rarely compete in them, switching to skirts or dresses for match play.

Page 67: Maria Sharapova at Wimbledon, 2007, shaking hands with Venus Williams. Her Nike dress featured a diaphanous back panel and a three tiered skirt. The deep shoulder cutouts allowed full arm mobility. Fitted bodices remain a standard tennis design, incorporating internal structures to support breast tissue, which can affect posture and gait during play.

Page 68: From left: Maria Sharapova, Roland Garros, 2007. Her Nike dress featured a sea blue chiffon overlay and a dropped waist dress in mesh tricot (an eyelet patterned fabric commonly used in sportswear). Naomi Osaka said that "this was the prettiest dress she had seen" (YouTube × Hana Kuma, 2024).

Page 69: Blue wrapover top made of Dri-Fit. French Open dress, 2007.

Page 69 BOTTOM LEFT: French Open, 2009—Nike layered tier dress by designer Natalie Candrian: "The sheer overlays were constructed of individual polyester/nylon tricot mesh panels dyed in custom colors. The underlayer was custom dyed polyester Nike Dri-FIT fabric. We always worked with a mannequin measured to Maria's size and body." BOTTOM RIGHT: Flat of 2009 French Open tiered dress.

Page 72: René Lacoste wearing his custom jacket with embroidered crocodile motif, Wimbledon, 1927.

Page 74 (Right): First iteration of the polo shirt drawing, taken from *Lacoste* by Laurence Benaim.

Page 74 (Left): Original embroidery of the Lacoste logo on René Lacoste's jacket.

Page 79: Venus Williams in *Vogue*, photographed by Stas Komarovski, 2022.

Page 80: *Chris Evert*, 2023, oil on canvas by Rachel Bos. Detail of Chris Evert wearing a lace tennis dress, US Open, 1971.

Page 85: Chris Evert, Wimbledon, 1978, wearing her famous tennis bracelet.

Page 86: Alex de Minaur getting his hair cut by Julien Farel, US Open, 2025. His lucky mother of pearl clover Van Cleef & Arpels bracelet peeks out.

Page 87: Helen Wills's charm bracelet with a Cartier tennis racquet charm. Cartier produced bespoke sporting charms for elite clients circa the 1920s–30s.

Page 88: Elina Svitolina, Wimbledon, 2019.

Page 90: Roger Federer, Wimbledon, 2012, wearing his Rolex Day Date II in 18K Everose gold, with black dial and baguette cut diamond hour markers.

Page 92: Marta Kostyuk wearing the tennis dress that later became the blueprint for her wedding dress, Wimbledon.

Page 92 (Continuation): Marta Kostyuk and Joelle discussing the design; Marta on her wedding day, 2023.

Page 96: Tory Burch illustration of the Billie Blue official jacket for the Billie Jean King Cup, 2022.

Page 101: Coco Gauff, 2024, wearing her New Balance (NB) U.S. Olympics dress. The bodice features a graphic print of a dégradé scatter of red stars, a knife pleated skirt, and her custom CG2 shoe.

Page 103: Sketch of the Coco Gauff Signature (CG1) shoe. Coco Gauff wearing the shoe during her 2023 US Open final victory. BELOW: Coco in her vision meetings with the New Balance design team.

Page 104: French Open 2025 CAD drawings and color swatches. The entire dress was created from a graphic developed by the New Balance team, with the skirt yoke woven into pleats.

Page 104 (Right, Page 105): Inspiration board for the 2024 US Open, featuring an outfit inspired by the Statue of Liberty and the tournament's signature colors.

Page 106: Coco Gauff hand signature: the graphic swatch from New Balance for the CG1 shoe.

Page 109: Coco Gauff, Wimbledon, 2025.

Page 110: Coco Gauff's embroidered bodice swatch and full 2025 Wimbledon look at New Balance HQ, Boston, USA.

Page 112: Coco Gauff wearing Miu Miu to celebrate her French Open 2025 win.

Page 112 (Right, Page 113): Campaign images of Coco Gauff wearing her NB × Miu

Miu collaboration outfit.

Page 115: The T500 shoe.

Page 115 (Continuation): Sunita Kumar Nair at New Balance HQ holding Coco's winning US Open 2023 outfit.

Page 116: Coco Gauff × NB × Miu Miu.

Page 119: Coco Gauff back detail on court, 2024, and her Miu Miu 2025 *Vanity Fair* party dress featuring jewel encrusted back detailing.

Page 125: Rafael Nadal preparing to go on court at the Rolex Paris Masters, 2022. His jacket bears the luminescent Nike swoosh alongside his custom Rafa bull logo—distinctive emblems that read like dual house crests.

Page 127: Tennis balls made of yarn—courtesy of Jaipur Rugs.

Pages 128–129: (From left)

– Ted Tinling sketch of Gussy Moran, 1949.

– Lea Pericoli, Wimbledon, 1964, in an ostrich feather dress. As she once told *The New York Times*: "You must be a little careful, because if you go out there with feathers and you lose, you're dead because the press will kill you—they will pluck you like a chicken."

– Maria Bueno, 1959. Tailored dress with lapel collar, subtly embroidered front placket, couture buttons, and a pleated skirt revealing a pastel pink underskirt.

– Detail from a Ted Tinling skirt for Nell Truman.

– Evonne Goolagong, 1972, wearing a dress embellished with aqua and floral embroidery and hand painted details referencing her Wiradjuri heritage and the Australian landscape.

– Ted Tinling's design board for Billie Jean King, 1973, with fabric swatches and sketches.

– Detail from Nell Truman's skirt.

– Rosie Casals, Wimbledon, 1972, wearing a Virginia Slims–branded dress—a bold declaration of allegiance to the women's professional circuit that challenged Wimbledon's strict anti advertising rules.

– Billie Jean King, Wimbledon, 1975, wearing a button down dress with shirt lapels and exaggerated collar, trimmed with lilac floral borders and paired with a blue cardigan embroidered with her initials.

– Gussy Moran, 1949, revealing her infamous lace knickers—an act that caused public uproar at Wimbledon.

– Ted Tinling, undated.

– Tracy Austin, US Open, 1979. White cotton piqué dress with eyelet embroidery, paired with a pastel pink cardigan.

– Ted Tinling gold shoes for Ann Jones, ca. 1970.

– Anne White, 1985, in her Lycra catsuit with long sleeves, fitted legs, and a high zippered neckline creating a streamlined, aerodynamic silhouette.

– Detail from Ted Tinling's 1973 design for Billie Jean King.

Page 133: Chris Evert with John Lloyd, 1979, in her wedding dress. The lace overlay, long sleeved bodice, and full skirt with train were quintessential Tinling—overtly romantic and flamboyantly feminine. Tinling operated his own bridal couture house from 1931–1939.

Page 138: Vijay Amritraj, 1974, wearing an adidas shirt, gold chain, and shorts—key tennis trends of the 1970s.

Page 139: Vijay Amritraj, Roger Moore, and Desmond Llewellyn in a scene from the James Bond film *Octopussy*, 1983.

Page 143: Boris Becker in front of the Fred Perry statue, Wimbledon, 2014.

Page 145: Boris Becker, Wimbledon, 1989, wearing a Fila shirt printed with vivid geometric panels in blue, teal, and navy on a white base. He was asked to change, as it failed to meet the tournament's requirement that attire be "predominantly white."

Page 145: Boris Becker, Wimbledon, 1985. The signature navy, red, and white pinstripe Fila shirt referenced Björn Borg's original design—a sartorial passing of the torch.

Page 146: Player entryway to Centre Court with a stanza from the Rudyard Kipling poem "If—" (1895) inscribed above the wall.

Page 149: Clockwise from left: Gucci campaign photographed by Sam Rock, 2025; craftsman's notebooks at Gucci, ca. 1950s; the first designer sneaker, ca. 1977; Gucci Diamante Canvas racquet bag, ca. 1950s; Gucci runway, Fall/Winter 2022–23, a modern take on Mrs. Phelps Stokes's skirt and the garden attire of the early 20th century.

Page 150: Gucci campaign featuring Jannik Sinner and his Head × Gucci bag, 2024.

Page 152: Jannik Sinner in a Gucci monogrammed suit, photographed by Philip Gay, 2021.

Page 154: Venus Williams, Australian Open, 1999, wearing African hair beads. She first wore the beads in 1994 at age 14 for her debut against Arantxa Sánchez Vicario.

Page 157: Rafael Nadal, French Open, 2019. Nike AeroReact technology opens its fibers as body temperature rises. The volt yellow color signals energy and power, while the matching headband and wristbands unify the chartreuse palette—creating a vivid, high impact visual statement for opponents, spectators, and media alike.

Page 159: Andre Agassi, 1992 US Open, demonstrating his signature power forehand; drawing by Wilson Smith III.

Page 160: Andre Agassi, drawing by Tinker Hatfield, 1989. Hatfield—Nike's lead designer, renowned for his Air Jordan creations—designed the Air Tech Challenge II featuring explosive "lava" neon graphics in hot pink, orange, and purple. The anti establishment aesthetic was paired with innovation: revolutionary Air cushioning in the heel and forefoot provided enhanced stability on hard courts.

Page 162: Agassi, French Open, 1990. Wearing "hot lava" leggings beneath black denim shorts paired with acid bright printed tops in pink and purple—establishing his rebellious, against the grain style language.

Page 162 (Continuation): Agassi practicing in 1991 in signature neon Lycra—still a visual and technical hallmark.

Page 162 (Continuation): US Open, 1991. The colorway shifted from hot pink to teal, lime, and aqua, rendered in a spray paint airbrush graphic and paired with his Nike Air Challenge line.

Pages 164–165: John McEnroe, 1998 Davis Cup warm-up jacket (not Nike). Boxy but tapered at the waist with detailing at the waist and neck, this style was a classic silhouette of the 1980s. Courtesy of the Department of Nike Archives.

Page 167: Naomi Osaka, US Open 2025. Her second collaboration with designer Yoon Ahn and Nike featured a crystal embellished jacket, a structured fitted bodice, and a voluminous bubble skirt. Accessories included red crystal roses in her hair, crystal covered headphones, and a crystal encrusted Labubu charm doll attached to her bag.

Pages 168–169: Naomi Osaka, US Open 2024, wearing her Harajuku inspired look: a ruffled mini dress with an oversized bow and bomber jacket designed by Yoon Ahn for Nike.

Pages 168–169 (Below): CAD drawings for Osaka's 2024 look and a design sketch of the dress.

Pages 168–169 (Right): Osaka at the Met Gala, 2021, wearing a gown by Nicolas Ghesquière for Louis Vuitton—a tribute to her Japanese, Haitian, and American heritage. The design fused kimono structure with a sculpted corset, ruffled jacquard layers (a recurring on court silhouette), and rich red and purple textile artistry.

Page 171: Rafael Nadal, Roland Garros, 2022, wearing a lemon and teal color blocked V neck T shirt with an extended back hem. The central front panel formed a V shaped heat energy map. Bonded shoulder seams—a common performance design feature—helped prevent chafing around the arms.

Page 172: Rafael Nadal's shoes with "RAFA." His footwear frequently matched his vibrant kit colors. "Last Match," Roland Garros, 2024.

Page 174: Serena Williams, Australian Open, 2014. A precisely tailored jacket merging fashion and performance, featuring soft lapels, welded zippered pockets, and the Nike swoosh. Although used primarily for aesthetic effect here, zippers—originally known as "hookless fasteners"—became a key sportswear innovation in the 1930s, enabling greater ease and autonomy in dressing.

Page 176: Serena Williams, Wimbledon, 2021. A custom Nike piece: an all white asymmetrical dress fitted through the torso and flaring into a full skirt. The bodice featured a single long sleeve, while a detachable flowing train created the defining gesture of romantic athleticism—Serena once again commanding the stage in a seamless monochromatic look.

Page 177: Serena Williams. Nike swoosh embellished with thirty-four Swarovski crystals—coded reference to Serena's age when she last won Wimbledon. The swoosh was designed by graphic design student Carolyn Davidson in 1971, symbolizing the wing of the Greek goddess of victory: movement, speed, and triumph.

Page 177 (Continuation): Serena Williams, Wimbledon, 2019. Her Nike court dress was crafted from a soft sweater knit fabric that molded to the body. The cut out bodice evoked the lines of a corset, while the skater style skirt—a favorite silhouette for Serena throughout the 2010s—balanced structure with movement.

Page 178: Serena Williams, US Open, 2004. A standout look that marked the beginning of Serena's redefinition of tennis fashion. She was the first to wear black on court, pairing a faux leather jacket and dress with studded embellishments. The cut and silhouette carried a Greco Roman influence, complemented by gladiator boots that fused athleticism with rock star edge.

Page 178 (Second Look): A stretch denim engineered for performance—an evolution of couture sportswear—paired with a fitted tank adorned with rivets and studs, her signature leather jacket, and gladiator boots, completing a look that balanced strength and style.

Page 179: Drawings and digital renderings by Wilson W. Smith III. Courtesy of the Department of Nike Archives.

Page 184: Serena Williams, US Open, 2018. A one-shouldered tulle piece fusing ballerina grace with athletic power.

Page 187: Virgil Abloh dress, 2018—detail.

Page 189: Virgil Abloh and Serena Williams, 2019. Serena wearing the famous Off-White™ dress designed for Roland Garros.

Page 190: Roger Federer with Off-White × Nike "The Ten" (2017), a custom pair designed by Virgil Abloh, photographed at the US Open Kids' Day.

Page 199: Arthur Ashe, 1968 US Open Final. Wearing his personalized Fred Perry shirt and cotton twill shorts. He later paired the look with a lightweight zip up warm up jacket featuring striped ribbed cuffs and hem to receive his trophy.

Page 200: Arthur Ashe, 1978. Wearing a Le Coq Sportif shirt featuring a navy windowpane grid. The design drew on modernist principles associated with Le Corbusier and the Bauhaus. This expression of French rationalism was later echoed by Italian label Fila under Pierluigi Rolando, whose use of grids, stripes, and color blocks articulated a distinctly Italian geometry.

Page 201: Arthur Ashe, 1968, with Harry Belafonte. His off court look—cravat, pocket handkerchief, mismatched jacket and trousers, and a striped shirt—reveals his quiet sartorial confidence and innate sense of style.

Page 202: Arthur Ashe, Johannesburg, South Africa, 1973. After being repeatedly denied entry due to apartheid, Ashe became the first Black man to compete in the South African Open. Pictured in a defiant red Le Coq Sportif polo shirt, navy shorts, and his stainless steel Rolex Cosmograph Daytona with matte dial, he embodied composure, elegance, and quiet strength.

Page 204: Fred Perry, Wimbledon, 1935, wearing the customary full flannel trousers. Perry's polo shirt is unidentified—not yet his own design, but soon to come.

Page 205: Original Fred Perry prototype shirt.

Page 205 (Continuation): The first Fred Perry sweatband with the laurel motif embroidered.

Page 207: Steffi Graf, 1982. A young Steffi Graf wearing Fred Perry.

Page 207 (Continuation): Fred Perry winners' Wimbledon coin.

Page 208: Amy Winehouse, c. 2007, London—a collaboration that fused her signature retro style with the brand's mod heritage, creating a look both nostalgic and defiantly modern.

Page 209: Barry, Neville, Gavin—Gavin Watson, 1984. Street subversive wear at its best in the 1980s.

Page 211: Björn Borg, Wimbledon, 1980. Wearing his signature pinstripe polo with a solid color collar by Fila from the *Linea Bianca* collection, designed by Pierluigi Rolando. The bold geometric bands of Fila and Le Coq Sportif's fine grids transformed tenniswear into a dialogue between Italian sensual modernism and French rational elegance.

Page 212: Björn Borg, July 1980, Wimbledon. Wearing his signature stripes, which made his look iconic, as he kisses the men's trophy.

Page 213: Björn Borg, 1980—detail of his carmine red Fila top featuring ribbed collar, cuffs, and hem, hallmarks of the brand's design. Custom made in luxury Italian mills from fine tricot, the piece included premium details such as an enamel zipper and hand woven logos—Italian luxury tailoring for a sports celebrity at its finest.

Page 213 (Continuation): Fila F Box logo design, introduced in the early 1970s, was created to reflect the brand's Italian modernist identity: its bold "F" within a navy frame symbolized strength and refined simplicity.

Pages 214–215: AO 2025—Radka Leitmeritz and The Cumberland Club, 2025.

Page 216: Gabriela Sabatini, 1988 US Open, wearing a white dress designed by Sergio Tacchini featuring vibrant semicircular graphics along the left side of the bodice and an A line skirt. The curved motifs evoke movement, motion, and grace—hallmarks of Sabatini's elegant playing style.

Page 216: Gabriela Sabatini, 1992 French Open. A coordinated two piece ensemble combining striped and floral graphics across the top and skirt. Stripes, a perennial motif in sports design, suggest speed while conveying a sense of timelessness and effortless style.

Page 219: Andy and Judy Murray celebrating his Wimbledon win, July 7, 2013.

Page 220: Film Still of Richie and Margot Tenenbaum. Richie wears his signature luxe pseudo sportswear, while Margot appears in a custom Lacoste dress, together capturing Wes Anderson's stylized vision of nostalgia and eccentric elegance.

Page 224: John F. Kennedy Jr. and Carolyn Bessette, Central Park, New York—John Jr. wears a T shirt reading "I Told Ya," a playful nod to a New York inflection and a witty echo of his father's presidential campaign button, "I Told You So." Designer Jonathan Anderson later revived the T shirt for the 2024 tennis film *Challengers*, evoking Kennedy's effortless East Coast insouciance and affluence.

Page 224: Zendaya as Tashi Duncan in *Challengers* (Dir. Luca Guadagnino)—she wears the "I Told Ya" shirt, referencing John F. Kennedy Jr.'s iconic look. The film explores class tension within the world of tennis—contrasting Tashi, who comes from privilege, with two working class players whose intertwined journeys lead them into the professional circuit and into Tashi's heart.

Page 227: RFK Tournament. Top: Actor Dustin Hoffman with a friend at the 7th Annual RFK Pro Celebrity Tennis Tournament, Forest Hills, New York, 1978.

Left: Arnold Schwarzenegger and Clint Eastwood at the 6th Annual RFK Tennis Tournament, Forest Hills, New York, 1977.

Page 228: Marianne Faithfull, Kate Moss, and Lucie de la Falaise at the Longwood Club, Upper Street, Regis Lake, New York, photographed by Bruce Weber, 1997.

Page 231: *Future Mythology* by Thibaut Grevet, 2022.

Page 232: adidas HQ, Germany, photographed by Sunita Kumar Nair.

Page 234: Alexander Zverev, adidas Originals Collection.

Page 235: Personal photographs by Sunita Kumar Nair of laser cut patterns for adidas fabric development.

Page 236: Close up of adidas Originals Collection, with personal photographs on Page 237 (right) and center page by Sunita Kumar Nair.

Page 238: Archive adidas shoe box, circa 1950s, featuring the same laser cut design.

Page 239: Félix Auger Aliassime at the US Open 2025 wearing Y-3.

Page 241: Y-3 fabric design for 2025 and Ana Ivanovic wearing Y-3 in 2015 at Roland Garros.

Page 242: Personal photograph of Stan Smith shoes at the adidas HQ, Germany.

Page 244: Billie Jean King, 1979 Federation Cup, Spain, wearing a custom Ted Tinling dress featuring an American flag motif—a patriotic, made for television statement piece blending national color with couture style tailoring.

Page 247: Stefanos Tsitsipas wearing adidas London Originals Collection '25.

Page 248: Pharrell x Viviane Sassen, 2018.

Page 250: From *Blurred Book* by Thibaut Grevet.

Page 253: Palace x adidas, 2015, photographed by Alasdair McLellan.

ABRAMS TEAM
Editor: Rebecca Kaplan
Design Manager: Heesang Lee
Managing Editor: Jodi Wong
Production Manager: Katie Gaffney

AUTHOR TEAM
Design Director: Alexandra Carr

Library of Congress Control Number: 2025943907
ISBN: 978-1-4197-8399-9
e-ISBN: 979-8-88707-847-2

Photography credits can be found on page 269.

Printed and bound in China

10 9 8 7 6 5 4 3 2 1

ABRAMS is represented in the UK and Europe by Abrams & Chronicle Books, 1 West Smithfield, London EC1A 9JU and Média-Participations, 57 rue Gaston Tessier, 75166 Paris, France.

abramsandchronicle.co.uk and media-participations.com

info@abramsandchronicle.co.uk

ABRAMS The Art of Books
195 Broadway, New York, NY 10007
abramsbooks.com

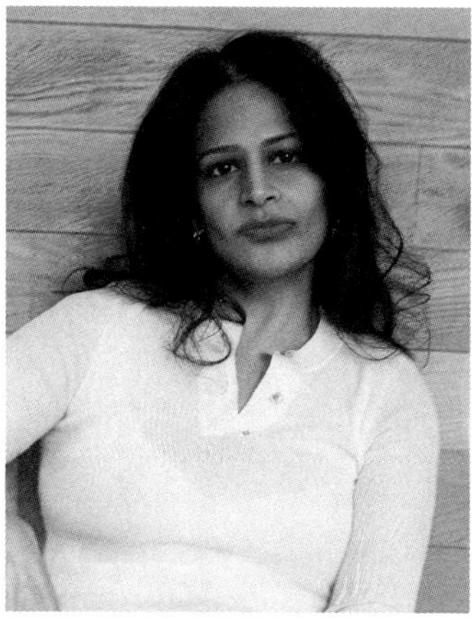

Sunita Kumar Nair is a fashion creative director and writer with contributions to *W Magazine*, *WWD*, and *Vanity Fair*. Known for charting untouched fashion terrain, her acclaimed book, *CBK: Carolyn Bessette Kennedy: A Life in Fashion*, was the first of its kind—a study of fashion classicism and cultural nuance. Her book, *ACE: The Times & Style of Tennis*, lends the same elegant eye to the world of sport and style.

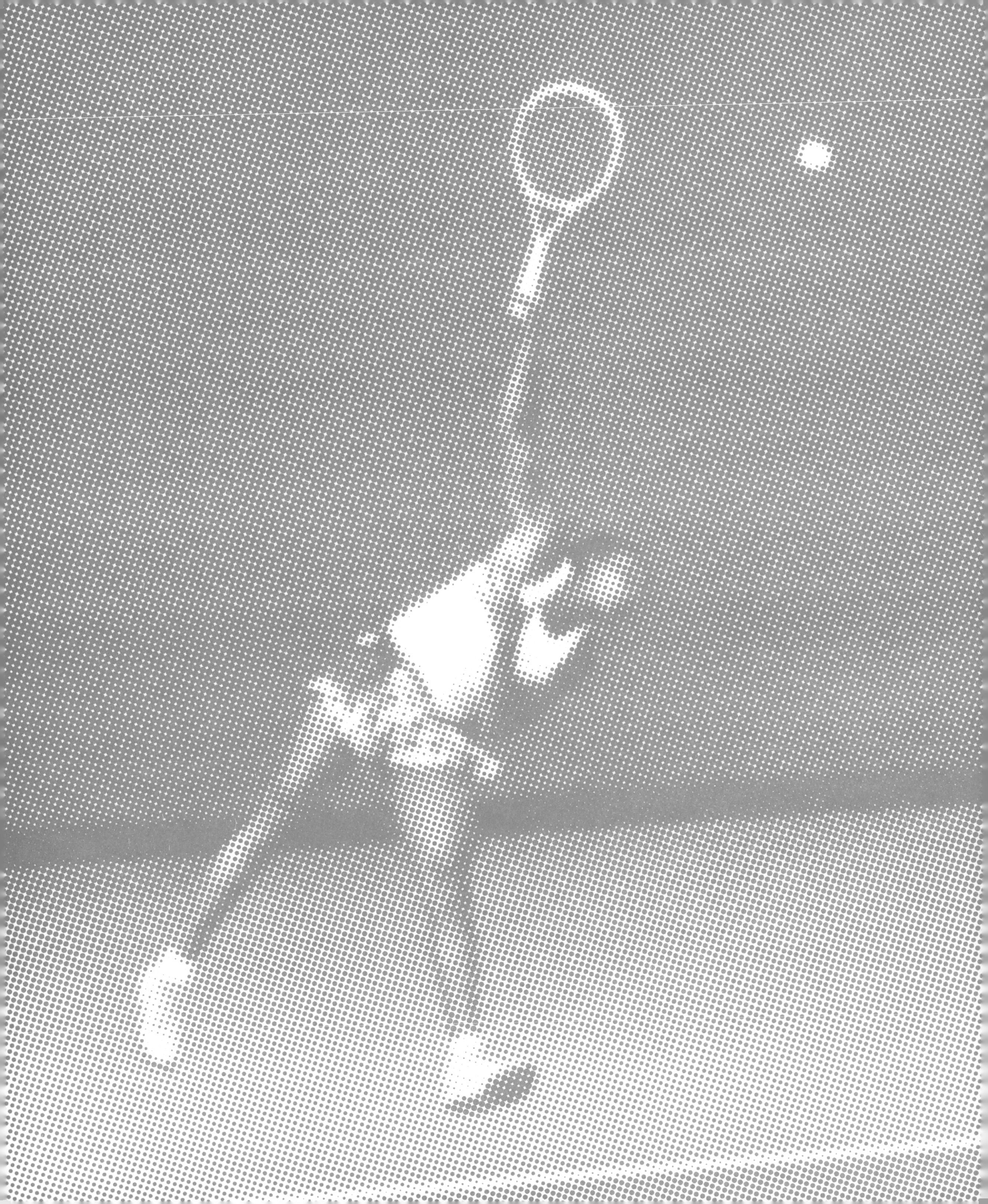